# Sustainable Audiovisual Collections Through Collaboration

# SUSTAINABLE AUDIOVISUAL COLLECTIONS THROUGH COLLABORATION

## PROCEEDINGS OF THE 2016 JOINT TECHNICAL SYMPOSIUM

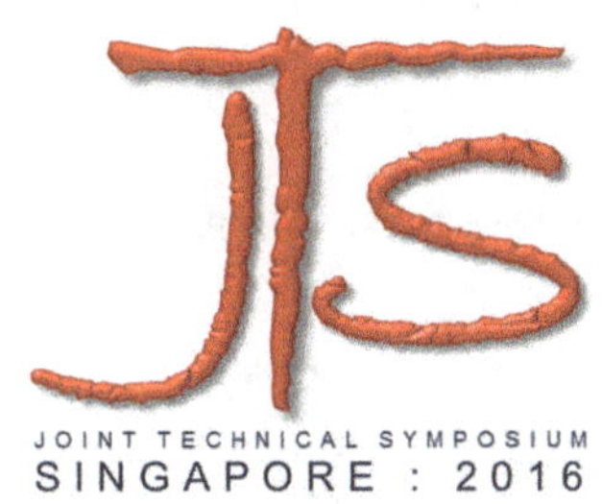


EDITED BY **RACHAEL STOELTJE, VICKI SHIVELY, GEORGE BOSTON, LARS GAUSTAD,** AND **DIETRICH SCHÜLLER**

Indiana University Press

*This book is a publication of*

**Indiana University Press**
Office of Scholarly Publishing
Herman B Wells Library 350
1320 East 10th Street
Bloomington, Indiana 47405 USA

iupress.indiana.edu



The paper used in this publication meets the minimum requirements of the American National Standard for Information Sciences—Permanence of Paper for Printed Library Materials, ANSI Z39.48-1992.

*Manufactured in the United States of America*

*Sustainable Audiovisual Collections* (2017): 1—219.
DOI: 10.2979/jts2016.0.0.0

Library of Congress Cataloging-in-Publication Data

Names: Joint Technical Symposium (9th : 2016 : Singapore), author. | Stoeltje, Rachael, editor. | South East Asia-Pacific Audio Visual Archive Association, host institution. | National Archives (Singapore), host institution. | Coordinating Council of Audiovisual Archives Association, sponsoring body.

Title: Sustainable audiovisual collections through collaboration : proceedings of the 2016 Joint Technical Symposium / edited by Rachael Stoeltje, Vicki Shively, George Boston, Lars Gaustad, and Dietrich Schuller.

Description: Bloomington, Indiana, USA : Indiana University Press, [2017] | Essays derived from presentations made at the 2016 Joint Technical Symposium (JTS), the ninth, co-organized by the Southeast Asia-Pacific Audiovisual Archive Association (SEAPAVAA) and the National Archives of Singapore under the auspices of the Coordinating Council of Audiovisual Archives (CCAAA) held March 7–9, 2016 in Singapore. | Includes bibliographical references and index.

Identifiers: LCCN 2017029250 (print) | LCCN 2017028571 (ebook) | ISBN 9780253027139 (e-book) | ISBN 9780253027023 (pbk. : alk. paper)

Subjects: LCSH: Motion picture film—Preservation—Congresses. | Audio-visual materials—Conservation and restoration—Congresses. | Sound recordings—Preservation—Congresses. | Sound recordings—Conservation and restoration—Congresses. | Film archives—Congresses. | Motion picture film collections—Congresses. | Audio-visual archives—Congresses.

Classification: LCC TR886.3 (print) | LCC TR886.3 .J645 2017 (ebook) | DDC 777—dc23

LC record available at https://lccn.loc.gov/2017029250

1 2 3 4 5 22 21 20 19 18 17

# Contents

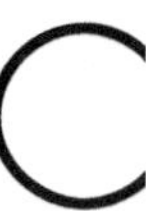

The following papers were presented at JTS 2016 Singapore but are not included in this publication:

FILMIC: A New Approach to Film Preservation / Jim Lindner

Automation to a Point: Processing the Radio-Television Hong Kong Archive / Joe Kelly and Andrew Martin

Uses of Shared Identifiers / Raymond Drewery

Access to the Information Held within Objects and Collections, including Metadata and Intellectual Property / Simon Jenkins

The Media Factory Approach to Restore Audiovisual Archive Files to Standard Compliance and Improved Interoperability / Jorg Houpert

# Sustainable Audiovisual Collections Through Collaboration

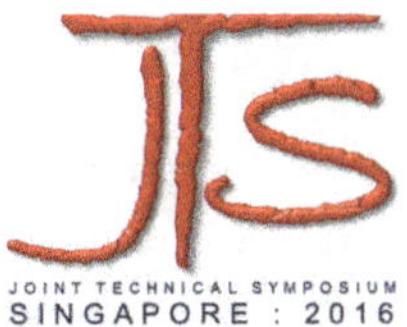


# Introduction

**Rachael Stoeltje**

With the unique city-state of Singapore providing the backdrop, the most recent Joint Technical Symposium (JTS) was held March 7–9, 2016, and addressed the theme, "Sustainable Audiovisual Collections Through Collaboration." This ninth JTS was co-organized by the Southeast Asia–Pacific Audiovisual Archive Association (SEAPAVAA) and the National Archives of Singapore under the auspices of the Coordinating Council of Audiovisual Archives (CCAAA).

The symposium attendees, 210 registrants representing 29 different countries, not only represented a wide and vast swath of the globe, but also a broad array of the wide-ranging professions that make up our field of audiovisual preservation and archiving today.

Singapore, famously known as the garden city, afforded us the special privilege of enjoying one of the most distinctive cityscapes anywhere. The primary host location, the elegant modern addition of the National Museum of Singapore was no exception. In contrast to the original historic structure, which serves as the public face of the Museum, the addition features a light-filled atrium made of glass walls and ceilings creating a venue that mirrors the architecture and culture of the city. The juxtaposition of contemporary structures with historic, colonial ones elevates contrast to a defining feature of the city. Especially apparent in the downtown harbor area are dramatic, bold new creations such as the hard-to-miss Marina Bay Sands, a three-towered structure topped with a Skypark shaped like a boat. This astonishing edifice, built as a focal point of the harbor, faces the ingress of the river, its banks reminiscent of the city's not so distant past.

Turning to the symposia and the JTS itself, this 2016 iteration followed the format of the eight prior symposia. At the core and throughout each event, the JTS has been a dedicated conference focused on the international scientific and technical issues pertaining to audiovisual archives and archivists. A review of the past 23 years of JTS programs reveals that the changes in symposia have reflected current technological advancements while maintaining a core focus on efforts to preserve the collections: film, audio, video, and now digital.

The very first JTS, for example, included papers covering the basic handling of nitrate film, long-term storage of videotape and, what were at the time, some of the newest storage, reformatting options—in one case, optical storage discs for preservation masters. As the symposium has evolved over time, discussions of digital storage and reformatting options appear more frequently. Indeed, as digitization and digital collections are now fully integrated into the routines of archival work, this year's symposium included relevant topics such as video codecs and open-source tools for management of archives expanding digital collections. George Blood, a frequent JTS attendee, noted that, "in the past, the symposium's emphasis was on research projects. Media was deteriorating, machines falling out of production, while digital was new and untested, and digital production flows and standards were non-existent. This year's presentations reflect the JTS community influence over the years and how to approach these new technical problems and workflows."

Consistently, the symposium has served as a record of the newest and best preservation practices and tools in our fields and of the technological breakthroughs that are being developed and placed on the market today. Moreover, as we plunge into the digital age, we can anticipate that more and more papers will address these new technologies that impact the preservation of and access to our collections.

*Sustainable Audiovisual Collections* (2017): 1–2. DOI: 10.2979/jts2016.0.0.01

The core topics from the last two decades have consistently focused on those mentioned above. However, it is important to note that the primary purpose of the JTS from the beginning has been to assemble representatives from the various organizations that operate with similar goals in order to address technical issues commonly encountered in our ever more frequently overlapping worlds. The earliest JTS was, after all, created by the very group that would eventually become the CCAAA (by 2000), and all following JTS symposia have been sponsored by CCAAA and hosted by its member organizations.

Pre-CCAAA, this little group was simply known as the Roundtable of Audiovisual Records. It produced the very first symposium in 1983 in Stockholm, cohosted by CCAAA organizations FIAF and FIAT. This original Round Table, which itself was the result of a 1980 UNESCO report entitled "Recommendation for the Safeguarding and Preservation of Moving Images," evolved into CCAAA. As the umbrella organization for its member groups, it has now produced nine Joint Technical Symposia over 23 years in different global locations. Moreover, it hosts World Day for Audiovisual Heritage, Archives at Risk, and many other initiatives through efforts by all partnering international organizations.

At this year's event in Singapore, almost all CCAAA organizations were represented either through presentations or through the intense preparation required for such a significant international conference. Most importantly, though, it is impossible to express an adequate level of thanks to the multi-talented organizers, SEAPAVAA General Secretary Irene Lim and SEAPAVAA President Mick Newnham, and their teams. They must be commended for their months of detailed planning, which gave consideration to all possible contingencies, resulting in a smooth, efficient and memorable symposium. On top of the success of the symposium, our hosts also provided a night safari tour, a remarkable dinner from the thirteenth floor of the National Library with views of the city, visits to the National Archives, and specific cultural tours.

Additionally, the Conference Program Committee created a program representing the many and varied voices of our broad field. Members of the Committee included CCAAA member representatives David Walsh and myself from FIAF, Brecht Declercq from FIAT, Kate Murray, Dietrich Schüller and Lars Gaustad from IASA, and Mick Newnham representing SEAPAVAA, all of whom assisted in the production of a program that reflected current issues and concerns in global preservation and access.

Also, I want to express my gratitude for the continued support provided in the process of transforming presentations into this publication. Special thanks are due to JTS publication co-editors George Boston, Lars Gaustad, Dietrich Schüller, and Indiana University Libraries Moving Image Archive's assistant archivist, Vicki Shively. I am especially grateful to her for her contagious enthusiasm and ability to juggle multiple authors and tasks, all the while paying immaculate attention to detail and maintaining an unfailingly good spirit.

Lastly, I wish to extend my appreciation to FIAF Senior Administrator and historian, Christophe Dupin, for his most recent creation of the new CCAAA website where he has compiled and digitized the histories of CCAAA, the JTS, and World Day for Audiovisual Heritage. For more information on the history of CCAAA and the JTS, the new CCAAA website and the new FIAF website are now available and contain newly digitized historical documents.

# Brief History of the Joint Technical Symposium

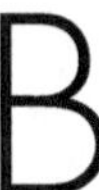

**Christophe Dupin**

The Joint Technical Symposium (JTS) is an international scientific and technical event dealing with matters of particular importance to audiovisual archives and archivists. Organized every few years since 1983 by the various audiovisual archives associations now forming the Coordinating Council of Audiovisual Archives (CCAAA), it provides an opportunity for colleagues around the world and those interested in the field to meet and share information about the preservation of original image and sound materials. The 2016 JTS, which took place in Singapore in March 2016, was the ninth since 1983.

The first Joint Technical Symposium, entitled "Archiving of the Moving Image in the 21st Century," took place at the Swedish Film Institute in Stockholm, 1–4 June, 1983. Co-organized by FIAF and FIAT (now FIAT-IFTA), it was part of that year's FIAF Congress. It dealt primarily with film and video, and included high-quality technical papers, workshops, visits to film and video institutions, and a small exhibition of film equipment with potential use in archives. The papers reflected the concerns of the day: the handling of film and videotape, the preservation of nitrate film stock, and the impact of new technologies such as optical discs.

The title of the second JTS was "Archiving the Audiovisual Heritage." The event took place in May 1987 in the International Congress Center in West Berlin, and was hosted by the Stiftung Deutsche Kinemathek. It was once again attached to the annual FIAF Congress. The symposium's organizing committee consisted of members of the Technical Commissions of FIAF, FIAT, and IASA, thus recognizing the need for film, video, and sound archivists to discuss similar challenges. The Symposium attracted over 300 delegates. UNESCO supported the event by offering a number of travelling grants for delegates from developing countries. The proceedings of the Symposium were published by the Stiftung Deutsche Kinemathek in 1988 under the title *Archiving the Audiovisual Heritage: A Joint Symposium.*

The third JTS took place at the Canadian Museum of Civilization in Ottawa, 3–5 May 1990. It was organized by the Technical Coordinating Committee of the International Round Table on Audio-Visual Records (predecessor of the CCAAA), and was composed of representatives of FIAF, FIAT, IASA, ICA, and IFLA. One of the main concerns was the chemical stability of carriers, as delegates discussed the need to copy images and sound stored on carriers previously thought to be indestructible. Digital recording techniques were also part of the discussions. The proceedings of the Symposium were published in 1992 by UNESCO and the Technical Coordinating Committee, under the title *Archiving the Audiovisual Heritage: Third Joint Symposium*.

The next JTS took place at the National Film Theatre in London in January 1995. Organized once again by the Technical Coordinating Committee on behalf of FIAF, FIAT, and IASA, its title was "Technology and our Audio Visual Heritage: Technology's Role in Preserving the Memory of the World." Topics discussed included the ethics of archiving and the breakdown of the components of signal carriers with age; methods and projects concerning restoration and conservation of signals and carriers; and the use of computer techniques in audiovisual archiving. The proceedings were published in 1999 by the Technical Coordinating Committee.

The fifth Joint Technical Symposium, entitled "Image and Sound Archiving and Access: The Challenges of the 3rd Millennium," took place in Paris 20–22 January 2000. The proceedings were once again published (with an accompanying CD-ROM), this time by the CNC.

The next two Joint Technical Symposia, in 2004 and 2007, took place in Toronto and were both organized by AMIA on behalf of the CCAAA. The Programme Committee for both events was cochaired by Grover Crisp and Michael Friend. Their titles—"Preserving the Audiovisual Heritage: Transition and Access" and "Audiovisual Heritage and the Digital Universe"—confirmed the urgent need for audiovisual archivists around the world to discuss the challenges of the digital revolution.

The 2010 JTS was organized by FIAF on behalf of the CCAAA, and took place 2–5 May 2010, immediately after the FIAF Congress in Oslo. Its theme was "Digital Challenges and Digital Opportunities in Audiovisual Archiving." The Programme Committee was chaired by Thomas Christensen, Head of the FIAF Technical Commission.

The ninth Joint Technical Symposium took place in Singapore in March 2016. Co-organized by SEAPAVAA and the National Archives of Singapore on behalf of CCAAA, its theme will be "Sustainable Audiovisual Collections Through Collaboration." The organizing committee recognized that the audiovisual archiving world has seen many dramatic changes and advancements in the technologies that enable preservation since the last JTS. It considered that the rate and magnitude of these changes requires a collaborative approach to enable all archives to make sense of the best way to keep collections alive for future generations. The official website of the 2016 JTS was jts2016.com.

Digitized historical documents are now available on the CCAAA website at http://www.ccaaa.org/.

# Let's Emulate the Sound of Colours!

1

**Reto Kromer**

**Abstract**

Let's emulate the sound of colours from the past through the best techniques that are technologically available today. By keeping all the possibilities available for our successors, they will be free to debate, modify and improve on our own work.

**Keywords**

digital film restoration, audiovisual preservation, analogue, digital, photochemical, colour reproduction, ProRes, TI/A, FFV1, FLAC, Matroska, FFmpeg, QCTools, MediaConch, DCP, OpenDCP, data archiving, conservation, restoration, migration.

## Collaboration

Very little of the available technology and tools have been designed and manufactured especially for audiovisual archiving purposes. On the contrary, most of the technology and tools that we are using in our daily archival work have been designed and developed for today's production and post-production needs. Archivists, conservators, and restorers are continuously adapting this technology and tools to fulfill specific preservation and access needs. Therefore, we only rarely have, for example, a carbon-arc projection of a toned and stenciled nitrate print, but usually, we will enjoy a modern digital projection that emulates, as best as possible, that specific historical look through a file. Emulation can, of course, also be seen in a pedagogic sense: a master teaching to his disciples. So this is indeed important!

## Analogue and Digital

In the late 1980s and the early 1990s, when I started considering digital methods for both film restoration and audiovisual conservation, I was mainly regarded as a fool—or at best a candid dreamer. Many years after, before the end of 2013, when I closed down our photochemical laboratory, I was often considered a person who missed the boat in the switch to the new digital world because, occasionally, I still preferred to apply the "old-school" analogue, photochemical methods. Ironically, what I was actually doing was capitalizing on the best potential offered by both worlds and mixing them together to achieve the best possible results. This method created the most historically accurate presentation of a masterpiece or a document in the modern screening context. The penultimate job my photochemical lab did was the preservation of amateur films shot on Kodachrome film stock. Generally, for this type of preservation, we would use the Fujifilm daylight 64 ASA camera negative as an intermediate film stock because it provides the best possible quality in analogue colour reproduction. Sadly, by then that film stock was no longer manufactured, and we used the very last reels stored in our refrigerator.

The Joint Technical Symposium's (JTS) audience is a very special one. As the JTS name implies, this is a symposium of technically interested individuals with crossover specializations.

The audio community was the first, and the quickest, to move from analogue to digital, and the relatively small size of their data files aided in their early technological adaption. Also, audio technicians seemed to adapt to the new technology easier than other film disciplines, most likely because the move from analogue mechanical recording, to analogue magnetic recording, to digital magnetic recording, to file-based recording was more natural and less polemic in the sound fields.

The broadcast community shifted to digital just after the audio communities to take advantage of the digital possibilities for production and postproduction. At this early stage, they rarely took into account the new challenges for preservation in this digital medium, as well as not understanding the fundamental differences between restoration and enhancement.

Unfortunately, the film preservation community is still in the middle of paranoiac contradictions. It appears that most of their energy, time and money is used for the continuous and duplicitous restoration of a few dozen films they call "canon." Some film purists think that even digital-born films should be preserved onto film stock. In today's worst/best scenario we can record onto film only 1/64 of the image quality from the digital file. That is less than 2%. This data loss means that more than 98% of the data are tossed into the rubbish bin. This situation, regrettably, exists because while camera sensors are continuously improving, re-recorders onto film are not. The market for this particular type of recording equipment is gone.

If analogue storage is the answer to all audiovisual preservation needs, why do we have to struggle that much with analogue conservation and restoration issues?

## Standardisation

The proceeding three examples are relevant file formats to the film preservation field. If one could be established as a standard principle for the moving image community, collaboration would be more effective and efficient.

ProRes is often hated by archivists because it is a proprietary format of Apple. However, this is a de facto standard in postproduction. The Society of Motion Picture & Television Engineers (SMPTE) wishes to standardise this recording format. At this time it is unclear if it is only the Apple ProRes 422 HQ that is meant to be standardised, or the entire ProRes format family, such as the 4444 XQ. The hope is that the community avoids the mistakes they made with the standardisation of the CineForm or VC-5 codec. Essential information is still kept secret by GoPro, and not all metadata described in the standard matches the metadata generated by GoPro's products. An unfortunate situation indeed!

A group of scholars from the University of Basel in Switzerland has the goal to define a TIFF format that contains all the technical metadata that is relevant to preservation. Adobe, having refused the name TIFF/A as analogous to PDF/A, has chosen to name the new file format TI/A (Tagged Image for Archival). ISO (International Organisation for Standardisation) is the body where this new recommendation should be submitted, possibly amended, accepted, and finally published.

The IETF (Internet Engineering Task Force) has established a workgroup called CELLAR (codec encoding for lossless archiving and real-time transmission). Cellar is currently standardising the lossless video codec FFV1, the lossless audio codec FLAC, and the extensible media container Matroska, which is based on EBML (extensible binary meta language), a binary XML format. Once adopted, these standards could also be submitted to ISO and SMPTE for additional validation.

## Open-Source Software

Today, there are plenty of open-source software options which do not require you to be an engineer to use them. These digital tools form a complete archival ecosystem. The following software is extremely useful and highly recommended.

FFmpeg is a complete, cross-platform solution to record, convert, and stream audio and video. It would benefit every audiovisual archivist to be literate in FFmpeg.

QCTools offers an extremely wide range of strong quality control tools for video preservation, developed by the Bay Area Video Coalition and Dave Rice.

Most audiovisual archivists are familiar with MediaArea's MediaInfo. MediaArea is currently developing the new tool MediaConch. This tool consists of an implementation checker, policy checker, reporter, and fixer that targets preservation-level audiovisual files; specifically Matroska, LPCM (linear pulse-code modulation) and FFV1, for use in memory institutions.

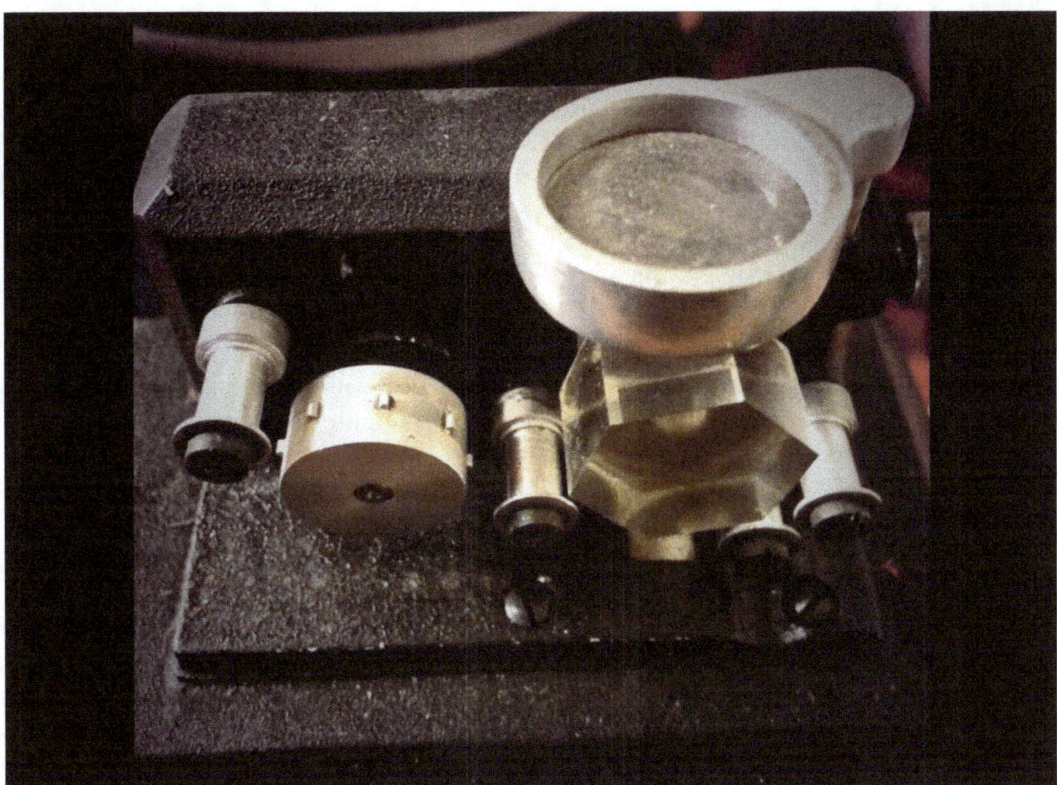

**Figure 1.** The minimal equipment needed so see the images of a silent 9.5 mm film in movement. This format is also called *Pathé Baby.*

The Digital Cinema Package (DCP) has replaced prints in commercial film distribution for theatrical projection. DCP is a unique format that was designed by the movie industry, conversely, because of how it is constructed, it can make a film archivists' preservation work difficult.

Despite these issues, the archivist should give consideration to DCP when deciding the best software tools for their collections. It allows greater control over the manner in which the audience sees a historical film. The archivist can encode the right colours, the correct aspect ratio, an adequate projection speed, and the DCP will be screened that way in all cinema theatres worldwide. OpenDCP is one of the tools that makes this possible.

## Open-Source Hardware?

In the analogue world, things may appear simple. Figure 1 shows the minimal equipment needed to create the illusion of movement. In the digital world, equipment with that kind of simplicity is currently not available.

Twelve years ago, when we built our first scanner, we only modified one camera part within an optical step printer. The projector part, the lenses, the pre-wet device that we had previously developed, as well as the mechanical movement was retained without modification.

Also, the optical camera, number 128 from Richard Craß in Berlin, was the first one we converted from analogue to digital. Many others made similar conversions.

It is possible to build, in your kitchen, a relatively simple machine for cleaning all kinds of magnetic tapes.

For archiving large amounts of audiovisual data, LTO is often chosen. The magnetic tape based solution LTO (linear tape-open) with LTST (linear tape file system) is indeed a good solution for data archiving in the real world.

## Conservation

In short, analogue conservation focuses on the chemistry of the base, and the emulsion or the magnetic coating, and concludes that one should store materials in a cool and dry environment.

On the other hand, digital conservation concludes that one should keep every single bit unchanged, and instead focuses on the container, codes and the so-called "raw" data.

Briefly, as for the migration process, from January through June of 2014, we migrated the digital archive of our company from LTO-4 to LTO-6. It was decided to change some file formats, and to convert them *en passant* into other more robust formats for future accessibility. We started with roughly 1000 tapes and ended up with fewer than 300 tapes. Although we reduced the storage volume in the security cabinet by more than two-thirds, there are now more consistent data. Additionally, we have migrated 5.7 PB of data and only encountered one single error. This was resolved by using the archive's second back-up copy.

This kind of work must be done through an automated process to avoid the "human error" factor. However, archivists do need to have the skills to deal with technical issues. It is crucial to be able to read and understand the technical information provided by the industry, and to choose the solution that best fits their archival needs.

## Restoration

Throughout my life, I have spoken many times about the ethics of conservation and restoration, including organizing a full conference in 2010 about this very topic. Through age and experience, I have come to agree thoroughly with the thought: "Restoration consists of replicated errors of the past." We, as a professional community, should be able to do more in our restoration work than just replicate the errors of the past.

The first software for digital image restoration, primarily, selected the region where a problem occurred, called ROI (region of interest), and that area would be defocused a small amount resulting in the problem becoming less visible. To mask the fact that the image is less sharp, the contrast is increased to compensate, and the viewer has the illusion that the problem is resolved.

Modern restoration programs work at the pixel level. The software tries to fix the actual problem that a pixel has, or that a small group of pixels has, rather than try to mask it. Additionally, these newer programs are more complex and need more powerful computer processing for optimal efficiency. This assortment of tools was developed mainly by the game industry for their special effects. If the archivist uses them *cum grano salis*, then true restoration work can be performed, and not simply camouflage the existence of a problem. Just as importantly, any restorative interventions need to be carefully documented. It can be a difficult but essential task.

## Recent developments

Significant advances have been made in the audiovisual and game industry software.

The accessibility of high dynamic range allows the image reproduction to contain a more accurate colour representation (for example of Dufaycolor, Kodachrome, or Technicolor), and can be used to improve audiovisual archiving.

The higher frame rate options allow the archivist to encode precisely the frame rates used during the silent film era. Also, by multiplying frames and adding black frames to emulate the projector's shutter blades, it gives a more accurate, as well as a more pleasant viewing experience. Additionally, theatrical access is improved dramatically.

Furthermore, other technological fields, such as forensic science, has developed new tools, allowing us to read all the information off of a magnetic tape, and to interpret it by using their software. Also, the algorithms developed for DNA sequencing can be used to process the optical soundtrack from an archival scan. This should be done frame by frame and edge to edge, with a little vertical overscan. By utilizing diverse technologies, these programs will open the most doors for more accurate conservation and restoration work.

*Summa summarum:* Let's emulate the sound of colour through the best techniques that are technologically available today. By keeping all the possibilities available for our successors, they will be free to debate, modify and improve our own work.

Having graduated in mathematics and computer science, Reto Kromer became involved in audiovisual conservation and restoration thirty years ago. He was head of preservation at the Swiss National Film Archive and lecturer at the University of Lausanne. He has been running his own preservation companies and lecturing at the Bern University of Applied Sciences and the Academy of Fine Arts Vienna. His current research includes colour spaces, CLUT, and codec programming and emulation.

## Acknowledgments

I entered this field in late October 1986. During these past 30 years, I have had the pleasure to meet many individuals who have been fundamental in developing my career. I would like to thank, warmly, all the persons who have been most crucial for my own professional development: Marguerite Engberg, Alan Masson, John Pytlak, Dominic Case, Paul Collard, Luigi Pintarelli, Paul Read, Kris Kolodziejski, Martin Sawyer, Carole Delessert, Hermann Wetter, Rémy Pithon, László Gloetzer, Charly Huser, Sam Kula, Ray Edmondson, Jim Lindner, Grover Crisp, Michael Friend, Peter Adelstein, Jean-Louis Bigourdan, Charles Poynton, John Graham-Cumming, Nicole Martin, Dave Rice, Misty De Meo, Yvonne Ng, Agathe Jarczyk, and David Pfluger. My work and the work of the teams I have had the privilege to lead has always been collaborative—collaboration on different levels: between institutions, individuals, companies, and institutions, and/or individuals, and/or companies.

I also wish to acknowledge the help provided by Adrian Wood.

2

# BFI Film Forever: Unlocking Film Heritage

**Charles Fairall**


## Abstract

*Unlocking Film Heritage* (UFH) is one of the three key strategic aims within the BFI's 2012–17 National Lottery-funded *Film Forever* strategy. With an ambition to digitise, preserve, and make accessible 10,000 film titles, the BFI has consulted with partners across UK collections to harmonise and document technical standards for both essence and metadata and negotiated a common tariff on behalf of the project for commercial digitisation and restoration services. All films digitised through UFH are being presented to the UK public through the web-based *BFI Player*, with the majority being free to view.

In addition to the curation, digitisation and presentation of 10,000 films, the BFI has built a state of the art data centre, and is creating a new Digital Preservation Infrastructure, designed to operate seamlessly with the existing collections database (CID). It will enable processes for ingest, media asset management, long-term preservation, and access to benefit all BFI digital collections. Through the UFH project, technology transformation is being applied across the BFI conservation centre with the introduction of the latest digital film image/sound scanning and restoration systems. While maintaining all essential analogue expertise, existing conservation staff, through a programme of training and hands-on practice, will develop new skills and processes, enabling full end to end archive workflows to meet the needs and demands for both analogue and digital preservation and access.



## Keywords

digitisation, preservation, collaboration, public access, online, commercial, archive sector.


## Strategy

Priority three of the British Film Institute's 2012–17 Film Forever strategic plan[1] declared a very clear and determined message: "Access to screen heritage is integral to the BFI's ambitions to develop British film talent, and to provide a programme which attracts new audiences, public and professional, to a richer experience of film." The programme that followed, known as Unlocking Film Heritage, represents a major commitment to ensure that UK's screen heritage is safeguarded for future generations and made available to discover and enjoy through web delivery on BFI Player[2] and in venues across the UK. Core to the ambition is *Britain on Film*, a programme of 10,000 titles selected from the BFI National Archive, Regional and National Archives and rights holders across the UK.

At the time of writing, Unlocking Film Heritage nears the programme's final year; this paper sets out to describe the essential technical and practical necessities facing film archivists from across the UK as together we embraced the digital challenge.

## Partnership

As the UK's lead body for Film, the BFI has navigated a central but consultative path to achieve the cultural and technical aims of Unlocking Film Heritage. Engaging with stakeholders from the very beginnings of the programme has been key to progress and success. Following an initial series of workshops, where colleagues representing conservation, collections, and data management representing a wide selection of film collections across the UK gathered together, a common understanding of technical capabilities and ambitions was rapidly gained, and a sense of cordial agreement achieved through the iterative compilation of a Technical Standards & Deliverables document. Through this process, not only was it possible to agree and specify technical

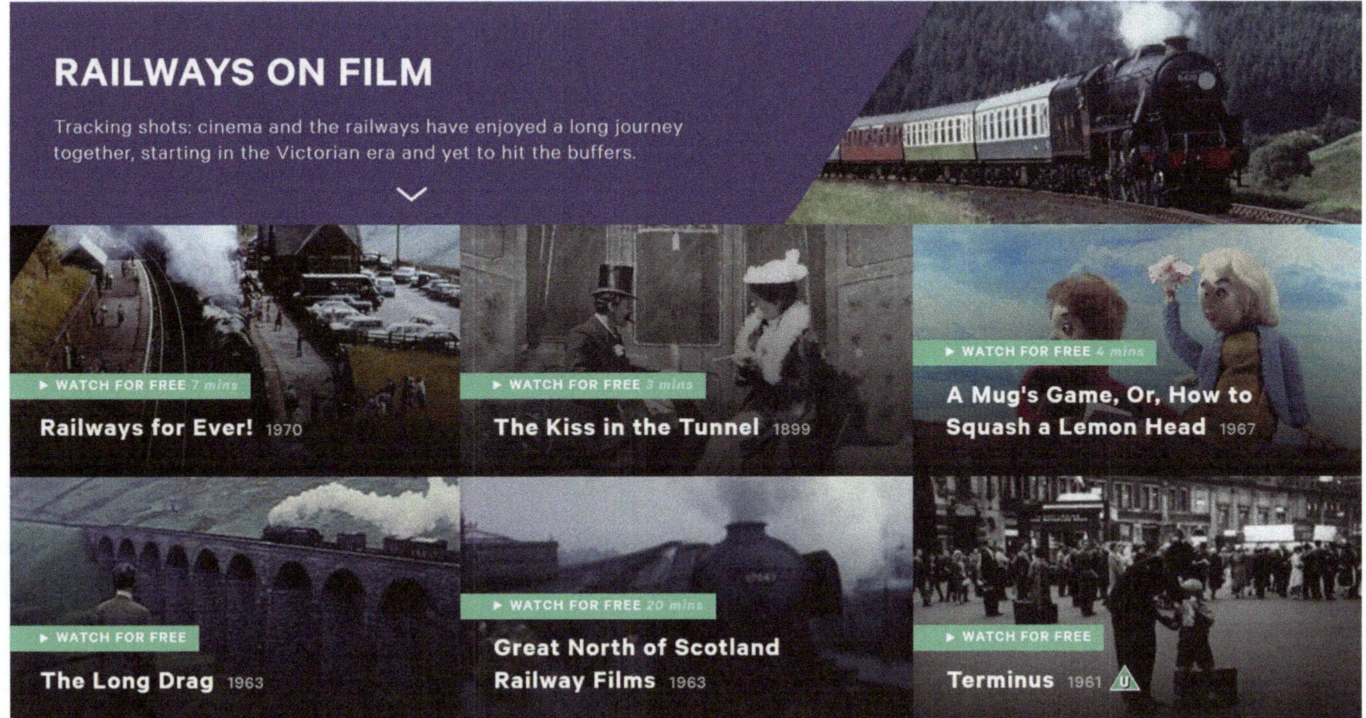


parameters for digital preservation and access for the entire programme, but also to consider and address the broadest range of film collections, capabilities within individual organisations, and practical guidelines for each partner to achieve the highest standards possible.

## Technical Standards & Deliverables

Having consulted widely and thoroughly with partners, it became apparent that while a single set of standards was essential for delivery to the BFI Player and presentation of preservation essence and metadata to the BFI National Archive, there was not necessarily a single specification for image scanning. All agreed that each film element selected for digitisation should be judged on its own merits and that the professionals who understand the physical and aesthetic quality of their collections best should decide upon the most appropriate path to take for digitisation. However, with the overwhelming majority of UK cinemas in the UK set up for 2K resolution, an agreement was reached that wherever possible a resolution of 2K with 10-bit quantisation in DPX format should be the standard to aim for.

Through a necessity of government procurement rules and desire for best practice, in advance of the UFH project, the BFI had the benefit of a technical services framework for procurement, comprising six specialised businesses that had been selected by firstly meeting a stringent set of requirements, and subsequently, succeeding in a competitive tender process. At an early stage, the six companies were invited to sense check the Technical Standards and Deliverables document, with a view to extending the BFI's framework coverage to all UFH partners.

The paragraphs that follow illustrate the key technical details agreed with participating UK partners.

### Image Digitisation Standard

The ambition for UFH is to scan film, preferably at 2K 10-bit log to create the best quality digital preservation file affordable within the Programme. If 2K scanning is not achievable or considered practical then the aim is to capture the data at the highest quality available, choosing a digitisation approach that best suits material type and condition, with SD 4:2:2, 4:3 PAL being the minimum standard. For HD digitisation, the preferred standard is 1080P, with 720P being the minimum standard. Correct film running speed must be determined and identified within metadata for all transfers. It is recommended that original film frame rates be represented in finished files by repetition of existing film frames. For all digitisation, the original film image aperture should be captured.

### Audio Digitisation Standard

Digital sound files, derived from either optical or magnetic film tracks, should be in .wav or broadcast .wav format as appropriate, at a minimum standard of 48 kHz/24 bit, with 96 kHz/24 bit being the preferred standard. Digital sound files created simultaneously with image scans can be kept in AIFF format.

### Mezzanine File Standard

Finished files represent the scanned, conformed, dust-busted, and graded film materials. The finished file in the original aspect ratio, with accompanying synced audio (where applicable), should be presented for use within the BFI Player as a ProRes 4:2:2 file, with HQ HD specification and resolution being preferred.

### DCP Creation

- Film scan, preferably 2K 10-bit log DPX files—a scan capturing the full dynamic range without gamma applied
- Preservation standard audio files (48 kHz or 96 kHz, 24-bit .wav)
- Finished ProRes 4:2:2 HQ Mezzanine HD file
- Finished MPEG4 h.264 file @ 1.25 Mb/s DCDM—to include final audio .wav files and the final image files as a 16-bit .tif image sequence, in X, Y, Z colour space

### Viewing File Standard

An MPEG4 h.264 viewing file created from the finished ProRes 4:2:2 file should be set for streaming at 1.25 Mb/s with the pixel resolution scaled for a frame height of 540 and the frame width according to aspect ratio, e.g., 960 for 16:9.

### Fixity File

All files intended for preservation should be supplied with accompanying fixity data as an MD5 checksum or hash value, provided at the source.

MD5 files should be provided at the following levels:

- DPX: at folder level (i.e. folder per reel)
- Other choice preservation files: at file level
- DCDM: at folder level
- ProRes 4:2:2: at file level
- WAV: at file level
- MD5 files should match either folder level or file level naming conventions.

## Technical Metadata

"It is to be expected that audio visual files will have sufficient Metadata embedded in them and/or associated with them to describe their Content to the production . . . systems with which they will interact."[3]

- The purpose of this metadata within the Unlocking Film Heritage project is to allow accurate identification of digital files within archive catalogues and the National Catalogue.
- To maximise data workflow efficiency (automatic information extraction and import of metadata into desired systems, thereby reducing the cataloguing challenge for each selected item) our strong preference for delivery of technical metadata is a separate discrete XML file or sidecar XML file, but technical metadata can also be embedded in file headers or containers (e.g. MXF).
- XML files can be generated from the digital video or audio files using commonly available media information extraction tools. In general, the XML file should share its filename with the video or audio file it describes, to aid association between the two.

## Technical Delivery

All the required file deliverables will be committed to two sets of LTO5 data tapes with LTFS file structure to be retained within the BFI National Archive or relevant collection for preservation purposes.

All files for preservation within an archive should be supplied with accompanying fixity data as an MD5 checksum or hash value, provided at the source. Where generating an MD5 value for folders containing large numbers of DPX or TIFF image files is not practicable due to technical constraints, a record of folder size (in bytes) for each reel is acceptable as an alternative.

## Common Rate-Card for Technical Services

Following the great success of a collaborative approach to discussing and agreeing a range of common digital access and preservation technical standards, along with service provision through a trusted framework of suppliers for all UFH partners to enjoy throughout the programme, the BFI was technically well equipped to begin the process of distributing funds to achieve the agreed outcomes. It was clear that a number of different work paths would be required, depending on film material types and the intended digital outcomes. Working closely with partners and the framework of suppliers, it was agreed that a fixed price list would apply and be enjoyed by all partners. For simplicity, all work would be through one of three defined routes.

- Route 1: details digitisation costs when the source material is a Print (Silent or Combined)—35 mm / 16 mm / 9.5 mm / 8 mm
- Route 2: details digitisation costs when the source is either a BW or Colour Intermediate with Separate Sound—35 mm / 16 mm / 9.5 mm / 8 mm
- Route 3: details digitisation costs when the source is Original Negative either Silent or with Separate Sound—35 mm / 16 mm / 9.5 mm / 8 mm

## Digital Preservation Infrastructure

The BFI has included digitisation and data storage to complement traditional preservation methods for over a decade; a good example of this being for magnetic film audio tracks, where acetate decomposition advances at such a rapid rate and in such a destructive manner that there is virtually no alternative but to digitise. Additionally, whenever the opportunity has arisen, raw image scan and sound master files have been collected opportunistically and kept as digital preservation surrogates to supplement the physical masters. LTO2 tapes were adopted for this purpose initially, and subsequently in 2012, when the BFI's television archiving moved from videotape to data file workflows, LTO5 under LTFS was adopted.

Adopting good practices such as maintaining two copies of data, linking essence to metadata, and migrating to later tape formats as they became available, this entirely manual approach to digital asset management proved workable but—from a strategic perspective—clearly fell short in a number of ways. For example: storing LTO tapes on shelves in a vault, with access and preservation activities dependent on retrieval by personnel did not align with growing expectations of *digital* being immediate and globally accessible technology. Migrating from one LTO generation to the next in a model where the number of new digital files was escalating yet reliant on human interaction was also unsustainable beyond the very short term.

So with thousands of additional titles being added to the BFI's digital collections, to provide robust preservation for this growth and the already substantial legacy, along with accessibility befitting of a digital world, an entirely new approach was needed. Although considerable thought and research had taken place over several years, the task of creating a new digital preservation infrastructure began in earnest when budgets were secured through the Unlocking Film Heritage project. Given the specific nature of the BFI's digital preservation challenge, a special form of procurement known as competitive dialogue procedure[4] was chosen, where instead of inviting the commercial markets to respond to a specification by means of consultation workshops, to which prospective bidders would be asked to discuss individually. With over 100 expressions of interest, a shortlist of six companies were selected and the dialogue, which spanned almost a year, proceeded.

The resulting solution, which integrates an Imagen MAM system with BFI's Collections Information Database (CID) includes sophisticated technologies and processes for automated digital storage through two Spectra Logic T950 data tape libraries (LTO6 and IBM TS1150), managed by Black Pearl appliances, with mass access to low-bit-rate proxies from Isilon NAS, and successive data migration for preservation built-in was contracted to a single supplier, Ovation Data Services. A 10 Gb/s fibre network connects archive staff to the system through high-performance PCs, allowing ingest and retrieval of preservation files along with a variety of tools for encoding from analogue sources, editing, and transcoding. With legacy preservation ingest set as a priority, the system began to roll out during late 2015 and is due to become fully operational in 2016.

## Enhanced Digital Capabilities

In addition to the creation of a digital preservation infrastructure, the Unlocking Film Heritage project sought, as a fundamental requirement, to enhance capabilities for digitisation and digital delivery from the BFI National Archive. Previous investment over the preceding decade in the Master Film Store (MFS), Collections Information Database (CID), along with modern film preparation equipment, and an Arriscan film scanner, provided the archive with excellent

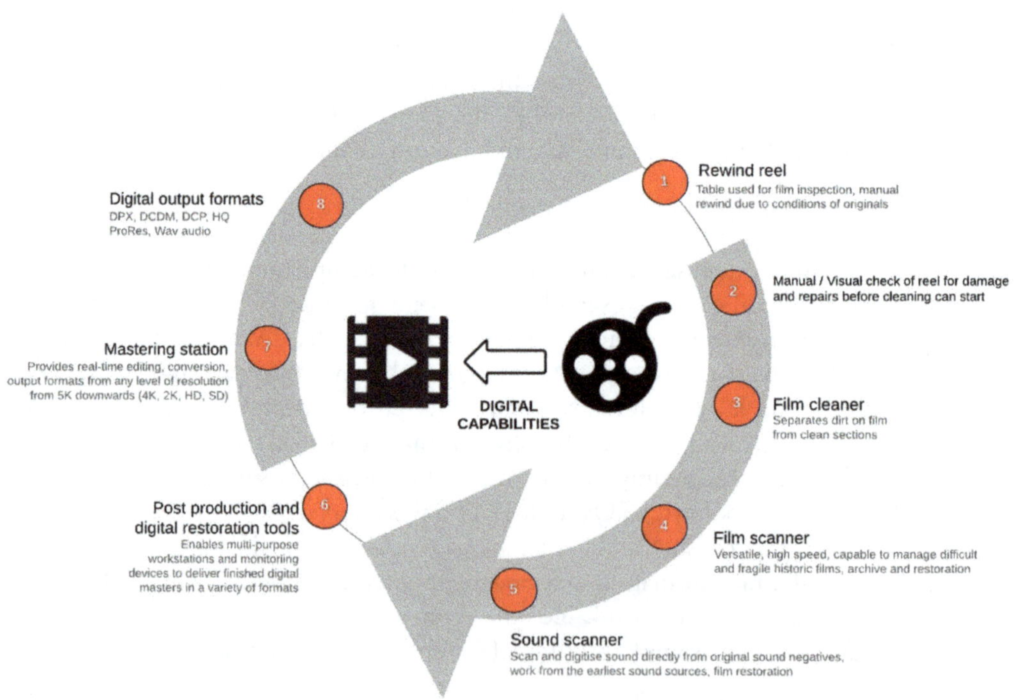

foundations from which to continue its transformation. During 2015, procurement through traditional tendering resulted in the addition of a new Scanity 2K film scanner from Digital Film Technologies, Phoenix, and Nucoda restoration, and editing systems from Digital Vision, along with a new film-cleaning machine from RTI.

Latest technology equipment and systems are unquestionably essential to progression, but most important are the skills and processes that will enable an archive to function effectively into the future. Throughout the Unlocking Film Heritage project, staff at the BFI Conservation Centre have been closely involved with each stage of the transformation to digital. Procurement teams for each area of technology enhancement were led by key archive staff, whose extensive knowledge and experience in respective fields removed the need for external consultants. The staff has been encouraged to engage with internal seminars, where new concepts, along with revisions of fundamental principles are discussed. As procurement and installation of new equipment have progressed, more specific workshops have been held to involve the whole team in the creation of new workflows and practices.

## Collaboration

Unlocking Film Heritage has been a project enjoying many facets of collaboration, embracing archives and collections across the many UK regions and nations. Archivists have forged new relationships with commercial service providers, and the common language of digital has been spoken by all.

Charles Fairall has worked at the BFI National Archive, UK, for 29 years and as Head of Conservation has primary responsibility for leading the technical teams to preserve and make accessible the extensive moving image collections which constitute the BFI National Archive. Significant recent projects that Charles has contributed to include: creation of the BFI Master Film Store, restoration of Alfred Hitchcock's earliest films, and transformation of the archive's operations to meet the challenges of a digital world. Charles is currently leading initiatives within the BFI's Unlocking Film Heritage project on technical standards and procedures and the further enhancement of the archive's digital capabilities and technical infrastructure. Charles is a Fellow of the Chartered Management Institute, a member of the Institution of Engineering and Technology, a member of the Royal Television Society, and a correspondent member of the FIAF Technical Commission.

## Notes

1. http://futureplan.bfi.org.uk/launch.aspx?pbid=62b10d3a-080b-4234-93d6-5fffb70b4509.
2. http://player.bfi.org.uk/.
3. Technical metadata as described within EBU Tech r 123.
4. https://www.gov.uk/government/uploads/system/uploads/attachment_data/file/225317/02_competitive_dialogue_procedure.pdf.

3

# New and Improved! Experiences from the Introduction of the National Library of Australia's Second Digital Collection Management System

**Mark Piva**


## Abstract

The National Library of Australia recently completed the implementation of its second iteration of a Library-wide digital collection management system. This paper presents a case study on the change in relation to the Oral History and Folklore Branch, comparing previous and current systems and discussing the system's development and implementation.



## Keywords

digital collection management system, Oral History and Folklore Branch, recorded interviews, Australians, social history, folkloric recordings, sounds database, tape-recorded collection, intelligent persistent identifier, persistent identifier, digital library infrastructure replacement, non-intelligent persistent identifier, accessioning workflow, preservation workflow, migration, audio.


## Introduction

The National Library of Australia recently completed the implementation of its second iteration of a Library-wide digital collection management system. This paper presents a case study on the impact of the system change in relation to the Oral History and Folklore Branch, and will discuss aspects such as the benefits and limitations of previous systems, development and implementation of the new system and an overview of the initial period after the new system went live. There is also discussion about the use of intelligent and non-intelligent permanent identifiers and how accessioning, preservation and delivery workflows were affected by the change.

## The Oral History and Folklore Collection

The National Library of Australia (the Library) holds the world's largest reference library of published and unpublished material relating to Australia and the Australian people, comprising of books, journals, magazines, pictures, photographs, maps, sheet music, audio recordings, manuscript papers, and ephemera. The Oral History and Folklore Branch (OH&F) manages a very successful program with original unpublished recordings dating back to the mid-1950s. It contains a wide range of recorded interviews with eminent Australians and social history and folkloric recordings. The collection currently comprises 46,500 hours, with newly commissioned interviews adding approximately 1,500 hours per year. Since November 2001, OH&F have been working through a digitisation plan to preserve all physical audio carriers to broadcast wave format (BWF). At February 2016, OH&F had preserved 88% (41,000 hours) of its collection.

## Collection Management System Precursor—Sounds Database

Although the title of this paper indicates discussion about the Library's second iteration of a digital management system, it is actually the third iteration of a collection management system for OH&F, as they used a standalone electronic database prior to the existence of a Library-wide system.



*Sustainable Audiovisual Collections* (2017): 16–20. DOI: 10.2979/jts2016.0.0.05

In 1996, a stocktake of all Oral History and Folklore collection carriers (originals and associated duplicates) was conducted, with the detailed information compiled into a Microsoft Access database named the "Sounds Database." The Sounds Database listed for each carrier: a unique intelligent identification number based on the Tape Recorded Collection (TRC) number, content description, and detailed technical information including size, duration, tape thickness, speed, type, equalisation, and brand.

Digital preservation of audio as BWF files commenced in November 2001, and the Sounds Database was used to generate descriptive and technical metadata for import into the file header. Technical information about the BWF master file and updated carrier duration was automatically reimported back into the database upon upload to mass storage.

The Sounds Database could also generate reports on the exact number of carriers in the collection at any particular time, along with their estimated duration, physical characteristics and digital preservation status.

## Collection Management System No. 1—DCM

In 2001, the Library designed and built the Digital Collections Manager (DCM), being the first iteration of a Library-wide system capable of centralising all digitised special collection copy records.

OH&F continued using the Sounds Database until 2005, at which time the DCM was enhanced to allow the import of physical carrier records. This enabled OH&F to continue managing their entire collection in DCM, in a similar fashion to the Sounds Database.

During migration, the TRC number used to identify carriers in the Sounds Database was converted to an intelligent persistent identifier (PI), which the DCM interpreted to organise material into a hierarchical structure of work records with a parent/child relationship.

An example of an intelligent PI is as follows: nla.oh-0121–0061–0001

- nla = National Library of Australia
- oh = Oral History and Folklore Collection
- 0121 = Mel Pratt Collection
- 0061 = Interview 61 – Sir Hubert Opperman interviewed by Mel Pratt
- 0001 = First session of the interview

The PI directly references the accessioning and holding number (TRC 121/61) and indicates the carrier's shelf location. Carrier information was attached to each work record as separate copy records. The PI formed the file name for audio preservation workflow files and gave necessary structure for mass storage purposes.

Compared to the Sounds Database, the DCM allowed integrated accessioning and digital preservation workflows and the creation of bibliographic links between the work record in DCM and the MARC catalogue record, as well as an increased number of data fields, allowing more advanced search capabilities and the generation of more complex reports.

In summary, the DCM became integral to the OH&F workflows and was used daily in all aspects of OH&F collection management: cataloguing, accessioning, preservation, online audio delivery, and access.

## Collection Management System No. 2—DLIR and Banjo

By 2011, DCM had reached the end of its effective life and a replacement system was required.

In terms of scope, the Digital Library Infrastructure Replacement (DLIR) program is the largest IT program ever undertaken by the Library. It involves all collection areas, as well as IT systems, IT storage, delivery, access and discovery areas. As the DLIR is a completely new infrastructure, and as the Library's needs were so complex and specific, the construction of the DLIR was conducted in-house. The expected completion date is 2017.

Key advantages the DLIR provides include:

- A new collections management system named "Banjo" that is more flexible and scalable in design, allowing modular development of new workflows as they are identified.
- A true end-to-end environment for all of the Library's digital collections, allowing advanced integration and dynamic synchronisation of information between all relevant systems, such as the Voyager Integrated Library Management System containing MARC catalogue records, the Trove aggregator, ArchivesSpace, Preservica, Forensic Toolkit, rights management systems and the cube-tec Dobbin render farm.
- Support of all collection workflows in a unified and consistent manner, from small-scale, single-item uploads to high-volume automated batch ingest.
- A new mass storage system completely decoupled from the management system and improvements in the way digital collection objects are organised, stored, and validated.

The DLIR program adopted "agile" development methodologies to enable multiple concurrent streams of design, implementation, and user acceptance testing. System requirements were documented as "stories" allowing accurate tracking and feedback on stage completion.

## Use of Nonintelligent Persistent Identifiers

A major modification introduced by Banjo was the move from an intelligent to a nonintelligent PI. The ongoing use of an intelligent PI became unsustainable, as long-term storage of the file necessitated the creation of restrictive hierarchical structures which caused file management difficulties.

To address this, Banjo allocates nonintelligent running number PIs to all digital objects. Continuing the example of the interview with Sir Hubert Opperman, the first session of his interview now has the following nonintelligent PI: nla.obj-214897814.

The lack of contextual information in the PI means the object's work record is free to be integrated into or removed from a structural relationship without damage to the integrity of the object or associated works.

However, the move to a nonintelligent PI posed a special risk to OH&F, given the time and effort spent to ensure the intelligent PI contained reliable and consistent contextual information. OH&F considered the sole use of a nonintelligent PI, but preexisting workflows and processes were too reliant on the intelligent PI structure.

Fortunately the flexibility of the new system allowed the incorporation of both PI types into each record, so the new nonintelligent PI can act as the definitive identifier for the object, whilst the older intelligent PI exists for OH&F use as an "Alias PI" free text field. OH&F continue to apply and manage the Alias PI field for new content according to preexisting accessioning rules and are able to identify collection items using the Alias PI with similar search and reporting functionality to what was available in DCM. Banjo also allows the use of the Alias PI during the preservation workflow, which then converts the file name to the nonintelligent PI when uploaded to mass storage.

## Banjo—OH&F Design

Scoping, design and implementation of Banjo workflows began in 2012 for the books and journals collections, followed in 2013 by the pictures and manuscripts collections. General scoping and drafting requirements for OH&F commenced during October 2013.

As mentioned above, OH&F accessioning and preservation workflows were already well established within the DCM environment, but it was still necessary to objectively question workflows that were in some cases ten years old. This in turn identified redundancies, such as the production of access copies in obsolete formats and workflow gaps, such as the ability to manage time-coded transcripts/summaries and digitally preserved video.

System requirements were scoped as conceptual diagrams and transformed into detailed specification stories, which were repeatedly checked to confirm all requirements were documented and to ensure existing DCM functionality was not inadvertently lost in Banjo.

## Banjo—OH&F Development

Dedicated development for OH&F commenced in January 2015, with an estimated duration of eight months, to be followed by an additional month for data migration.

Banjo was designed with a single accessioning workflow to provide consistency of metadata across all collection records. This allows other collection areas to accession and manage collection content such as audio material, which previously had to be incorporated into the OH&F collection in order for it to be preserved.

Banjo was also designed to have a single preservation workflow, but it was recognised that existing OH&F audio preservation workflows were too complex and highly integrated with other systems to be altered. Therefore, it was agreed to recreate existing DCM audio preservation workflows in Banjo, with necessary improvements to reflect updated processing requirements.

## Banjo—OH&F User Acceptance Testing

A number of test environments were created, along with dedicated IT systems for logging and tracking bugs and issues (JIRA software). A significant amount of time was invested prior to testing to create accurate and sensible test data, as it was not possible to import existing work and copy records into the test environment. It was necessary to have a large number of records available, as in some cases it was not possible to reuse records for further testing.

Along with testing accessioning and preservation workflows, OH&F tested and assessed the interaction between Banjo and other Library systems such as the Voyager Integrated Library Management System and the Online Audio Delivery System. This included analysis of how work records automatically generated in one system would flow into another, along with identifying any subsequent impediments to the preservation process.

By August 2015, although much had been achieved, the test environment was very fragile and there were times when testing was limited to a specific aspect of a story, as other parts of the Banjo system were yet to be developed. In order to maintain progress, OH&F reviewed outstanding tasks and stories along with holding weekly meetings to report on findings. This provided an important venue for discussion and sharing of information and quickly became a fast-track method of finding solutions and forming small teams to solve more complex issues.

Towards the end of the testing period it became more possible to test end-to-end workflows, but it was also necessary to retest previously completed procedures, as constant development of Banjo meant new code could inadvertently introduce bugs.

## Banjo—OH&F Data Migration

DCM contained approximately 83,500 work records and 500,000 associated copy records for the OH&F collection. OH&F accessioning and preservation workflows prevented the use of Banjo and DCM at the same time, so it was essential that all OH&F DCM data and records be migrated to Banjo prior to production use.

In March 2015, OH&F commenced an analysis and categorisation of OH&F work and copy record structures in order to create a set of migration rules. Work records were separated into two categories: those which were delivered online (31%—25,900 work records) and those which were not (69%—57,600 work records). Migration of works not delivered online was relatively straightforward. However, the migration of online delivered works was much more complicated.

DCM was unable to deliver audio directly from the work record holding the audio objects. So in order to deliver audio online, it was necessary to create an intermediate work record to act as a bridge between the DCM and the Online Audio Delivery System. The intermediate work was then subsequently linked to the work record holding the audio objects. Many intermediate works held time-coded transcripts and summaries relating to the audio, which resulted in fragmented management of copies relating to a single work.

In contrast, Banjo allows audio delivery directly from a single work record without the need for an additional intermediate work. Time-coded transcripts and summaries can be attached to the same work record as the audio, thereby drawing together all relevant copies.

A flat migration of work records from DCM would have included now-redundant intermediate work records, so the solution was to "fold in" intermediate work records into the works they were delivering. This strategy was of high risk, as the folding in of records had to take place at the same time the records were migrated. The creation, testing, and refinement of these specific migration rules took two months.

On 28 October 2015, OH&F ceased DCM data entry to allow necessary premigration file and record audits. Data migration for work and copy records commenced on November 17, 2015 and was successfully completed on November 30, 2015. Another month of data quality checks were carried out to ensure all information was transferred correctly, with amendments due to inconsistent DCM data required for only 950 records.

## Banjo—OH&F Production

OH&F commenced using production Banjo on December 9, 2015, and whilst the system is still being tested and refined, a number of benefits and increased efficiencies have already been experienced, including:

- Synchronised transfer of information between Library systems, increased search capabilities, enhanced preservation workflows for metadata creation and upload, and the ability to bulk ingest collection material
- Advanced delivery functionality, including online delivery of audio directly from work records, and automatic online release of time-coded transcripts and summaries
- The ability for collection areas to accession material of any format and add new carrier types

However, the biggest advantage provided by Banjo and the DLIR stems from the flexibility offered by the use of a nonintelligent PI. The Library now has a highly flexible and adaptable collection management system, allowing collection areas to accession items in any order with the ability to easily rearrange their structure and relationship at any future time. Audio from different collection areas can be grouped together and delivered online, without disturbing the context of the audio within a particular collection, nor the structural integrity of the audio files, work and copy records, and their long-term storage. Alongside these advancements, system flexibility has maintained established OH&F collection management processes through the retention of the older intelligent PI as the "Alias PI" free text field.

The replacement of the Library's digital infrastructure was a complex and difficult undertaking, however the Library's collection is now in a much better position to be sustained and made accessible for future generations.

Mark Piva is the Manager of Sound Preservation and Technical Services within the Oral History and Folklore Branch of the National Library of Australia in Canberra, Australia. He is responsible for the management and development of the digital audio preservation program for the Library, including preservation of newly commissioned born digital recordings and supervision of preservation of legacy audiovisual material in the Library's special collections.

He was significantly involved in the transition of the Oral History and Folklore Collection to a new digital collection management system, including specification of the required system's functionality, coordination of user acceptance testing and supervision of the associated migration of 580,000 work and copy records.

# Changing Gears: Fast-Lane Design for Accelerated Innovation in Memory Organisations

4

**Johan Oomen, Maarten Brinkerink, Bouke Huurnink, and Josefien Schuurman**

## Abstract

Audiovisual archives are embracing the opportunities offered by digitisation for managing their work processes and offering new services to a wide array of user groups. Organisation strategy, working processes, and software development need to be able to support a culture where innovation can flourish. Some institutions are beginning to adopt the concept of "two-speed IT." The core strategy aims to accommodate two tracks simultaneously: foundational but "slow," and innovative but flexible and "fast." This paper outlines the rationale behind the two-speed IT strategy. It highlights a specific implementation at the Netherlands Institute for Sound and Vision, a large audiovisual archive and museum. Two-speed IT is enabling Sound and Vision to reach its business objectives.

## Keywords

strategy, participatory culture, infrastructure, innovation, asset management, software development.

## Introduction

Museums benefit from fostering a "culture of innovation" as a way to effectively manage ever-changing expectations of user groups, and at the same time make the most of new opportunities offered by technology (Simon, 2011). The fundamental challenge is how to achieve the public missions (i.e., supporting a myriad of users to utilize heritage collections so that they can actively learn, experience, and create). As Douglas Rushkoff (2014) notes, "It's not about how digital technology changes us, but how we change ourselves and one another now that we live so digitally." For this, it is essential for museums to have access to technical infrastructure that allows not only for digital assets management but also to "pursue contemporary objectives" (Johnson et al., 2015)—for instance, using new channels for content distribution, (e.g., YouTube, Instagram) to engage with new user groups, or using technologies (e.g., linked open data, NLP) to enrich and optimize work processes or allow for creative ways to access collections (Gorgels, 2013).

In this paper, we propose the fostering of innovation for heritage organisations through "two-speed IT" (Bossert, 2015) and the accompanying organisational structure to realise it. We first zoom in on some of the most urgent challenges audiovisual archives face today, and then we highlight the necessity for audiovisual archives to invest in innovative capital to ensure long-term impact. In next section, we introduce the concept of two-speed IT as a way to ensure uptake of innovative IT solutions in a production environment, and then we illustrate how two-speed IT can function in practice.

## Audiovisual Archives and the Future

Audiovisual materials will be as much a part of the future fabric of information as text-based materials are today. As creation continues to expand, archives will be storing and managing increasingly large collections of assets. Archives operate within a dynamic and multifaceted context. They will grow to become nodes in a network of communities along with other content providers and a variety of stakeholders from industries ranging across education and research, creative industries (publishing, broadcasting, game industry), tourism, journalism, and so on. Recent studies indicate that by around 2025, analogue carriers will need to have been digitised. After that date, it will be impossible to transfer the carriers, due to either technical obsolescence of the playback devices or the physical state of the carriers (Casey, 2015; National Film and Sound Archive, 2015; Wright, 2012).

For many archives, managing "born digital" is already the norm, with analogue collections growing only through donations or acquisitions. So, the future of audiovisual archives is digital. Multiple formats will need to be supported, from the highest industry standards to emerging open-video formats and wrappers. Content, in various formats, will continue to be managed through specialised asset management systems. Metadata will be fine-grained, allowing access at shot or scene level (W3C, 2011). Standards will be adopted to allow interchange between collections (Resource Description Framework, Simple Knowledge Organisation System, Persistent Identifiers, schema.org, etc.) and to maintain a record of provenance or metadata records as content is distributed online. Navigation across the combination of semantic data and a diverse range of media types is essential. In terms of the value chain of media consumption and production, the position of archives and roles of archive staff will evolve. Already today, we see the transformation of the traditional role of archivists/cataloguers. The future archivist plays a role as media manager; managing assets from their inception all the way through to distribution and long-term storage (Lydon and Kleinert, 2011).

In summary, we envision the future audiovisual archives as being smart, connected, and open, using smart technologies to optimise workflows for annotation and content distribution. Audiovisual archives can do so by:

1. Collaborating with third parties to codesign and codevelop new technologies in order to manifest themselves as front-runners rather than followers (Brynjolfsson and McAfee, 2014)

2. Connecting to other sources of information (other collections, contextual sources) and to a variety of often niche user communities, researchers, and the creative industries

3. Embracing the use of standards defined by external instances rather than by the cultural heritage communities themselves

4. Fully adopting "open" as the default to have maximum impact on society by applying open licenses for content delivery, using open-source software and open standards wherever possible, promoting open access to publications, and so on

Asset management systems will need to be able to manage various streams of metadata:

1. Metadata exported from production systems
2. Expert annotations
3. Machine-generated metadata
4. Crowd-sourced annotations and other sources
5. Knowledge extracted from secondary sources related to content

With respect to ensuring long-term storage, archives need to make fundamental choices between storing content on servers they own, using cloud storage, or opting for mixed models. Other choices relate to the type of storage media (tape, optical, solid state, hard drives) and adaptation of standardised working processes to endure digital durability.

The dynamics between the creative industries and archives will change. Archive staff and "creatives" will be working more closely together than ever before (Eskevich et al., 2013). These result in ample opportunities, for instance playing a more proactive role in the production process, and suggest topics for new programmes based on gems from the archive. This relates to the future role of archives as curators of vast materials of content. Filters need to be applied to provide meaningful access to vast collections. These files can be created by machines (recommender systems), by experts, or by a smart combination of both.

## Fostering A "Culture of Innovation"

The lawful foundation of archives differs from organisation to organisation. Some organisations are established by law as separate entities (legal deposits); others are part of larger organisations like museums, libraries, universities, or broadcasters. In many cases, audiovisual collections are maintained by public bodies and in effect serve public missions, but not exclusively. Commercial footage libraries and other commercial entities (e.g., search engines and video platforms) are also looking after growing bodies of audiovisual heritage, albeit with other primary motivations than providing access to gain knowledge or support creative processes. Growing areas of importance are private archives, notably created by the billions of people carrying smartphones that allow for high-quality multimedia recording. Personal archiving is starting to be addressed (Redwine, 2015) but is still a huge area of research. Established archives are investigating to what extent they can help ensure long-term access to these collections. Many commercial players are active in this domain, from social networks to cloud storage providers. Given this context, it is key for "traditional" archives to educate their constituents about the value they bring to society through securing the sharing of knowledge, a prerequisite for democracies to function; but also, perhaps more down to earth, to educate and entertain communities and individuals and to facilitate the exchange of ideas between various stakeholders.

Over the past years, we have participated in many online and offline discussions in the audiovisual archive domain. Below are some of the main subjects that will impact their future position given the context in which they operate.

Foremost, audiovisual archives are in a challenging position, operating as custodians of (mostly) in-copyright works whilst also managing the public's expectations in providing online access. Copyright rules need to be modified to allow memory organisations to provide access to their collections. A balance needs to be found between giving creators a remuneration for using their works and allowing the guardians of their works to provide public access for various user groups. As a fundamental rule, content added to the public domain should stay in the public domain (Communia, 2011). Also, memory organisations should consider adopting an "open by default" access policy, as to lead by example. Also, archives could consider liaising with rights owners and study the possibility to to provide access to commercially unviable (i.e., out-of-commerce) content with few restrictions (European Commission, 2012). Modernisation of copyright regulations should look at collective licensing and other ways that decrease the burden of obtaining copyright permissions. With respect to newly created material, creators should be encouraged to use Creative Commons licenses to foster a culture of innovation and creativity. For works commissioned by public institutions, the use of open licenses could be made compulsory (European Commission, 2015).

Impact needs to be measurable and measured wherever and whenever possible, not only because archives are asked to be accountable for how resources are spent, but also to build solid business cases that will enable future investments, be they in services or supporting infrastructures. Following the Balanced Value Impact Model, we can distinguish between internal, innovation, economic, and social impact (Tanner, 2012). Impact metrics also need to take into account new types of use. Already, material from archives is shared using open licenses (e.g., on platforms such as Wikipedia) (Brinkerink, 2015). Use on these third-party platforms needs to be monitored if possible; alternatively, qualitative evidence needs to be gathered. Audio and video fingerprinting can be used to track content usage over various platforms.

As a result of digitisation, archives and their users are sharing the same information space. To fully realise their potential, archives need to ensure that their collections are available where users reside. A practical implication of this truism is that institutionally maintained access points such as searchable archive catalogues should not be the only way to access collections. On the Web, content likes to travel, and archives must embrace this fact, at the least by making their catalogues findable for online search engines and shareable on social media platforms, but more fundamentally by providing developers with application program interface (API) access to the catalogue and content and by adopting machine-readable copyright labels to facilitate access (Chan and Cope, 2015). In this way, third parties can "build upon" online collections (e.g., publishers that integrate resources in learning environments). Following this "liberalisation" of content, a new paradigm emerges that allows archives to focus their efforts on "super serving" niche communities such as filmmakers, media scholars, and amateur historians.

Archives benefit from fostering a "culture of innovation"as a way to effectively manage ever-changing expectations of user groups, and at the same time make the most of new opportunities offered by technology (Mckeown, 2012). For this, it is essential for archives to have access to technical infrastructure that allows not only management of digital assets, but also the pursuit of contemporary objectives in line with user expectations. For instance: using new channels for content distribution such as YouTube and Instagram to engage with new user groups; using technologies such as linked open data and natural language processing to augment and optimize work processes; or allowing for creative ways to access collections. A "culture of innovation" will also open possibilities to increase the level of cooperation with academia in areas ranging from digital humanities to computer science.

## Introducing Two-Speed IT

Bossert (2014) outlines how organisations need to have capabilities in four distinct areas in order for them to remain successful as their operations and services are increasingly digitised:

First, because the digital business model allows the creation of digital products and services, companies need to become skilled at digital-product innovation that meets changing customer expectations.

Second, companies need to provide a seamless multichannel (digital and physical) experience so consumers can move effortlessly from one channel to another. For example, many shoppers use smartphones to reserve a product online and pick it up in a store.

Third, companies should use big data and advanced analytics to better understand customer behavior. For example, gaining insight into customers' buying habits—with their consent, of course—can lead to an improved customer experience and increased sales through more effective cross-selling. Fourth, companies need to improve their capabilities in automating operations and digitizing business processes. This is important because it enables quicker response times to customers while cutting operating waste and costs.

In order to deliver on a timely basis, software development of "testing, failing, learning, adapting, and iterating rapidly" (Bossert, 2014) needs to be in place. However, applying an "experimental" development approach in an operational context that includes critical back-end (legacy) systems is hardly possible, nor is it appropriate. As a way to cope with this fundamental incompatibility, organisations can choose to adopt a digital product management model, coined "two-speed IT." This accommodates two tracks, or "speeds," simultaneously: a "slow" foundational speed and a "fast" innovative speed. Below, we introduce the concept as it may be used in the heritage domain.

### Two-Speed IT in the Heritage Domain

In the heritage domain, managing digital assets and embracing innovation are characterised by very different dimensions—in terms of standards used, in terms of partnerships, in terms of managing investments over time, in terms of accountability, in terms of staff expertise, and so on.

For the "slow" speed, standardised and off-the shelf solutions are used to secure 24/7 service. The solutions are updated following service-level agreements with suppliers. In the heritage domain, good examples are systems for managing storage, cataloguing, play-out, and ordering. Given the impact, the frequency of updating applications in the "slow" ecosystem is not high and is measured in months or years rather than weeks.

The "fast" speed features mostly tailor-made solutions that cater to very specific user requirements and are used to experiment with new technologies. The applications do not have very stringent requirement regarding stability and minimum "uptime" (i.e., they are in some cases maintained by developers themselves). For instance: experimental visualisations of data sets, automatic metadata extraction services, and online magazines linked to current exhibits. This is the "speed" most closely connected to creating highly personalised experiences (Rodney, 2016).

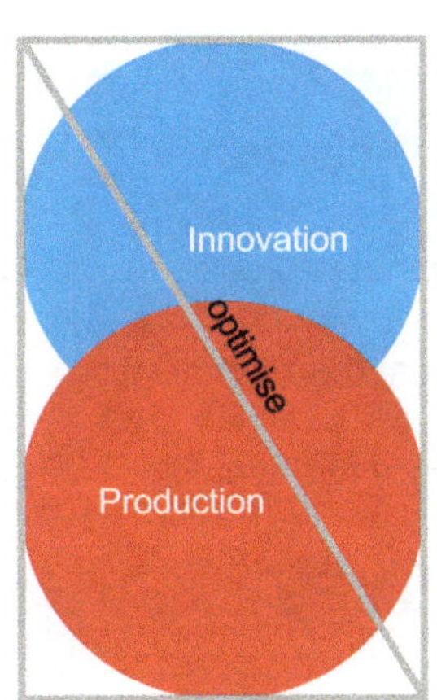


**Figure 1.** The two-speed IT ecosystems.

Both ecosystems have their specific infrastructures, applications, development, and staging environments, as well as suppliers. As highlighted in figure 1, they overlap partly, for instance when ecosystems make use of similar underlying streams of data. In practice, the "conversion" from slow to fast is a process driven by business requirements. What's key is to optimise systems and processes.

Our illustrative use case is the Netherlands Institute for Sound and Vision (hereafter also referred to as "Sound and Vision" and "the institute"). Sound and Vision is a leading audiovisual archive with a growing digitised collection of 1.9 million objects (ranging from film, television, and radio broadcasts to music recordings and Web videos) and a museum that attracts approximately 250,000 visitors annually. Born-digital assets are ingested in a state-of-the-art digital repository accessible both online and in the museum.

While putting two-speed IT into practice, Sound and Vision has been inspired by leading examples in the cultural field, which have been putting a similar "culture of innovation" into practice, also bringing the two-speeds together. For instance, the Rijksmuseum has built a state-of-the art, high-quality, and immense online collection on top of the data from its internal ADLIB catalogue, while taking the idea of an active audience more than seriously with their Rijksstudio (Gorgels, 2013). Also, the award-winning and Webby-nominated Walker Art Center website couldn't have been built without a strong emphasis on in-house and iterative Web development (Simon, 2011).

Another source of inspiration is the API-driven technology "stack" of the Cooper Hewitt, enabling innovative ways to unlock the TMS collection database, both online and on site (Chan and Cope, 2015). The stack of the Cooper Hewitt connects two proprietary servers: the collection database (TMS) and the database that knows about the visitors. In the context of this paper, these servers are positioned in the "slow" speed ecosystem. An API allows the creation of a range software applications, including the website and the interactives in the exhibits. As Meyer (2015) notes, "the [Cooper Hewitt] museum made a piece of infrastructure for the public. But the museum will benefit in the long term, because the infrastructure will permit them to plan for the near future."

The API is also connected to third-party sources including social media platforms such as Flickr and Instagram, creating richer and more personalised experiences for visitors.

## Two-Speed IT in Practice

Sound and Vision has ensured the successful transition to the digital domain after completing a seven-year, 90 million euro programme to digitise its analogue assets. Today, it has one of the

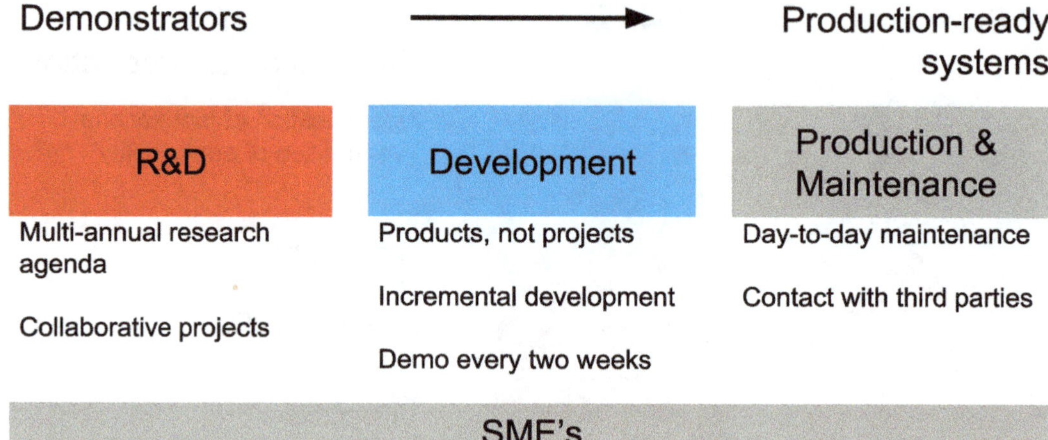


**Figure 2.** Departments working on two-speed IT at the institute.

largest collections of digital heritage assets in the world, totalling over 15 petabytes. Recently, a multiannual innovation agenda was adopted, consisting of five research themes:

1. Automatic metadata extraction and big data analysis
2. Explore new access paradigms
3. Understand users
4. Ensure digital durability
5. Study the impact of media

An integral part of the transition to the digital domain, a new mission statement, a new strategic plan (covering 2016 to 2020), and a new organisational structure were defined and implemented. A guiding principle was the conviction that the success of memory organisations lies in their ability to make the abovementioned notions of "smart," "connected," and "open" an integral part of their strategies (Oomen and Aroyo, 2011; Ridge, 2014). Sound and Vision adopted two-speed IT as one of the key design principles.

Before implementing two-speed IT, software development had been mainly executed by third-party software developers. Also, there were few formalised connections between research and development (RandD) and the rest of the organisations, making it hardly possible to implement results from RandD in daily operations.

Hence, two-speed IT needed to be grounded also in the organisational structure. Today, three department are jointly responsible for delivering successful IT solutions: RandD, Development, and Production and Maintenance (fig. 2).

The departments have the following responsibilities:

1. R & D (Research and Development): implementing the research agenda through participation in research projects. Software development by scientific programmers.

2. Development: translating business requirements into functional requirements. Development following SCRUM. Evaluating output of R & D projects. Creating services and applications that foster and adopt innovation.

3. Production and Maintenance: ensuring the uptime of applications, installing new versions and patches from third-party suppliers according to set service-level agreements.

Small and medium enterprises (SMEs) also play a key role, as they are involved in the successive stages; they are partners in R & D programmes and are involved.

Note that the three departments are not responsible for the business requirements and product ownership of the services developed. The business units, Archive (responsible for the collection management and access) and Museum (operating the Sound and Vision museum and online presentation), are responsible for this.

Handling of the flow and resources between the teams will be addressed by adopting the concept of (living) labs that allow Sound and Vision to experiment and explore innovative concepts in a near-production environment, in close-to-real-life scenarios with realistic data sets. As we require the labs to be based upon production system infrastructure and protocols, the uptake of successful concepts in the production environment can be much smoother. Obviously this requires close tuning and synchronisation between the three departments involved.

### First Adoptions: Speaker Labeling and Entity Extraction

At Sound and Vision, an off-the-shelf asset management system (DAAN, Digital Audiovisual Archive Netherlands) from supplier Vizrt forms the foundation of the "slow" ecosystem (Vizrt, 2015). The asset management is the "core" of the archive and includes services to search, view, select, license, and order digital media assets. Next to DAAN is a more agile "fast" ecosystem of tailor-made solutions for distinct functionalities, notably open-source search and automatic metadata extraction. This is the layer where output of research can be implemented in production workflows.

Following the two-speed IT, Sound and Vision successfully deployed automatic speaker labelling (a result from a research project with Radboud University) in 2014, speeding up the annotation process and offering a new access point to the collections. In 2015, technology to extract names of people, places, events, and organisations from subtitle files was introduced. This was originally developed in collaboration with the University of Amsterdam. In both cases, spin-off companies from universities are playing an important role in the process, as they were involved in developing the initial demonstrators with academics and currently are working under a service-level agreement with the Production and Maintenance department.

### Scaling Up Two-Speed IT for Online Availability

Plans are underway for a major revision of the access strategy. Using the off-the-shelf asset management system as the back end, distinct access scenarios will be supported. This will be the ultimate test case for the "two-speed IT" approach, as it impacts multiple departments and requires significant investments in the infrastructure.

Revising the access strategy starting with identifying three ways to make collections available online that are in line with the strategic plan for 2016 to 2020:

1. Public accessibility: providing access to the collections for everyone. This is one of the core missions of the institute. It ensures everyone can search through the entire catalogue online and—if possible—also directly consult the material. If the material isn't digitized yet, or if rights are not cleared for online consultation, alternative options for accessing the material will be presented to the user.

2. Online presentation: highlighting core parts and specific items from the collection, in high quality. This allows the institute to enact its role as a museum in an online environment. It involves interpretation and contextualisation of the collection through singling out and featuring individual objects. Being able to to experiment with different online forms of presentation is key here. Active participation of the online audience will play an important role in ensuring that production of meaning is not limited to the perspective of the museum curator.

3. Open reusability: enabling reuse of the "open" metadata and content by individuals and by third-party applications (through APIs). This supports the "open by default" access policy that the institute adheres to, allowing third parties to reuse collections that fall in the public domain or, where relevant, IPR is held by Sound and Vision.

These three forms (fig. 3) together clarify what online availability constitutes for the institute. Subsequently, they provide a starting point for the formulation of functional and technical requirements for the infrastructure that is required to support them.

The three forms of online availability are not tied to a particular service or organisational department, as they transcend the business units Museum, Archive, and RandD. Furthermore,

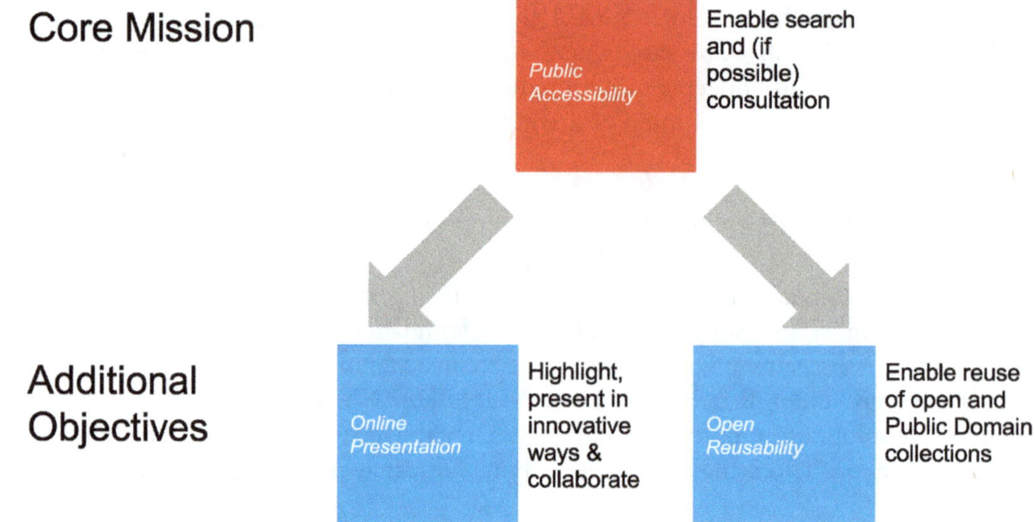


**Figure 3.** Schematic overview of the three forms of online availability.

they provide insight into the different ways in which the institute achieves its tasks and goals in relation to online availability of its collections. The different forms of online availability are complementary to, and interdependent on, each other. The realisation of the three forms of online availability is an important step towards a holistic online strategy for Sound and Vision. Therefore, it is crucial to ensure that these forms are realised simultaneously. This averts fragmentation of the online services provided by the institute and reflects the complementary nature and mutual reinforcement of the three forms.

The next step in defining the online strategy was making an inventory of the functional and technical requirements for the three forms of online availability:

For public accessibility, it is of prime importance that the entire collection is found easily. This requires proper integration into popular search engines, detailed metadata, and search functionality that meets the needs of the user. Navigating the collection must be intuitive and insightful (e.g., supported with automated recommendations and contextualised with links to internal and external collections). When material can be made available online, it is important that the quality and user experience meet the expectations of everyday consumers of online media services. These are constantly evolving. When only metadata is available for online consultation, alternative viewing options (in situ consultation or ordering a physical copy) need to be offered. All of this relies heavily on sound administration of the relevant features and information in the catalogue.

Online presentation is about highlighting specific items from the collection and placing them in a rich, meaningful context. This is managed through curation, research, and editorial work and is supported by automatic, data-driven curation mechanisms. It is the ambition of the Museum unit to experiment and innovate in the online presentation forms. The user's own voice is of great importance here. An important requirement is therefore to support public participation, enable a dialogue with the user, and give the audience an active role in the production of meaning.

The open reusability of the collection is primarily supported by capturing specific (IPR) information about the collection in the catalogue, particularly the application of open licenses or the fact that an item is part of the public domain. This information will then be made explicit in the appropriate form for both humans and (search) machines. To support various types of use of the content, it should be available in high-quality and open-media formats (both consultation copies and source files). For automated forms of reuse by third parties, programmatic access to the collection (metadata and content) through an open API—without login—is a requirement.

The three forms of online availability provide opportunities to strengthen each other. For example, the contextualisation (automated or curated) that results from the Online Presentation could greatly enhance the intuitive navigation of the online catalogue that is provided under Public Accessibility, and vice versa.

To meet the functional and technical requirements for the three forms of online availability summarised above, several new components need to be introduced into the digital infrastructure of Sound and Vision. Here are the three most important ones:

*Transcoding and online consultation copies.* Online consultation copies are intended as end products that enable the user to consult the archival material online (and also to reuse the material in the case of Open Reusability). Playback quality and the file formats that are utilized must be in line with the expectations of everyday consumers of online media services (like YouTube and Netflix), which are constantly evolving. Important to note here is that the online consultation copies must be generated for only a small part of the entire archive, namely where the IPR status permits online consultation. In the current situation, this is an estimated 0.180 percent of the entire collection (and 0.600 percent of the digital collection). The proportion available for reuse is estimated to be 0.032 percent of the entire collection. The nature of the online consultation copies comes with higher demands on the playback quality (for an optimal user experience) and the variety of file formats (for different purposes and devices, in a rapidly changing technical environment). This differs from the so-called low-res preview proxies that have already been generated for the entire digital archive, for use in the media asset management (MAM) system.

*Data processing and enrichment.* Online availability of the Sound and Vision archive is reliant on four sources. Source files are stored in the Digital Archive, which can be accessed via the MAM. The MAM also serves as a catalog and contains the metadata of all objects. The Thesaurus ensures consistent use of descriptive terms and serves as a bridge to link to the various collections in the archive and (external) context sources. To assist navigation and automated contextualisation, based on the abovementioned sources a media and data analysis component is required. Automatic annotation and linking is performed by various algorithms. The resulting annotations are, if possible, put back into the MAM catalogue (as metadata enrichments).

*Flexible back end.* The flexible back end is an API service architecture that combines data from multiple internal and external collections and context sources. It functions as an intermediate layer in the digital infrastructure, in order to extend the standard functionality provided by the MAM with specific functionality required for the three forms of online availability. The resulting combined data is exposed via various service APIs to which online platforms and third parties can connect (depending on the goal).

The abovementioned functional and technical requirements and proposed components also offer new possibilities beyond the three forms of online availability. First, the flexible back end can support experimentation, innovation, and incubation based on the Sound and Vision archive by combining direct access to the digital archive and collection metadata with new forms of media and data analysis and/or audience participation. This is relevant for internal RandD, but also for experimentation and innovation on the basis of the archive by (research) partners and startups. It allows the various parties to experiment (casually, exploratively, or in a defined lab setting) with the enrichment of the archive. This corresponds with the desirable behavior in ecosystem “fast” of two-speed IT. Second, the infrastructure described above offers opportunities for new ways to provide access to and/or present the digital collection within the walls of the institution. Besides exploiting the digital archive and collection metadata, the (automated) enrichment, contextualisation, and linking of the items is reused in the museum context. This provides opportunities for better integration of online and on-site museum experiences.

On the one hand, continuity of the museum exhibitions during the opening hours of the museum are of high importance and should therefore reside in ecosystem “slow” of two-speed IT. However, to provide a more contextualised, dynamic, and personalised experience for the visitor, it is also important to be able to expose the museum visitor to the innovations happening in ecosystem “fast” from the outset. This allows for incremental development of new museum experiences and also provides opportunities for audience engagement, beyond what ecosystem “slow” can offer.

## Conclusions

In this paper, we proposed that heritage institutions consider adopting "two-speed IT" to enable innovation in parallel to maintaining a stable core digital infrastructure. In presenting our case, we sketched our vision of the potential future role of archives and some of the challenges that they will face to fulfill that potential. We also give a brief outline of the concept of two-speed IT and propose its embedding as a dual pair of ecosystems for cultural heritage organisations.

Our proposal is based on the successful implementation of two-speed IT at the Netherlands Institute for Sound and Vision, which has adapted the approach to enable it to innovate with new technology while maintaining a stable, standardised basis for IT infrastructure. This has had impact on the strategy and organisational structure of the institute. Following the implementation of this approach, cutting-edge speaker identification and automatic entity-extraction techniques were successfully implemented in production systems in 2014 and 2015. This year, an ambitious programme on online access has been initiated (see "Two-Speed IT in Practice").

Over the past two years, we have learned a lot regarding two-speed IT and have found it to be a well-suited strategy for ensuring that the outcomes of research and innovation projects can find their way to production systems. With the experience gained over the past years, we look forward to implementing the new access strategy and further developing the two-speed IT model within our own organisation. We hope other museums and memory organisations think about creating and maintaining the technical prerequisites to flourish in an online networked environment.

In future work, we will compare how different organisations are adopting similar or alternative approaches to the two-speed challenge with the aim to substantiate our initial findings further.

Johan Oomen, Maarten Brinkerink, Bouke Huurnink, and Josefien Schuurman are with the Netherlands Institute for Sound and Vision, The Netherlands.

## References

Besser, H. (2015). Personal digital archiving: Issues for libraries and a summary of the PDA conference. *IFLA WLIC 2015*. Cape Town, South Africa. Retrieved from http://library.ifla.org/1218/1/197-besser-en.pdf.

Bossert, O. (2015). Organizing for digital acceleration: Making a two-speed IT operating model work. *McKinsey and Company*. Retrieved from http://www.mckinsey.com/industries/high-tech/our-insights/organizing-for-digital-acceleration-making-a-two-speed-it-operating-model-work.

Brinkerink, M. (2015, June 17). Dutch cultural heritage reaches millions every month. *Netherlands Institute for Sound and Vision*. Retrieved from https://www.beeldengeluid.nl/en/blogs/research-amp-development-en/201506/dutch-cultural-heritage-reaches-millions-every-month.

Brynjolfsson, E., and McAfee, A. (2014). *The second machine age: Work, progress, and prosperity in a time of brilliant technologies*. New York: W. W. Norton.

Casey, M. (2015, January). Why media preservation can't wait: The gathering storm. *IASA Journal* 44, 14–22.

Chan, S., and Cope, A. (2015, April 6). Strategies against architecture: interactive media and transformative technology at Cooper Hewitt. *MW2015: Museums and the Web 2015*. Retrieved from http://mw2015.museumsandtheweb.com/paper/strategies-against-architecture-interactive-media-and-transformative-technology-at-cooper-hewitt/.

Communia. (2011, June). Policy recommendations. Retrieved from http://www.communia-association.org/recommendations/.

Eskevich, M., Jones, G. J. F., Aly, R., Ordelman, R., Chen, S., Nadeem, D., Guinaudeau, C., Gravier, G., Sébillot, P., De Nies, T., Debevere, P., Van de Walle, R., Galuscáková, P., Pecina, P., and Larson, M. (2013). Multimedia information seeking through search and hyperlinking. *Proceedings of the 3rd ACM conference on International conference on multimedia retrieval.* Dallas, Texas. Retrieved from http://hal.archives-ouvertes/icmr106-eskevich.pdf.

European Commission. (2012, September 20). Memorandum of understanding (MoU) on key principles on the digitisation and making available of out-of-commerce works. Retrieved from http://ec.europa.eu/internal_market/copyright/out-of-commerce/index_en.htm.
European Commission. (2015, July 23). European legislation on reuse of public sector information. Retrieved from https://ec.europa.eu/digital-agenda/en/european-legislation-reuse-public-sector-information.
Gorgels, P. (2013, January 28). Rijksstudio: Make your own masterpiece! In N. Proctor and R. Cherry (eds.), *Museums and the Web 2013*. Silver Spring, MD. Retrieved from http://mw2013.museumsandtheweb.com/paper/rijksstudio-make-your-own-masterpiece/.
Johnson, L., Adams Becker, S., Estrada, V., and Freeman, A. (2015). NMC Horizon report: 2015 museum edition. Austin, Texas: The New Media Consortium.
Maggie, L., and Kleinert, A. (2011). BBC roles for archivists: Developments of archivists roles and competencies.
Mckeown, M. (2012). *Adaptability: The art of winning in an age of uncertainty*. London: Kogan Page Limited.
Meyer, Robinson. (2015, January 20). The Museum of the future is here. *The Atlantic*. Retrieved from http://www.theatlantic.com/technology/archive/2015/01/how-to-build-the-museum-of-the-future/384646/.
National Film and Sound Archive. (2015). Deadline 2025: Collections at risk. Retrieved from http://www.nfsa.gov.au/site_media/uploads/file/2015/10/29/Deadline_2025_Collections_at_risk.pdf.
Oomen, J., and Aroyo, L. (2011). Crowdsourcing in the cultural heritage domain: Opportunities and challenges. In *Proceedings of the 5th International Conference on Communities and Technologies*. (pp. 138–149) ACM.
Redwine, G. (2015, December). Personal digital archiving. *Technology Watch Report*. Digital Preservation Coalition.
Ridge, M. (2014). *Crowdsourcing our cultural heritage*. London: Asgate.
Rodney, S. (2016, January 22). The Evolution of the museum visit, from privilege to personalized experience. *Hyperallergic*. Retrieved from http://hyperallergic.com/267096/the-evolution-of-the-museum-visit-from-privilege-to-personalized-experience/.
Rushkoff, D. (2013). *Present shock: when everything happens now*. New York: Penguin.
Simon, N. (2011, December 7). Digital museums reconsidered: Exploring the Walker Art Center website redesign. *Museum 2.0*. Retrieved from http://museumtwo.blogspot.nl/2011/12/digital-museums-reconsidered-exploring.html.
Tanner, S. (2012). Measuring the impact of digital resources: The balanced value impact model. Report, Open Content Exchange Platform. *King's College London*.
Vizrt. (2015, March 18). Dutch national TV and film archive choose Viz One for MAM. Retrieved from http://www.vizrt.com/casestudies/44774/Dutch_national_TV_and_film_archive_choose_Viz_One_for_MAM.
Media Fragments Working Group. (2011, December 1). Media fragments URI 1.0. W3C. Retrieved from https://www.w3.org/2008/WebVideo/Fragments/#deliverables.
Wright, R. (2012, March). Preserving moving pictures and sound. DPC Technology Watch Report 12–01 March 2012. *Digital Preservation Coalition*. Retrieved from http://dx.doi.org/10.7207/twr12-01.

# 5

# Organized Metadata Management Using Autogenerated Program Scripts

**Nobu Yamashita**


## Abstract

NHK (Japan Broadcasting Corporation) recently launched an autogenerated program script system in its archive database. Files of news and other programs are transmitted from the play-out server to the archive server after broadcast. At the same time, all the metadata (including copyright information) is sent to the archive information system. The autogenerated program script system automatically generates a program outline table containing descriptions of sequences and shots, narration scripts, subtitles, copyright information, and conditions of use for each program. This system can recognize the breaks of each shot automatically, so it places an image of the first frame of each shot in the thumbnail column. It takes narration scripts from a closed-captioning service. This new system has dramatically enhanced the functionality of the archive database. The outline table is very useful for producers as they can easily grasp the content of each program by browsing. Every word in the script will be made retrievable using a search engine in the database. By clicking a thumbnail, users can watch a reference video. By clicking a checkbox, users can request a copy of the sequences or shots. Users can also access detailed copyright information (e.g., payment information, PDF files of contracts, and trouble reports) on each shot or sequence. This complete metadata management will simplify the procedure for reuse of content for productions, online services, and distribution. NHK hopes that it will promote utilization of stored programs and eventually help reduce location expenses.



## Keywords

metadata, database, copyright, autotagging, STT, MAM, script, user-friendliness.


## Introduction

What is the most important key to establishing a digital TV archive? One possible answer to this question is error-free digital filing. Another is management of users' access authorizations for security. In my view, however, the answer is the manner in which we manage metadata (including copyright information). Does a particular TV program contain footage for which we do not hold the copyright? Who performed in the program? Under what conditions? Without such information, we cannot reuse the content in other programs or distribute content over the internet. In this paper, I will describe a system that enables NHK (Japan Broadcasting Corporation) to safely manage enriched metadata in a user-friendly manner. (I will use the word "metadata" to refer to cataloguing information, not technical metadata.)

We can consider metadata management from two perspectives: the perspective of the manager of the database and the perspective of the user of the database. From the viewpoint of the manager, data entry is essential. The more you try to enrich your metadata, the more information you must enter into the database. The workload can become heavy. One option for creating a sustainable database is automatic input, that is, a basic system linkage that allows detailed program information such as the broadcast schedule to be sent automatically to the archive database.

From the user's viewpoint, a user-friendly interface is essential. A user may immediately need an overview of a particular TV program with details of every sequence, for example, what kinds of scenes are contained and who is performing at which points in a long program. In response



*Sustainable Audiovisual Collections* (2017): 32–38. DOI: 10.2979/jts2016.0.0.07

to users' requests, NHK developed a means for autogeneration of program scripts that provide users with easy-to-see program outlines. Some background information on the NHK archives is important at this point. NHK began radio broadcasts in 1925 and television broadcasts in 1953. We began systematic preservation in the early 1980s. As for metadata management, we began to use a computer-based database (instead of a paper-based database) in 1985. We changed our archive system from tapes to file servers in 2013. At the same time, we started to use a new archive information system. The greatest merit of our file-based archive system is that we can preserve all aired programs automatically without fail. Preserved programs can be rebroadcast without technical checking.

## Increasing Need for Metadata Management

There are many advantages to a file-based database. In this paper, I focus on the system that enables NHK to safely manage enriched metadata in a user-friendly manner.

Let us briefly consider why management of metadata and copyright in detail has become important. In 2015, twelve countries including Japan reached a broad agreement on the Trans-Pacific Partnership, a trade pact that will, inter alia, lead to elimination of tariffs on goods and services. A provision on copyrights will cause copyright protection terms to be extended from 50 years after the author's death to 70 years after the author's death (or 70 years after the release of the work). Further, the agreement entitles a party other than the copyright holder to bring a charge against an infringer. (Thus far in Japan, copyright infringement has been prosecutable only upon a complaint from the copyright holder.) As copyright protection is strengthened, legal sanctions for infringements of copyrights will become stricter. Consequently, the importance of copyright information on audiovisual content will grow.

NHK operates broadcasting services in accordance with Japan's Broadcast Law. A revision of this law in April 2015 enabled NHK to launch a wider range of internet services to keep up with a need for integration of broadcasting and telecommunications. To use aired programs for online services, NHK must clear copyrights for their use separately. (In Japan, a system to allow us to clear copyrights for broadcasting and online services at the same time has not been fully established.) To post content online, we need to select and use parts of programs by means of editing and/or by dividing long footage into chapters or sequences. Consequently, it is increasingly necessary for us to manage metadata with copyright information for each sequence.

## Autogenerated Program Scripts

An autogenerated program script is shown in figure 1. From left to right: it consists of sequence, thumbnail of each shot, shot name, narration script, subtitle, copyrights, and cautions for use. In this autogenerated program script, segmentation of sequences and naming of shots are currently done manually. The system recognizes the first frame of each shot and creates thumbnails automatically.

You (the user) can preview a reference video from the exact shot you want to see by clicking the thumbnail. You can order a copy of the sequence or shot by ticking the check box. The "script" column is completed when closed-caption text is sent automatically.

Shot names can be retrieved. For the time being, full text is excluded from the search object as the data is too big. We want eventually to accomplish full-text search.

To summarize, thumbnails and narration scripts are generated automatically. We need to manually split a video into sequences, name shots, and enter subtitles and, if necessary, add cautions for use. For programs with many shots (for instance, a music program), you (the user) can combine some shots. You can also split long shots as needed.

With the selector switch, you can change from portrait mode to landscape mode. The landscape mode (fig. 2) looks similar to the editing software interface with which program-makers are familiar. You can watch the reference video from any point you wish. You can select the mod

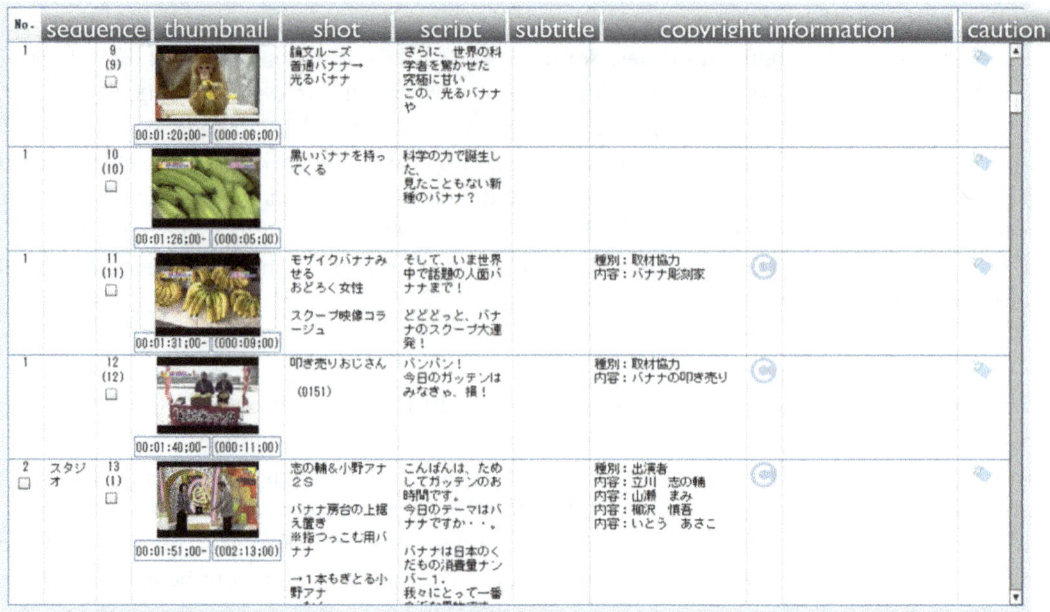


**Figure 1.** Autogenerated program script.

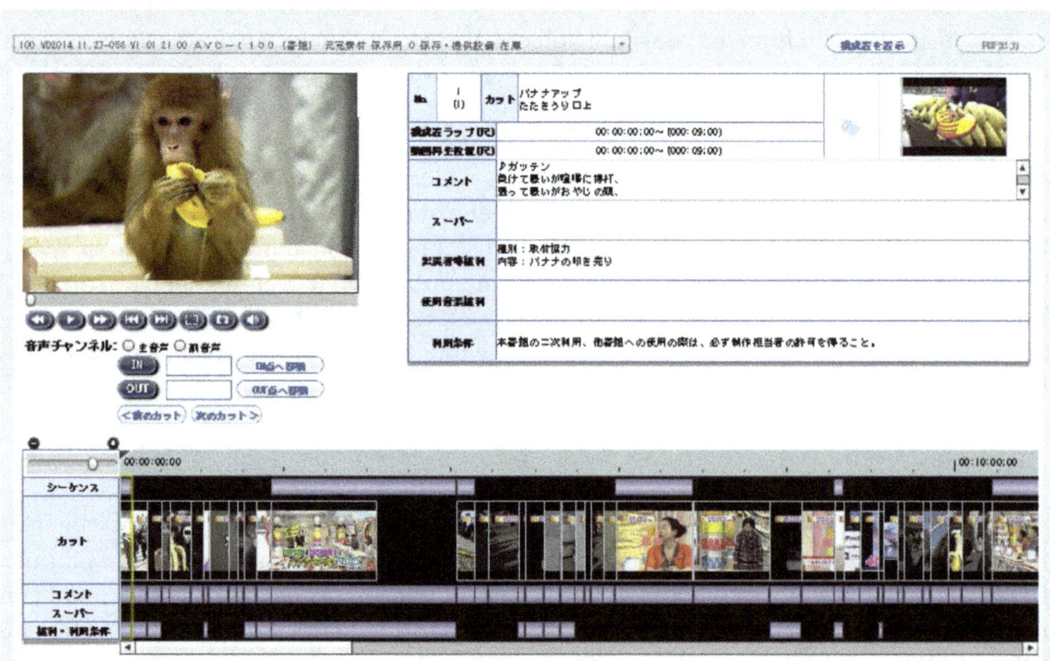

**Figure 2.** Landscape mode.

## Copyright Information Management

Figure 3 shows a page of the integrated copyright information for the entire program. Clicking words with a blue underline causes detailed information on the copyright holder to be shown on the right-hand side.

If footage produced by a film or computer-graphics production company is used, NHK must pay a license fee for the use. The "Copyrights" section in the program script is linked to a screen with copyright information on the acquired footage. It gives contact information for copyright holders and conditions for the use of copyrighted material, for example, the period and number of runs approved and whether the content may be posted on the internet.

NHK's play-out server, archive information system, and storage facility are connected (see fig. 4). From the play-out server, metadata (along with audiovisual content) is transferred to the archives server. For people with hearing difficulties, closed captions are available for over 70%

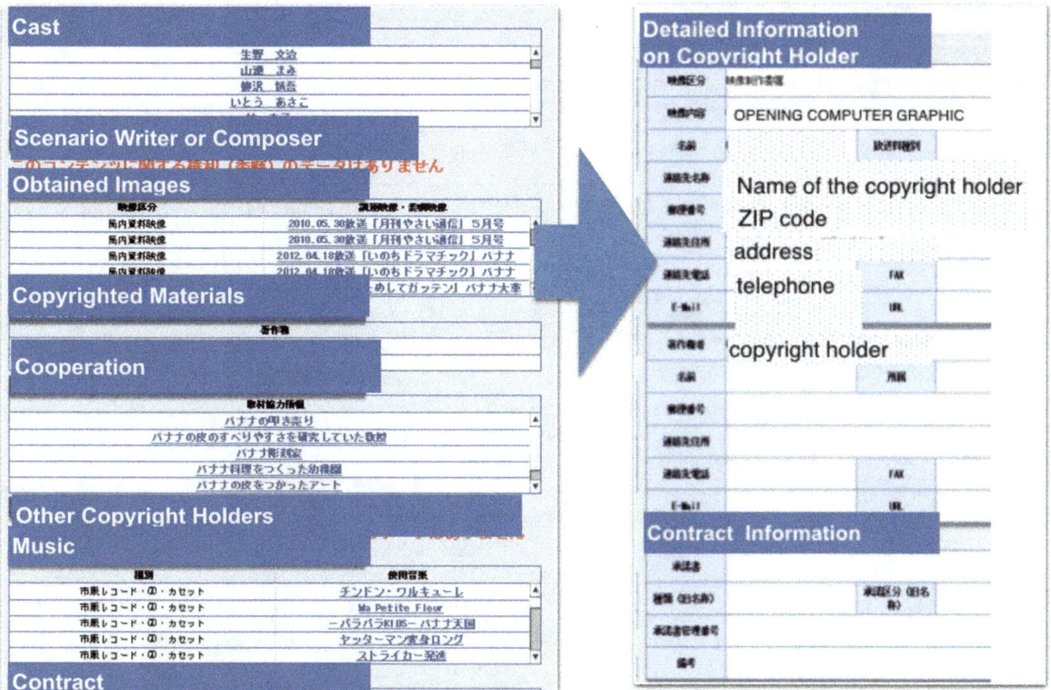


**Figure 3.** Copyright information.

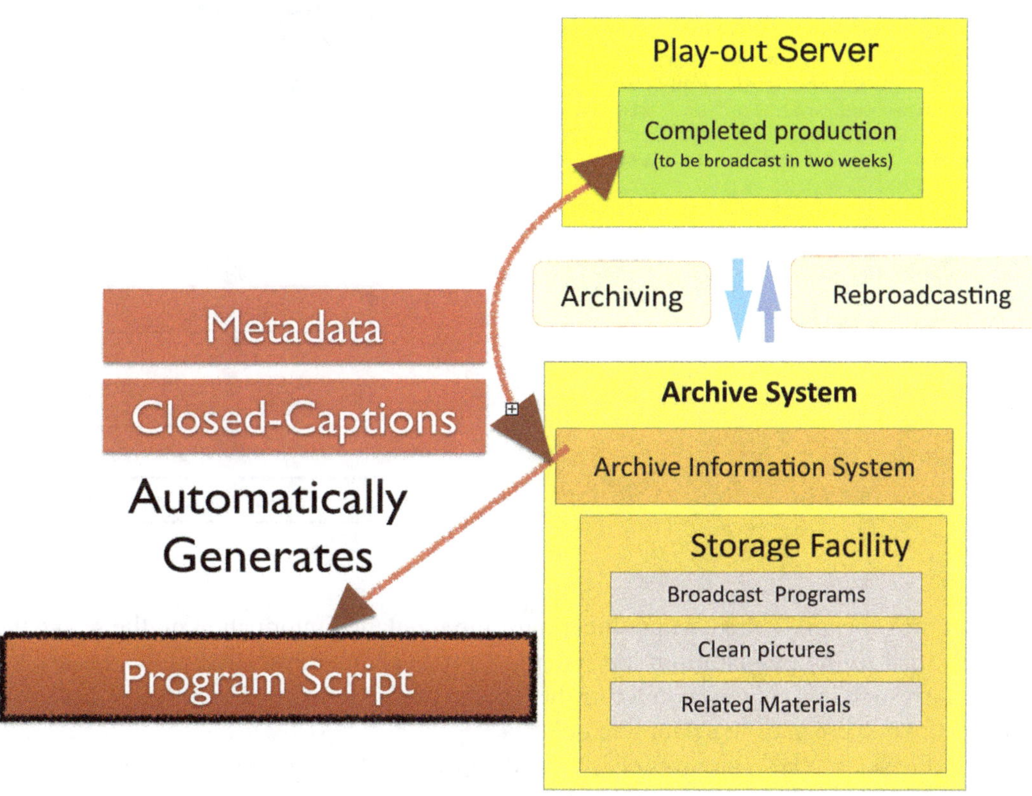


**Figure 4.** Connected play-out server, archive information system, and storage facility.

of NHK programs. Such text is also sent to the archive system. In short, most of the metadata are integrated into the autogenerated program script.

Figure 5 shows a screen for setting the search criteria on the database. Users can search content by entering keywords including program title, cast, broadcast date, channel, and shot name. The more metadata the program contains, the more options users have for search conditions. The autogenerated program script contributes to the enrichment of metadata and to the user-friendliness of the search system.

**Figure 5.** Screen for setting search criteria.

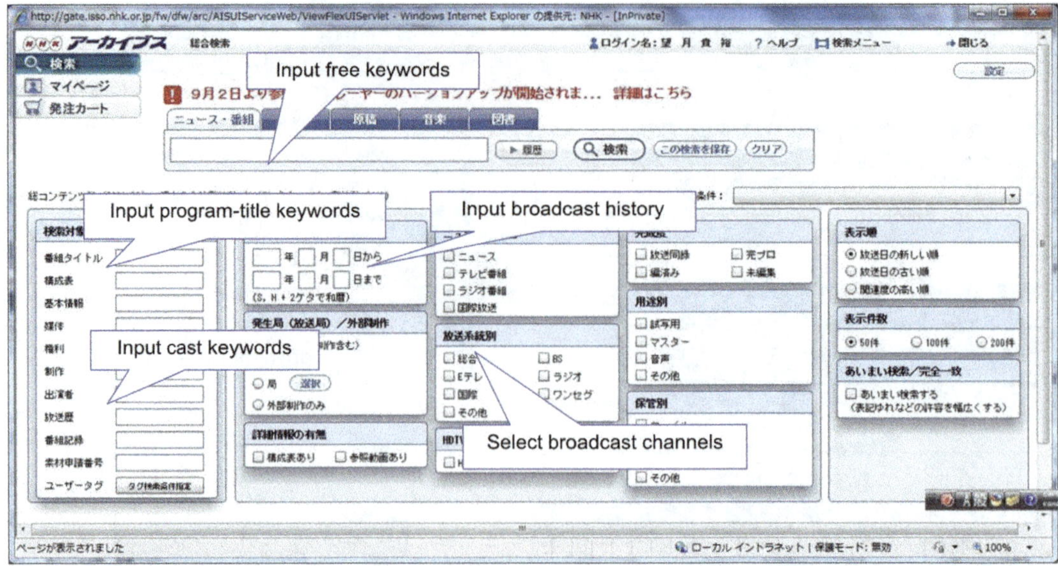


**Figure 6.** Monitoring of status of producer's entry of copyright information

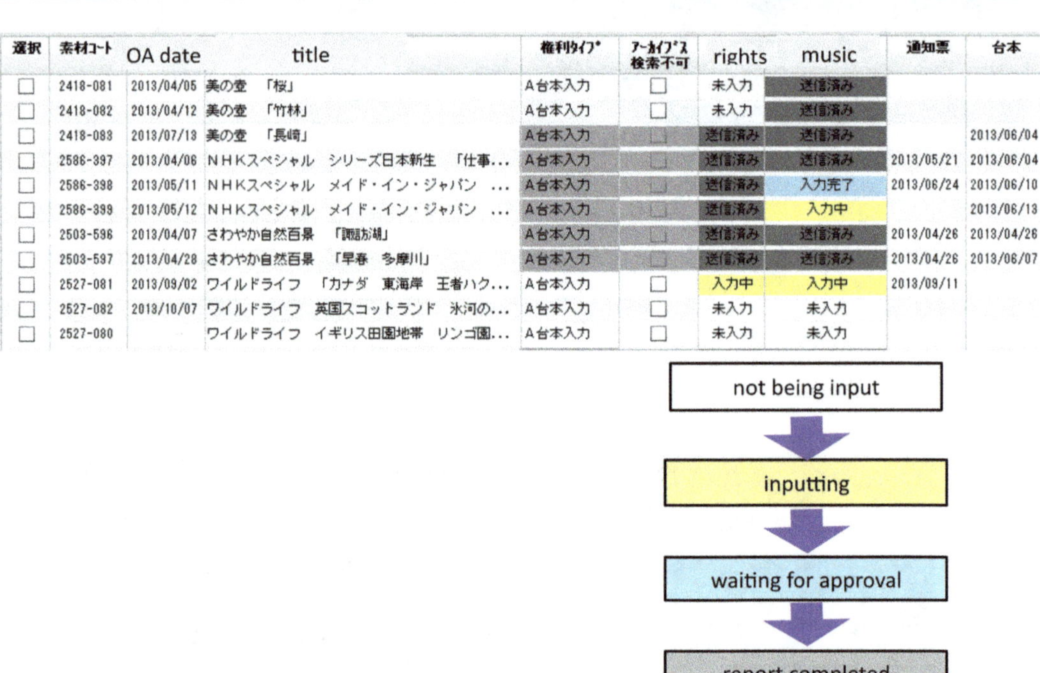

| 選択 | 素材コード | OA date | title | 権利タイプ | アーカイブス検索不可 | rights | music | 通知票 | 台本 |
|---|---|---|---|---|---|---|---|---|---|
| ☐ | 2418-081 | 2013/04/05 | 美の壺　「桜」 | A台本入力 | ☐ | 未入力 | 送信済み | | |
| ☐ | 2418-082 | 2013/04/12 | 美の壺　「竹林」 | A台本入力 | ☐ | 未入力 | 送信済み | | |
| ☐ | 2418-083 | 2013/07/13 | 美の壺　「長崎」 | A台本入力 | ☐ | 送信済み | 送信済み | | 2013/06/04 |
| ☐ | 2586-397 | 2013/04/06 | ＮＨＫスペシャル　シリーズ日本新生　「仕事… | A台本入力 | ☐ | 送信済み | 送信済み | 2013/05/21 | 2013/06/04 |
| ☐ | 2586-398 | 2013/05/11 | ＮＨＫスペシャル　メイド・イン・ジャパン　… | A台本入力 | ☐ | 送信済み | 入力完了 | 2013/06/24 | 2013/06/10 |
| ☐ | 2586-399 | 2013/05/12 | ＮＨＫスペシャル　メイド・イン・ジャパン　… | A台本入力 | ☐ | 送信済み | 入力中 | | 2013/06/13 |
| ☐ | 2503-596 | 2013/04/07 | さわやか自然百景　「諏訪湖」 | A台本入力 | ☐ | 送信済み | 送信済み | 2013/04/26 | 2013/04/26 |
| ☐ | 2503-597 | 2013/04/28 | さわやか自然百景　「早春　多摩川」 | A台本入力 | ☐ | 送信済み | 送信済み | 2013/04/26 | 2013/06/07 |
| ☐ | 2527-081 | 2013/09/02 | ワイルドライフ　「カナダ　東海岸　王者ハク… | A台本入力 | ☐ | 入力中 | 入力中 | 2013/09/11 | |
| ☐ | 2527-082 | 2013/10/07 | ワイルドライフ　英国スコットランド　氷河の… | A台本入力 | ☐ | 未入力 | 未入力 | | |
| ☐ | 2527-080 | | ワイルドライフ　イギリス田園地帯　リンゴ園… | A台本入力 | ☐ | 未入力 | 未入力 | | |



After the program is aired, its producer must input detailed information on the works and materials used in the program into the system. It has been a concern that producers are too busy to enter such information as entering the data for a huge number of shots (sometimes over 300 shots for one program) is a daunting task.

Over the years, NHK's archives division and copyrights division have instructed producers that copyrights are indispensable for the reuse and/or distribution of content and that lack of copyright information can lead to unauthorized use of footage and possibly to a lawsuit.

The progress of the entry status is monitored through the system. Each status is indicated by a different color. White indicates that no copyright information has been input. Yellow indicates that input is in progress. Blue indicates that inputted data are waiting for the approval. Gray indicates completion.

NHK's copyrights division also makes a list of the copyright information status for newly aired programs per program or division in charge and submits the report to the executive board. If producers neglect the duty, they are reproached by the management.

Producers are not required to enter all the items for every program. In fact, they only need to input all the information for programs that are expected to be reused later. Such programs account for several percent (7%–8%) of NHK's programs. When producers cannot enter the information themselves, archiving staff sometimes do so on their behalf.

Producers' workload is further reduced by interlocking of systems. The archive database is integrated with 20 other systems. One of those is the payment system for the cast. For instance, if NHK pays 100,000 yen to a group of singers, the payment information goes to the archive database, which gives authorized users access.

Fees for performers are paid in accordance with predetermined standards in most cases. When a separate negotiation is necessary, it is very useful for the user to see the payment history in this integrated database. The database is linked to payments not only for cast members but also for other contributors such as scriptwriters, music composers, and calligraphers.

## Other Useful Functions of Autogenerated Program Scripts

Some of NHK's stored footage has been made public on the internet and other media. However, NHK's archive system is for professional use; only producers and those who distribute NHK content are authorized. The users observe strict confidentiality requirements as the database contains personal information.

Users can take out the search results in Excel files and autogenerated scripts and individual copyright information in PDF files. They then enjoy the convenience of viewing the data on their personal computers even while offline. Japan has strengthened its legal measures to protect personal information. In this context, balancing information security with convenience is a difficult challenge.

Program scripts can be also downloaded in Excel format. Producers can add or correct data in the Excel sheet then upload the updated sheet to the system. Corrected data including copyright information are reflected in the system. NHK has recently reduced in-house program production and increased its outsourcing of production. The ability to enter data in an Excel sheet is especially helpful for outside producers who cannot access the system. They can name shots and input copyright information into the Excel sheet at their own office and send it back to the NHK producer, who uploads the updated sheet to the system.

## Autoannotation Functionality

Other functions are also related to NHK's archive database. For instance, staff at the NHK Science and Technology Research Laboratories are proceeding with research on content-based image retrieval. The system detects distinctive features of a query image and searches for similar images through analysis of colors, textures, and layouts.

With this system, users can easily search for target shots based on similar shots stored in the database. They do not need to use keywords.

An autotagging system is also under development at the NHK Science and Technology Research Laboratories. With an image of a flower, for example, the system analyzes the color and texture and automatically generates the keyword "flower." This system will save time for producers by saving them from needing to name every shot in an autogenerated program script.

Also, we are developing a system that recognizes patterns in images and automatically segments footage into sequences. For example, if there is an indoor sequence followed by an outdoor sequence, the system recognizes the change. We hope this technology will help reduce the burden of manual work for video segmentation.

We are also developing an integrated news retrieval system. This system converts newscasters' voices into digital text automatically. It also enables users to search for words in the text and for relevant news scripts.

## Conclusion

New copyright legislation will, as stated, extend the copyright protection term and allow people to more easily demand damages for infringements. Broadcasters therefore face a growing risk

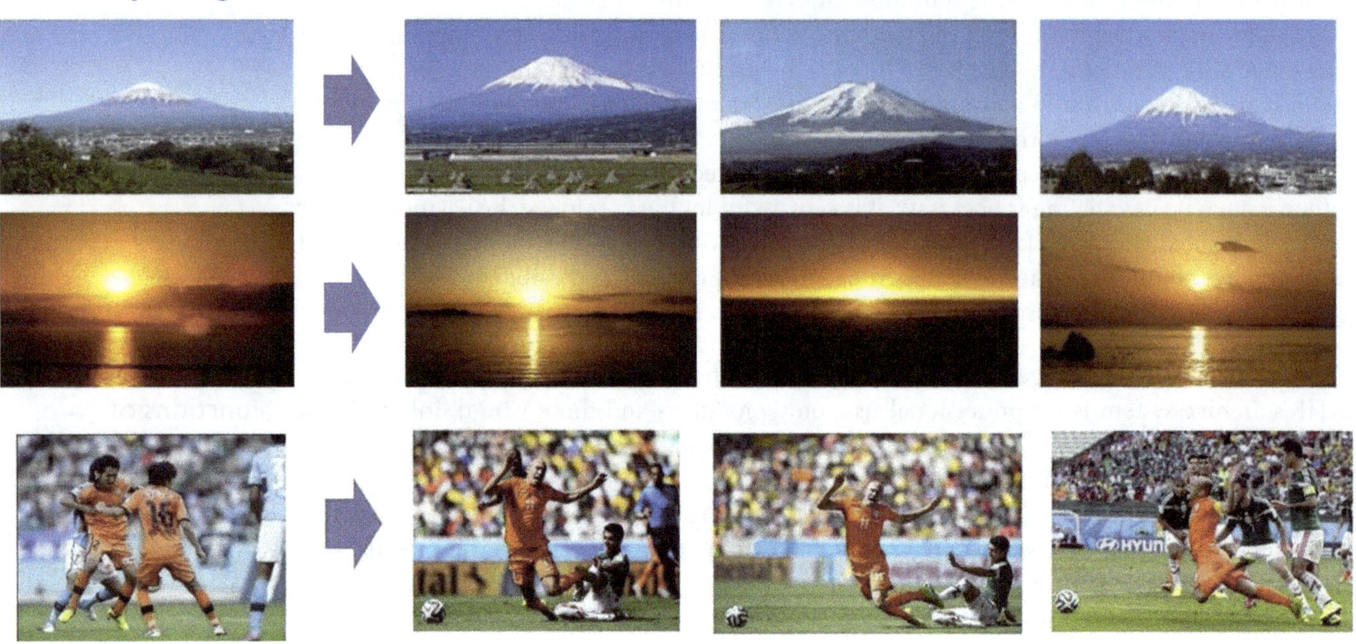


**Figure 7.** Content-based image retrieval.

of being sued. Copyright handling will become more important for broadcasters around the world.

As online services expand, detailed metadata management will be increasingly necessary for utilizing footage. It will also enable broadcasters to improve search functionality to respond to the trend for chapter division for personalizing of content. It is also useful for broadcasters and audiovisual archives who often sell portions of content.

There is a growing tendency for people to look at smartphones and tablets while they watch television. If the metadata for past programs is enriched, it will help broadcasters develop services and applications for such devices. One conceivable service would display a list of dramas featuring a specific actor or actress. Another would enable viewers to watch other scenes in which the actor or actress appears.

Increased automation of metadata management will help reduce labor costs and, notwithstanding a high initial investment, eventually pay for itself.

Audiovisual archives can be expected to make more profits from distribution of content and/or a wider range of online services (including VOD services) than ever before. Metadata management with well-organized functions will therefore become indispensable.

Nobu Yamashita joined NHK (Japan Broadcasting Corporation) in 1984. He has produced numerous television documentaries, mainly on modern Japanese history and Japanese and Western fine art. For the past six years, he has been in charge of media preservation and rights management in the NHK Archives division. He is also responsible for making an extensive collection of NHK footage available to the public and for academic use. In 2013, the NHK Archives Division changed its archive system to a cutting-edge file-based system. In 2015, it commemorated the 90th anniversary of NHK broadcasting in Japan by launching a website that includes about 2,000 video clips giving an overview of Japan's modern history. Nobu's involvement with these initiatives has given him a wider perspective on the future of television and mass communication.

# Canalizing the Maelstrom of Metadata: Extensions on the Hourglass Model

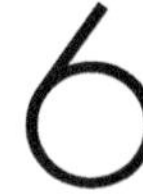

**Brecht Declercq**

## Abstract

This article presents the Hourglass Model, a theoretical framework allowing to redesign the strategies for the creation and use of mainly descriptive metadata in audiovisual archives. The model outlines four main categories of metadata creation (manual annotation by archivists, metadata coming from production, user-generated metadata, and automatically extracted metadata) and three main categories of use (preservation and collection management, search and retrieval, and enhancement and contextualization). Archives can plan an effective and efficient metadata strategy by connecting one or more creation methods with one or more purposes. Next, recent developments in the creation and use of descriptive metadata are discussed. The fact that these recent developments can be fit in easily show that the model is future-proof. Furthermore, it is suggested that the implementation of the Hourglass Model has consequences for the archive not only on the technical level, but also on the institutional and organizational ones. It stresses the importance of archival openness as an institutional leitmotiv, a new role for the archivists from the organizational perspective, and modular and exchangeable services as a key characteristic of the archive's IT infrastructure.

## Keywords

archives, audiovisual media, documentation, cataloging, metadata, strategy.

## Introduction

The quantity of audiovisual media (audio, video, and film) to be processed by audiovisual archives is globally in a constant increase. The growth of born digital items is accelerating and additionally digitization projects are going on, often aiming to digitize the entire collection of an archive (just a few recent examples: Monette, 2015; Messmer and Houpert, 2015; or Casey and Merten, 2015). Of the objects to be digitized large parts are not or only very superficially described or cataloged.

Metadata (descriptive, administrative, technical) are indispensable for archives in general for several key tasks such as storage management, preservation and making the collection searchable. In digital audiovisual archives in particular, this indispensability is by no means lower. Moreover, the user groups asking for access to these collections are becoming not only larger but also more diverse. New (actual or potential) user groups of the audiovisual archive additionally have their own needs in terms of access. Not only when it comes to the interface features, but also in metadata: types, form, vocabulary and level of detail in the descriptions (de Jong, 2010). Finally, television and radio broadcasters managing huge quantities of media are shifting their focus from the delivery challenge to the discovery challenge.[1] Also this factor stresses the essential role of descriptive metadata.

The history of documentation of audiovisual archives—or should we say audiovisual content in general?—was dominated until the 2000s by manual description by archivists. This method is known as particularly time-consuming, taking five times the duration of the media itself easily. But since then there has been a rapid evolution underway in the area of alternatives to the manual creation of metadata. In addition, there is an equally rapid evolution in the field of the use of these metadata. Previously metadata were quite commonly divided into administrative, technical and descriptive metadata, but since the second half of the 2000s terms as automatically extracted metadata, user generated metadata, preservation metadata, linked metadata, and so on have become ever more common, albeit mainly in theoretical literature and proofs of concept of all kinds. Despite this rapid conceptual change a big delay can be observed in the adoption in daily practice of the processes behind these terms.[2] On technological, organizational as well as institutional levels audiovisual archives seem to have difficulties with their implementation.[3]

## The Hourglass Model

The Hourglass Model has the ambition to serve as a theoretical framework for developing strategies for the creation and use of (descriptive) metadata. Originally developed in 2013 for the archives department of the Danish public broadcaster DR, it describes the place that metadata hold in contemporary audiovisual archiving, starting from the question how the different types of metadata relate to each other.

Preservation metadata for example, are sometimes automatically extracted. Still, no one will consider them synonymous terms. When analyzing the terms, it appears that some terms describe the way metadata are created, while others describe the purpose that they are used for. This leads us to situating them on different levels (fig. 1): a creation level, grouping the ways in which metadata are created or collected, and a purpose level, describing the goals that the metadata serve. These two levels are connected by archival processes, on which we will come back later on in this article.

Creating and collecting metadata and associating them with their corresponding essence today take very different forms. If we take a closer look however, it shows that the most significant differences between the methods of creation are in the moment of their creation (i.e., the point in the audiovisual value chain), and who or what is their creator or collector (fig. 2).

In fact, the creation methods can be divided into four different groups: first, there is the *manual annotation by archivists*, ideally right before giving the item its final place in the archive (but often much later), but at least after the production of the media object. Secondly, there are *production metadata*, a group holding a wide variety of metadata, which can be created both human and automatically. In any case they are created before entering the archives, during the production phase[4], in many cases with other purposes than strictly archival ones.

*User-generated metadata* are a third group of metadata creation methods. These are metadata created by the user, at any given moment, consciously or unconsciously, and through any technology. Finally there are *automatically extracted metadata*: they are the outcome of a broad range of technologies allowing the content of sound, moving pictures or still images to be described automatically without human intervention other than applying a specific algorithm to the media essence. Broadly speaking, these technologies can again be divided into classification, segmentation, recognition, identification, and transcription. The result can consist out of a text (such as a transcript of what is said in the media) but also for example out of a series of time codes indicating meaningful changes in the media, for example the transition of human speech to music or a new person coming into the picture. These transitions are often displayed in the user interface of the access platform[5] in the form of markers on a timeline.

At the purpose level we find the final objectives for which these metadata are used. We stress the word "final" here, because the human or automatic retrieval of the essence is rarely a goal in itself, but nearly always the starting point of a further purpose. Analyzing these purposes we can in fact identify three of them, the first being preservation and collection management. Evidently the term *preservation metadata* rises here: data about provenance, quality control (whether or not after one or more migration processes in any form) and all other kinds of actions of file management that the media object undergoes throughout its lifecycle.

Second, there is the most classical focus of archival disclosure: search and retrieval for reuse in whatever context. And finally there is enhancement and contextualization: linking the content from one collection with other content (where also the concept of linked metadata can

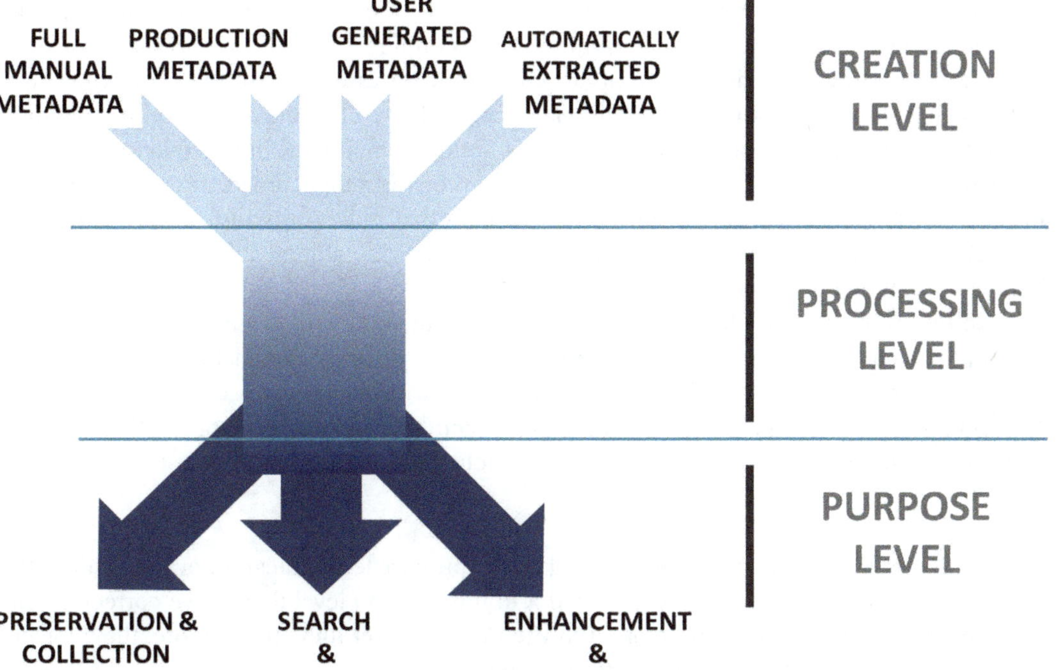


**Figure 1.** The Hourglass Model featuring the creation, processing, and purpose levels.

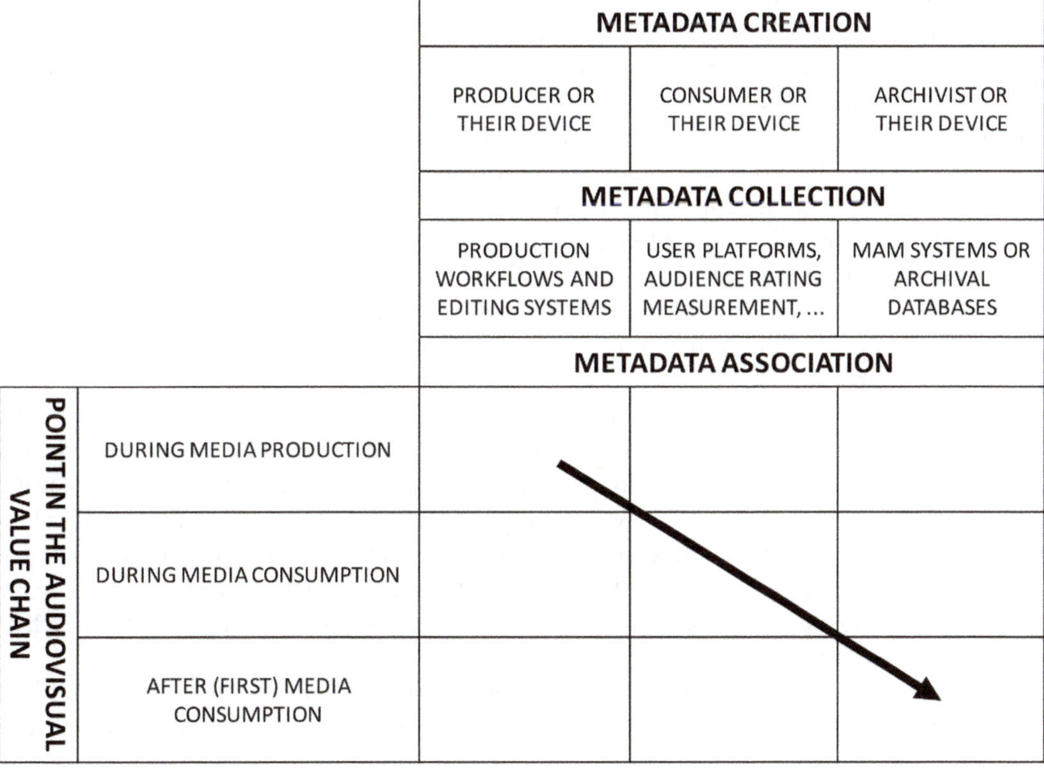


**Figure 2.** Metadata creation, collection, and association with the corresponding essence, versus the point in the audiovisual value chain. The arrow indicates the usual chronological order of methods applied.

be situated).[6] The most obvious use of the Hourglass Model involves a way of creating metadata being associated with a purpose that one wants to achieve. In fact, any of the four ways of creating metadata can be combined with any of the three purposes. The model thus results in twelve interesting combinations, some of which have been known for centuries (using full manual annotation for managing the collection for example) and others were born only recently. Based on the purpose, some form of metadata creation is chosen, taking into account the characteristics of the essence and the strengths and weaknesses of the creation method. It is therefore important that the archivist is well aware of these aspects. For example:

A radio broadcaster's archive wants to connect a series of undescribed interviews with politicians with pictures of the same politicians from other collections, via an online platform. To save time, the annotation of the interviews is not done manually, but by making use of the introduction texts written by the journalists while preparing their broadcasts. A disadvantage of these texts that the archivist should be aware of is that radio journalists often write names phonetically, instead of using the correct spelling. This will evidently obstruct the automatic connection of the collections.

Nothing however should stop the archivist from using different annotation methods for different parts of the collection, or to make sure that one source of metadata can serve multiple purposes. Furthermore, it could be interesting to cope with the weaknesses of one method, via the strengths of another one. A good example of the combination of metadata creation of all four categories, is the BBC World Service Archive Prototype (Raimond, 2013).

## Extending the Model

In recent years, both on the creation level and on the purpose level a clear innovation and further detailing of existing methods can be noticed. On the creation level these have corrected some weaknesses as they were known before. On the purpose level they furthermore allow for new possibilities within the three groups of reuse listed above.

With regard to production metadata, two evolutions are clearly visible. On the one hand there are some recent technological innovations. Production platforms (sometimes referred to as a *production asset management system* [PAM]) keeping track of the essence in various phases of the production process ever more acknowledge the importance of descriptive metadata already at that stage of the media value chain. Capturing metadata at that point in a structured and uniform way is beneficial not only to the efficiency of the production, but also later on during the archiving processes (Verwaest, 2014). On the other hand, the digitization of paper archive collections and the (semi-) automatic extraction of their content, serving as descriptive metadata is ever more common. BBC's Genome Project is a nice example of this trend (O'Dwyer, 2012). This shows that the use of production metadata is not limited anymore to recently produced content and that the full collaboration of the producers is not always required. If they can be harvested easily, the reuse of production metadata is the low-hanging fruit of metadata creation for the archive, offering often quite detailed metadata in an inexpensive and quick way.

Regarding user generated metadata an interesting distinction can recently be made between the conscious and unconscious creation of metadata. Consciously creating user generated metadata is usually associated with crowd-sourcing, though it does not necessarily have to be located there. It can be done in a high-tech way (Noordegraaf, 2012) as well as in a way that requires little technological investment. The Irish public broadcaster RTÉ managed for example to cancel out a number of question marks from its catalog via Twitter calls to the general public. The fact that this project reinforced the archive's connection with the general audience was more than just a positive side effect (Wylie, 2013).

As metadata created unconsciously by the user we consider data about the essence collected mostly automatically during the use or reuse (i.e., consumption) of the media, without the user taking specific action for this to happen, often even without being aware that this is happening. Since a few years already the term *consumer-generated metadata* is being used for this (Rule, 2008). In a certain sense, television audience ratings for example can be considered consumer generated metadata. But also other data on the perception of the media by the public can be considered metadata of interest to the archive. Monitoring and analysis of the viewer's emotions, based on *second screen* social media activity for example, is an ever-more common part of audience research, done or commissioned by broadcasters. In more general terms, we can state that particularly in broadcasting the archive and the audience research department are increasingly partners. Whether it is about use statistics or specific characteristics of the content, they ever more become customers and suppliers of each other's data. Since audiovisual archives are increasingly becoming platforms for media access, a thorough monitoring of customer behavior is also a matter of self-interest for the archive. Not only these traces of media consumption enable them to match supply directly with customer demand, it also makes their collections better described in the longer run.

It is even possible to create user-generated metadata via crowdsourcing, without the collaborators being aware that what they consciously create, actually serves as metadata. Collaborative subtitling platforms such as Amara are originally not intended to generate descriptive metadata, but for captions, translations and subtitling (Jansen, 2015). However, it is evident that these can also serve as descriptive metadata, just as the subtitling made by professionals. In summary user generated metadata in all their new forms are a very promising form of descriptive metadata. Some older objections, such as the doubts about reliability, the risk of vandalism and issues of labor intensity are virtually gone.

In the field of automatically extracted metadata two particularly important and partly linked evolutions can recently be observed. First and foremost this way of creating metadata (i.e., metadata generated via automatic speech recognition) has made its long-awaited entry in the daily practice of audiovisual archives. At the Swiss Italian-speaking public broadcaster RSI for example the technology was commissioned in 2012 as part of a new media asset management (MAM) system (Aziz et al., 2013). The second evolution, providing automatical extraction of metadata via a software-as-a-service (SaaS) model and an application programming interface (API)[7], has also led to a series of other implementations, usually on a project basis, but still in daily practice: the Studs Terkel Radio Archive calls on the API of Audiosearch (Schein, 2015) and the French-speaking Swiss public broadcaster RTS uses the Vocapia service for the annotation of its digitized audio tape collection (Lorenz, Seigneur and Wenger, 2015). On the SaaS market it is very easy to find other APIs offering various other technologies such as recognition or even identification of persons or objects.

Innovations at the purpose level often show a rather slow pace when it comes to MAM systems[8], but platforms targeting the end user tend to evolve quicker, as they're often built ad hoc, for particular projects and/or target groups. Three particularly interesting applications draw our attention.

Regarding preservation and collection management, harvesting the metadata generated by one or more devices in the digitization chain allow for a constant monitoring by the customers of outsourced digitization projects, as was demonstrated by Lorenz et al. (2015). Regarding search and retrieval the increasing quantities of essence and metadata pose a particular challenge. Search queries tend to have more results, but not per se more accurate ones. Graphic user interfaces (GUI) should therefore avoid overwhelming the user, by making use of features like improved relevancy ranking or refining results via facets. Also the idea of a slide switch meets this requirement: if a user chooses for less, but more accurate results, only the results of very reliable metadata sources are shown. To get more, but potentially also less accurate results, the search algorithm makes use of a gradually increasing number of metadata sources, also the less reliable ones. The results from the second option may also meet the need for a more serendipitous way of searching through media collections (Sauer, 2016).

Last but not least, descriptive metadata are used for innovative ways of enhancement and contextualization. Semantic linking is on the radar of audiovisual archives since a little less than ten years. It goes beyond the scope of this article to explain the functioning and the full possibilities of semantically linking audiovisual archive collections, but we will suffice by pointing to one of the more spectacular proofs of concept set up in recent years: RTBF's GEMS project, as explained by Jacques-Jourion (2013). For this project, the available metadata from more traditional archival databases were complemented by keywords spotted in texts generated by a speech-to-text engine. These were linked to each other and to external knowledge gathered in Linked Open Data sources such as DBpedia via an Open Service

Bus (OSB). The result is a web interface allowing serendipitous browsing through the media archive by journalists and revealing even unexpected links between keywords and media fragments.

## Implementing the Model

To implement the Hourglass Model in an audiovisual archive is not only a matter of installing new technology, just as a MAM system is more than just a new database. The Hourglass Model can fully come into its own only if new technologies to create and use—usually designed as services around the archival database—are mirrored into the archive's strategy and its organizational structure.

Metadata strategies in line with the Hourglass Model assume the acceptance and even the full embrace of openness as an institutional leitmotiv, leaving behind the old image of archives as fortresses of protected knowledge and archivists as omniscient gatekeepers. Metadata creation methods as well as their purposes are and will become even more linked to the outside world in the future. In this regard the Hourglass Model fully connects with what Oomen (2014) calls "open, smart and connected audiovisual archives." The main emanation of this openness at the creation level is clearly in accepting the user as a legitimate creator of descriptive metadata[9], while at the purpose level the output of the archive should connect also to the outside world, for example by considering the use of the archival content as the true value of it, as professed by Golodnoff and Lerkenfeld Smith (2011).

On the organizational level, implementing the Hourglass Model mainly translates into new roles for the archivist. Standing in the middle of it, at the process level, he or she should be aware of the new technological possibilities and the new institutional context of the archive, but also of the new needs of old and new target groups. Although it is likely that traditional manual annotation will still survive for a while, recognizing and connecting creation methods to purposes, while managing these processes and checking metadata quality will become ever more important. Knowing and respecting the strengths and weaknesses of each creation method and the characteristics of the collection to be annotated will help the archivist to make the most effective and powerful combinations.

When it comes to the archive as an IT architecture, the Hourglass Model is particularly suited in a flexible environment, where systems are modular and exchangeable. It assumes all but monolithic, one-purpose systems. The speed of technological evolutions together with ever more external connections calls for gradual adaptations (instead of the usual "big bang" when for example a new MAM system is taken into use) but also for solid standards[10]. The tendency of working with well documented micro-services clearly meets this requirement.

## Conclusion

In this article we have presented the Hourglass Model, we have elaborated further on recent evolutions in metadata creation and use, and we have suggested that the implementation of the Hourglass Model has consequences for the archive on institutional, organizational and technical levels.

The Hourglass Model is not a concrete tool, but a theoretical framework for everyone who's confronted with the redesign of the strategies for metadata creation. It is a framework for helping audiovisual archives to allow their metadata creation strategy to evolve. It is future-proof, because it allows new technologies to be fitted in easily. Evidently the metadata sources are related with four kinds of metadata creators: the maker of the essence, its user, the archivist and their devices. Next to that, also the moment of creation is an interesting, distinguishing factor.

The Hourglass Model also encourages to think out of the box when it comes to create metadata. In fact archives should consider all data surrounding the media value chain (from production to consumption, conservation and reuse) as potential metadata, in an open minded way. This means: how can these data be collected, associated with the essence and used for the strategy of the archives, the prospering of the collection and the needs of its users.

For those determining the strategies of audiovisual archives, the challenge is to redesign the existing ones, often mainly based on old-school manual annotation. In this context it is important to know these new methods, including their strengths and weaknesses. Next to that, business cases should be elaborated, taking into account the content wise characteristics of the collection (e.g. the rights situation) and the environments from which the archive acquires the content (e.g. the production methods of the broadcasting industry).

Parallels between the Hourglass Model and the Open Archival Information System (OAIS) are clearly visible. Both serve as a theoretical framework with three major components, focusing on input, output and processes in between (de Jong, Delaney and Steinmeier, 2013). This suggests that audiovisual archives who work OAIS compliant will also find it easier to think along with the Hourglass Model's logic. This way the Hourglass Model can be considered as a way to apply OAIS but limited to the descriptive metadata aspects of it.

*If all you have is a hammer, everything looks like a nail.* The archivist used to have only the full manual annotation method available. Soon however, this multipurpose goody will be exchanged for a whole toolbox. Then the archivist has to become acquainted with the strengths and weaknesses of each tool and to make informed decisions which one to use. Since the archivist will manually intervene less, it will also be more important to monitor the quality of the processes well. Ultimately a good overview will be required, because the ever-faster growing collection not only has to be made searchable, enhanced and contextualized but also has to be managed and preserved.

BRECHT DECLERCQ is the Digitization and Acquisition Manager at VIAA, the national audiovisual archive of Flanders, Belgium, since 2013. He is responsible for the overall digitization strategy of the Flemish audiovisual heritage. Previously, he worked for the Belgian public broadcaster VRT for almost 10 years as a radio archivist and as a project lead in several digitizations, media asset management, and access projects. He is the current Chair of the FIAT/IFTA Preservation and Migration Commission and Member of the FIAT/IFTA Executive Council. He writes, presents, reviews, and advises to several European broadcasters and audiovisual archives.

## Notes

1. In the world of linear analog broadcasting television and radio stations struggled with delivering their content to their audiences at the right time. In a world of internet based, nonlinear media consumption, their challenge is to make sure their content is discovered amongst the enormous supply of online media (Solheim and Børdalen, 2015).
2. For example and according to our research it took no less than 18 years between the first research of speech-to-text as an interesting technology for describing audiovisual archive items and the actual first implementation in the daily practice of a Western European broadcasting archive. See Christel, Stevens and Watclar (1994), as compared to Aziz, Vassallo and Veri (2013).
3. Gazendam (2015) reports that cataloguers at the Netherlands Institute for Sound and Vision manage to annotate roughly one-third of all audio and video material coming in, with the annotations reaching their final stage roughly two months after the first broadcast date.
4. For example: journalist's texts, interview transcriptions, subtitles, location data created by the built-in GPS-data in a recording device, etc.
5. To use a generic term; in many cases this will be a *media asset management system* (MAM).
6. This link could be considered not only a form of metadata use, but also of metadata creation: by linking one document to another, the first one forms a kind of descriptive metadatum for the other.
7. Of course, this supposes that the architecture of the archive's IT system is at least partially service oriented (SOA).
8. Recent research by Brodie Kusa, Declercq and Stanz (2015) with almost 50 audiovisual archives showed that more than one out of three archivists called the graphic user interface

(GUI) of their current MAM system "an unsolved or dissatisfying aspect," while almost two out of three held high hopes for improvement in this regard for their next MAM system.

9. An interesting example can be found in the Origo radio asset management system of the Norwegian public broadcaster NRK (Engels and Wettmark, 2015). The borders between users and producers of metadata are becoming very vague in this system, as journalists are allowed and even encouraged to alter metadata in the Origo interface.
10. We refer to the work of the FIMS task force (Framework for Interoperable Media Services), a joint initiative of EBU and AMWA (Dimino, Evain, Footen and Gilmer, 2013).

## References


Aziz, S.H., Vassallo, L., and Veri, F. (2013). Speech to text and semantic analysis. Our working experience. In: FIAT/IFTA Media Management Commission (Eds.), *Metadata as the cornerstone of digital archiving. Changing sceneries, changing roles, part VI. Selected papers from the MMC Seminar, Hilversum, 16–17th May 2013* (pp. 126–133). Stockholm – Vienna – Dubai: FIAT/IFTA.

Bailer, W., Höller, F., and Messina, A. e.a. (2005). *State of the art of content analysis tools for video, audio and speech.* Rome – Paris: PrestoSpace.

Brodie Kusa, E., Declercq, B., and Stanz, G. (2015). The FIAT/IFTA MAM Survey. An interim assessment of one decade of file-based audiovisual archiving. In: FIAT/IFTA Media Management Commission (Eds.), *Setting the standard in 2nd generation MAMs and metadata. Changing sceneries, changing roles, part VII. Selected papers from the MMC Seminar, Glasgow, 22–23 May 2015* (pp. 135–167). Stockholm – Vienna – Hilversum: FIAT/IFTA.

Casey, M., and Merten, M. (2015, September 30). *Media Preservation at Scale: The Indiana University Media Digitization and Preservation Initiative.* Presentation, 46th Annual IASA Conference. Paris.

Christel, M., Stevens, S., and Wactlar, H. (1994). Informedia Digital Video Library. *Proceedings of the Second ACM International Conference on Multimedia, Video Program.* New York, NY: ACM.

De Jong, A. (2010). *De nieuwe toegang tot audiovisuele content. Ontwikkelingen in de netwerkcultuur.* Hilversum: Nederlands Instituut voor Beeld en Geluid.

De Jong, A., Delaney, B., and Steinmeier, D. (2013). AV Preservation workflows: requirements for OAIS compliant workflow modelling. In: FIAT/IFTA Media Management Commission (Eds.), *Metadata as the cornerstone of digital archiving. Changing sceneries, changing roles, part VI. Selected papers from the MMC Seminar, Hilversum, 16–17th May 2013* (pp. 62–84). Stockholm – Vienna – Dubai: FIAT/IFTA.

Dimino, G., Evain, J.-P., Footen, J., and Gilmer, B. (2013). FIMS, a Framework for Interoperable Media Services. *SMPTE Motion Imaging Journal.* 122(6), 93.

Engels, R., and Wettmark, M. (2015, May 22). *Major changes at NRK or how to overhaul your metadata infrastructure using semantic web.* Presentation, FIAT/IFTA Media Management Seminar 'Changing Sceneries, changing roles. Part VII'. Glasgow.

Gazendam, L. (2015). *Cataloguer support in cultural heritage* (Unpublished doctoral dissertation). Vrije Universiteit, Amsterdam.

Golodnoff, T., and Lerkenfeld Smith, M. (2011). *Exploring cultural heritage and value creation. A case study of DR's Cultural Heritage Project* (Unpublished master thesis). IT University, Copenhagen.

Lopez, O., Moens, M.F., and Matton, M. (2013). *State of the art on semantic retrieval of AV content beyond text resources.* Geneva: EBU.

Lorenz, T., Seigneur, J.M., and Wenger, O. (2015, October 1). *Use case: large scale outsourced digitization project with automatic supervision.* Presentation, 46th Annual IASA Conference. Paris.

Jacques-Jourion, X. (2013). GEMS. Semantics for audiovisual dummies. In: FIAT/IFTA Management Commission (Eds.), *Metadata as the cornerstone of digital archiving. Changing sceneries, changing roles, part VI. Selected papers from the MMC Seminar, Hilversum, 16–17th May 2013* (pp. 32–41). Stockholm – Vienna – Dubai: FIAT/IFTA.

Jansen, D. (2015, December 4). *Community driven video accessibility.* Presentation, EUScreenXL Conference. Warsaw.

Messmer, R., and Houpert, J. (2015, October 10). *Quality control in ORF Broadcast and Archive Migration Workflows.* Presentation, FIAT/IFTA World Conference. Vienna.

Monette, P. (2015, October 10). *Radio Canada: Digitization of the audio, video and film collections.* Presentation, FIAT/IFTA World Conference. Vienna.

Noordegraaf, J. (2012). Crowdsourcing Television's Past. The State of Knowledge in Digital Archives. *Tijdschrift voor Mediageschiedenis. 14*(2), 108–120.

O'Dwyer, A. (2012). Digitising Context. The Case of the Radio Times. *VIEW. Journal of European Television History and Culture.* 1 [1], Utrecht – Maastricht – London. Igitur Publishing.

Oomen, J. (2014, October 29). *Towards more open, connected and smart audiovisual archives.* Presentation, Simpósio Internacional de Preservación Audiovisual y Digital. Archivos Contemporaneos. Mexico City.

Raimond, Y. (2013). The BBC World Service. An alternative approach to publishing large archives. In: FIAT/IFTA Media Management Commission (Eds.), *Metadata as the cornerstone of digital archiving. Changing sceneries, changing roles, part VI. Selected papers from the MMC Seminar, Hilversum, 16–17th May 2013* (pp. 136–144). Stockholm – Vienna – Dubai: FIAT/IFTA.

Rule, D. (2008). Professional Development: Classification Defined—Taxonomies, Ontologies and Folksonomies. *Incite*, 29(11), 21.

Sauer, S. (2016, March 17). *User-centered design and search practices: understanding user improvisation to support creative retrieval.* Presentation, 'The Serendipity Factor: Evaluating the Affordances of Digital Environments (SEADE)', CHIIR 2016. Chapel Hill, NC.

Schein, A. (2015, September 27). *The Studs Terkel Radio Archive: Take it easy, but take it . . . to new places.* Presentation, 46th Annual IASA Conference. Paris.

Solheim, E., and Børdalen, G. (2015, January 26). *From broadcasting to publishing: creating the new foundation for NRK's stories.* Presentation, EBU Production Technology Seminar. Geneva.

Verwaest, M. (2014, June 3). *The Value of Production Metadata (or the lack thereof).* Presentation, EBU MDN Workshop. Geneva.

Wylie, L. (2013). RTÉ Twitter Project. In: FIAT/IFTA Media Management Commission (Eds.), *Metadata as the cornerstone of digital archiving. Changing sceneries, changing roles, part VI. Selected papers from the MMC Seminar, Hilversum, 16–17th May 2013* (pp. 146–153). Stockholm – Vienna – Dubai: FIAT/IFTA.

# 7

# Using a Film Annotation Tool as Part of the Restoration Process

**Franz Hoeller**

Abstract

This paper demonstrates the advantages of using a dedicated annotation tool for documenting the film conditions and its importance in preparing a film restoration project. This will be shown on behalf of a real world project which has been carried out in the NITROFILM project at Filmoteka Narodowa in Poland.

Keywords

film annotation, film restoration, video annotation.

## Introduction

The NITROFILM (2010) project (www.nitrofilm.pl) in Poland was about the "Conservation and Digitalisation of Pre-War Feature Films at The National Film Archive in Warsaw." This collection contains about 159 Polish prewar feature films. Forty-three titles from the collection have been selected for digitalisation, comparative studies and reconstruction. The goal was to make it possible to produce a new copy of a given film in the fullest possible detail.

Three titles have been selected for full reconstruction and restoration:

- *Mania. Historia pracownicy fabryki papierosów* (*Mania: Story of a Cigarette Factory Worker*) (*Mania. Die Geschichte einer Zigarettenarbeiterin*). Directed by Eugen Illes, Germany 1918
- *Pan Tadeusz* (*Sir Thaddeus*). Directed by Ryszard Ordyński, Poland 1928
- *Zew Morza* (*Call of the Sea*). Directed by Henryk Szaro, Poland 1927

The other forty titles have been digitalised using a 4K scanner and were prepared for the reconstruction using detailed annotations to describe film conditions and defects.

For this large amount of material it soon became clear that a good tool support for annotation is crucial. Several film experts were working simultaneously on different parts of a film or even on different films. To ensure consistency, a common vocabulary is very important.

But there is still no standard available to describe film conditions and defects in a standardised way. MPEG-7, which is a multimedia-content description standard which was standardized in ISO/IEC 15938 (multimedia content description interface) in 2002 and is described in detail in Manjunath et al. (2002) and Martinez et al. (2002), gives a standardized way to describe multimedia content in an XML format. However, this was not sufficient to describe film- and video-related defects. The detailed audiovisual profile as described by Bailer and Schallauer (2006) is defining a more feasible MPEG-7 profile to describe multimedia content in the film- and video-defect domain. During the BRAVA project from 2000 to 2002, the Brava Broadcast Archive Programme Impairments Dictionary was created which gives a good reference list for problems related to film and video. At the moment, the EBU.io Quality Control group is quite active in defining video quality control items describing common defects mainly related to broadcast and video. There are some attempts to define and standardize the description for film and video defects, but there is still no widely adopted standard fulfilling the need to describe the defects in the NITROFILM project.



*Sustainable Audiovisual Collections* (2017): 48–53. DOI: 10.2979/jts2016.0.0.09

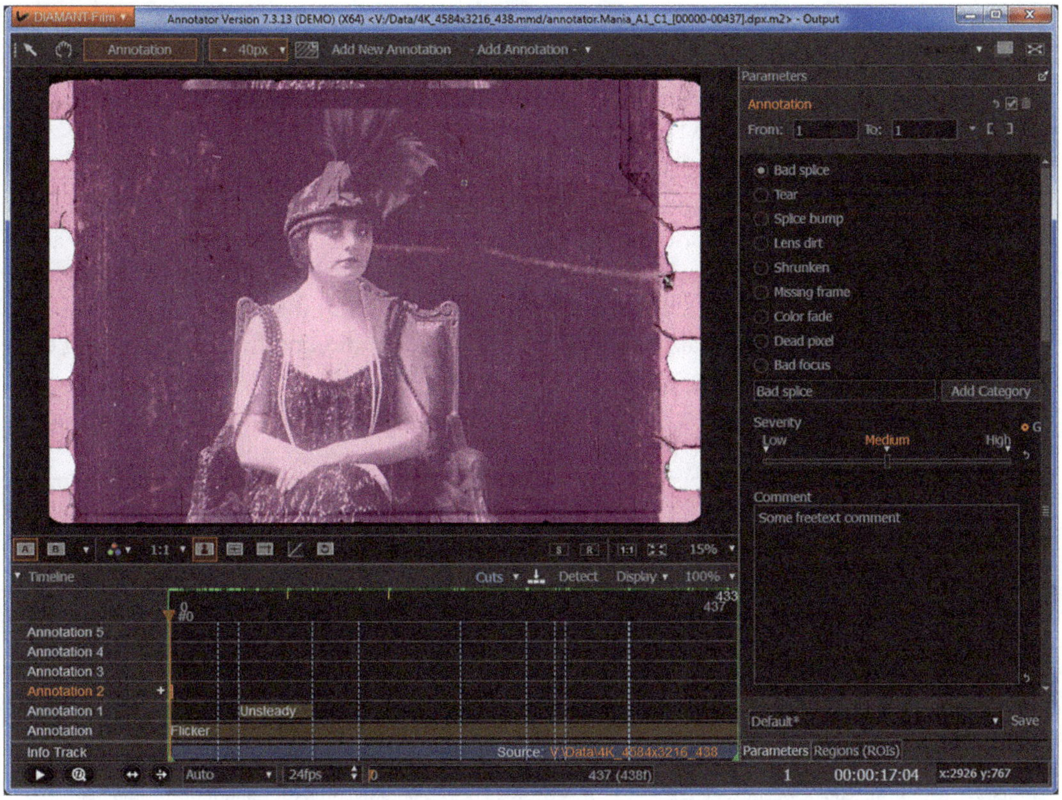

**Figure 1.** DIAMANT-Film ANNOTATOR by HS-ART Digital.

Therefore, it was necessary either to adopt an existing vocabulary or standard, or create a new or improved annotation vocabulary that could be shared among all annotating experts in a simple and futureproof way.

The annotation tool also needed features to support the viewing and analysing the scanned pictures in a fast and convenient way:

- View digitized film sequence in DPX 4K+
- Inspect channels separately
- View alpha channel with potential IR masks from the scanner
- Easy and quick zoom, pan and navigate
- See structure information live shots/scenes
- Fast playback eventually on a generated proxy
- Image analysis via histogram, waveform, pixel value view

In order to actually annotate the film conditions and defects, the tool must support various annotation functionalities:

- Frame level, shot level, or any free-range level annotations
- Annotation types or categories from a given vocabulary
- A severity indicator (medium, low, and high)
- A comment area for user comments
- Possibility to draw freeform marks in the picture

As a result of the annotation process, it should be possible to create reports out of the tool which show the detailed documentation of the film conditions and defects. Also this information should be used to decide which type of restoration should be used, or how restorations of various film items should be prioritized. Finally, an estimation of the time and cost for the restoration should be made easier with the annotation metadata at hand.

## DIAMANT-Film ANNOTATOR

It soon became clear that developing a new software fulfilling all the requirements from scratch was out of the scope for this project. After analyzing the requirements in depth, we found a way we could create the annotation features as add-on to the existing DIAMANT-Film Restoration software. So the idea of the DIAMANT-Film ANNOTATOR was born as described in HS-ART Digital--Annotator (Hoeller 2014). First it was made as an add-on in the RestorationManager+ software, but it also became a stand-alone software later on.

The ANNOTATOR allows you to create your own vocabulary simply by adding new annotation categories in the user interface. Vocabularies can be saved and loaded to files for easy exchange with other ANNOTATOR applications to ensure a common vocabulary set. HS-ART Digital has created a default vocabulary, respectively an annotation profile, for describing common film defects.

### DIAMANT-FILM ANNOTATOR Vocabulary

| Annotation category | Defect | Description |
|---|---|---|
| Annotation | Generic annotation | This is not a defect but a general annotation |
| SF Defect | Generic single frame defect | Defect which just appears on one image but does not fit in any existing category |
| | Reel-change marks | Also known as cue dots or cue marks. Look like punch holes |
| | Random scratches | Scratches appearing randomly in the image |
| | Random hairs | Hairs appearing randomly in the image |
| | Other physical damage | Not classified physical damage |
| Defect | Generic defect or artefact | Defect which does not fit in any existing category |
| Unsteady | Unsteadiness, shake, jitter, weave, bounce, instability, frame misalignment | Unsteadiness is an unwanted movement of the image in projection |
| Flicker | Flicker | Random or regular short period variations of luminance or chrominance intensity |
| Dust | Dust, dirt, blotches (single frame defects) | Random small particles covering the film and creating dark or bright spots in projection/digitalization |
| Scratch | Scratches, line scratches, tramline scratches, base scratches, emulsion scratch | Vertical lines usually caused by a piece of machinery that comes in contact with the film surface. Those scratches very often appear on multiple frames on the same position |
| Noise | Grain and noise issues | Unwanted random variation of brightness or color information in images. It can be produced by a sensor in a camera or scanner or also originate in film grain |
| Warp | Warp | Nonuniform distorted image. |
| Hair | Static hair, gate hair, camera hair | Hair in the gate, camera, or printer creating a static artefact |
| Bad splice | Bad splice | A splice is when a film has to be taped or glued together because of breakage or as part of the editing process |
| Tear | Tear (single frame defect) | Film tends to tear when exposed to high tension, especially when the material is old and brittle. An irregular tear line remains visible in the image of the affected frames |
| Splice bump | Splice bump | Unsteadiness caused by a bad splice in the telecine/scanner |
| Lens dirt | Lens dirt | Static spot caused by some dirt on the lens |
| Shrunken | Film shrinkage | The result of moisture and solvent loss in a film |
| Missing frame | Missing frame | An image is missing in the sequence |
| Color fade | Color fading / dye fading | Dyes of tinted films or colour layers can be subject to fading |
| Dead pixel | Dead pixel, hot pixel, frozen pixel, stuck pixel | A pixel or a group of pixels causing a position static damage over time |
| Bad focus | Out of focus | Resulting in a blurry picture |
| Stains | Generic stains | Not further classified stains. Can be caused by surface stains, mold, bacteria or chemical decay |
| | Surface stains | Stains on the surface of the film caused by water, oil, chemical or other |
| | Mold, fungus | Degradation due to mold |
| | Bacteria | Degradation due to bacteria. |
| | Vinegar syndrome (acetate decay) | Chemical acetate film base degradation |
| Bad focus | Misalignment from B&W separation film | Tri-Strip/YCM Recombine misalignment from B&W separation film |

S:/Projekte/Annotator/AnnotationData/reel_01_wet.#######.jpg[0090000-0093377]

Overview | Shots | Operations | Timeline | Summary | Help

DIAMANT-Film Restoration Report

Search:

| Icon | # | Start | Frames | Start TC | End TC | Duration | Filters | Tools | Annotations |
|---|---|---|---|---|---|---|---|---|---|
| | 1 | 90000 | 76 | 01:00:00:00 | 01:00:03:00 | 00:00:03:01 | | | Stability<br>Splice (2)<br>BigSpot<br>Luminance |
| | 2 | 90076 | 113 | 01:00:03:01 | 01:00:07:13 | 00:00:04:13 | | | Stability<br>Luminance |
| | 3 | 90189 | 9 | 01:00:07:14 | 01:00:07:22 | 00:00:00:09 | | | Stability<br>Splice<br>BigSpot |
| | 4 | 90198 | 208 | 01:00:07:23 | 01:00:16:05 | 00:00:08:08 | | | Stability (3)<br>Splice (2)<br>Luminance (15)<br>Warp (2)<br>BigSpot (6) |

**Figure 2.** Shot-based report.

S:/Projekte/Annotator/AnnotationData/reel_01_wet.#######.jpg[0090000-0093377] Overview Shots Operations Timeline Summary Help

DIAMANT-Film Restoration Report

Annotations

Search:

| # | Name | Start | End | Frames | Start TC | End TC | Duration | Comment | Track |
|---|---|---|---|---|---|---|---|---|---|
| 1 | Stability | 90000 | 90006 | 7 | 01:00:00:00 | 01:00:00:06 | 00:00:00:07 | | Annotation 1 |
| 2 | Splice | 90000 | 90000 | 1 | 01:00:00:00 | 01:00:00:00 | 00:00:00:01 | | Annotation |
| 3 | BigSpot | 90032 | 90032 | 1 | 01:00:01:07 | 01:00:01:07 | 00:00:00:01 | | Annotation |
| 4 | Luminance | 90063 | 90063 | 1 | 01:00:02:13 | 01:00:02:13 | 00:00:00:01 | | Annotation |
| 5 | Splice | 90075 | 90075 | 1 | 01:00:03:00 | 01:00:03:00 | 00:00:00:01 | | Annotation |
| 6 | Luminance | 90076 | 90076 | 1 | 01:00:03:01 | 01:00:03:01 | 00:00:00:01 | | Annotation |
| 7 | Stability | 90186 | 90188 | 3 | 01:00:07:11 | 01:00:07:13 | 00:00:00:03 | | Annotation 1 |
| 8 | Stability | 90189 | 90193 | 5 | 01:00:07:14 | 01:00:07:18 | 00:00:00:05 | | Annotation 1 |
| 9 | Splice | 90189 | 90189 | 1 | 01:00:07:14 | 01:00:07:14 | 00:00:00:01 | | Annotation |
| 10 | BigSpot | 90192 | 90192 | 1 | 01:00:07:17 | 01:00:07:17 | 00:00:00:01 | | Annotation |
| 11 | Stability | 90198 | 90208 | 11 | 01:00:07:23 | 01:00:08:08 | 00:00:00:11 | | Annotation 1 |
| 12 | Splice | 90198 | 90198 | 1 | 01:00:07:23 | 01:00:07:23 | 00:00:00:01 | | Annotation |
| 13 | Luminance | 90212 | 90212 | 1 | 01:00:08:12 | 01:00:08:12 | 00:00:00:01 | | Annotation |
| 14 | Luminance | 90213 | 90213 | 1 | 01:00:08:13 | 01:00:08:13 | 00:00:00:01 | | Annotation |
| 15 | Luminance | 90214 | 90214 | 1 | 01:00:08:14 | 01:00:08:14 | 00:00:00:01 | | Annotation |
| 16 | Warp | 90215 | 90215 | 1 | 01:00:08:15 | 01:00:08:15 | 00:00:00:01 | | Annotation |
| 17 | Warp | 90216 | 90216 | 1 | 01:00:08:16 | 01:00:08:16 | 00:00:00:01 | | Annotation |

**Figure 3.** Detailed report.

The vocabulary can be downloaded at http://www.hs-art.com/annotator.

The user interface of the ANNOTATOR allows the creation of annotations simply and quickly. At the end of the annotation process it is possible the export the annotations in various report types like in HTML to view or XML to further process the information in other third-party tools. Figure 2 shows a shot-based report and figure 3 is an example of a detailed report. Finally, figure 4 shows the statistics of the whole annotation project.

Figure 4. Annotation summary.

S:/Projekte/Annotator/AnnotationData/reel_01_wet.#######.jpg[0090000-0093377]

Overview Shots Operations Timeline Summary

DIAMANT-Film Restoration Report

Annotations

| # | Name | Count | Annotation Frames |
|---|---|---|---|
| 1 | BigSpot | 111 | 488 |
| 2 | Luminance | 27 | 368 |
| 3 | Splice | 19 | 19 |
| 4 | Stability | 19 | 195 |
| 5 | Warp | 2 | 2 |
| | Total | 178 | 1072 |
| | Affected Frames | | 903 |

## Conclusion

- For larger annotation projects, a good tool support is important in order to allow efficient viewing and inspection of the digitized film material.
- A flexible vocabulary helps to adapt to various situations but still guarantees consistency. Simple methods to share the vocabulary with other experts will help to ensure consistency between several users of the annotation tool.
- Report and export functionality allow for exchange with other solutions.
- Annotations can be valuable in prioritizing and guiding the restoration process. Annotations can be imported into DIAMANT-Film Restoration Software and help with the communication with the film restorers.
- The Annotator was used in a pilot project where forty-three feature films have been fully annotated.

Franz Hoeller is the managing director of HS-ART Digital, and the product manager for the DIAMANT-Film Restoration software. He is working as trainer and consultant in the fields of digital film restoration. As project manager, he was involved in several international research projects in the digital media area. He has a master's degree in telematics from the technical university in Graz and has worked as R & D software engineer in the fields of image restoration and processing at Joanneum Research in Austria and Pandora-International in the UK.

## References

NITROFILM–Konserwacja i digitalizacja przedwojennych filmów fabularnych w Filmotece Narodowej. (2010). Retrieved February 17, 2016, from http://www.nitrofilm.pl.

Hoeller, F. (2014). DIAMANT-Film Restoration / HS-ART Digital–Annotator. Retrieved February 17, 2016, from http://www.hs-art.com/annotator.

Martinez, J., Koenen, R., and Pereira, F. (2002). MPEG-7: The generic multimedia content description standard, part 1. *IEEE Multimedia*, 9(2), 78–87.

Manjunath, B. S., Sikora, T., and Salembier, P. (2002). *Introduction to MPEG-7: Multimedia content description interface*. Chichester: Wiley.

Bailer, W., and Schallauer, P. (2006). The Detailed Audiovisual Profile: Enabling Interoperability between MPEG-7 Based Systems. *2006 12th International Multi-Media Modelling Conference.*

The Brava broadcast archive programme impairments dictionary. (n.d.). Retrieved February 17, 2016, from http://brava.ina.fr/brava_public_impairments_list.en.html.

EBU.io—Quality Control. (n.d.). Retrieved February 17, 2016, from http://ebu.io/qc /items/0001W.

# 8

# The Restoration of *The Thousand-Stitch Belt* (1937): Utilizing Analog and Digital Techniques to Retrieve the Color of a Two-Color System

**Masaki Daibo, Tomohiro Hasegawa, and Kazuki Miura**

**Abstract**

*The Thousand-Stitch Belt*, produced by Dainihon Tennenshoku Eiga Seisakusho (Greater Japan Natural Color Productions), uses a two-color system and is the oldest surviving Japanese color talkie. Greater Japan Natural Color Production is known to be the first production to adopt the Multicolor process, called "Shanghai color" at the time. This essay will demonstrate the process by which we revived the color of the two-color system through analog and digital technologies. We could neither ship the original material, a nitrate color positive, to Japan, nor rely on technical supervision. In spite of these limitations, we were able to devise a new method of digital restoration with the production companies, IMAGICA Corporation and IMAGICA WEST Corporation. By analyzing the data resulting from photochemical simulations at IMAGICA WEST, we determined the color range that the two-color system could not reproduce, kept that range from being picked up in color grading, and thereby retrieved the color of *The Thousand-Stitch Belt*.

**Keyword**

two-color system, Multicolor, Cinecolor, analog simulation, a dedicated LUT, *The Thousand-Stitch Belt*, the oldest surviving Japanese color talkie.

## Preface

We conducted two careful field investigations at Gosfilmodond (the National Film Foundation of the Russian Federation) and "repatriated" three hundred and forty-seven Japanese films from Russia. The repatriation projects seemed complete, however Gosfilmofond informed us that there still remained nearly two hundred tins of fragments. Thus, as part of our third field investigation in 2014, we closely examined a print of *The Thousand-Stitch Belt* (dir. Genjiro Saegusa, 1937)[1] that was confirmed in the late 1990s by Adrian Wood, a well-known supervisor of various film restoration projects, and Victor Belyakov, an independent film researcher.

*The Thousand-Stitch Belt*, produced by Dainihon Tennenshoku Eiga Seisakusho (Greater Japan Natural Color Productions), uses a two-color system and is the oldest surviving Japanese color talkie. This field investigation identified the print as a 35 mm color nitrate positive with soundtrack, 534 meters (approximately 19 min.), and about half the length of a complete release print. Greater Japan Natural Color Production is known to be the first production to adopt the Multicolor process, called "Shanghai color" at the time (Motion Picture and Television Engineering Society of Japan, Inc. 1997, pp. 57–58). We can assume that this title was also produced with the same two-color system, because the print on Kodak positive stock was struck from the Dupont negative, and both Kodak and Dupont were known for marketing special film for Multicolor. Amongst many color processes that appeared from the 1930s to 1940s when film was shifting from the silent era to talkies, together with Three-strip Technicolor used for feature films, Multicolor (from 1928 to 1932) competed for market share worldwide. Its successor was Cinecolor (from 1932 to 1950), used for short films including documentaries, or animations (Belton, 2000, pp. 344–357).



*Sustainable Audiovisual Collections* (2017): 54–59. DOI: 10.2979/jts2016.0.0.10

This essay will demonstrate the process by which we revived the color of the two-color system through analog and digital technologies. We could neither ship the original material, a nitrate color positive, to Japan, nor rely on technical supervision. In spite of these limitations, we were able to devise a new method of digital restoration with the production companies, IMAGICA Corporation and IMAGICA WEST Corporation. By analyzing the data resulting from photochemical simulations at IMAGICA WEST, we determined the color range that the two-color system could not reproduce, kept that range from being picked up in color grading, and thereby retrieved the color of *The Thousand-Stitch Belt*. To be more precise, we constructed the restoration workflow as follows for image and sound respectively.

## The Restoration Workflow of *The Thousand-Stitch Belt*

### Restoration of the Image

(a) We scanned the original material—35 mm nitrate print—at Gosfilmofond, to receive 4K 10-bit log DPX file.
(b) We converted the resolution of above scanned data from 4K (4096×3112 pix.) to 2K (2048×1556 pix.) at IMAGICA. Then we excluded the soundtrack section (1828×1556 pix.) from it to make pretreatment data, and conducted such processes as removing the dirt on the image, stabilizing the motion of the image, and eliminating scratches or stains.
(c) Then, before color grading, we made an attempt to simulate the two-color system by photochemical means and to analyze the results to clarify the color range that the two-color system cannot reproduce, and set a restriction of this range, finally, creating the Digital Source Master (DSM).

### Restoration of the Sound

(d) We scanned the original material at Gosfilmofond, to receive a 24-bit 48 KHz WAV file.
(e) We conducted processes at IMAGICA, such as reducing a clicking noise, humming noise, and distortion.
(f) Finally, by using all the data gained by the above-mentioned processes, we created a 35 mm projection print, and a Digital Cinema Package (DCP).

## 1. Color Retrieval by Photochemical Simulation

Before any discussion of the actual color retrieval of *The Thousand-Stitch Belt*, we should begin by taking a look at the two-color system itself. Negative films for two-color separation shooting apply a "bi-pack system," which uses black-and-white panchromatic film, and black-and-white orthochromatic film tinted in red. These specialized films were marketed by Eastman Kodak and Dupont. In this system, light from the lens reaches the orthochromatic film's side, but it is not exposed by red light waves, so only the wavelength between blue and green is recorded, and only the light that goes through the orthochromatic film reaches the panchromatic film's side. Panchromatic film, on the other hand, has photographic sensitivity for all the wavelengths of red, green, and blue, but because the emulsion of orthochromatic film is tinted, so that it absorbs blue light, only the red waves are recorded. To gain a positive image from the negative used for shooting in this way, special film was used with emulsion on both sides (Cornwell-Clyne, 1951, p. 338). The emulsion used for this special film was only sensitive to blue, and it could be printed from two strips of negatives onto both sides at the same time. To prevent the light waves affecting each other, the emulsion was tinted in yellow so that it absorbed blue light, and this tinting was washed away in the process of development. Black-and-white positive images could thus be created on both sides.

The next step was to immerse the film into a tank whose structure allows only one side of the film to touch the chemical liquid. By doing this, a silver image on positive film made from the panchromatic side was toned in Prussian blue (Fe7 [CN] 18). Then, the whole film went through the uranium liquid for toning, so that the silver image of blue-filtered positive was toned in orange, and further went through the red-dye liquid to supplement the color, because the orange image is easily affected by basic dye. This is the system of Multicolor. The generation method of the color of orange has changed from the mixture with uranium toning, in case of Multicolor, to a dye only in the case of Cinecolor.

This two-colored system's process is referenced in Cornwell-Clyne's *Colour Cinematography* (1936/1951). We confirmed the information gained from the literature with a currently available film: *Riou gindenka Osaka Kaikosha syogakko gohomon* [tentative title] (4 mins.). Among the films stored at NFC, as with *The Thousand-Stitch Belt*, this 1940 35 mm nitrate print was also produced by Greater Japan Natural Color Productions. It most likely used the same two-color system and helped us tremendously in understanding the features of the Shanghai color. According to the analysis of this nitrate print by IMAGICA WEST, red toning was tinted by a mordant dye of magenta color for the image part after the uranium toning, and the soundtrack was only toned in blue. This information matched the description of basic texts on film color.

Keeping in mind the color process of the two-color system explained in detail previously, we will now proceed to understand the features of the same process more precisely by photochemical simulation. First, we used Kodak T-MAX100, black-and-white film for photography to shoot the color chart and vegetation, and made black-and-white separation negatives by shooting with Wratten No. 44 and No. 23 filters.[2] In this way, we tried to get results closer to the spectral sensitivity recorded by panchromatic and orthochromatic films respectively, as introduced in the thesis titled "Multicolor process" published in *SMPTE* journal by Russell Otis in 1931.

Secondly, to replicate the Multicolor process, we printed a positive film, using Eastman Kodak 2302, from two separately treated black-and-white negative films. Initially, we shot the first negative film stock with a red filter, applying blue toning on the exposed positive image. As this was toned by iron, it was possible to employ the original toning process described in Cornwell-Clyne's *Colour Cinematography* (1936/1951). However, we were unable to follow the 1930s procedure on the second black-and-white negative film stock. The positive exposure gained by the blue filter would have required basic dye and uranium to be used to tone the red. Because of environmental issues this process is no longer possible. Therefore, for this procedure we found it necessary to employ the Desmet method. After applying this process, these two-toned positive films were cemented together to recreate colors through this two-color system. Comparisons of the images after the toning was applied, as well as after the two negatives were printed onto a single positive film stock, were similar with Cornwell-Clyne's descriptions of the original method.

## 2. Restoration Using Digital Technology: Making a Dedicated LUT And Grading

We conducted a detailed analysis of the data gained by photochemical simulation in the previous section, then we identified the area of color gamut which the two-color system cannot generate and for grading set restrictions so that the area in question was ignored. In order to achieve this, we made a dedicated LUT by using a supplementary tool which prevents adopting colors the two-color system cannot express in the grading stage. The LUT keeps an input value if it is within the range that the two-color system can express, and if it is outside of that range, converts it to be shown in vivid green as a warning sign (fig. 1). The LUT itself is just a numerical table, but the main challenge in developing its unique color limiting capabilities is centered entirely on making the algorithm to determine if the input value is within the two-color system's color gamut (the capacity of expression) or not. To identify the color gamut, we prepared a chart which showed both a 21-step blue toning gradation, and a 21-step red toning gradation (by the Desmet method) using the photochemical simulation explained in the previous section. The chart suggests color samples that blue toning and red toning can express. We measured these with a

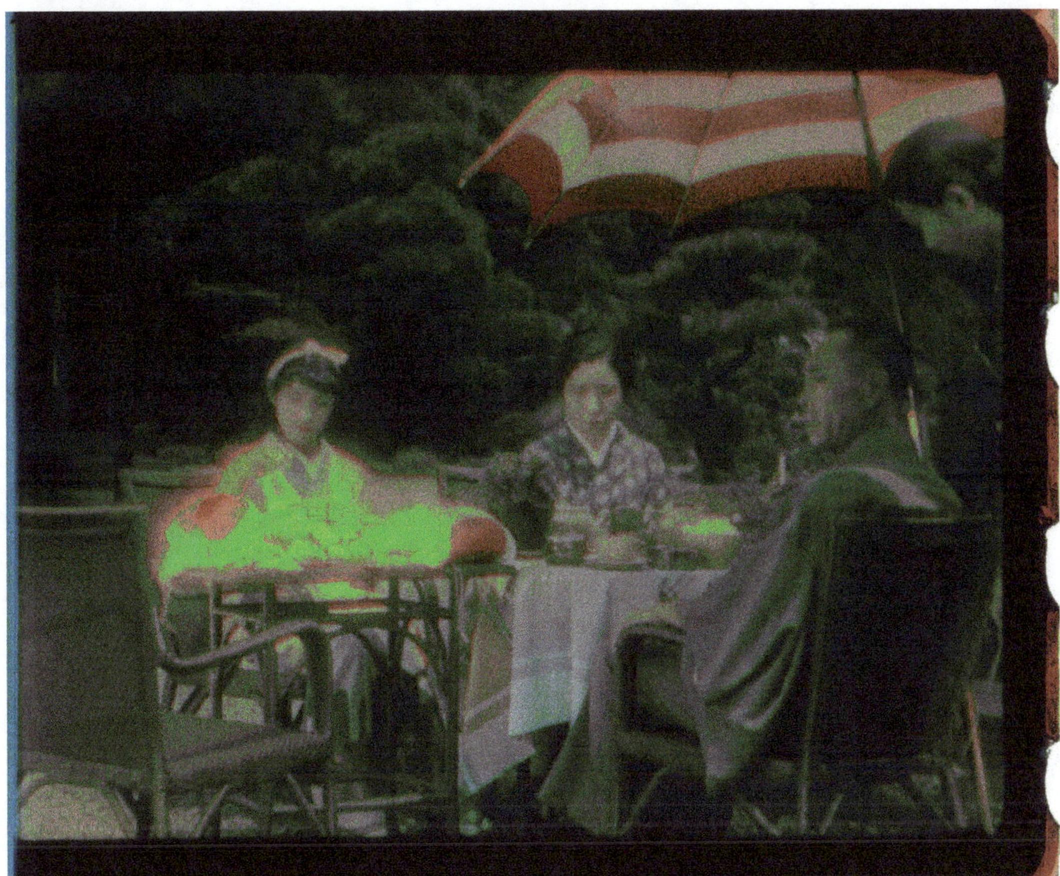

**Figure 1.** The warning sign shown in color on the women's kimonos by the dedicated LUT.

spectral radiometer (Topcon SR-UL1R) and gained each coordinate in the XYZ colorimetric system. The colors that can be expressed by the mixture of these two colors are an aggregated combination of coordinates (21×21=441) gained from the samples, so we considered it to be the expected color gamut of the two-color system.

Also, we expected to make a DCP after completion, which is a file format for digital projection, and grading was done in accordance with DCP's standard specification for the viewing environment, DCI-P3 color space, with gamma 2.6 and white point 6300K. For the DCI-P3 color gamut and the above mentioned expected color gamut of the two-color system, if you compare how each volume (three-dimensional color gamut in a color space) overlaps, you can identify the range of the two-color system within the DCI-P3 color gamut. However, we visualized the actual measured value gained from the previous simulation on a three-dimensional scatter diagram, and found out that it was in too complicated a form, and with too much distortion to define how each color gamut volume overlaps. Therefore, we first converted each color gamut into CIE Lab color space, then determined the range by considering that the aggregation of the colors on DCI-P3, whose color difference (quantitative description of color's perceptive difference) from actual measured value is within a defined area: 9.2,[3] is the aggregation of colors which the two-color system is able to express.

After such verification, the dedicated LUT for the restoration of two-color system, showing vivid green as a warning sign when an input value lies outside of the two-color system's color gamut, is made. By using this LUT, when it comes to the colors that remain in the range that the two-color system can create, it is possible to proceed with the same grading as usual, but when they exceed the range, only the exceeded area appears in vivid green. By repeating this feedback, efficient color-grading becomes possible within the range that the two-color system can express (fig. 2).

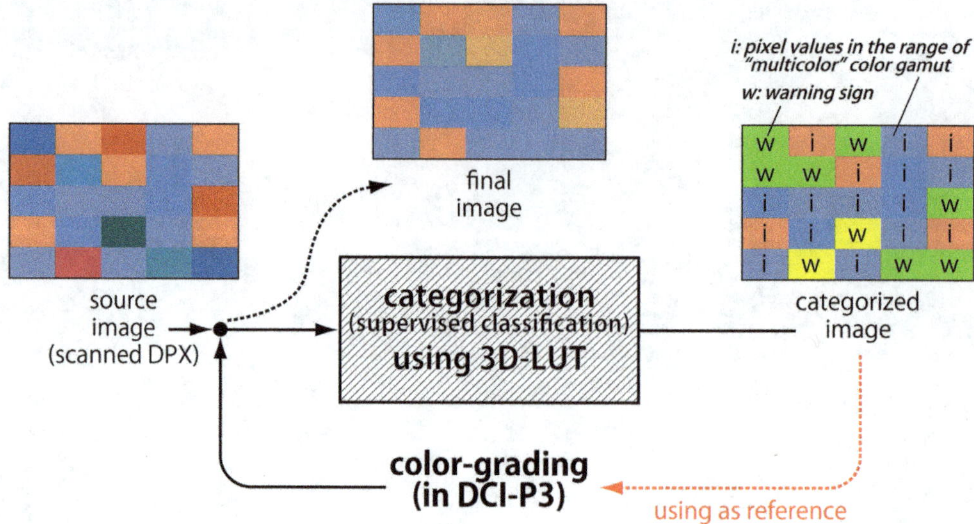


**Figure 2.** The feedback loop for conforming to two-color system's color gamut.

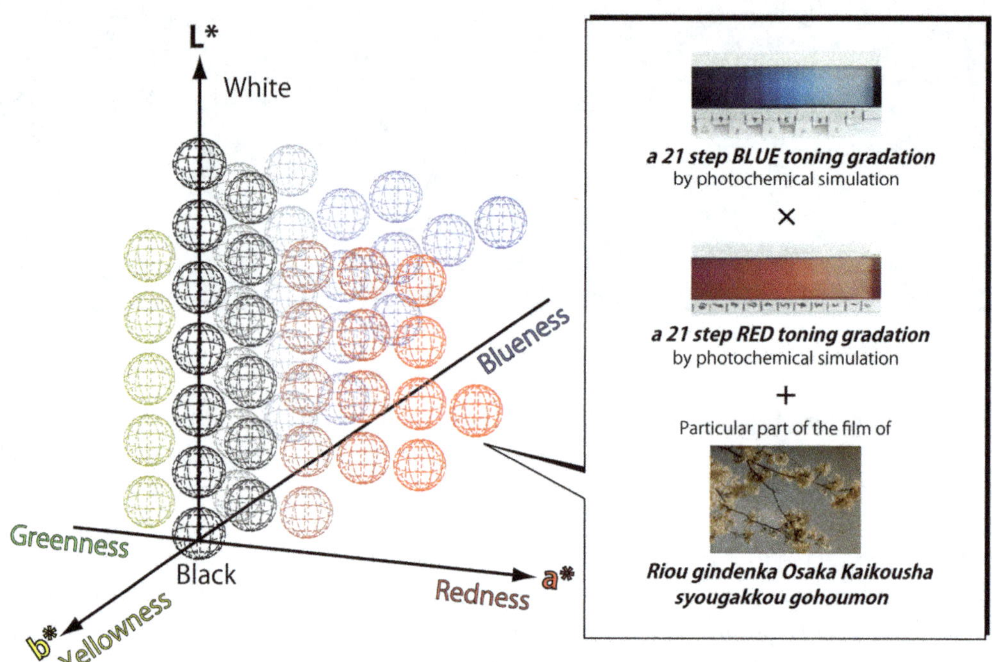


**Figure 3.** The concept image of measured data converted to CIE Lab color space.

However, as the identification of color gamut depended too much on our limited sample size, we measured the color palette in *Riou gindenka Osaka Kaikousha syougakkou gohoumon*, which theoretically, used the same sort of color system. By adding the data to identify the range of the color gamut, and altering the LUT (fig. 3), this revised LUT became the final version in this restoration.

## Conclusion

Aiming as far as possible at retrieving the probable colors made by this special process, we implemented a new method of digital restoration. For this, the limitation of the color gamut that the two-color system cannot express actually became a key factor. This means that we first clarified the features of the two-color system by actual measured values gained through a photochemical simulation that was based on an historically relevant reference book, then specified areas of the color gamut which this process cannot generate, and color graded the restored data with a color value restrictive LUT, allowing us to reproduce the colors of *The Thousand-Stitch Belt.* This methodical combination of digital and analog techniques is extremely effective at revealing features from original materials that may be inaccessible because of restrictions like physical deterioration. Moreover, this new approach allowed us to analyze results not only indirectly, as a reference for grading, but also directly in the actual restoration workflow, when we altered the LUT for grading.

MASAKI DAIBO is Assistant Curator at National Film Center, The National Museum of Modern Art, Tokyo. He is in charge of film acquisitions and also manages the restoration of film and preservation of the NFC collection. He received a PhD in Human and Environmental Studies (Film Studies) from the University of Kyoto in 2013. His most recent article is "The Multiple Versions of Joseph Rosenthal's Siege and Surrender of Port Arthur (1905)," Journal of Film Preservation, vol.92, 2015, pp.53–62.

TOMOHIRO HASEGAWA is a color scientist and also manages several R & D projects focusing on color reproduction of the film. He holds a master of engineering in electrical engineering and computer science from the Shibaura Institute of Technology (2012).

KAZUKI MIURA is Researcher of the National Research Project for Sustainability of Born-Digital Cinema at the National Film Center, the National Museum of Modern Art, Tokyo (2014). He managed several digital restoration projects as a technical director at IMAGICA Corp.

## Acknowledgments

We would like to express appreciation to Yoshihiro Matsuo of IMAGICA WEST for his special knowledge of Multicolor and Cinecolor, as well as his initiative and implementation of photochemical simulation.

(Translated by Kae Ishihara)

## Notes

1. The thousand-stitch belt refers to a hand-made amulet for Japanese soldiers on their way to war.
2. Kodak, Wratten Light Filters. Retrieved February 18, 2016, from https://archive.org/details/WrattenLightFilters.
3. This color difference (9.2) was employed as an acceptable value when the dedicated LUT was made, in terms of ease of controlling grading and color reproducibility.

## References

Belton, J. (2000). Cinecolor. *Film History*, 12(4).

Cornwell-Clyne, A. (1936/1951). *Colour Cinematography* (3rd ed). London: Chapman & Hall.

Kodak Limited London, (1953). Wratten Light Filters, (1st ed.). Retrieved from https://archive.org/stream/WrattenLightFilters/Kodak-WrattenFilters#page/n2/mode/1up.

Motion Picture and Television Society of Japan, Inc. (1997). *Nihon eiga gijyutsushi* (*A history of motion picture technologies in Japan*).

Otis, R. (July, 1931). Multicolor process. *Journal of the Society of Motion Pictures Engineers*, 17(1), 5–10. Doi:10.5594/J08027.

# Migration of Archived Video Footage: Challenges and Solutions for Hardware, Software, and Workflow Issues

**Franz Pavuza**


## Abstract

Vienna's Phonogrammarchiv is currently in the middle of the first migration of video data. The archive developed solutions for the challenging transfer procedures from mostly outdated but still operating equipment to modern hardware, and for linking legacy software for the playback process with today's programs for recording and storage. Relying on rugged tape recorders backed by major manufacturers, and on a future-proof philosophy for the compatibility of playback devices over more than a decade turned out to be a good choice. Software solutions for parts of the migration process that replaced the originally expected hardware operations will be discussed, specifically the lossless transfer from a proprietary file format to more common or open standard formats.

The presentation will also point out workflow issues, recommending—at least for small archives—manual rather than automatic metadata processing for the first migration, done in tight cooperation of the archivist and the technician, in order to streamline the migrated data with respect to formats and metadata notations, and to correct a few errors in the archives database that inevitably occurred during the initial phase of the archiving process, when the workflow underwent occasional modifications. The primary goal for this admittedly time-consuming process is a mostly automatic second migration in the future.



## Keywords

audiovisual archive, video department, technical issues, obsolete formats, analog sources, uncompressed file format, video data migration.


## Introduction

Archiving of video footage at the Phonogrammarchiv in Vienna started in 2003 after an extensive investigation within the academic community (universities, museums, academy of sciences), covering holdings and properties—for example, formats—of video tapes ready for archiving.

The subsequent process of acquiring hard- and software for the archiving procedure followed three basic guidelines: quality, affordability and easy maintenance of the archiving system by an Austrian vendor. Therefore, the philosophy that has already been proven for audio archiving—analog sources being digitized in the best available process and stored in an uncompressed or lossless-compressed format, and digital sources nearly unchanged during processing and transfer to their final storage device—could also be applied, accordingly, to the video footage. Also, financial support was provided by the Academy of Sciences, and the local vendor guaranteed short response times in case of hard- or software problems with the archiving system.

The archive finally agreed to accept, temporarily, a proprietary, non-standard format for the archived video and audio files (DPS/DVA) because there was a safe loophole (SDI-connector) for the first migration to extract the standard format data sequence (ITU-601) included in the proprietary DPS/DVA container.

The workflow to be developed should also follow, as closely as possible, the task sequence already used for audio footage. However, modifications resulting from specific properties of the video stream, such as much higher data rates and larger files were inevitable.

According to recommendations, the start of the first migration was expected to be between six and ten years after the first archiving tasks, in order to switch from aging hardware to a new one, and to stay within the time frame of the final archiving media generations (LTO tapes) with backwards compatibility in reading the previous two generations.

The worldwide economic crisis at the end of the last decade affected Austria as well, and resulted in heavy cuts in personnel and budget, even threatening the existence of the archive for a while. So the start of the migration was delayed significantly.

## Migration Workflow

Initial contemplations about the temporal structure of the migration offered many possible approaches ranging from a concentrated migration period of a few months, focusing almost all activities of the archive on the migration process, to a more or less continuous migration over the whole migration period of nearly a decade, and in parallel to the regular archiving tasks.

For future migrations, a fully automatic process certainly is a must. However, to ensure a smooth automatic data transfer in the future, it is advisable to correct, manually, all errors of the initial phase where workflow and technical issues had frequently been modified due to the lack of experience. Thus, the current procedures include a step-by-step transfer of the data, with both a technician and an archivist closely watching the process, correcting or complimenting data, and making relevant remarks for the archive's internal database.

As an example, on some initial files, keyframes (as a support for a search in the archive's database) were missing, so they have been added during the migration procedure. Also, some metadata describing scene changes were linked to displaced pointers at the timeline, because they were written down before the material was stripped from empty frames at the beginning of the file. These errors have been corrected, as well.

The technical issues were much more extensive. Back then, the nature of the archiving software suggested the time-saving storage of the original unaltered file together with an additional file that included a list of "virtual" files (representing the actual subfiles, had the original one been cut into "real" smaller parts). Time saving was of high priority due to the backlog of material ten years ago. Also, this constraint prevented us from creating integrity files. It simply took too long to calculate them. We accepted this status of limited data security—having only two copies of the archived files (two pieces of LTO-tape, of different manufacturers, stored in different places in Vienna).

Clearing backlogs are of less importance now. Consequently, the archive decided that, in parallel with the transfer from the proprietary DPS-container to a more standardized AVI-file, it was the right moment to create "real" files from the virtual ones. Furthermore, integrity checks will accompany the actual files from now on.

## Hardware Issues

For the archiving process, our vendor supplied two good quality personal computers with extra dedicated hardware (to handle uncompressed files), and for the I/O-channels—for example, for the external striped hard disk arrays.

Naturally, after more than ten years of archiving there were signs of wear, so we replaced the heavily used hard disks with new ones. This was just in time, because now SCSI hard disks are more difficult to find on the market and more expensive. One SCSI controller failed during the initial migration phase and was replaced. The graphics card, unfortunately, belonged to a device family prone to failure after a couple of years because of an improper seal of the main chip, so it had to be replaced. The other components of the two computers still work without any problems.

Our final storage media for the first decade had been LTO tapes of generation 1 and 3. The three LTO-1 recorders had been heavily used, so when there was extra budget available we bought an additional LTO-2 that was available as a bargain when LTO-3 devices became the best-selling family of recorders, and another LTO-3 when LTO-4 and -5 were current products. Luckily, all of them operate flawlessly, with the LTO-3 recorders being slightly more sensitive to low humidity in the studio during the wintertime. The recorders did refuse to operate properly below 25% humidity, but stated the reason clearly on the error report. A small humidifier solved the problem.

As for the tapes themselves, among the few hundred tapes of LTO-1 and LTO-3, only three pieces were rejected initially by the recorder during the archiving process, and three others showed a reading error during migration, with two of them being capable of delivering the file by a second playback run. One single file could not be recovered, so we used the second copy for playback.

## Software Issues

The original "archiving" software came together with the hardware ingest card of the PC. This was standard editing software, but was only used for virtual cutting of the original file and creating a description file with the transition points between the scenes. This piece of software had some minor issues that had never been corrected by updates, but we found workaround procedures to circumvent them and avoid the problems. One of these flaws was the susceptibility to rapid brightness changes in a scene, such as a flash, or on the three-second overlap period we initially provided to prove that no scenes or frames had been removed. We later omitted the overlap that stemmed from the analog times of archiving audio or video material.

For the first migration we decided to create real files, which takes some time and makes use of the copy command within the player window of the editing program. This feature is not typically used during the archiving process. Furthermore, we had to get used to another bug that prevented the system from creating files with more than about 44,000 frames. To this day, we do not know the reason for this behavior. It is definitively not a matter of internal storage space (RAM or hard disk), but there is a theory that it may be a driver problem with the outdated operating system, Windows 2000. Since most of the real files are smaller than that, it is not a big problem. We create larger files by calculating two smaller, slightly overlapping ones, and then glue them together with a frame-accurate open-source utility.

The original backup software that came with the operating system, Windows XP, was fairly stable during archiving, although it still contained a few harmless bugs. For example, compared to the first recorded copy, the recording time for the second copy of the LTO tape was significantly longer, making the procedure slower. However, rebooting before making the second copy solved the problem. Also, the software gave warnings when the tape was played back on another system, as opposed to the one it was actually recorded on. This was a particular issue when playing back multi-session recordings. This problem seemed to stem from operating systems that varied slightly because of minor update differences, but, fortunately, no files were lost.

Multi-session recordings had to be read back separately in order to ensure that the description was not overwritten on previously recorded files. This issue is preventable by paying attention during the migration process. Additionally, it was also a potential source of errors back then, because somebody could forget to store the correct description files. In that case, the original file was edited using the metadata from the archive's database which accurately listed the timestamps of the scenes. This process, of course, is extra time-consuming work.

After the rendering of "real" files, pairs of DPS and DVA Files, we used a commercially available format converter that combined the contents of the DPS and DVA container to one single AVI-file. Also, we made use of a filter provided by the DPS community, downloading it from the webpage of the company that later on acquired the DPS/DVA vendor. This process is now a fairly quick procedure. In the case of problems with the software conversion, we still could make use of the ITU-601-output on the SDI-terminal of the DPS-System as a base for further processing.

There are occasional mistakes to be corrected, such as denomination, typing errors in the database or on the LTO-cassette leaflet, missing keyframes, or incorrectly rendered "browsing" files with wrong field order. Therefore, the transfer to the new storage media, LTO-5 tape, includes a careful check of these issues against the archive's database.

The original backup software is no longer supported on systems using Windows 7 and upwards, so we switched to the new linear tape file system, known as LTFS-format, and used command line software and drivers provided by the tape recorder manufacturers. This process is a relatively easy job. In contrast to the archiving process from years ago, these migration recordings, as well as all future recordings during the archiving process, using LTFS will be done by the system operators in order to correctly mount the recorder and provide an adequately fast data stream for the recorder from the hard disk array. The huge amount of storage space of LTO-5 (1.5 TB) requires an intelligent preparation of the sum of projects to be recorded on tape, preferably in one session, and directly from an internal hard disk over a SAN-connection (LTO-1 tapes could be properly fed with data from an external hard disk using the popular but slower USB2-connection).

## Recommendations

For the first migration, we recommend an admittedly time-consuming, but in the long run, rewarding manual migration in tight cooperation between an archivist and a technician. This process applies, particularly, to material created during the initial phase of archiving, where workflow, formats, and equipment may have been modified frequently, and when a more uniform structure of the stored material is highly desirable.

Since migration usually has to include original hard- and software, it pays to keep the systems in good condition with occasional checks. Two complete sets of archiving computers, plus backup tape recorders, or other storage devices are recommended. It is also advisable to get the latest possible updates and drivers for backup- and editing software, and to buy some spare parts as long as they are available (e.g., SCSI-controller).

If LTO or similar systems are used, it is also a good idea to acquire additional recorders that offer backward-reading compatibility.

In conclusion, video data migration should, in our opinion, be seen as a continuous process in parallel to the regular archiving tasks. It should be repeated within a period of six to eight years, thus having the fully functional hard- and software technologies that enable a smooth transition from one storage media generation to the next one.

Franz Pavuza has been with the Phonogrammarchiv of the Austrian Academy of Sciences since 2002 and is responsible for the installation and operation of the videographic section (technical issues). He has an master's degree in electronics from the Vienna University of Technology and until 2002 worked at the university as an R & D assistant for projects in cooperation with industry partners and government-supported funds in audio, video (basic research, applications in test & measurement) and industrial electronics (development of prototypes). He is a member of the AMIA (Association of Moving Image Archivists) and the German FKTG (Fernseh- und Kinotechnische Gesellschaft).

His job at the Phonogrammarchiv includes presentations for training sessions and workshops (ERPANET, National Library of Austria) and conferences (AMIA, IASA, FIAT, DELOS).

He currently supervises the first major video data migration at the Phonogrammarchiv.

# 10

# An Investigation into the Restoration of 1950s Wire Recordings

**Nie Manying, Wang Xi, Zhang Shuxia, and Yan Jie**


## Abstract

Wire recordings constitute a remarkable percentage of the audio records from the early years of the founding of the Peoples Republic of China. Most of them suffer from degradation and shortage of playback devices, hindering access to the precious records. Consequently, a project was conducted to establish a wire recording restoration platform and the digitization of wire recordings from several archival agencies. This paper describes the processes of machine and records restoration, with encouraging results obtained for the rescue of wire recordings from local archives.



## Keywords

wire recordings, wire recorder, audio records, restoration, steel wire recording, magnetic wire recording, audiovisual archives.


## Introduction

The idea of recording sound on steel wire dates back to the 1870s. Magnetic wire recorders became available in the late 1940s, and these devices were widely used in China in the early and mid-1950s. As magnetic tape recording and long-playing records opened up the HI-FI era in the 1950s wire recorders gradually stepped off the stage. Although the history of wire recordings was not long, a great deal of wire recordings was preserved in China's archival institutions. However, replay of and access to these precious historical records is getting difficult due to vanishing playback equipment and degrading wires—that is, by oxidation.

To deal with this challenge, the Institute of Scientific and Technical Research on Archives of the State Archives Administration of China (SAAC) launched a project in 2011 on wire recordings restoration in 2011. During 2013 and 2015, the research team safeguarded approximately eighty spools of wire recordings from local archival agencies following the digitization procedure we developed. After restoration of the wires in bad condition and digitization the recorded contents, these recordings are now accessible and available for research by the public.

### Number and Type of the Wire Recordings in China

## Challenges

From January to March 2011, the research team surveyed wire recordings preserved in some forty potential collections in China, including thirty-one provincial archives, one departmental archive, two broadcasting stations, and six musical institutions. Twenty-five of the forty institutions held wire recordings, with an estimated number of almost three thousand spools in total.

In China, wire recorders are mainly used for the recording of major events (e.g., the great ceremony of the foundation of PRC on Oct. 1, 1949). The major topics of the wire recording the archives include speeches of important leaders (e.g., Mao Zedong, Zhou Enlai), conference recordings, broadcast shows, music played by famous musicians, and original folk music. These recordings of traditional music are an important part of the diverse cultures within the common heritage of China.



*Sustainable Audiovisual Collections* (2017): 64–71. DOI: 10.2979/jts2016.0.0.12

### Problems

Wire recording technology has been obsolete now for more than half a century, and replay equipment has become scarce. The remaining pieces are in poor shape, and spare parts are hard to find. Without wire recorders, most organizations that hold such recordings have never been able to listen to the recorded contents, and there is little information about the content from the original catalogues: a situation hindering access to the recordings for curators as well as for researchers.

Half of the investigated organizations that hold wire recordings are in great need of assistance to safeguard their collections. Some have already transferred the recordings to other types of media like cassettes or open-reel tapes some time ago, but now neither the wires nor the tapes can be replayed; both are in need of another round of transfer. Some wire recordings are in poor condition, and archivists are unable to properly handle them.

## Search and Repair of Playback Equipment

### Search of Wire Recorders

The first task of the team to rescue the wire recordings was focused on the search for appropriate wire recorders. Unfortunately, the equipment widespread at the time is now very hard to find. The research team searched around vintage markets, visited old equipment collectors, looked for information online, and finally acquired six wire recorders, all of from Webster-Chicago: four of model 80–1, one 181–1, and one 288–1.

Webster-Chicago model 80–1 was relatively easier to find, and we used them as the basic playback equipment. Model 288–1 was used as a supplement, being the latest model available. As the project went on, the search for equipment was continued and a dozen of wire recorders of different brands and models have been gradually acquired.

### Repair of Wire Recorders

Amongst the six wire recorders, two 80–1, the 181–1, and the 288–1 are in good shape. The other two 80–1 wire recorders are also in good overall shape, but one of them mildly jitters while the other has a less sensitive audio output.

Winding the wire evenly onto the spool is essential. We experienced two cases in which the recording head was slightly high, which resulted in a wind pack thicker on the top and thinner on the bottom of the spool. As more wire winds up on the take-up drum, its cross section takes a trapezoidal shape. We used test spools to check whether the height of the recording head is at the appropriate level. If the wire did not wind evenly from the very top to the very bottom, we opened up the cover of the wire recorder and adjusted the height of the recording head accordingly.

The wire recorders run on 110 volts AC, whereas the voltage in China is 220 volts AC. Therefore, the wire recorders were plugged into a transformer.

## Restoration of the Wires

After adjustment of the playback equipment, the next step is to solve the problems concerning the wires. Having been unused and out of care for quite some time, some of the wires suffer from a variety of problems: dust, dirt or grease, and more serious defects like breakage, kinks, curls, or snarls. All these require careful repair before running the wires through the machines.

### Cleaning

There was dust on the surface of most of the wire recordings received by the team. Some were also greasy, which required physical cleaning. In order not to damage the wire and its tightness and even packing, a soft brush was used to wipe off the dirt, striking in the direction of the wind of the wire.

Sometimes, dirt or light grease on the wires appeared also inside the wind, which gradually accumulated in the groove of the recording head. In this case, the groove was cleaned with a soft brush moistened with alcohol after each replay in order to prevent contamination of other wires.

### Removing Rust

Steel wires for recording will generally not get rusty. Some may become rusty, however, if stored in a humid environment or because the steel quality is less resistant against oxidation. Though the signal from the wire might not be affected significantly, the magnetic recording head would be damaged quickly by the rust. Therefore the rust must be removed by application of a rust remover (e.g., WD-40) with a soft cloth.

### Tying and Untying Knots

The recording wire is almost as thin as human hair (generally 0.10–0.15 mm). Though it is pliable, it can always have kinks (see fig. 1) and even break if not handled properly. During replay and rewind, the wire should pass smoothly through the recording head from one reel to the other. The wire runs at a high speed, but mild kinks would not interrupt the smooth movement of the wire, nor produce any audible artefacts. However, when the kink is more severe, the tension of the wire could possibly break the wire at the kink, which could result in a major entanglement. In order to prevent this from happening, the kinks need to be straightened out, broken wires need to be tied together, and badly tied knots need to be trimmed. Unfortunately, the three aforementioned problems were frequently encountered by the team, and had to be dealt with separately.

There are two alternatives to flatten the kinks. The first is using a toothpick. This applies to mild kinks, where the wire has twisted itself into a bending curve.

We point the tip of the toothpick into the curve, twist and gently squeeze its way deeper through to enlarge the curve, then turn the toothpick to open up the curve, and finally gently pull the wire straight. The second method is to use two pliers with pointed heads. This applies to more severe condition, where the curve was twisted and pulled tight into a folding point. We hold the wire at both the sides of the folding point with the pliers, gently untwist the wire and pull it straight. Sometimes this has solved the problem, but sometimes the wire breaks anyway. This means fixing the wire with a knot, but this has to be done anyway, because a well-tied knot is far stronger and more stable than a kink.

For broken wires, we tie a square knot for securing. To make the knot strong, we tie two overhand knots, first right over left and twist, and then left over right and twist. Then, pull the knot tight (usually with the help of two pincers), and trim the loose ends close to the knot. (See fig. 2.) If done properly, the knot should pass through the groove of the recording head without catching. Fortunately, because of the recording speed, a knot would result in only a very short loss of recorded content, which is hardly recognizable.

For the knots already found on the wire, it is important to check their status, and redo improperly-made knots, or shorten the loose ends if not trimmed close enough to the knot. This is to avoid the groove of the recording head catching the knot, which might result in unwanted popping noise in the replay signal.

### Untangling the Wire Snarls

We came across several occasions of snarled wires. It often happens during rewind, as the rewinding speed is six times faster than replay speed, thus increasing the tension on the wire. Once snarls happen, a repair could easily take up dozens, or even hundreds, of hours and always requires

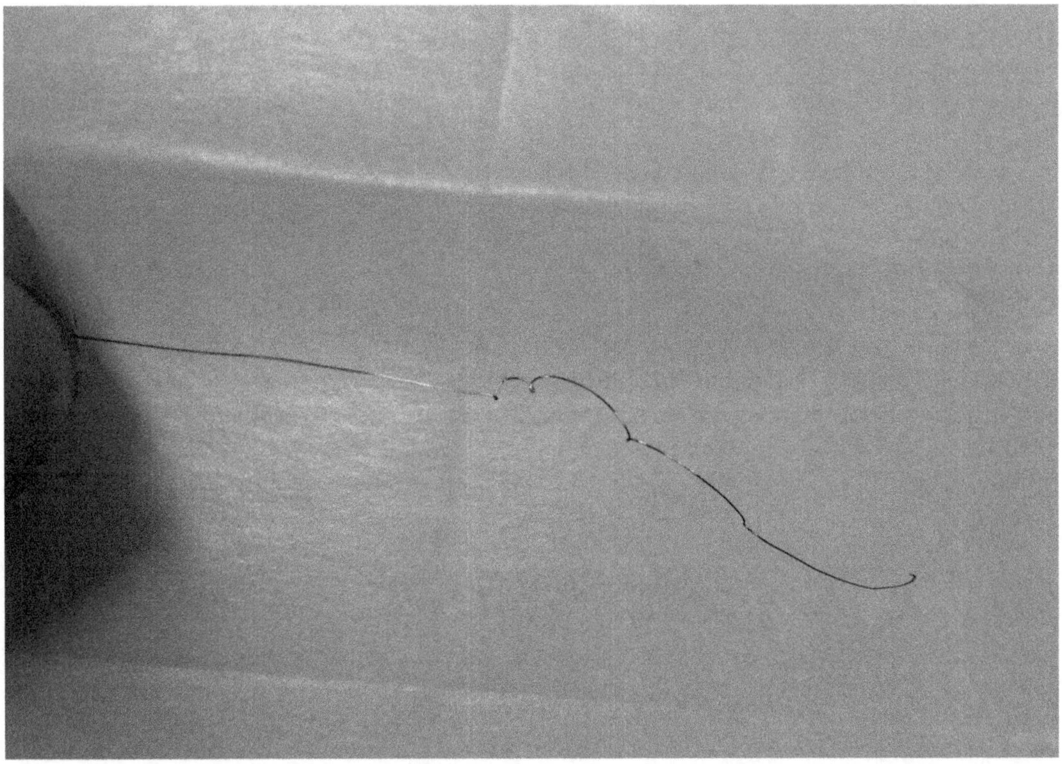

**Figure 1.** Four kinks in a short piece of wire.

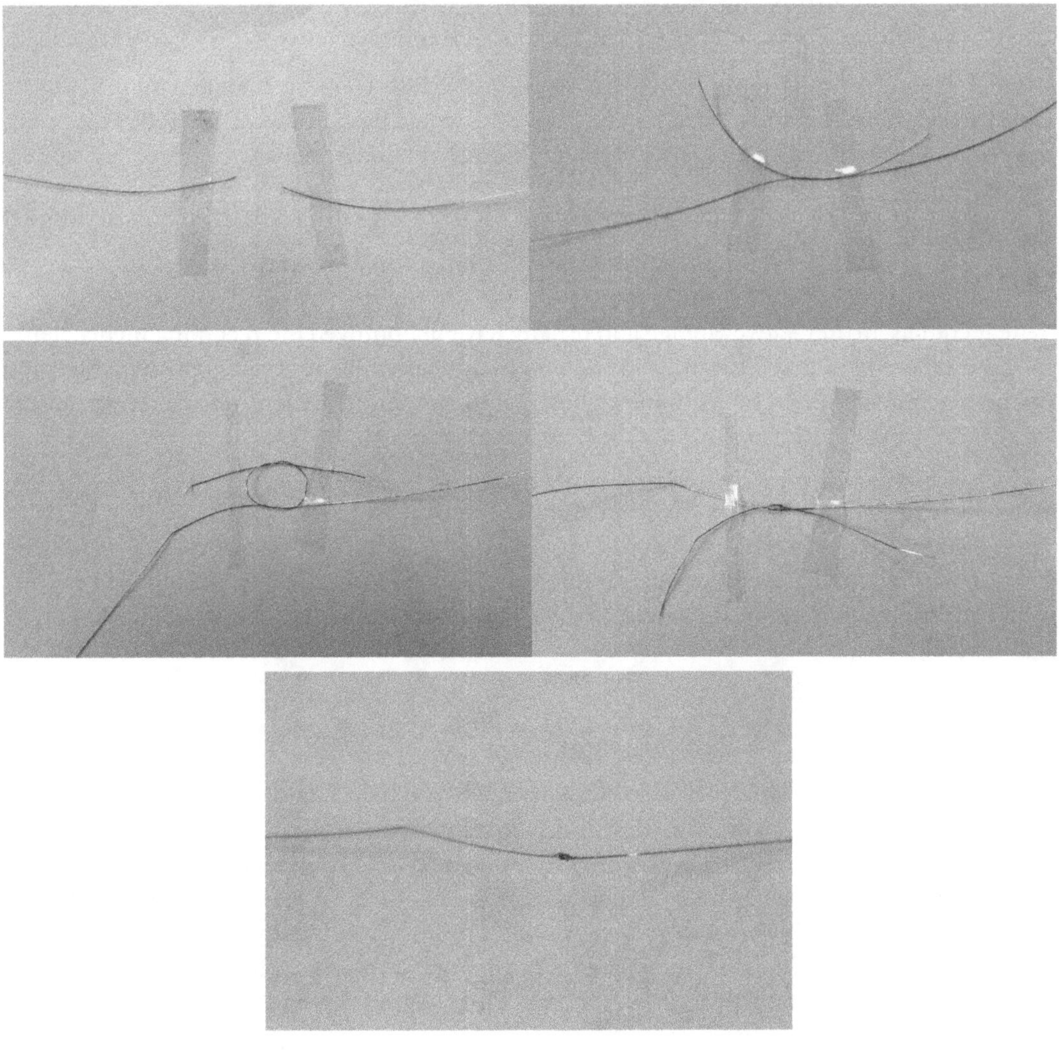

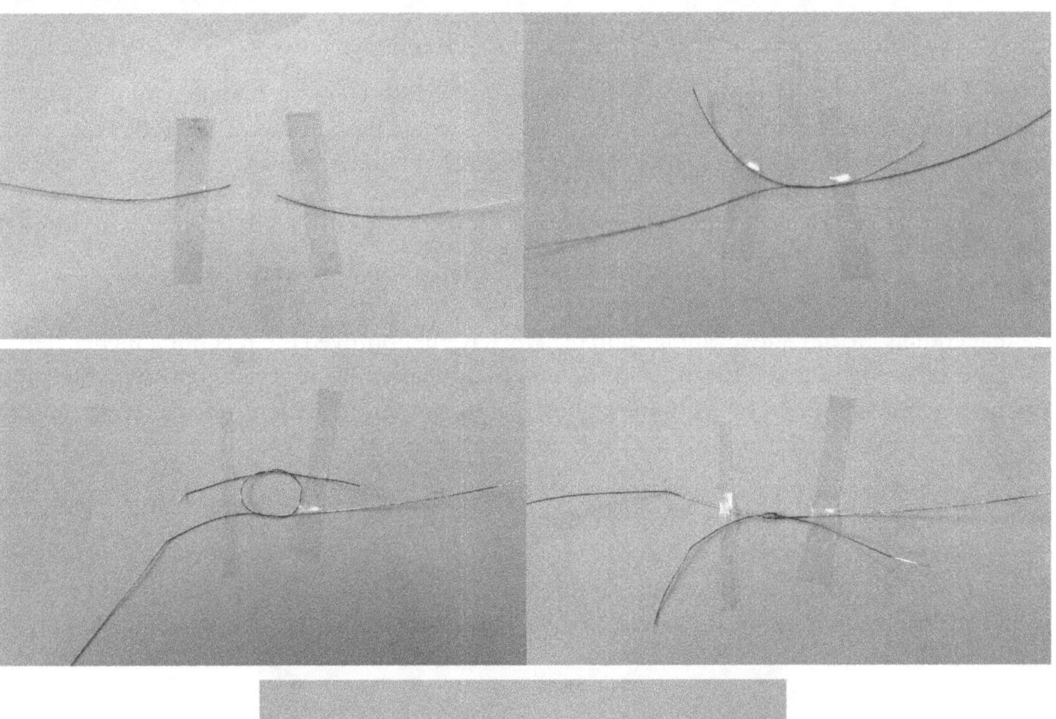

**Figures 2–6.** A showcase of the process of tying a broken wire.

the help of other people. Pliers, pincers, sharp needles, toothpicks, adhesive tape and labels, pencils, and clips are needed for untangling. To distinguish the overlapping relations between several parts of the wire, we used white paper as a background to provide a contrast against the colour of the wire.

If there is only one end, all you have to do is try to sort out the overlapping sequence. But if there are multiple ends in the snarl, broken sections need to be sorted out first. We do not cut the wire unless there is no other way to sort out the mess.

When broken sections are separated from the snarl, a clip is attached on both ends to prevent it from contracting into a snarl once again. Then we attach a leading thread between two sections, thus connecting all sections into a whole wire to make the transfer.

If a kink breaks in the untangling process, we stick a label on the two ends and mark it with the same number, indicating the two ends that should be attached together later. This is done, in the sequence of the numbers, at the end of the restoration process.

By this method, even rather discouraging situations could successfully be solved, as figures 7–10 show.

### Attaching the Leading Thread

The leading thread, attached at the two ends of the wire, is used to tightly fix the steel on the spool and the take-up drum. If some wires come without a leader at the outside end, we attach one for the convenience of replay. The tying of the leading thread differs from that of the steel wire.

### The Procedure of Wire Recording Restoration

## Organizing Restoration

In order to ensure the authentic, complete, and accurate transfer of the recorded information on the wire recordings, a standardized procedure for the whole process was developed. This procedure involves assessment, pre-treatment, digital transformation, metadata capture, description, evaluation, storage, etc.

### Maintain Appropriate Working Temperature

Wire recorders are of relative vintage and usually have not outlived the recording media. Thus, they should be maintained carefully to prolong their operability as long as possible. We warm up the machine for ten to fifteen minutes before use, and only use them twice a day to prevent overheating: once in the morning and once in the afternoon.

### Electromagnetic Interference

In their transfer, audio signals are prone to electromagnetic interference. In order to prevent those, all wireless communication devices, specifically mobile phones, were not allowed in the transfer laboratories.

### Mechanical Malfunctions

Apart from the wire recordings we received already in a tangled state, snarls could also occur during transfer. This is usually caused by mechanical malfunction. For example, the recording head gets stuck at a higher level during movement, or it is held back in the rewinding mode.

When the mechanism of the recording head is jammed by the lack of lubricant (e.g., by dried out grease), the head would stop at the top for several seconds and then suddenly drop to the bottom, leading to improper wire wrapping and snarls. Cotton swabs were used to wipe off the dried grease with alcohol, thereafter lubricating the mechanism with timepiece lubricant oil.

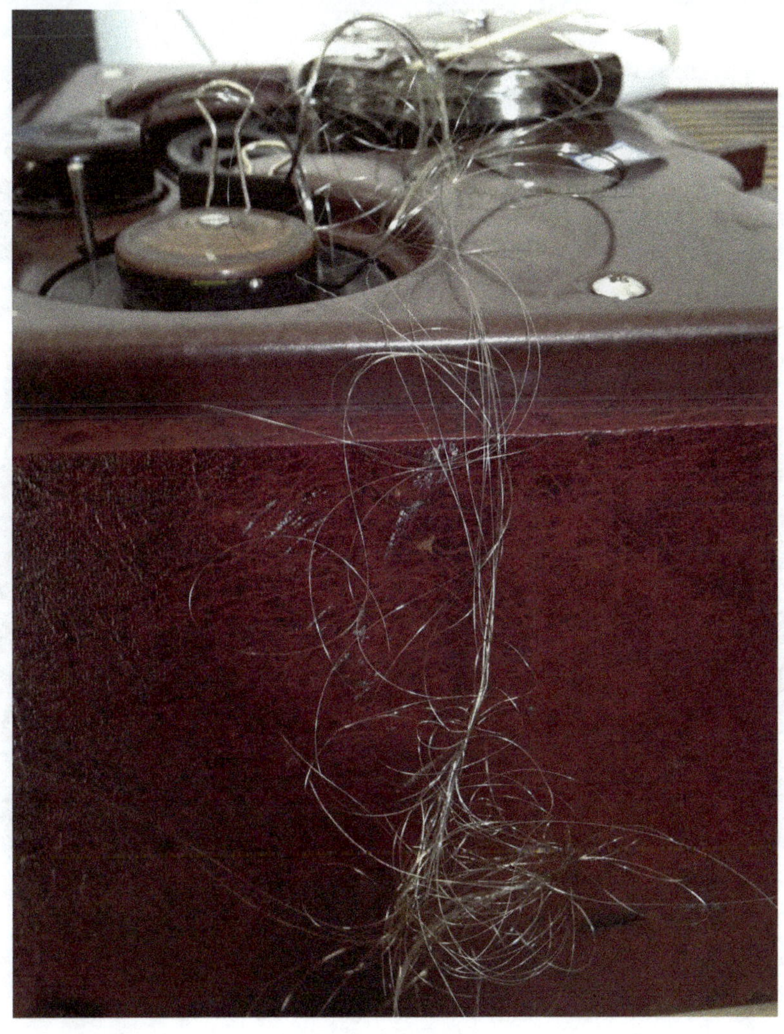

**Figures 7–10.** A severe case of wire disorder and how it was solved.

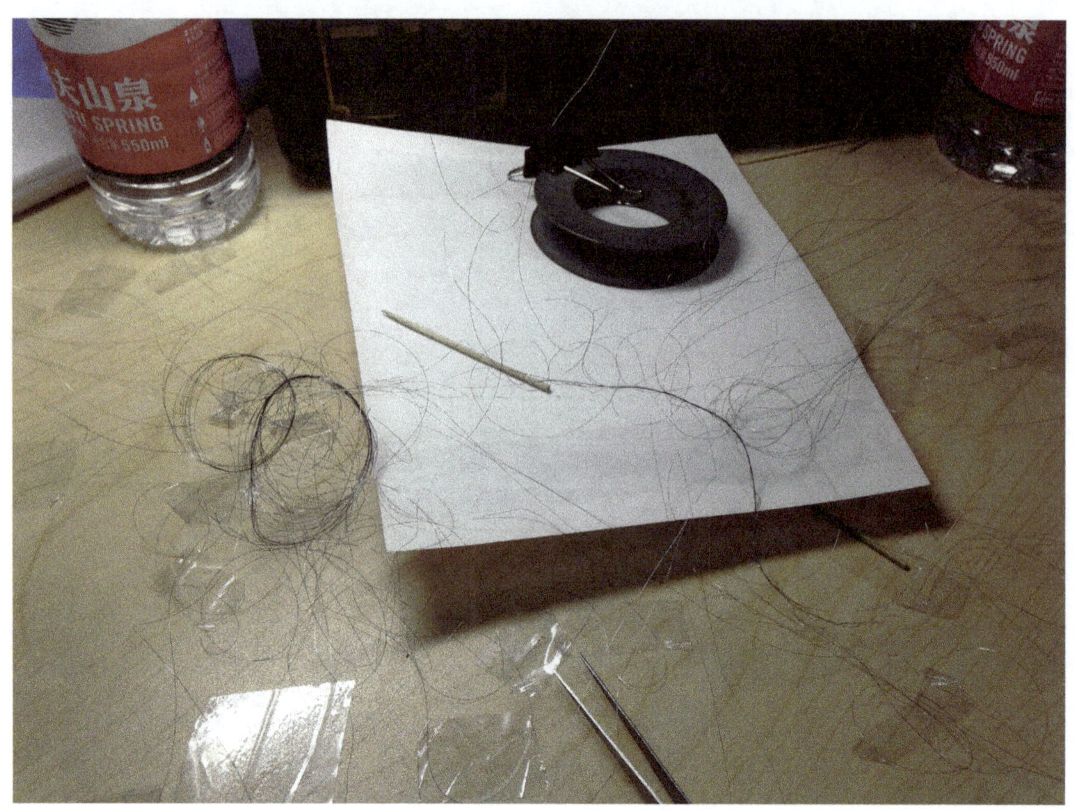
SPRING
550ml

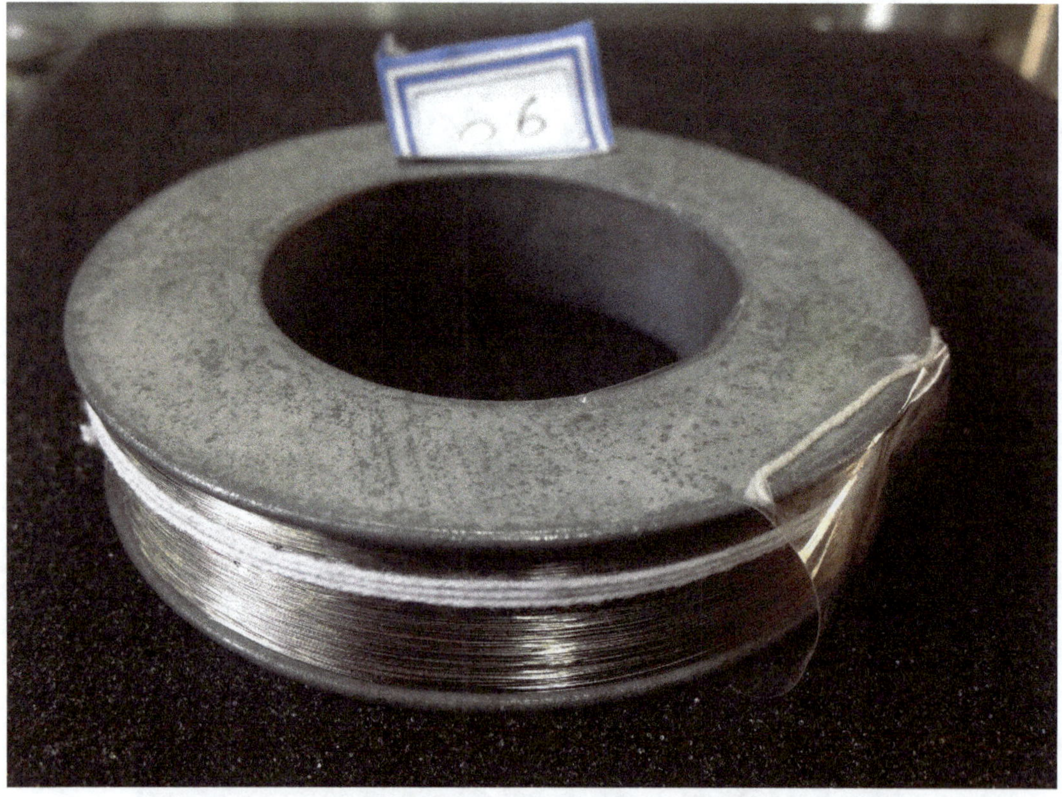

### Sound Editing

Following international standards, it is important to maintain the unmodified, original state of the transfers. Consequently, we store two WAV format versions of the audio after digitization. One is the unaltered original digitized audio signal, and the other a slightly sound restored one for later editing.

### Checksum

In order to control the authenticity of the digitized audio file, the checksum, using the MD5 algorithm, is added. This allows to verify the integrity of the originally produced audio file, as any modification would change the checksum.

## Conclusion

In the course of the establishment of the transfer platform, some eighty reels of wire recordings from local collections have been transferred and preserved after extensive work on the restoration of the degraded and partly damaged wires.

The principle of "retaining the original state" has been followed during the entire processes of transfer of the selected wire recordings, by following the standards and recommendations drafted by International Association of Sound and Audiovisual Archives.

Although valuable experiences have been accumulated in the experimental development of the restoration of the wires and appropriate transfer procedures, lots of investigations are still needed to improve magnetic wire transfer, as information transfer technology further develops. Along with the rise of awareness for the protection of cultural heritage in general and for audio-visual archives in particular, we believe that the interest for early audiovisual documents will increase, leading to further research for the improvement of their transfer.

NIE MANYING is a research archivist and Chief of the Information and Standardization Division at the Institute of Scientific and Technological Research on Archives (ISTRA). She graduated from Nanjing University with a double degree in Information and Biology and has worked in ISTRA ever since. Her research focuses on standardization, preservation, and the management of archives. She is also one of the Chinese editors for the ICA journal, COMMA.

WANG XI graduated from university in 2007 and then joined ISTRA. She was engaged in the application of new technologies in archival and records management. She participated in several projects and delivered several papers and presentations.

ZHANG SHUXIA is a research archivist at the Information and Standardization Division at ISTRA, as well as a member of the work group. She graduated from Renmin University with a master degree in Archival Science.

YAN JIE is an archivist at the Information and Standardization Division at ISTRA, and also a member of the work group. He graduated from Beijing Electronic Science and Technology Institute with a degree in Communication Engineering.

## Reference

Schüller, D. (2005). IASA Technical Committee, Standards, Recommended Practices and Strategies: The Safeguarding of the Audio Heritage: Ethics, Principles and Preservation Strategy (IASA-TC 03). Version 3.

# 11 Findings from the Digitization of 78 rpm Discs

**George Blood**

## Abstract

The early decades of sound recording were a period of rapid change in both recording technology and performance practice. Primitive recording equipment, minimal documentation, and musical pitch varying by time and location make it difficult for archivists to know the proper playback stylus size and playback speed. Using four very large data sets of both pristine and worn media, combined with a highly consistent selection methodology, this study investigates the level of accuracy attainable when selecting stylus size and determining playback speed. The analysis shows it is possible to determine, with high certainty, the correct playback stylus size per record label during this period of early sound recording. The analysis then shows that the distribution of pitch follows a Gaussian distribution of randomness, meaning it is not possible to know with certainty the proper playback speed. Commentary discusses the cultural environment of the early recording era and the implications for archival practice today.

## Keywords

acoustic era, acoustic recording, Association for Recorded Sound Collections, Brylawski, Samuel, Edison Diamond Discs, Thomas Edison National Historic Park, Encyclopedic Discography of Victor Recordings/American Discography Project, Fabris, Gerald, Eldridge Johnson Museum, Free Library of Philadelphia, hill and dale, IASA/International Association of Sound and Audiovisual Archives, ISO 16, lateral cut, Library of Congress, Mick Moloney Collection of Irish-American Music and Popular Culture, National Jukebox, New York University, OKeh Records, Packard Campus of the National Audio-Visual Conservation Center, playback speed, Sixtonics, standard pitch, stylus, stylus size, Sueiro Bal, Marcos, Victor Talking Machine Company.

## Historical Context

Every field of critical inquiry that engages with the past inevitably must address questions that are very difficult, if not impossible to answer. What color were dinosaurs? What was before the Big Bang? On what day was Henry V born? Was Thomas Jefferson a good violinist or a bad violinist? Aristotle wrote, "Everyone desires to know." Our desire for knowledge and certainty propels human inquiry, especially when that inquiry involves the roots of our identity. The insatiable need to know leads us to uncover the previously unknown, even though the answer, if ultimately found, may prove dissatisfying, either because it challenges our assumptions, or is simply not very interesting after all. Furthermore, we must embrace and apply new information and knowledge appropriately, accept when we do not and may not ever know certain information, and accept that our actions are based on assumptions and opinion, rather than facts, however well founded.

On the front of the Stephansdom Cathedral in Vienna are two iron bars, each about a meter long, one about a hand's width longer than the other. Installed in the Middle Ages, these were the official Viennese measurements of a yard for use by local and traveling merchants for general commerce in the city. There was a measure for linen, and a separate measure for drapery. A traveling merchant adjusted his practice to the local standards. For hundreds of years, this was the state of standardization in the world.

The early part of the twentieth century was a time of great changes. The Industrial Revolution brought prosperity to a new middle class. New modes of transportation brought far-flung parts of the world into contact. As manufacturing expanded with the introduction of interchangeable



*Sustainable Audiovisual Collections* (2017): 72–89. DOI: 10.2979/jts2016.0.0.13

parts, the need for standards in weights and measures became apparent. Likewise, manufacturers soon found ways to create entertainment goods for the new mass market.

At the same time, many technologies were new and poorly understood. Electricity was lighting homes before anyone understood grounding. Electric motors and microphones[1] were crude. Their use in sound recordings was limited prior to the development of electrical recordings in about 1923. Speed was hard to measure and regulate.[2] There was no understanding of, much less the means to measure, distortion. There were no definitions for frequency response and level, speed fluctuation, gain, or linearity.

Standards as we understand and use them today, were taking root in the early decades of the twentieth century. As the formerly isolated peoples of the world began to interact more frequently, they shared their goods and cultures. To work together they needed to adapt or adopt the things they wished to share. For musicians to play together they needed a common pitch and tuning system. Between 1895 and 1910 there were three international meetings to define the frequency of the A above middle C. At those meetings the standard rose from 430 to 435, then to 440 Hz.[3] It takes a long time for a standard like this to become widely practiced. Musicians, like people in all walks of life, can be slow to adopt change. More practically, instruments are not replaced very frequently. Church organs and string instruments may last centuries.[4] The physical dimensions of an instrument affect its characteristic pitch.

Into this brave new world of evolving standards, fluid pitch, and new inventions arrives recorded sound. One might reasonably say the early technicians and recording engineers were "making it up as they went along." For some experimenters we have lab notes that document the goals, methods, and discoveries of their work.[5] For some recording sessions, the recording staff kept notes. Thomas Edison left behind some very detailed technical drawings. Unfortunately, just as they were "making it up as they went along," they didn't really know what information might be worthwhile to keep—either for the benefit of their developing profession, or for future researchers.

Despite the many limitations of weight driven lathes and large acoustic horns, and the uncertainties about practices in the early decades, we nonetheless have documents of the cultural record that do not exist from earlier times. Audiovisual records are what distinguishes the cultural record of the twentieth century. This is what drives our curiosity to understand these media. We gain both a better understanding of our history during this important period of change, and as audiovisual archivists, an appreciation for the roots of our profession.

## The Problem

There are serious challenges to determining the correct way to reproduce these recordings. At what speed was the lathe turning on the day this particular recording was made? What pitch did the musicians tune to? How accurately regulated was the speed of the lathe? Did the musicians retune between takes? Were the musicians from different traditions and did they choose a compromise pitch for the recording date?[6]

As we can see, there are many contextual problems to determining "what is the correct speed" of an acoustic 78 rpm disc. Lacking strong documentation from a period of general uncertainty, we are forced to work with the recording engineer's final product—that is, the discs themselves. The overwhelming majority of the discs in existence are heavily worn from many years of use and enjoyment. This wear means our work in reproduction, especially stylus selection, must take this deterioration into account in the data we gather. Just as archaeologists must interpret fossils and astronomers must compensate for the affect of the Earth's atmosphere when peering into the heavens, record wear obscures our data.[7]

## The Digitization Process

The playback and digitization process followed the widely adopted best practices of the trade:

- Hand-delivered from home institutions
- Cleaned with Keith Monks Record Cleaning Machine (distilled water)

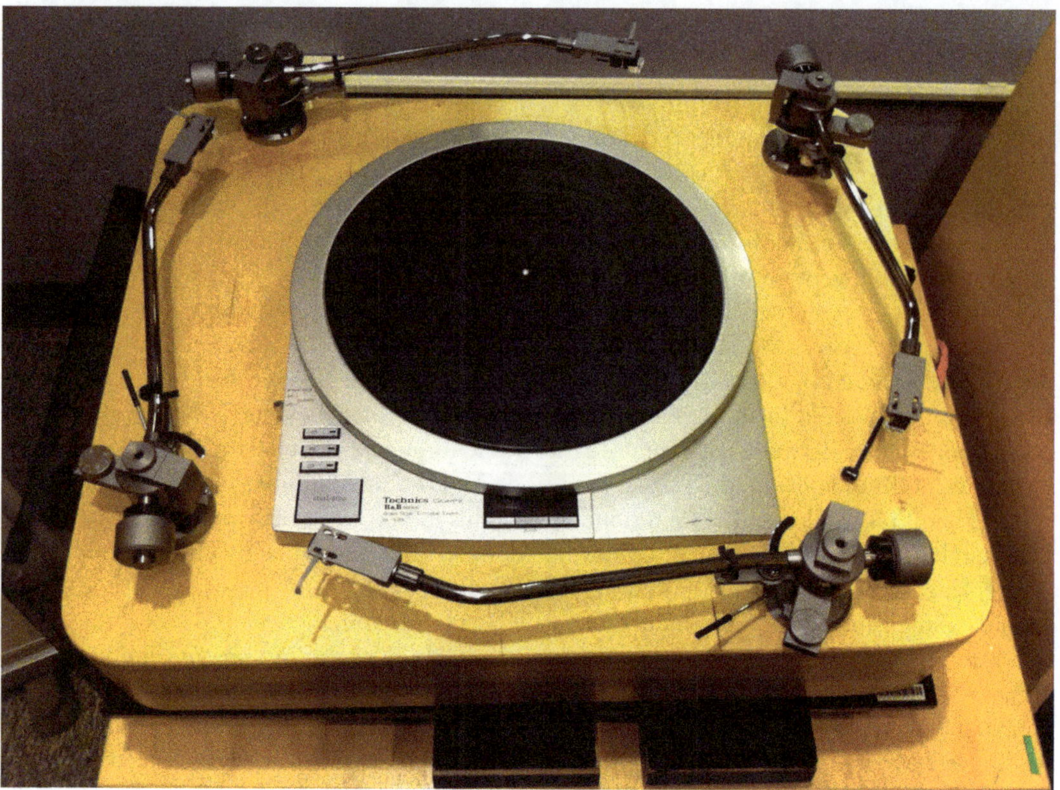

**Figure 1.** This is the playback system built for this work. By mounting four tone arms, four different styli can be reproducing at the same time. The engineer can compare, in real time, the sound of each stylus and rapidly switch between them. Compared to the traditional method of manually changing the stylus, then replacing with another, then changing back, etc., there is no need to remember what one stylus sounded like. With the push a button the operator can compare, not two but four, different styli rapidly.

- Pictures of the label and matrix (Nikon D810 at 400ppi TIFF)
- Technics SP-15 Turntable fitted with needles by Expert Stylus
- 4 KAB preamps
- 8 Channel PrismSound ADA-8XR (96k Hz/24 bit)
- Pitch detection
- Trim and render derivatives for National Jukebox[8]
- Harvest and store AES-57 metadata

## The Data

The core sources[9] for this study have several attributes that make the data especially relevant:

- The sample sets are large: more than 9,000 disc sides.
- The data include international sources.
- A period of approximately twenty years of early recording practice is covered.
- All work was performed to the same specifications.
- All work was performed with the same equipment.
- All work was performed by the same engineer.

These are the four data sets used in this study:

- Victor Talking Machine Company

The Victor discs are the stuff collectors, engineers, and historians dream of. They are in pristine condition, beautifully preserved at the Eldridge Johnson Museum. Most of the rare and international titles in this study are in this collection.

- Edison Diamond Discs

These are factory originals, also in pristine condition ("reference discs" they might be called), under the care of Gerald Fabris at the Edison National Historic Park. This data set includes multiple takes of the same selection.

- OKeh Records

Unlike the Victor and Edison discs, the OKeh disc collection was assembled from discs that had circulated in the wild. They had been bought in stores, played, enjoyed, and handled under a random set of circumstances. They are far more representative of the samples available to most studies. They are holdings of the Library of Congress, at the Packard Campus of the National Audio-Visual Conservation Center in Culpeper, Virginia.

- Mick Moloney Collection of Irish-American Music and Popular Culture

This New York University Collection is included to represent the general population, as a control and for comparison.[10] Insofar as the focus of the collection is Irish music, there is no preference for a given label. Like the OKeh Records samples, these are discs that had circulated in the wild.

The highly uniform digitization process allows us to investigate variation within each collection and between the four sets, and to explore the sources of those variations.

The findings from each data set are first presented separately.

### Victor Talking Machine Company

**Part 1, Stylus Size**

The Victor recordings data represents 3,500 sides. When the Victor Talking Machine Company operated in Camden, New Jersey, they sent copies of each title to the Free Library of Philadelphia. Like all libraries, only about 2% of their holdings circulate, and the sound recordings followed this pattern. When the Library chose to deaccession their analog sound recordings, the Victor discs moved to the Eldridge Johnson Museum, run by the Delaware Department of Parks and Recreation. This is an enormous collection of rarely played discs.

Most of the recordings at the Eldridge Johnson Museum are widely distributed. The selection of discs to digitize was led by Samuel Brylawski, Editor/Project Manager of the Encyclopedic Discography of Victor Recordings/American Discography Project at the University of California at Santa Barbara, someone who we can reasonably assume to know a thing or two about the Victor catalog. This project selected very rare recordings of Eastern European, South American, and ethnic recordings. Therefore, we have an international distribution over a range of two decades, making our sample set both large and widely representative.

This sample bias is the result of selection focused on rare ethnic titles. While this gives the sample a highly desirable international distribution, the results are less evenly representative of the time period. A more carefully designed study might have added samples where the distribution has a low number of titles. However, the data will show this would not have had a significant impact on the results.

During this period there was great variation of performance practice by region. This is very important for the investigation of speed and pitch, which will be discussed in the second half of this paper. The sample set has the advantage that the recordings were made by teams from the same label.

Data from the Victor discs show this remarkably clear finding. One stylus size, 2.8 mil, was chosen for more than half the Victor sides digitized. The data were next examined for an explanation of the secondary strengths at 2.0, 2.3, and 2.5 mil.

The data were analyzed to determine whether the distribution of sizes matched the distribution over time. Higher numbers of sides are expected in the subsets at 1916–1917 and later because there are more data points to begin with (cf. fig. 2).

And indeed that is what we see in the data. The peaks in the stylus size subsets mirror the peaks in the aggregate data. Further, no trend appears in the data. The data do not show size A being used in the early 1910s, then a few years later, toward the 1920s, a shift to a different size's dominance, and so on. The distribution of 2.0, 2.3, and 2.5 mil is fairly even, with significantly more 2.8 mil across all time periods.

**Figure 2.** illustrates that within out sample set, some time periods are better represented than others.

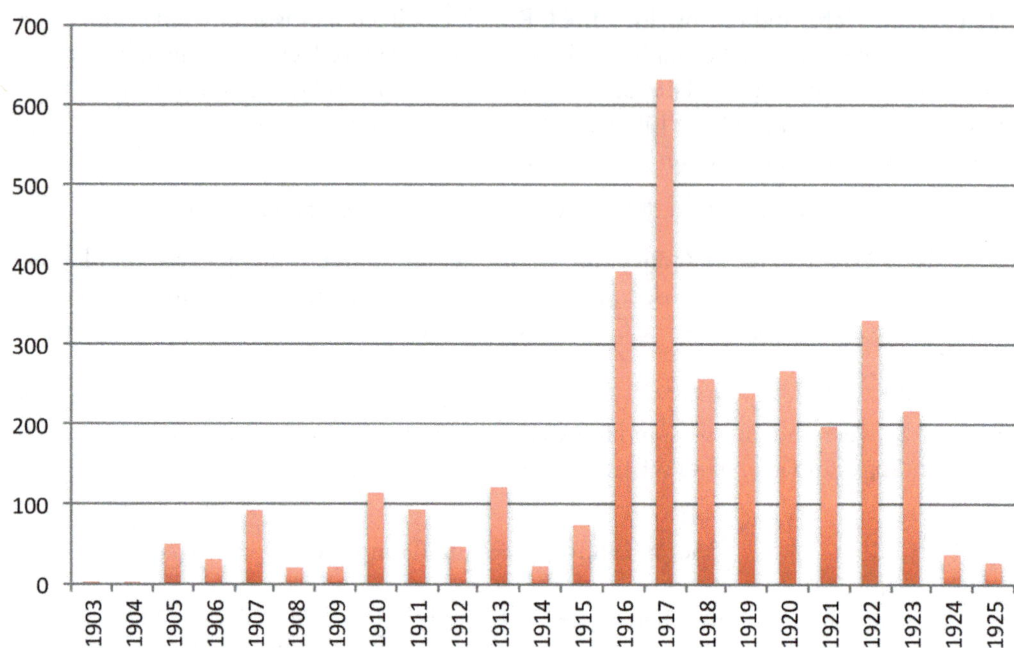


**Figure 3.**[11]

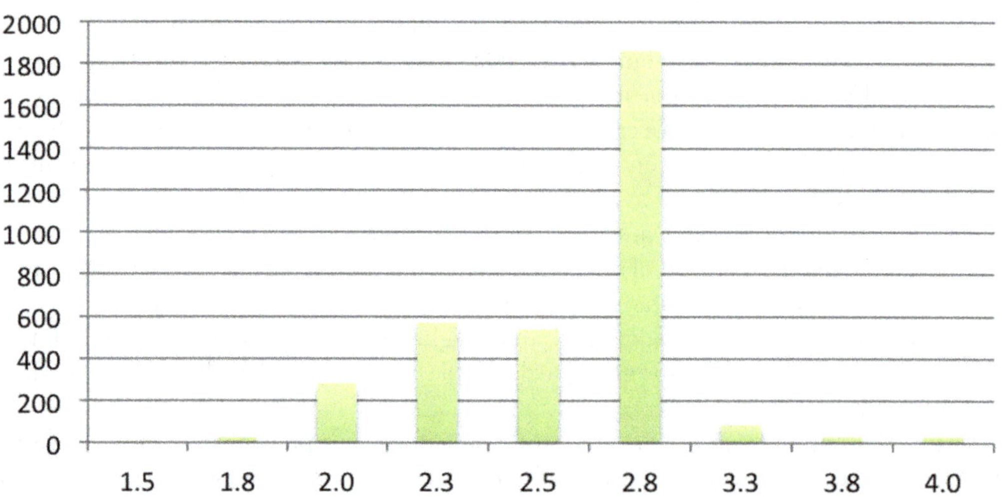


The data were next analyzed by the recording location. Just as with the distribution of the stylus size by catalog number, we find the same pattern: all locations dominated by 2.8 mil, followed by smaller sizes, as shown in figures 5a–d.

In conclusion, when working with acoustic Victor discs, a 95% certainty for proper stylus size is obtain by reviewing just four stylus sizes. If this sample were random, that is, if it followed the normal distribution under a bell curve, the data would be symmetrical, with an equal distribution of samples to left and right of the peak. However, there are nearly 100 times more samples of smaller stylus sizes to the left of 2.8 mil than larger stylus sizes to the right of 2.8 mil, indicating something is causing the nonrandom distribution.

Might the intended cutting stylus size have been 2.8 mil? As the cutter was used, was it worn down, to a smaller and smaller size until it was replaced?

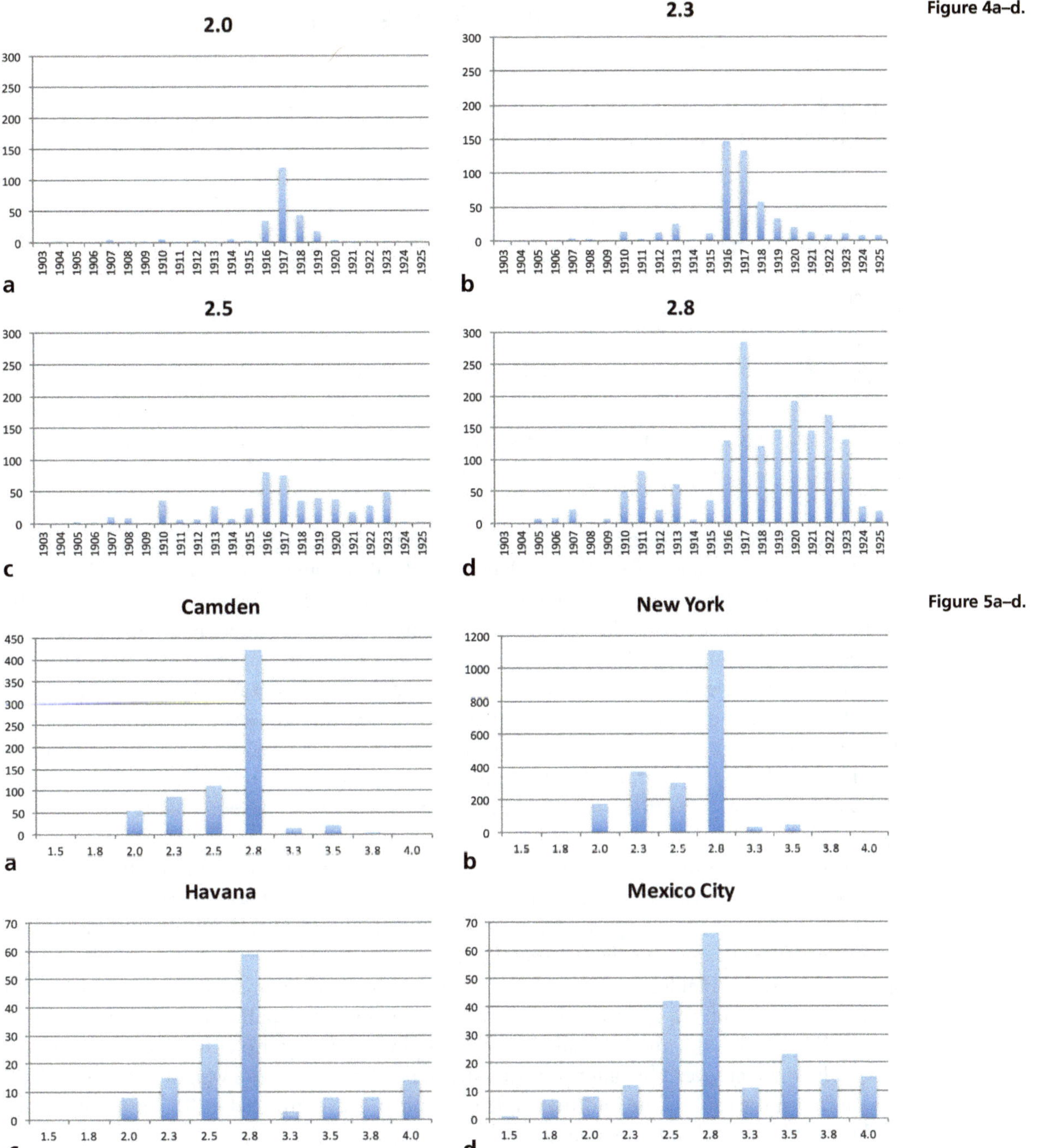


Figure 4a–d.

Figure 5a–d.

## Edison Diamond Discs

The Edison recordings are represented by 2,500 sides. Edison's company retained samples of most discs it recorded. The collection includes released discs, multiple takes from which the released version or versions were selected, as well as unreleased material. Similar in scope and condition to the Victor discs, this is an enormous collection of rarely played discs.

The results of analyzing stylus selection for Edison Diamond Discs (fig. 6) are likewise very clear. They are also very puzzling. Edison, as an engineer, was meticulous in the specifications for his inventions, their manufacture, and use.[12] Engineers, collectors and historians have long struggled with a great disparity: we generally agree that Diamond Discs "sound better" (whatever that means), when played with a very small stylus; and yet, the documentation left by Edison indicates a larger, 3.5 or 3.3 mil, stylus size should be used for playback.

Figure 6.

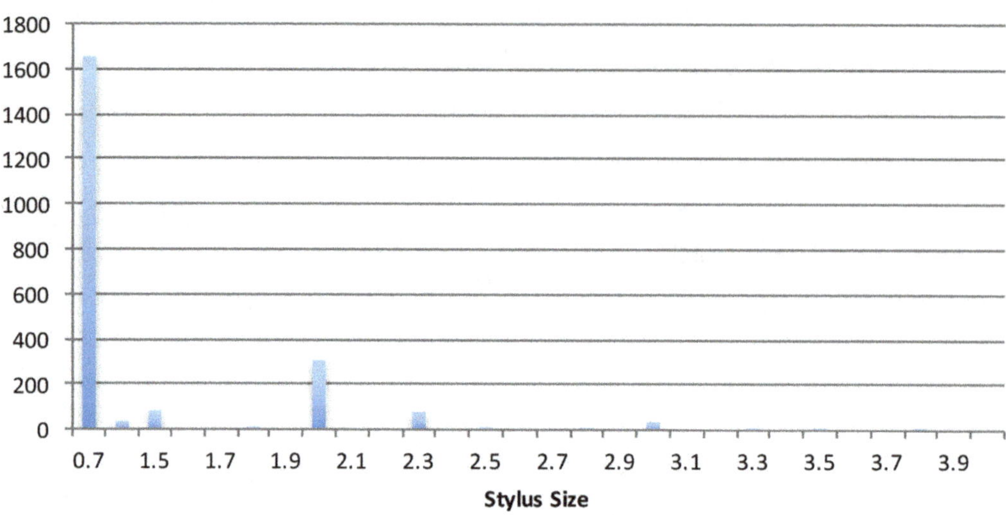


Disc grooves are three-dimensional: top to bottom, left to right, and along their length. In practice, either the lateral (in hill and dale) or vertical (in lateral cut) component is absent.[13] Discussions of stylus shape focus on the cross-sectional view of the "stylus in the groove"—that is, how the stylus fits and tracks side-to-side or up-and-down. Less frequent are discussions that consider the relationship between the longitudinal shape and size of the cutter and that of the playback stylus. The cutter, by definition, will have a sharp point: it may be 3.5 mil across, but it is shaped (ground or cut) into a sharp point to cut into the recording medium (at first wax, then later lacquer). A playback stylus that had a sharp edge, and short longitudinal profile, would naturally tend to cut the disc while being played. Shellac is much harder than wax, but the problem remains. Further, remember how these media were played: a stylus wiggled in the groove, then transferred that wiggle to a diaphragm that transduced the motion into varying air pressure (a.k.a. sound) which was amplified by a horn—the larger the horn, the greater the amplification. The stylus both reproduced the sound in the groove, and moved the horn apparatus across the disc.[14] To keep the stylus in the groove firmly enough to move the horn, a great deal of pressure was needed. The nominal weight of the diaphragm and the suspended horn is 4–5 ounces. LP turntables track at below 3 grams! As the surface area of the playback stylus is reduced, the weight of 4–5 ounces is spread over a smaller and smaller area. This means more weight is applied to the groove, leading to increased wear. The sharp cutting stylus incises fine detail along the groove. The fatter playback stylus, needed to carry the weight of the diaphragm and horn, cannot capture the information left behind by the cutting stylus. It spans multiple hills and is unable to reach into the dales.[15]

Might it be that Edison's working assumptions regarding the relationship between the cutting stylus size and shape[16] and the playback stylus size and shape were incorrect?[17] Instead might it be that Edison's cutting stylus, especially in the hill and dale topology, resulted in a groove profile best reproduced by a very different stylus: a size and shape not easily obtained at that time?

## OKeh Records

The work on Victor and Edison discs was performed under a contract specifically intended to generate content for the Library of Congress' National Jukebox.[18] A later contract was awarded for digitization of general audiovisual holdings of the Library. The Moving Image Broadcast and Recorded Sound Division (MBRS) selected a large span of OKeh[19] Records for preservation digitization under this contract.

The samples are acoustic recordings, the earliest of which are sometimes vertically cut (like Edisons), spanning approximately a decade. Unlike the Victor and Edison discs in this study,

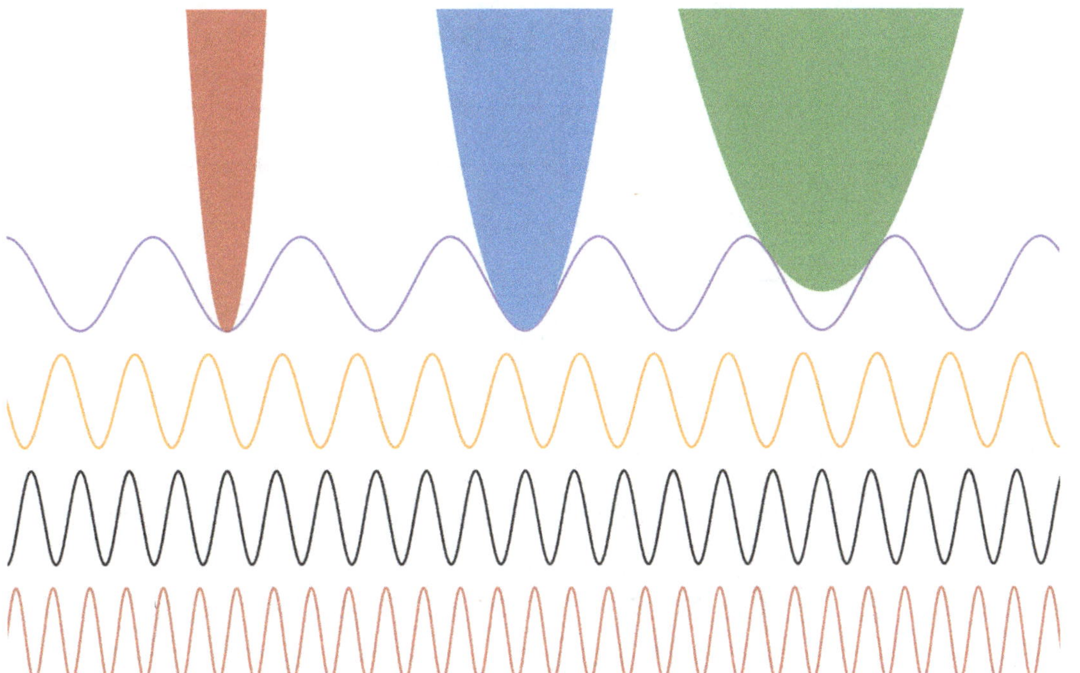

**Figure 7.** Higher frequencies have smaller wavelengths. Smaller wavelengths are smaller groove sizes (lower waves in the image). Large styli distribute the weight, but don't fit into the groove (right). The center stylus fits Edison's specification. The left stylus sounds better.

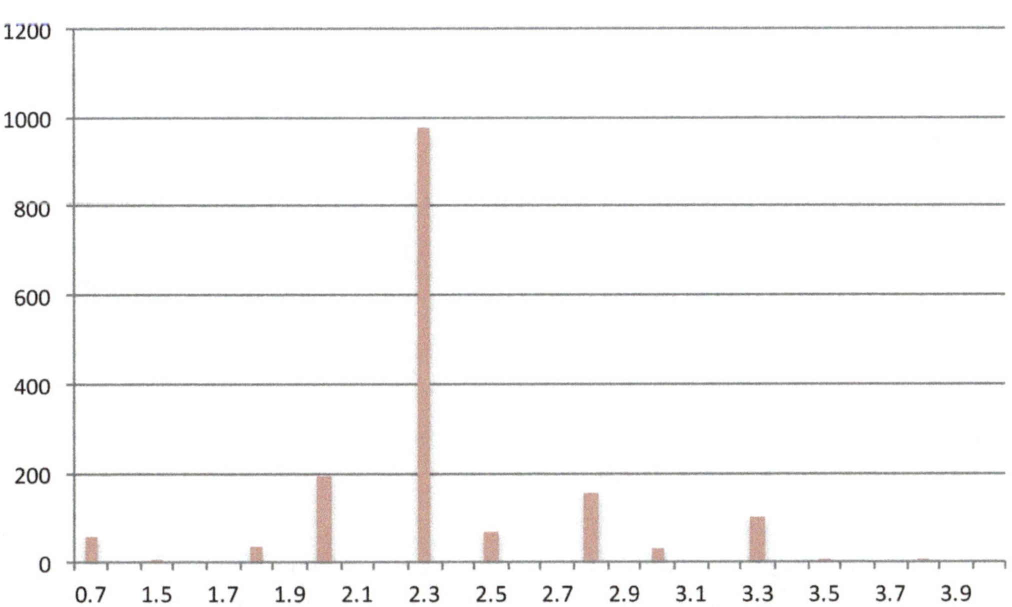


**Figure 8.**

these discs are heavily worn from general circulation and years of enjoyment by their owners. Their condition varies widely—very good to poor, and, rarely, very fine like the Victor and Edison discs. For our study, these discs are a contrasting label and contrasting condition. They are from the same time period and have been digitized using the exact methodology as the Victors and the Edisons (e.g., using four tone arms, etc.).

Whereas the Victors showed a clear preference for 2.8 mil and Edisons for 0.7 mil, OKeh acoustic discs have an equal preference for 2.3 mil. In contrast to where the Victors show the prominent 2.8 mil followed by the secondary peaks to the left of smaller sizes, the OKeh data show an even distribution to the left and right of the peak, of larger and smaller stylus sizes.

Might the engineers at OKeh have changed cutting styli more frequently than was the practice at Victor? Despite the clearly audible signs of wear and aging, the OKeh data on stylus

Figure 9.

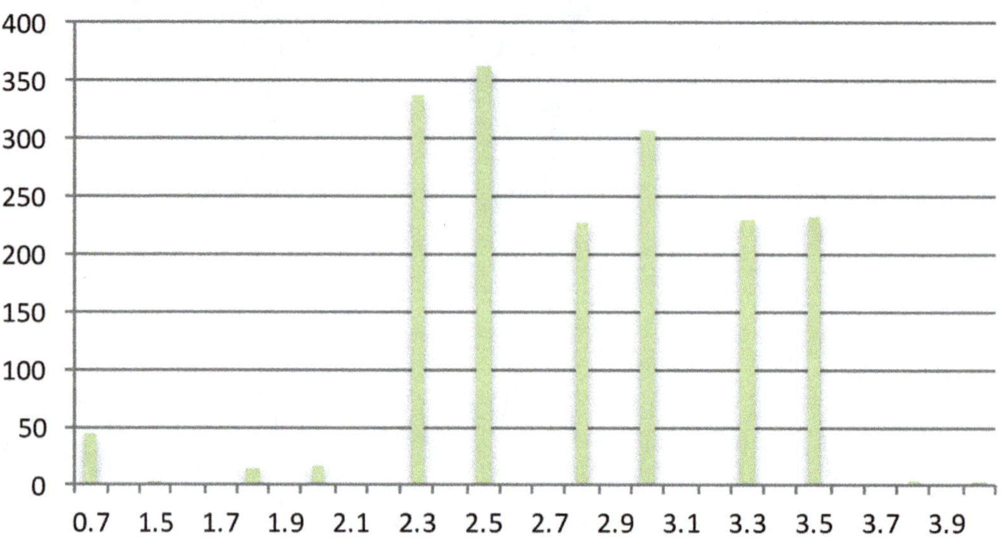


Figure 10.

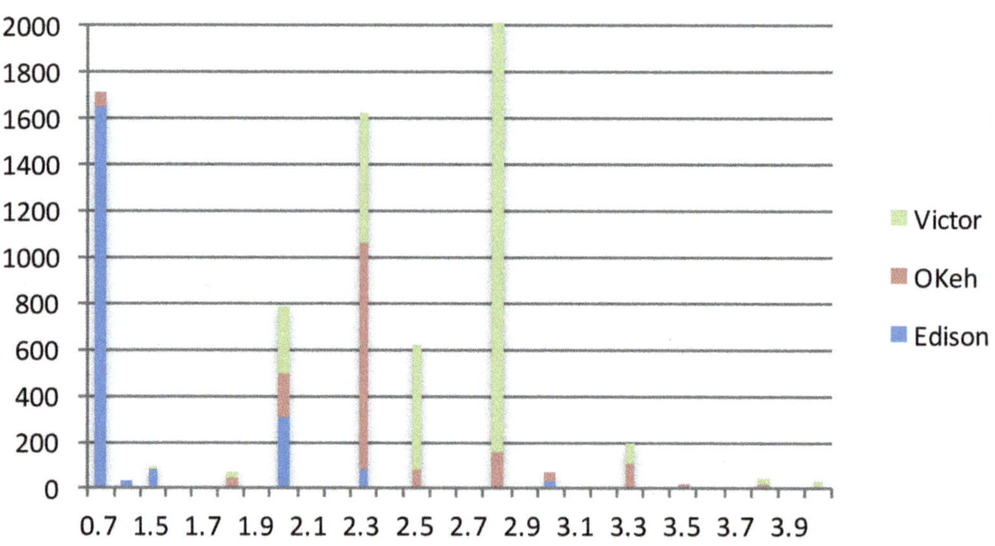


size are among the clearest of all the data sets in this study. Might the long-held assumption in our trade, that stylus selection includes compensating for groove wear, be wrong? Could it be that usage wear does not fundamentally warrant a stylus choice different than would be made on a pristine disc?

### Mick Moloney Collection of Irish-American Music and Popular Culture, New York University

The NYU/Moloney Collection focuses on genre rather than label. The playback stylus size selection for the discs shown in figure 9 is included to represent the distribution of stylus sizes in the general population of discs available throughout the 78 rpm era.

This data affirms that the single engineer who digitized all four sets (Victor, Edison, OKeh and Moloney discs), was thorough and considered multiple stylus sizes during his selection process. The chart also shows a distribution clearly different from those from the label-specific

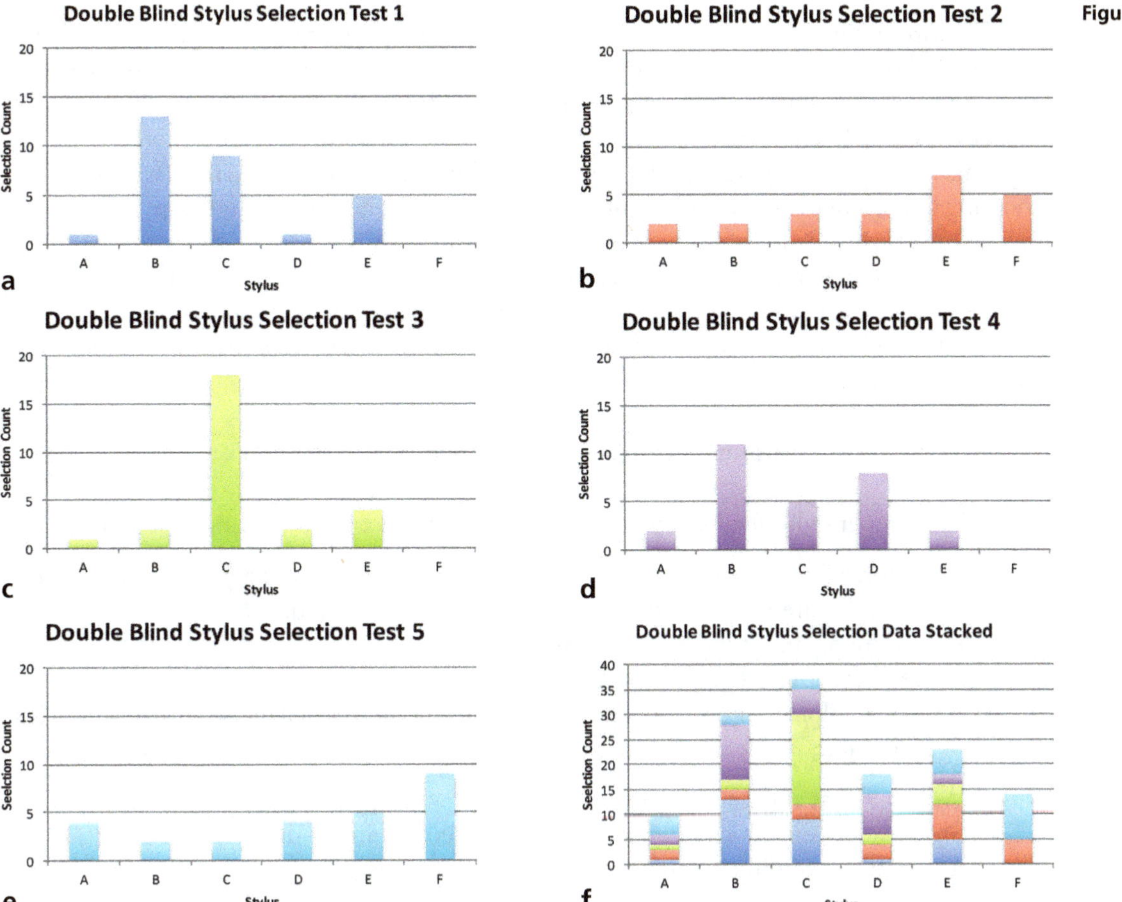


Figure 11 a-f.

data, where there is a clear preference for one size over all others. Here we see, in a random selection of labels, no clear choice of stylus size is evident.

The chart in figure 10 combines all the data from Victor, Edison and OKeh. Both show many strong peaks and no clear preference, supporting the assertion the NYU/Moloney collection is representative of the general population, and the label specific data is clearly different from the general population. The peaks do not match because the underlying labels are different. The goal is not to say the two charts match. It is to show that when multiple labels are present in the data there are multiple peaks. When a single label is examined in large quantities, a clear preference emerges.

One final data set for stylus selection:

### Marcos Sueiro Bal Double Blind Study on Stylus Selection

At the 2015 International Association of Sound and Audiovisual Archives (IASA) Conference in Paris Marcos Sueiro Bal, Senior Archivist at WNYC in New York and cochair of the Association for Recorded Sound Collections (ARSC) Technical Committee, presented preliminary results of his study on stylus selection. Sueiro Bal made short digital files of disc transfers. Each disc (presented below in its own chart, fig. 11a-e) is a different genre. Each disc was played multiple times, each time with a different stylus size and shape (A–E or A–F in the following examples). There were five or six stylus sizes for each of five different musical genres. In preparation for a double blind test, he asked a colleague to rename the samples to obscure information about the styli used for playback of the samples. Sueiro Bal asked respected audio transfer engineers to review the files at their leisure using their preferred playback environment, and to report their preferences. Two respondents[20] took the test twice. The responses provided 49 data points for each musical selection.

The assumption has been that an experienced engineer with training on what to listen for is needed to choose the proper stylus size; yet, only one test shows a consensus preference.

The results of the tests are presented in figure 11a–f.

The last chart, figure 11f, includes all the data points for all five tests together.

There is no distinct preference for any given ordinal choice; that is, there is not a bias toward choosing the first item heard, for instance. From this distribution it appears the engineers taking the test took their time to carefully consider all the alternatives.

The wide range of results for each sample calls into doubt whether we can assert that the choices of stylus size, even by professionals, results in the "best," "proper," or "correct" stylus. This doubt is reinforced by both respondents who took the test twice and gave different preferences in most instances.

### Summary Conclusions on Stylus Size Selection

- The proper stylus for a given label in a given era can be known with high certainty.
    - Victor: 2.8 mil is the best stylus size. In practice 2.0, 2.3, and 2.5 mil sizes are needed due to apparent wear in the cutting stylus on some recordings.
    - Edison: 0.7 mil is the best stylus size.
    - OKeh: 2.3 mil is the best stylus size.
    - NYU/Moloney: aggregate data demonstrates a wide range of practice during the period before 1923.
- Wear may not affect stylus choice after all.
- Stylus selection by experienced and respected engineers is highly variable and not repeatable according to the generally accepted standards of the scientific method.

## Part 2, Speed Determination

While pitch and speed are inextricably linked, they will vary independently of each other during recording. Just as two disc cutters might operate at a different speed, two artists performing to the same lathe might tune to a different pitch. During playback however, without additional information, it is not possible to separate the two effects. The result might be due to the cutting speed, or the tuning pitch, or a combination of both. Pitch A might be 435 Hz or 440 Hz. Rotational speed might be 71.29 rpm or 78.26 rpm. However, if A = 440 Hz = 78.26 rpm, then A = 435 Hz ≠ 71.29 rpm.

As discussed in the introduction, speed determination of recordings from the early twentieth century is challenging due to widely varying practices for reference pitch, difficulty controlling mechanical speed of the recording lathe and playback turntable, lack of documentation, and other technical and cultural factors.[21]

Parameters are moving targets:

- A =?
- How fast does a turntable spin?
- How do you control that speed?
- Regional differences in pitch and/or recording practice
- Ambient temperature changes pitch of the instrument between takes
- A work is otherwise too long to fit on one side
- Simply playing out of tune (or different temperament)
- Ego/Ability (want to appear to sing higher or play more "brilliantly")
- Who cares?
- Operator error (during recording or playback)

As demonstrated for stylus size in the example of the NYU Moloney Collection, our control group, it is possible the apparent randomness could be the result of many different variables laid

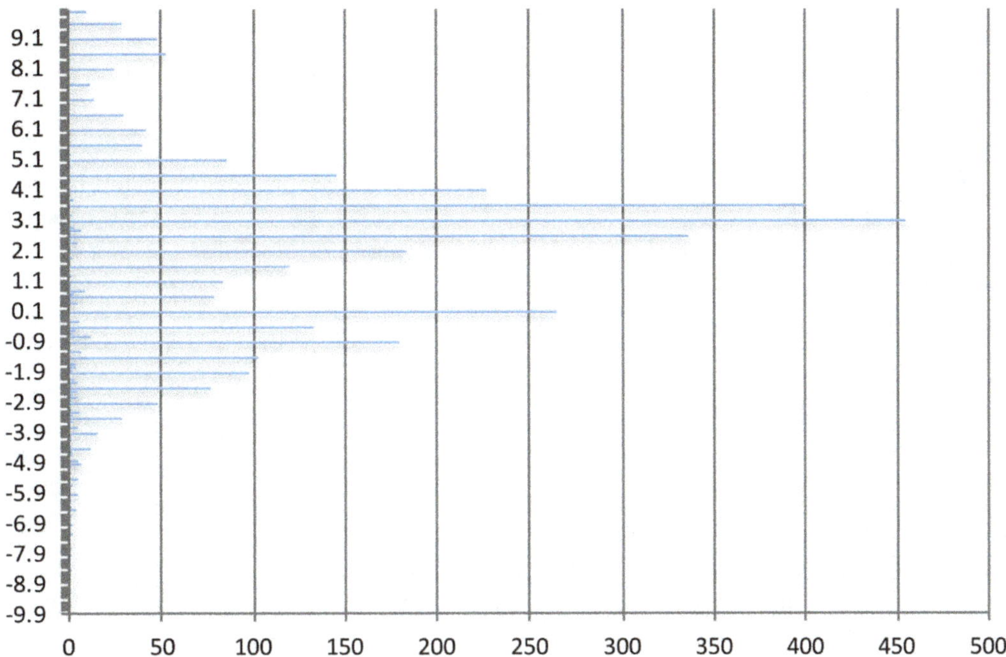


Figure 12.

on top of each other. That is, if the data is parsed into its component subsets, discrete causes might emerge.

Or they may not. Recall that the distribution of stylus sizes for the Victor discs did not vary over time or by location.

In the traditional method for pitch detection, the engineer matches an external pitch, whether it be from a tuning fork, pitch pipe, or other source, such as a small keyboard.[22]

Pitch detection for the work in this study used a polychromatic tuner.[23] This measures all twelve pitches, in real time, at the same time. Pitch is set very rapidly, very precisely, and with high repeatability. This is a significant advance over traditional methods.

For this project, the clients, the Library of Congress and New York University, specified that the speed of the discs be varied such that A = 440. Noting that discussion of the merits of that choice are beyond the scope of this paper, the author wishes only to point out that the choice is highly defensible and, for this study, the key to producing meaningful data on speed and pitch selection during the acoustic era. Because, if playback is to be subject to "what I like best," then the data will vary just as it did in Marcos Sueiro Bal's study on stylus selection. There would be no anchor around which to compare the results.

With the target fixed, investigation of variance from that target is possible. The same would be true if the target were A = 435 Hz or rpm = 78.26 or 77.92. The locus of the data changes, but the variation and distribution around the reference does not.

The charts are plotted with percentage deviation from A = 440 Hz on the vertical axis (±9.9%), and the number of samples at each 0.1% increment along the horizontal axis.

### Victor Talking Machine Company

This result on speed variation in the Victor discs is the exact opposite of the distribution found in the stylus sizes. Where the stylus data show cleared peaks, these data are random. They follow normal distribution—also known as a bell curve—as predicted by the central limit theorem.

*Annotations for Figure 13.* Since many of the recordings in this data set were made in remote locations under difficult circumstances, we can assume more chances for variation in the Victor recordings. However, as shown below, this distribution is found in all four data sets.

Figure 13.

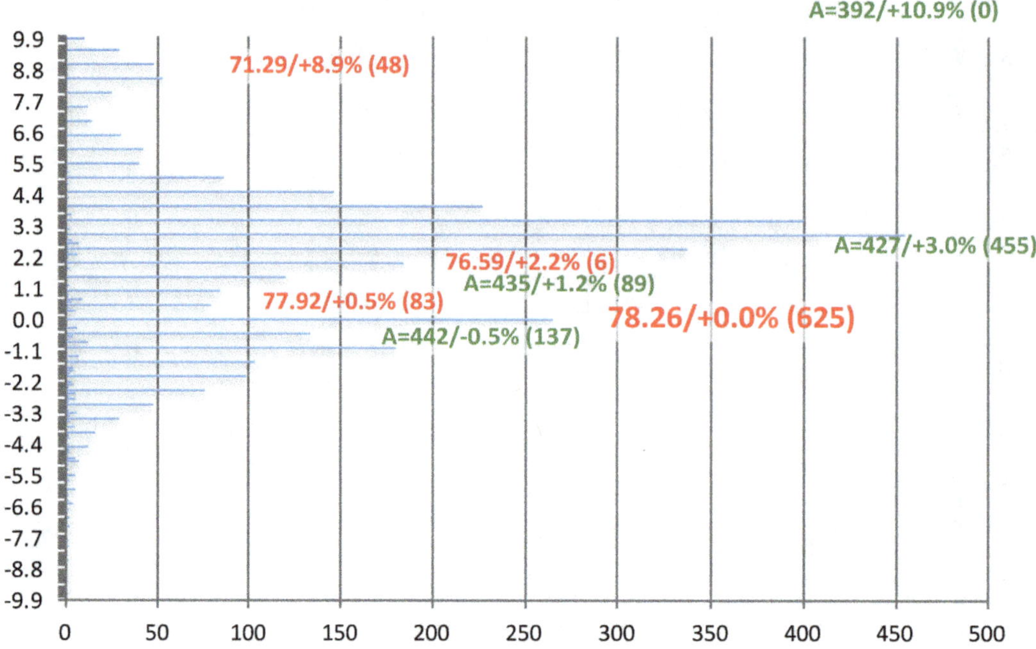


Figure 14a–d.

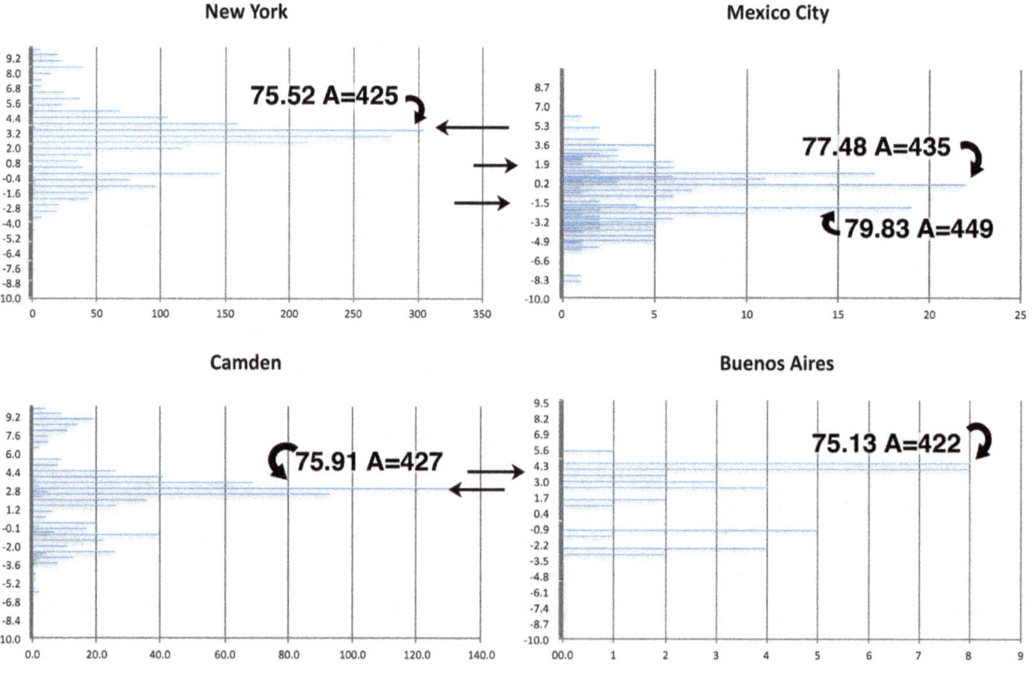


The historical record includes information on pitch over time and by location. The literature is full of information purporting to establish rotational speed as well. If either of these were true, we would anticipate peaks in the data. Anticipated peaks would include historical pitches, such as frequencies A = 415, 430, 435, as well as 440, and proposed target rpm speeds such as 71.29 and 77.92.

However, when the graph is annotated with these values where we *anticipate* peaks, we instead find areas of *low* sample count. Where there are peaks in the data they do not correspond to the speed and pitch values proposed by other authors and the historical record on pitch.

The Victor data were also analyzed by recording location.

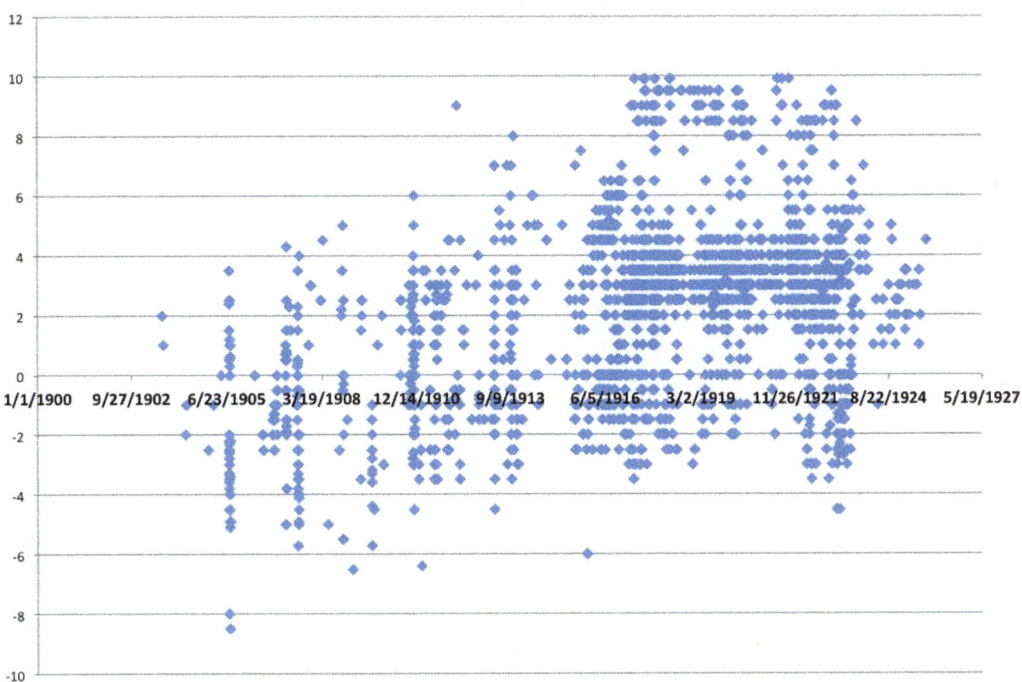


**Figure 15.**

The arrows highlight where the charts appear to indicate some dominance.

Here again we find the data peaks do not correspond to any anticipated pitch or speed values, with the exception of one peak in the Mexico City (fig. 14b) data for A = 435, or 17 out of the 3,500 sample points. This is not statistically significant.

This scatter plot (fig. 15) distributes the data by catalog number. It clearly demonstrates a very wide dispersion in each of the subsets of the catalog periods represented in the data.

The data does show a general slowing of the record speed over approximately twenty years, in that the amount of speed correction necessary to bring the discs to A = 440 increases. Slowing the discs allows longer works to be recorded.

An alternative explanation for this trend is that the reference pitch falls over this period. Since the historical record on pitch is an upward trend, this alternative explanation seems unlikely.

## Edison Diamond Discs

The Library of Congress contract that specified the Victors be pitched to A = 440 Hz also specified the Edison Diamond Discs be speed adjusted to 80 rpm. This speed selection is based on strong documentary evidence found in their corporate archives.

This work on pitch discovery was performed only near the end of the job with the specific goal of gathering data for this study, rather than as required by the contract. There are only 718 data points.

These early data show some interesting peaks that correspond to anecdotal information from other engineers: they often find Diamond Discs to fall not at 80 rpm, but at 78.26 or 79.04 rpm.

This data is inconclusive. When a larger number of sides have been digitized, a clearer pattern may develop, or it may demonstrate randomness as discovered with the other labels.

## OKeh Records

Speed variation (fig. 16) in the OKeh discs is also a random distribution.

Figure 16.

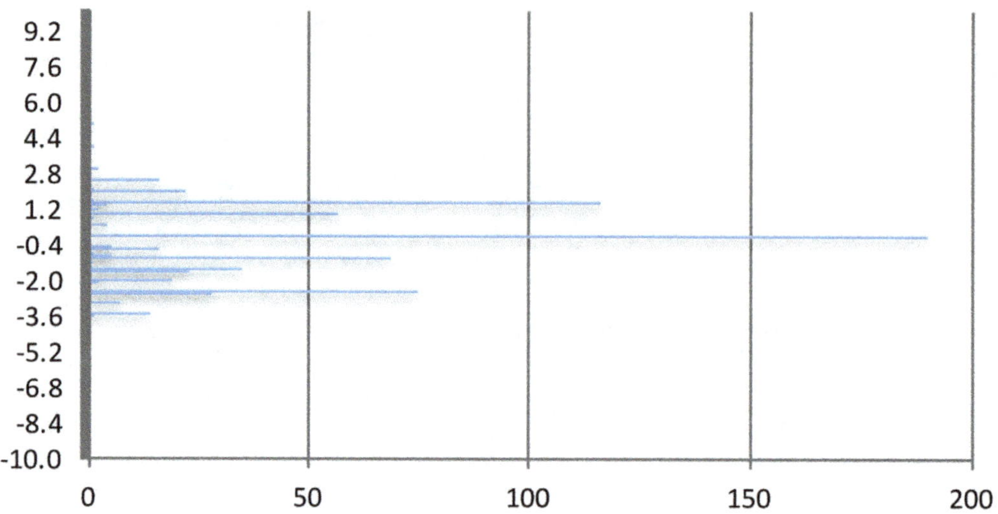


Figure 17.

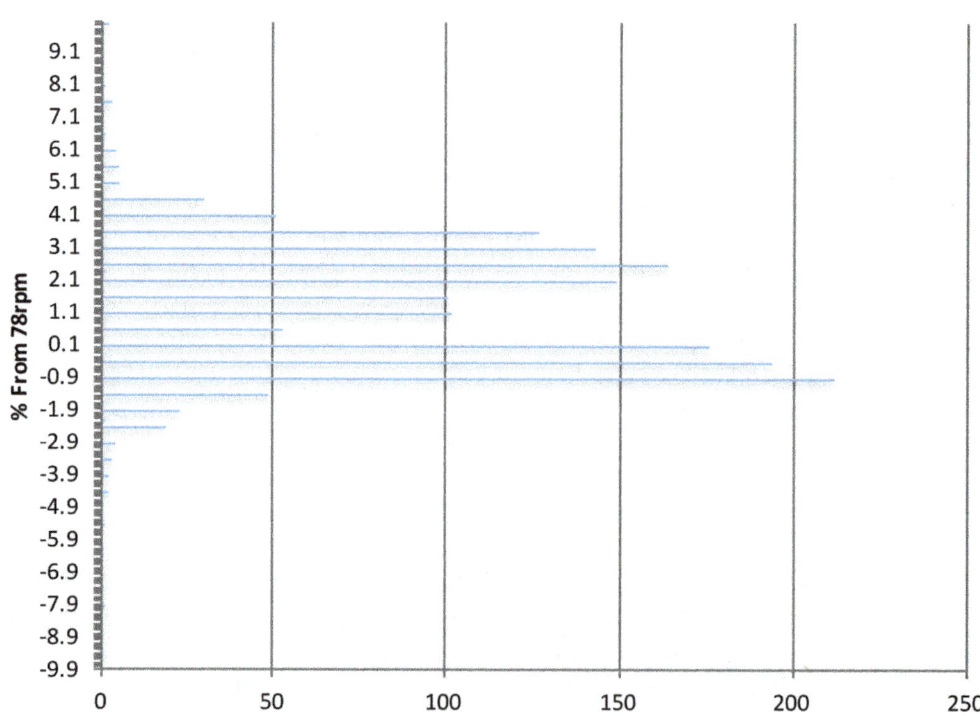


### Mick Moloney Collection of Irish-American Music and Popular Culture, New York University

The data drawn from the random labels in the NYU/Moloney Collection spans a larger time period than the other data sets, extending well into the electrical era.

Might these data indicate a convergence toward 78.26 rpm as the actual target speed of discs? Afterall, many of the challenges faced in the acoustic era working with purely mechanical systems, were either solved or improved over time with the regular use of reliable and accurate electric motors and standard line frequencies of 50 Hz and 60 Hz.

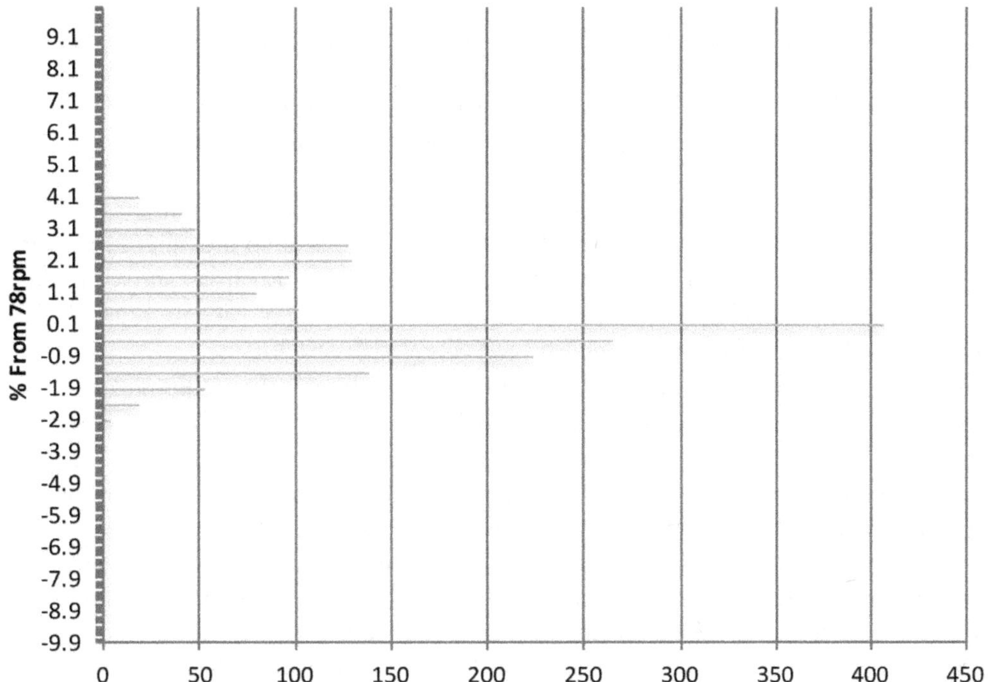


Figure 18.

### Additional Information on Speed Determination

We embrace that 78.26 rpm may not equal A = 440 Hz, but we want it to equal something. However, might we be imposing our early twenty-first century expectations on a late nineteenth century culture? Consider the following three anecdotes.

First: Attendees of the 2011 IASA Conference in Frankfurt were treated to a performance by the Sixtonics. The concert included a live recording demonstration using restored early electrical recording equipment. When the resulting lacquer disc was played back, one of the musicians asked why it played at a pitch higher than they had just performed? The drag of the cutting stylus had slowed down the lathe during recording. When the disc was played back there was less resistance and the turntable played up to speed.

- What is the proper way to play back this disc? At the originally performed pitch, or the pitch that would have been experienced in the home?
- Do we assume it took one hundred years for someone to notice this phenomenon? Or is it merely the case that one hundred years ago pitch varied so widely it was taken for granted?
- Might the 79.04 rpm speed observed in the small Edison sample correspond to this demonstration?

Second: In 2011 your author recorded all fourteen Bach keyboard concerti on a collection of restored antique harpsichords. The instruments were built between 1627 and 1707. When the instruments were built, pitch was trending from A = 392 to 415. During restoration each instrument was pitched differently according to the tradition of when and where it was originally made. To avoid strain on the instruments, and many broken strings during the recording, all the instruments were retuned to a compromise pitch of A = 400, a pitch with no historical foundation whatsoever. Other recordings have been made with these instruments in solo or continuo roles. In those recordings, made in the span of a few years, the instruments were tuned to their native pitches: 392, 405, 407, 410 and 415. If these had been among the Victor, OKeh and Moloney discs in this study pitched to A = 440, every one would be misrepresented, and each in a different way.

To anyone who presumes to know exactly the correct pitch to play any given acoustic era disc, we offer this YouTube video: https://www.youtube.com/watch?v=UnhlQUBsd6g.

### Summary Conclusions on Speed Determination

Analysis of four data sets totaling 9,000 sides, of pristine and worn discs, and of a random selection of labels, demonstrates no clear pattern to definitively determine the speed or pitch of acoustic-era 78 rpm recordings.

These findings inform the process of preservation. It is necessary to use the proper stylus because it is not possible for the listener to alter that choice. Speed, on the other hand, can be changed when playing a digital file. In practice it may make sense to choose a fixed reference (speed or pitch) for playback and leave it to the user to decide; and to provide multiple playbacks with different styli, and again leave it to users to choose which they prefer.

George Blood graduated from the University of Chicago with a degree in music theory. He was recording engineer at the Philadelphia Orchestra for twenty-one years, has engineered and produced six hundred radio programs and 250 CDs, five of which have received Grammy nominations. His company digitizes over one hundred thousand hours of sound, video, and motion picture film content each year. George is a frequent presenter, giving ten to twenty presentations and workshops annually, covering topics from audiovisual fundamentals to bit accuracy and quality control. He has served on standards committees for the Audio Engineering Society and the Advanced Media Workflow Association for MXF/AS-07, the board of the Conservation Center for Art and Historic Artifacts, and the technical committees of the Association for Recorded Sounds Collections and the International Association of Sound and Audiovisual Archives.

## Acknowledgments

I want to thank John Bolig, Victor discographer extraordinaire; Sam Brylawski, University of California Santa Barbara; Mari Carpenter, Travis Kirspel and Keith Minsinger; Eldridge Johnson Museum, Delaware State Division of Historical and Cultural Affairs; Brian Destremps, Senior Audio Engineer, George Blood, LP; Caitlin Hunter, Patrick Smetanick, Gene DeAnna, Library of Congress; Morgan Oscar Morel, IT Systems Admin, George Blood, LP; Kimberly Peach, Lead Archivist, The Winthrop Group; and Kimberly Tarr, Head, Media Preservation Unit, New York University.

## Notes

1. The microphone was developed independently by Emile Berliner and David Edward Hughes in the 1870s. It is one of the fundamental precursors of Alexander Graham Bell's telephone in 1876. Nonetheless the diaphragm at the base of a horn serves the same function: transducing from one form of energy to another, from sound pressure to electricity (microphone) or to mechanical motion (cutting a phonograph).
2. It's one thing to make an electric motor go around. It another thing to make it go around at a consistent speed, an imperative for sound recordings.
3. The issue of pitch would remain important. When the new International Standards Organization (ISO) was formed in 1955, one of their first tasks was to adopt a uniform frequency of A = 440 as ISO 16. This is where we get the expression "Standard Pitch," by which we mean A = 440.
4. Woodwind and brass instruments rarely last more than a generation. Professional musicians may "blow out" an instrument in five to ten years. This idea was put to me by Jay Krush, founding member of Chestnut Brass Company, an ensemble that specializes in playing early brass instruments. Most of the historic instruments they've been able to collect are real dogs. "The good ones were played until they died. The ones that survive were owned by amateurs who rarely played them, then threw them in a closet until their grandchildren found them."

5. An excellent summary of work by the Edison staff: *Stylus Shapes and Sizes: Preliminary Comments on Historical Edison Cylinder Styli*, by Bill Klinger, Chair of the ARSC Cylinder Committee.
6. The author is grateful to Clara Blood, DMA, for furnishing this fascinating discussion on this topic as viewed from a different vantage: Oboists as keeper of orchestral pitch. http://www.oboeclassics.com/Burgess.htm.
7. This assumption regarding the impact of record wear is brought into question later in this paper.
8. All the work for the Library of Congress is destined for this site: http://www.loc.gov/jukebox/.
9. The data for this paper was collected from two contracts performed for the Library of Congress and another contract for New York University. It is important to note that none of these contracts required the acquisition of data specifically for this study. Flaws in the methods of data gathering and analysis are evident throughout. However, the findings are extremely clear, more than overcoming these flaws. Efforts are taken throughout the paper to point out where a more disciplined approach could have been followed, and how better method may or may not have produced different results. The raw data are available at www.georgeblood.com.
10. It is important to point out the data from the Moloney Collection used in this study includes both acoustic and electrical recordings. Therefore, it is far from perfect for comparison with the Victor, Edison and OKeh data.
11. Please pay attention to the scaling on the left side of these charts. Some times it is scaled for maximum resolution, and other times scaled to a fixed unit to facilitate comparison between charts.
12. Cf. footnote 3.
13. Most discs are cut by modulating the groove side-to-side ("lateral cut"). Edison media are cut up and down ("vertical cut"), a.k.a. "hill and dale." Vertical cut discs have more consistent groove geometry. However, loud sounds tend to eject the stylus from the groove. Ultimately lateral cut was used by most manufacturers, and became the standard for LPs.
14. Edison Diamond Disc players include a feed screw to move the stylus and horn across the disc. This requires the pitch (number of turns per unit distance) of the disc and feed screw to match. Otherwise the feed screw would cause the disc to skip forward or backward.
15. For a discussion on tracing distortion see Di Toro, J. SMPTE 29, 493, 1937
16. Edison's grooved media used a geometry often called "door knob" shape, from the popular shape of Victorian era hardware. Other manufacturers used conical shape, triangular in profile, or a triangular shape with the point removed.
17. The assumption is the playback stylus should have the same profile as the cutting stylus. This is impossible to achieve. The shape might be very, very close, but due to irregularities in the recording medium, and the replication process, as well as wear of both the cutting and playback stylus, an exact match cannot be achieved.
18. www.loc.gov/jukebox.
19. Fun fact: At the beginning of the twentieth century "OK" was a popular, new expression. While the spelling evolved to "okay" or simply "OK," at this time it was spelled "okeh". The label's name is a play on this new expression and the founder's initials Otto K. E. Heinemann.
20. Marcos Sueiro Bal himself and George Blood, the author of this paper.
21. Other factors may introduce variation or noise into the data. These include digitization engineer choicing up or down to the nearest semitone, discs whose speed varies across the duration of the disc, wow and flutter, nonequal tempered tunings, etc. Each of these may impose additional considerations upon a given side. However, their frequency of occurrence is low, and therefore only noise in the data, not influencing the conclusions. Cf. the discussion and charts that follow.
22. A few practitioners have perfect pitch. Some choose to leave the discs at 78.26 rpm and avoid this topic entirely. Others choose what they like best based on their musical judgment, and may take into consideration a pitch detection method.
23. PitchLab is available for iPhone iOS and Android smart phones. Rare 12-pitch Stroboconn and Petersen tuners, no longer manufactured, are also suitable for this work.

12

# Playback Methods for Phonogram Images on Paper

**Patrick Feaster**

Abstract

The world's oldest sound recordings survive only as images on paper that were not originally intended for playback. Some of them have recently been made audible for the first time via techniques that rely on putting existing tools to new and unanticipated uses.

Keywords

lossless, video, encoding, codecs, compression ratio, FFV1, JPEG2000, Dirac, H.264, uncompressed, NLE, transcoding.

The practice of playing back recorded sounds dates back to Thomas Edison's phonograph of 1877. Numerous sound-recording formats intended for playback emerged then and in the following decades, ranging from indented tinfoil sheets to wax phonograph cylinders to gramophone discs in hard rubber and shellac. All of these formats pose greater or lesser challenges to those who want to hear and preserve their audio content today. But the world's oldest phonograms—dating back before Edison's phonograph—have come down to us only as paper documents: graphical records intended not for playback but for visual apprehension, analogous to the records of earthquakes traced by seismographs. During the last decade, some of these primeval recordings have been played back as sound for the first time, dramatically expanding the time depth of the historical audio available to modern listeners. Here I would like to discuss some innovations that have made the playback of these documents possible.

To put matters in context, we should begin with some history. The principle of using an eardrum-like membrane to pick up and record sound vibrations out of the air was first conceived in 1852 by Édouard-Léon Scott de Martinville, a Parisian typographer and scientific proofreader. Scott was inspired by an account of the mechanism of the human ear in a treatise on physiology to imagine creating an artificial ear which would pick sounds up out of the air in the same way a real ear does, but which, instead of passing the signal along to the brain, would record the vibrations by tracing them onto a moving surface. He conducted preliminary experiments in late 1853 or early 1854, but it wasn't until early 1857 that he began pursuing his idea in earnest and patented an instrument based on it, which he called the *phonautograph* or sound-self-writer. His initial design sought to replicate the middle ear and oval window as well as the outer ear and eardrum, but his phonautograph usually took a simpler form, much more like Edison's later phonograph: sounds were concentrated into a funnel, a membrane at the opposite end of the funnel vibrated in response to them, causing a stylus attached to the membrane to move back and forth as it traced a line onto a sheet of soot-blackened paper wrapped around a rotating drum.

Scott's goal wasn't to play back the sounds he recorded as sound, but to capture them graphically—to represent the subtleties of the living voice on paper that were missing from conventional writing and musical notation. However, his inscriptions, or *phonautograms*, represent sound waves according to the same logic as the grooves on LPs do: both are graphs of the displacement amplitudes of sound waves as a function of time. For many years past, the fact that phonautograms should theoretically be playable as sound was no great secret, the only necessities being a practical method of converting the data into playable form and a source of appreciable duration—that is, longer than a split second.



*Sustainable Audiovisual Collections* (2017): 90–95. DOI: 10.2979/jts2016.0.0.14

In 2007, David Giovannoni, Richard Martin, Meagan Hennessey, and I founded the First Sounds Initiative (FirstSounds.org), an informal collaboration with the goal of tracking down and making audible the world's oldest recorded sounds. We immediately set our sights on pre-Edisonian phonautograms and, by March 2008, had satisfied both of the necessities I mentioned. First, we had located some relatively long phonautograms which Scott himself had recorded in 1860 and deposited with the Academy of Sciences in Paris, and we had digitized them at 2400 dpi using an ordinary flatbed scanner. Second, we had identified a partner to convert the waveform images into WAV files: Carl Haber and his colleagues at Lawrence Berkeley National Laboratory had developed an optical playback system for analog grooved records, and their software for analyzing images of grooves on gramophone discs appeared suitable for phonautograms as well.

We chose one phonautogram labeled as representing the song "Au Clair de la Lune," and dated April 9, 1860, as our most promising candidate. As with most of Scott's phonautograms, it had been traced helically on a paper wrapped around a cylinder, but when the paper had been removed and flattened, it had become a rectangle with traces running across its width at a slight angle. Traces that had been made continuously around the cylinder—and across the join in the paper—were thus broken into strips, one strip per rotation. Moreover, all of the phonautograms Scott is known to have recorded in 1860 feature two parallel traces: one documenting the voice and another traced alongside it by a tuning fork as a time reference. For our initial playback in March 2008, David Giovannoni isolated each strip of the phonautogram into a separate image file; Earl Cornell carried out the raw conversion of the individual rotations into audio; and David connected the pieces into continuous tracks, with the voice in one stereo channel and the tuning fork in the other. Now the most conspicuous problem with the audio was that Scott had rotated the cylinder of his phonautograph by hand, and its speed was irregular enough to distort a sung melody beyond recognition. Fortunately, the tuning fork was available for use as a pilot tone. I stayed up into the wee hours on the morning of March 15, 2008 adjusting the tuning fork to 500 Hz five cycles at a time by hand in CoolEdit, and the voice track along with it, resulting in the version of the audio we unveiled two weeks later at the annual conference of the Association for Recorded Sound Collections in conjunction with a press release: "The World's Oldest Sound Recordings Played for the First Time." However, some noteworthy technical challenges remained.

The software designed for use with the IRENE system uses algorithms to try to identify the position of a groove—or in our case, a two-dimensional line—at each successive point along the time axis, as though it were being followed by a stylus on a turntable: a "virtual stylus," they call it. "Au Clair de la Lune" had presented us with fairly straightforward waveforms that fit this logic, which is why the software was able to convert them so readily into audio. Unfortunately, many remaining phonautograms displayed broad smudges or points where the trace loops backwards relative to the direction of recording, such that a single point along the time axis corresponds to two or more points along the amplitude axis (see fig. 1). These examples violate the basic assumptions of the "virtual stylus" approach; imagine trying to play a comparably shaped groove on a turntable and you'll appreciate why.

In the fall of 2008, I devised an alternative approach to phonautogram playback using Andrew Jaremko's ImageToSound, freeware designed to convert to convert any 24-bit bitmap image into a WAV file as though it were an optical film sound track. Such sound tracks consist of long, narrow bands that vary either in width ("area") or in opacity ("density"); when they move past a light source, they variably obstruct it such that the fluctuating intensity of light can be transduced into an audio signal. To simulate this process, ImageToSound calculates the average brightness of successive columns of pixels in a digital image and assigns the values to successive samples in a digital sound file. Scott's phonautograms might not seem to fit this model at first glance, but it occurred to me that by filling in the spaces above and below the trace with white in common graphics editing software, we could convert a phonautogram into a pair of bright bands of varying width which this software could then convert into two playable audio tracks that could be summed to mono in turn. Unlike our earlier approach, this method can accommodate

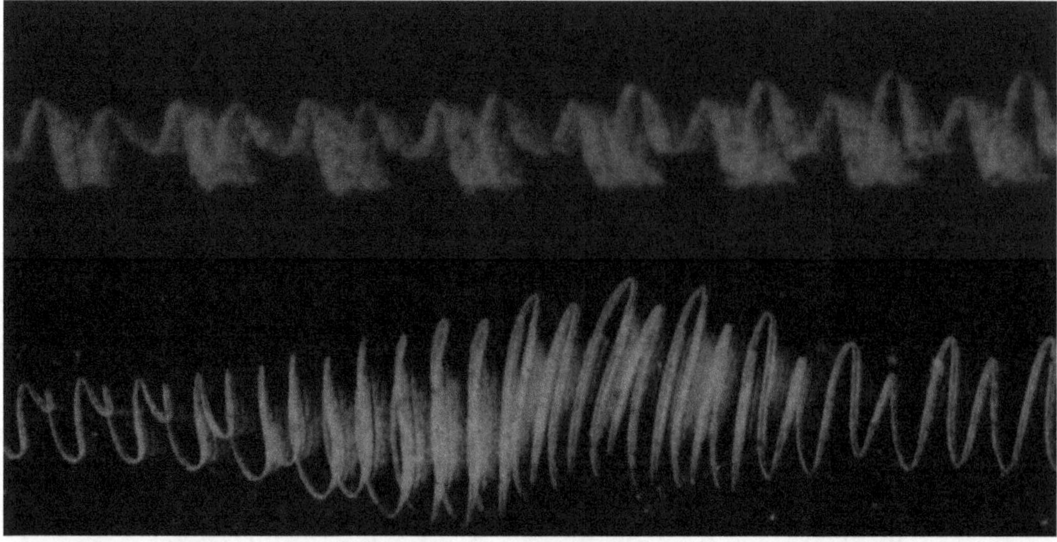

**Figure 1.** Phonautographic traces that violate assumptions of orthogonality. FirstSounds.org.

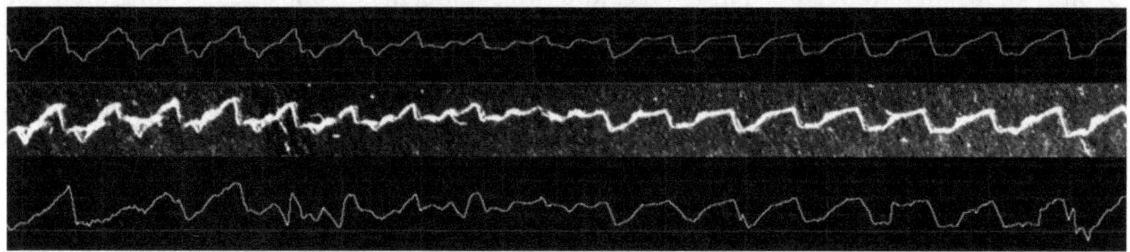

**Figure 2.** Analyses of a phonautographic trace (center) using ImageToSound (top) and "virtual stylus" approach (bottom). Griffonagedotcom .wordpress.com.

highly distorted traces without violating its basic logic, enabling us to hear *something* from them, although of course it doesn't correct the errors. Some of the most badly mangled phonautograms thereby came within reach of our playback efforts. Meanwhile, I found that I could obtain improved results using this technique even from well-recorded phonautograms such as "Au Clair de la Lune," if only because it relies on time-consuming manual image manipulation in Photoshop while the "virtual stylus" relies on algorithms that are more susceptible to confusion. Figure 2 shows a portion of the original trace of "Au Clair de la Lune" in the middle, the "virtual stylus" analysis from 2008 below, and an ImageToSound analysis from 2011 above.[1]

Meanwhile, as we took advantage of our ability to play back a wider range of phonautograms, we soon made a humbling discovery: our initial playback of "Au Clair de la Lune" had been set to twice the correct speed. We had misinterpreted Scott's notation of the tuning fork frequency "500 simple vibrations per second" as 500 Hz rather than 250 Hz, so what we had first taken to be the singing of a young girl turned out, on closer examination, to be a painfully slow rendition of "Au Clair de la Lune" by a deep male voice, presumably that of the inventor himself.[2]

Several aspects of phonautogram playback remain ripe for development, and none more so than those that involve speed-correction. Our current practice of correcting the speed of tuning-fork traces by hand—five cycles at a time—is far from ideal. In the past, Earl Cornell at Lawrence Berkeley National Laboratory and Jamie Howarth of Plangent Processes have both speed-corrected phonautograms on our behalf more programmatically and more accurately, but they are unable to contribute their services on a standing basis. More recently, David Giovannoni has experimented with applying the time-correction algorithms of Celemony's Capstan to phonautograms. In its current form, he finds that Capstan can improve the stability of a file that has already been manually speed-corrected, but it attempts by default to adjust an unaltered tuning-fork trace to the nearest half-tone, and until some provision is introduced for overriding this feature, it will remain unsuitable for speed-correcting phonautograms "from scratch."

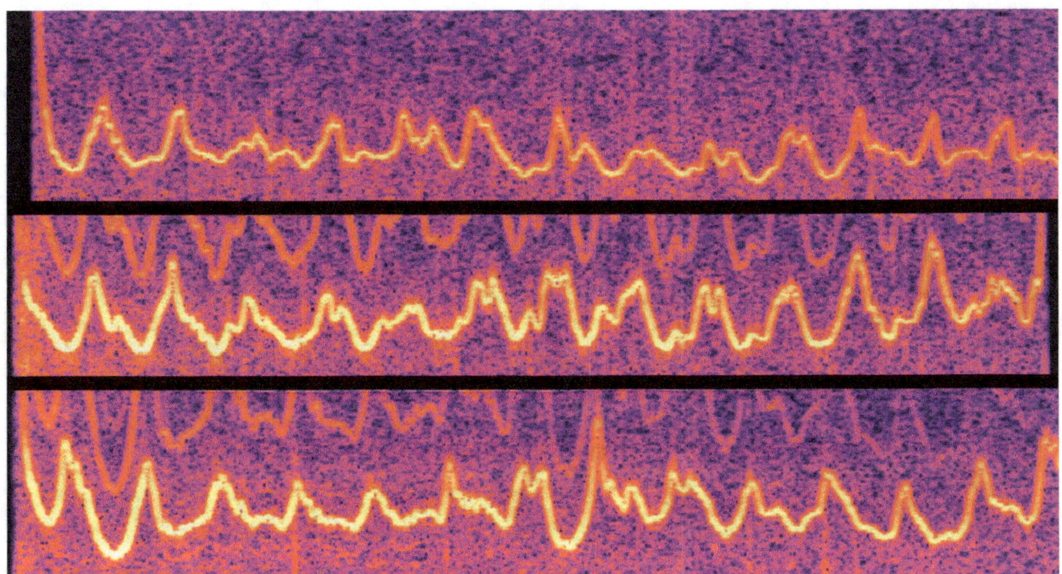

**Figure 3.** Spectrograms of tuning-fork pilot tones from three phonautograms recorded in 1860.

Further innovations in speed-correction could yield a significant breakthrough on another front. At present, the "Au Clair de la Lune" phonautogram from April 9, 1860, is the world's oldest playable sound recording with content that is readily recognizable by ear. Older phonautograms survive, but they don't feature the tuning fork trace as a time reference, leaving us with no objective means of correcting for the irregular speed of rotation during recording. We can still render them into audio at, say, a constant linear speed of 18.375 inches per second, combining a standard CD sampling rate with a scanning resolution of 2400 dots per inch;[3] but it might be misleading to characterize the result as "playback" or "reproduction," given how tenuous its connection to an originating sound is. My preference in this and other cases is to speak of *educing* phonograms—bringing forth the sound they embody from a latent condition. Even so, there may be hope for these earlier phonautograms. If we study the uncorrected tuning fork traces in the later phonautograms, some examples of which are shown in Figure 3, we find that there was some regularity to the speed changes, just as we might expect from the rhythms of manual cranking. If we can identify similar patterns in the earlier phonautograms, we may be able to compensate for them, mitigating the most egregious effects of the speed fluctuations, even if we cannot eliminate them entirely.

The phonautograms of Édouard-Léon Scott de Martinville constitute humanity's earliest recordings of its own voice, and their documentary significance was recognized through their inscription on the UNESCO Memory of the World Register in 2015. However, the playback technique I've been describing is by no means limited in scope to phonautograms. Among other things, I've applied it successfully to ink prints on paper of early gramophone discs. The only significant extra step in this case entails converting the spiral into phonautogram-like strips by applying a standard polar-to-rectangular-coordinates transform (see fig. 4).

No account of playback methods for phonogram images on paper would be complete without acknowledging that the waveform is only one way of displaying acoustic data: as a graph of time versus amplitude. Another option is the sound spectrogram: a graph of time versus frequency. These two forms of display are largely interchangeable, to the point that many pieces of audio editing software will let you toggle back and forth between them. And sound spectrograms can be played back as sound too. I've been using a program called AudioPaint by Nicolas Fournel for this purpose; like other similar software, it uses additive synthesis, combining together sine waves at frequencies corresponding to the height of pixels and amplitudes based on their brightness. I coined the term *paleospectrophony*, literally "old spectrum sounding," in the fall of 2008 to refer to the use of a reverse Fourier transform to render audible historical inscriptions that represent sound graphically in terms of a time axis and a frequency axis, such

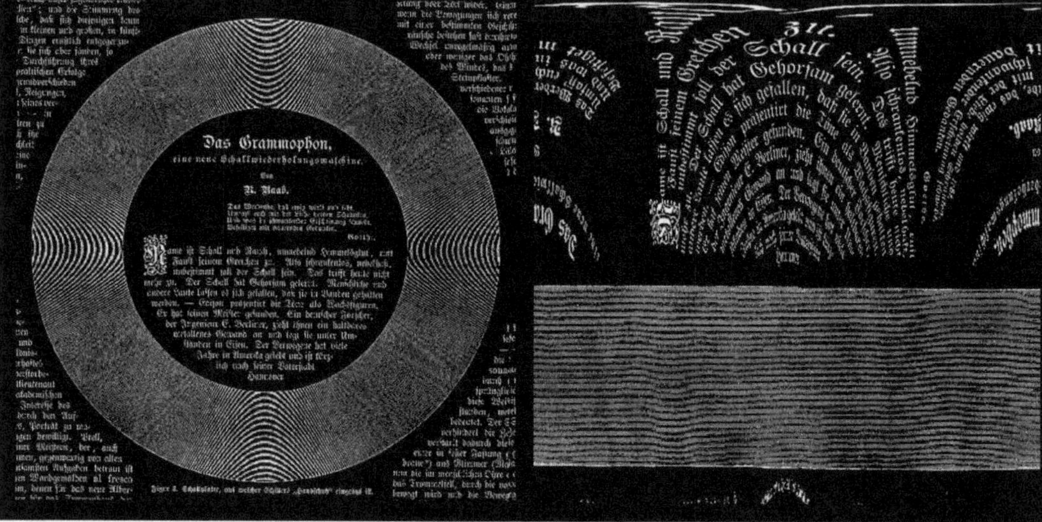


**Figure 4.** Image data for gramophone disc before (left) and after (right) polar to rectangular coordinates transform. Griffonagedotcom.wordpress.com.

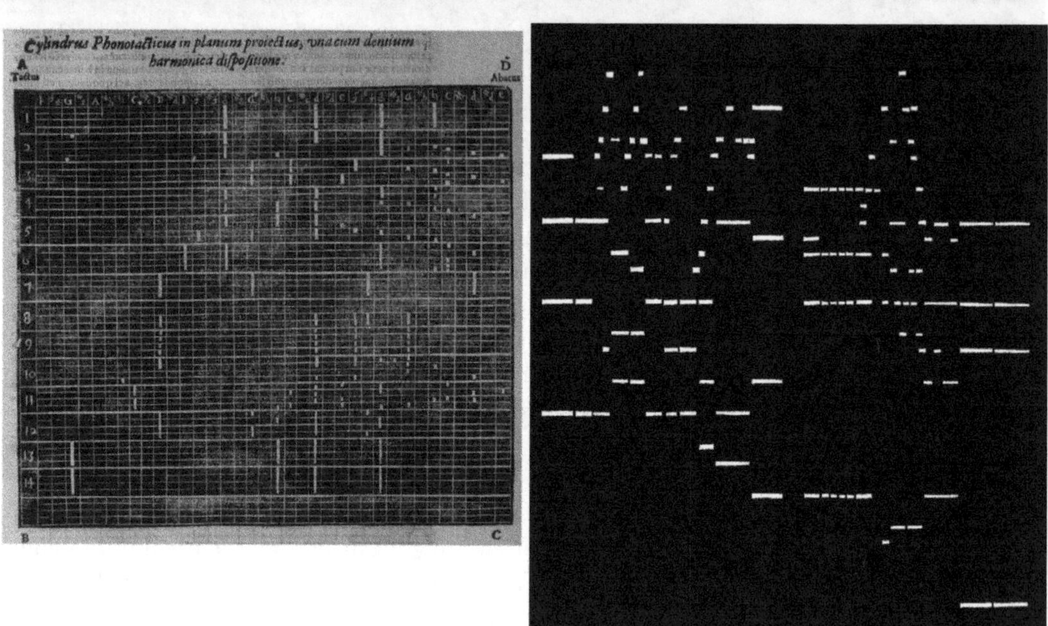


**Figure 5.** Plate from 1650 illustrating the pinning of a barrel organ, in original form (left) and as processed for eduction (right), from Feaster (2012), p. 91.

that the resulting sound bears a resemblance to the originally intended content. Automatically produced sound spectrograms date back only to the 1940s, so at first glance this technique may not seem to offer much in the way of time depth. However, we can use paleospectrophony to educe *any* inscription that can be interpreted as a graph of sound frequencies as a function of time, including early modern plates illustrating how to pin barrel organs (see fig. 5) and some kinds of medieval musical notation. For example, thousand-year-old manuscripts in Daseian notation happen to conform to the format expectations of a modern sound spectrogram as a graph of time versus frequency, and the music we hear when we treat it that way *is* approximately the music the scribe originally meant to encode.[4] In this case, the technological approach itself is relatively unremarkable; what's noteworthy is the identification of unexpected categories of historical documents that are suitable for it: sources that resemble phonograms closely enough that we can meaningfully listen to them *as* phonograms.

Indeed, in closing I want to emphasize that the solution of technical problems in the eduction of phonograms on paper has so far relied on putting existing tools to new and unanticipated uses rather than on the creation of new tools. With customized tools, we might yet be able to accomplish a great deal more.

Patrick Feaster is an independent consultant and developer, specializing in professional open-source solutions for long-term preservation needs and lossless audiovisual archiving workflows. He studied media computer science at the Technical University in Vienna and has worked as a project leader and developer in the field of digital preservation since 2002. As an employee of NOA Archiving Solutions, he set up and developed solutions for different broadcasting archives around the globe.

## Notes

1. The "shape" of the original trace and the "shapes" of the digital waveforms correspond because both digital files represent the source in a manner analogous to the output of an amplitude transducer such as a ceramic cartridge. For better or worse, all phonautogram transduction to date has been constant amplitude rather than constant velocity.
2. Updated versions of this phonautogram and others from 1860 are available online from FirstSounds.org, as well as in Feaster (2012), tracks 14 and 15.
3. Several such examples dating from 1857 appear in Feaster (2012), track 16.
4. Examples of these types may be found in Feaster (2012), tracks 1, 17, 21, 22, 24–25, and 28.

## Reference

Feaster, P. (2012). *Pictures of Sound: One Thousand Years of Educed Audio, 980–1980.* Retrieved from http://www.dust-digital.com/feaster/.

# 13

# Present and Future Applications of Optical Soundtrack Scan Technology

**Gilles Barberis**

Abstract

Over the past two decades, a few developers and researchers have been trying to solve the issue of image spread correction in variable area negative soundtracks. They were initially aiming to save time and money on the optical transfer process by avoiding the printing of new sound positives. With the present paper, I aim to emphasise the higher quality achievable with the features of the optical soundtrack scanners available nowadays, rather than just the economical advantages. After a brief technical explanation of what image spread is, how it is generated by optical recorders and fixed by either positive prints or scanners, this proposal will analyze some specific, yet broadly recurring issues in variable area optical soundtracks, and explain how these can now be solved by scanner technology. The approach proposed by this paper will link each setting of optical scanners to precise examples of audio and optical damage, or human mistakes, coming from a particular period, film stock, or film sound technology. Finally, we will try to envisage some possible developments of scanner technology, especially the increased collaboration between archives and laboratories, achieved by splitting raw scan and post processing and by deploying the two processes to their most suitable environment.

Keywords

variable area, variable density, optical soundtrack, soundtrack scanning, sound restoration, Western Electric, RCA photophone, Fox movietone, Tobis Klangfilm.

Facing the challenge of long-term accessibility of audio-visual collections leads to the need for analyzing the pros and cons of current optical soundtrack scanning technologies.

In this context, we will voluntarily overlook the dawn of the optical recording, like the early experiments of Édouard-Léon Scott de Martinville with his Phonautograms, or the first sound-on-film specimen of Eugène Lauste. These cases would require dedicated research and testing.

Focusing on what is worldwide and industrially recognized as the sound-on-film era, a huge majority of the elements we would run into, in the aim of sound digitization, is constituted by opticals. From the late 20s through the end of the 50s, the first generation element is generally an optical negative soundtrack. With the rise of the magnetic recording during the 50s, until the digital era, the first generation element would become the 35 mm magnetic film. It does not take an expert in the field to find out that, sadly, in several countries, mags have not been considered archival material; hence, they have been poorly preserved, or, in the worst-case scenario, erased and reused. Furthermore, the next resource for movie soundtracks from the 50s through the 90s was the sound negative.

Up until a few years ago, the standardized workflow for preservation and digitization of an optical soundtrack was based on photochemically copying master elements onto more stable film bases. The two main reasons for this are the natural deterioration of the original material, and some intrinsic characteristics of optical soundtrack negatives that require a track print to achieve a proper playback.

For variable area tracks, that characteristic is a phenomenon called "image spread." This term means that no photographic material is capable of an immediate and instantaneous transition from total transmission to total density. For instance, using a microdensitometer and



*Sustainable Audiovisual Collections* (2017): 96–100. DOI: 10.2979/jts2016.0.0.15

scanning across such a transition would show that there is always a slope between one state and the other. It is this slope on a variable area recording that derives the name "image spread." This problem could be cured by selecting the precise exposure level at which the image spread on the print exactly match and cancel out the image spread on the negative.

Soon after the introduction of optical soundtracks in the movie industry, the processing labs asked for a procedure to determine the optimum exposure conditions for both the negative and the print. Since the 40s, this industry-standard practice, commonly known as the cross-modulation test (Eastman Kodak Company, 2001), is a routine used for quality assurance. The test is based on the fact that a perfect sinusoid, comprising a high-frequency signal (about 10 kHz), modulated at 75% by a low-frequency one (typically 400 Hz), will have an average value of zero (the average light transmission will be constant). In the case of underexposure or overexposure, some of the low-frequency modulation components will be introduced into the average value of the signal and may be detected. A low-pass filter is connected to the optical pickup head to eliminate the high-frequency carrier, and the amount of the 400 Hertz signal remaining is analyzed to determine the exposure and printing conditions which result in the lowest-level signal. The exposure with the lowest measurable distortion is the optimum exposure.

For variable density tracks, the optical sound is affected by a complex array of issues: intermodulation distortion, loss of high frequencies, and reduced dynamic range. These physically complex phenomena are intertwined and relate to a subtle divergence from the ideal film exposure. In this case, the aim of the optical engineer is to print a series of exposures, known as a "wedge test," to find the correct gamma that would cause the least amount of distortion. In 1890, Hurter and Driffield studied the relation between film exposure and film density, developing a model known as the "H & D" curve (Hurter and Driffield, 1890). The toe of the curve is a horizontal segment, because, at low exposures, minor changes do not affect film density. The central segment of the curve is linear, with a 1 : 1 relation between density and exposure. The shoulder at the end of the graph is where the density of the film gets close to saturation, and even a big increase in exposure will not affect the darkness of the film. The wedge test points out the linear part of the curve as the exposure that would lead to the lowest distortion in the print.

Over the past two decades, a few developers and researchers have been trying to overcome the limit of the photochemical approach to sound transfers. There are multiple reasons for that.

- The tests mentioned previously are valid and effective only on soundtracks produced with the standardized cross-modulation practice. That leaves out early soundtracks, like single unilateral variable area, Movietone showreels, and Tobis-Klangfilm soundtracks. It also leaves out later productions coming from countries where those cross-modulation standards were adopted later on. Moreover, some standard operations were reliable and effective if the negative was printed on specific film bases that might not be available anymore.
- In this digital age, the continued existence of film manufacturing and laboratory processes is questionable. With Kodak and Hollywood's current effort to finalize a deal to keep film alive, and Fujifilm's decision to shift its business operation's focus on products and services designed for digital workflow; relying solely on the photochemical option for soundtrack archiving is a dangerous bet.
- There is a price for processing expenses and the environment. In a study conducted by Robert J. Heiber, the cost of printing one billion feet of optical soundtrack (that is the estimated amount of sound negative material to be preserved worldwide, according to the 1994 UNESCO survey), would easily reach $370m. According to the same research, the laboratory process for printing onto EK 2302 stock would consume 133,000,000 liters of water, create chemical waste of 2,432,000 kg, and solid waste of 5,500,000 kg (2015).
- Sound scanners offer problem-solving tools that were unthinkable with the photochemical option, or at least save hours of digital cleaning. The idea is to solve issues like dust,

scratches, lateral and azimuth offsets, as well as under and over exposure when the sound is still in the optical domain, thus avoiding time-consuming and artifacts-inducing algorithms, and digital plug-ins.

- Finally, the last burden of optical soundtrack transfers—moving and shipping numerous reels from archives all over the world to ultra-specialized film labs—might come to an end. It is our hope that "future applications" will help resolve this issue. Until now, sound scanners remove the need for a fully equipped photochemical laboratory; all that is needed is a sound room with a good acoustic, a sound technician with good ears, and reputable and assured shipment courier. Soundtrack scanner providers are aiming to offer, in the near future, the possibility of a split workflow, making it possible to separate the scanning from the processing operation. These two steps can then take place at different times, and if required, at different locations. In this scenario, an archive could temporarily acquire a scanner to digitize the images within its entire collection (a task that requires the skill to carefully handle weak film material), while the processing is done in a sound studio by an audio engineer (a task that requires a studio with acoustic treatment and sound engineering training).

This kind of research in the field of soundtrack scanning is laying the foundation for a new approach in film conservation and film restoration. Sound digitisation is the first step in this process, and one that may make a tremendous difference for future soundtrack preservation. The following information has been provided by developers of optical soundtrack scanners in order to show different approaches and tools.

### Deluxe COSP (Chris Reynolds, Deluxe Media)

Deluxe's COSP Xi2k (Chace Optical Sound Processore—Xtended *i*ntelligence2k) optical sound track reader is the culmination of over thirty years of hardware and software evolution, and features a sophisticated and comprehensive set of DSP technologies, enabling the playback of virtually any optical sound track. The foundation of the reader is a 4096 pixel, dual-line CMOS camera with a fully integrated and intuitive GUI that offers true 96 kHz transfers with 2048 pixel resolution. Using a red LED light source, the COSP Xi2k can be used on any OSTN or OSTP format and has the capability of transferring OSTNs with equivalent or better quality than would be achieved by making an OSTP.

Digital image and audio processing occurs on a proprietary PCIe card that features powerful field-programmable gate arrays (FPGAs), giving it the ability to process complex blocks of data that operate on all 2048 12-bit pixels at the full 96 kHz scan rate. This allows the COSP to support all three of its operating modes—Variable Density Mode, Variable Area Edge Detection and Thresholding Mode, and Variable Area Integration and Thresholding Mode—simultaneously, with eight separate 24-bit output channels at all times. It can be mounted to both MTM and Sondor film dubbers.

Additional features allow for the elimination or reduction of issues that cannot be corrected with traditional track printing including a pixel-exclusion mode, cross-modulation distortion compensation, clash compensation for VA tracks, a PEC (photoelectric cell) emulation mode, and more.

### Sondor RESONANCES (William Hungerbuehler, Sondor)

"RESONANCES" is the result of a collaboration between Sondor and the University of La Rochelle (France) and its MIA lab. It is an optical soundtrack scanning system, available for Sondor OMA E and VERSA film transports. It is based on a CCD line-scan camera combined with digital image processing, and enables the operator to remove optical defects of the soundtrack at the time of transfer before it is converted into audio.

The beauty of this approach is that the operator can visually inspect the soundtrack on the screen and determine which optical, electrical, and digital adjustments will work best to receive a proper result from the transfer. (S)he can use some visual monitoring tools like a histogram, spectrogram, and pre/post processing windows, as well as direct audio monitoring.

The sound output is either captured to disk using the operator's audio editor of choice, or through the supplied audio interface.

RESONANCES 22, and later, integrates metadata management. Resumed, this means that working with RESONANCES generates a so-called "Job" file, which contains descriptive metadata, as well as the history of actions (so-called "runs," recorded each time the "grab" button is hit; the "run" describes the action: date, frame counter, used plugins, and plugins parameters).

The aim is to provide data to help the RESONANCES user with workflow management tasks. RESONANCES write the data (descriptive data and action history) to an XML file locally, but can transmit the descriptive part (cinematographic work, film reel info, . . . ) to a server, allowing some centralized reporting or restoration supervision.

### Laser Interface SoundDirect (Henrik Lausen, Laser Interface Photonics)

SoundDirect is a laser soundtrack scanner. To understand what this is, let's make a simple comparison: In analog, the white and red light readers basic principle is light averaging. In reverse scan readers, Resonance and COSP, the basic detection principle is imaging. In the SoundDirect laser scanner, the basic principle is diffraction. Diffraction is a spread-of-light happening in micrometer scale when light encounters edges and openings—the light waves bend around corners and interferes, causing some blurry pattern. A laser beam is scanned over the front of the film and what comes through is caught by a detector. When the beam crosses the soundtrack edges, the detector generates a high-low-high pulse which represents the track width at that particular point. Each subsequent scan builds up a sequence of width-modulated pulses, describing the track in steps as small as 5 microns of film movement.

1. What diffraction does is to change the pulse duration. The negative black track appears to the detector narrower than it actually is, and the user can adjust, in real time interaction, exactly how much, so that the Image Spread is eliminated totally, as good as 30–40 dB. Interestingly, the elimination curve is logarithmic, which explains why exposure steps are somewhat critical, although variable area format is in many ways a more robust format. Note that the Image Spread reduction is not done by software, it is done by the light work itself. When the pulses are recombined into digital or analog sound, the cleanup has already taken place, although the software, of course, plays an important part for the settings of the system

Apart from Image Spread, there are additional improvements for the elimination of other characteristics.

2. As regards dust and scratches, the pulse time modulation is much cleaner than the original track. Small disturbances are ignored by the low trigger level—large spots, of course, affect the beam, but a resulting click has a short rise-time which is ideal for declicking software to detect as being separate from the actual sound. A popular analogy would be the beard-foam-razorblade principle.

3. The material density, and contrast of historic films come with enormous variations. The working principle (diffractive pulse-width) is very robust against this because the pulse timing, not the beam intensity, is what matters. Whether black and white, colour, cyan, or the low contrast of fine grain, as long as there is an acceptable signal, the system works on all these variations. Occasionally, you may come across a film with such low contrast that it cannot be handled, but that situation is extremely rare.

4. Another asset is an oscilloscope view of the track, which shows the scanning characteristics of the soundtrack. This gives an insight into what actually happens on the track, the same way you would use an X-ray to look through a painting, or at the internal workings of a body. In practice, different tracks have their own unique characteristic signature which you learn to recognize and understand.

5. Is there any back side to this? Well, the actual sound rendering is very accurate. That also means that faults in the soundtrack itself are rendered accurately. In other words, a good

soundtrack on bad material may sound very good, while a bad soundtrack on good material sounds as it sounds.

6. Unusual formats exist, such as experimental 3 and 4 multitracks, and even up to a 13-track format. The system is supplied with electronic masking gates which may be set by the users. Typically, two tracks are masked separately to enable stereo when it occurs, but you may combine tracks, or mask off bad edges quite freely.

7. A general note: SoundDirect may be said to represent a new paradigm in technology, called photonics, focusing on light itself as a basis for invention. That means that the actual wave properties of light are used as the workhorse, because they have been revealed and characterized by modern physics and quantum mechanics, and the invention of laser has made it possible to tailor-make those properties into a usable form.

Gilles Barberis has been the head of the sound department of L'immagine Ritrovata film restoration LAB since 2007. He is a lecturer for film restoration at the FIAF schools in Bologna, Singapore, and Mumbai, as well as a sound technology history expert. He has been working on soundtrack scanning for the past nine years.

## References

Eastman Kodak Company. (2001). Cross modulation distortion testing for motion picture laboratory. Retrieved from: http://motion.kodak.com/KodakGCG/uploadedfiles/motion/US_plugins_acrobat_en_motion_support_h44_h44.pdf.

Heiber, R. J. (2015). Considerations for optical soundtracks in a future without film. *Journal of Film Preservation*. Federation Internationale des Archives du Film. Retrieved June 22, 2016 from https://www.highbeam.com/doc/1P3-3710197301.html.

Hurter, F., and Driffield, V. C. (1890, May 31). Photochemical investigations and a new method of determination of the sensitiveness of photographic plates. *Journal of the Society of Chemical Industry*, IX(5), 76–122.

# Practical VisualAudio: A Long Journey to Tangible Results

14

**Stefano S. Cavaglieri**

**Abstract**

VisualAudio, the Swiss optical audio signal retrieval system for coarse-, as well as microgroove discs, based on analog high-resolution photography and subsequent film scanning, has just celebrated its fifteenth anniversary. This long journey eventually has produced a number of tangible results. A post-prototype was put in the production chain a couple of years ago and is has since been jointly operated on regular schedule by a re-recording engineer and a software developer at the Swiss National Sound Archives, proving the degree of maturity reached. We will illustrate some very practical aspects of this system, splitting the workflow into logical processing steps. We will point out the challenges, the ups and downs, as well as any room this technology may have for further improvements. We also mention and compare it to similar systems.

**Keywords**

optical signal retrieval, coarse-/microgroove discs, accurate high-resolution copy, freeze the degradation, preserve history without rewriting it.

## Introduction

The basic idea came from the microscopic observation of the surface of the disc.

If you look at the shape of the groove in figure 1, you may notice that:

- the shape of the groove visually represents the acoustic vibrations, which closely correspond to the electric signal of the recorded sound; and
- there is plenty of information available, but it requires a very high resolution photography or scanning.

## Concept

The following workflow (fig. 2) is quite straightforward:

- the disc is photographed (high resolution copy)
- the film is scanned (image digitization)
- the raw image is processed (groove reconstruction)
- the final image is transduced to sound (sound extraction)

## Hardware

Figures 3 and 4 show our third-generation photo camera. Our first-generation turntable scanner is shown in figure 5.

## Advantages

Why the analog photographic step?

- The photo is an accurate, high-resolution copy.
- It is a quick and reliable way to freeze the degradation of the surface of a disc.
- A certain depth of field is granted by well-known photographic principles.

**Figure 1.**

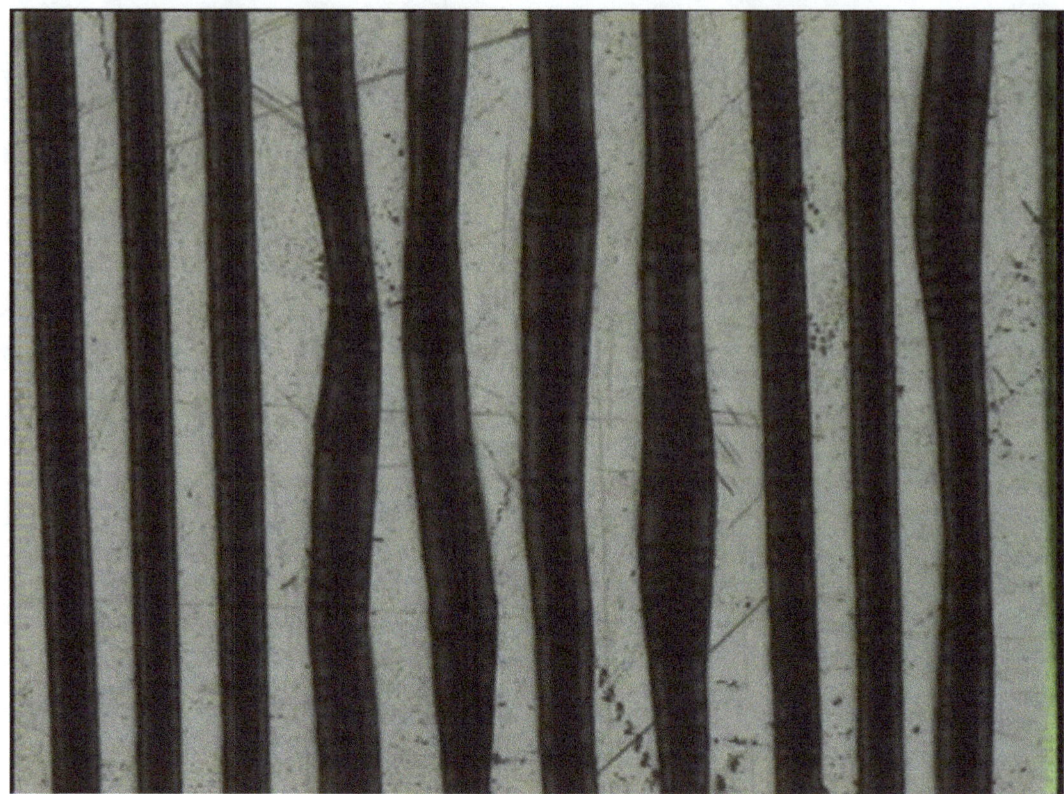

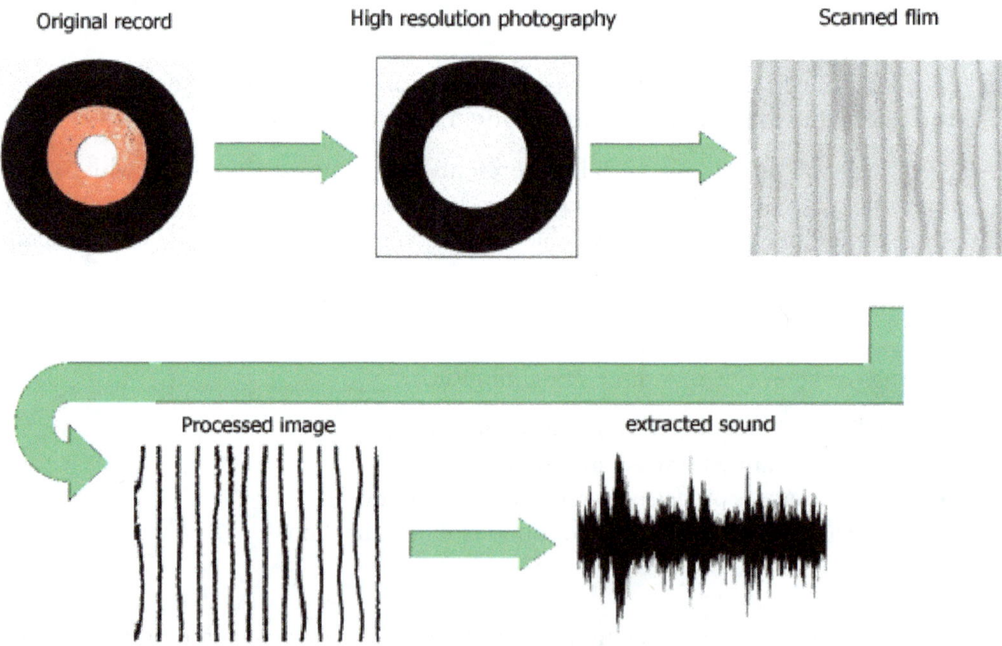


**Figure 2.** A schematic overview of the VisualAudio concept.

And there are a number of additional benefits of analog photography:

- The picture is shot without interfering with the surface of the disc. There is no need to manipulate the disc, except for placing it inside the photo camera. We can take pictures of discs in virtually any condition—delaminated, broken, deformed—and they can, later on, be read and the sound can be restored.
- Each and every disc format, regardless of the size, the speed, or the cutting, is read using the same equipment. We even tried to get a picture off a vertical-cut disc, a typical

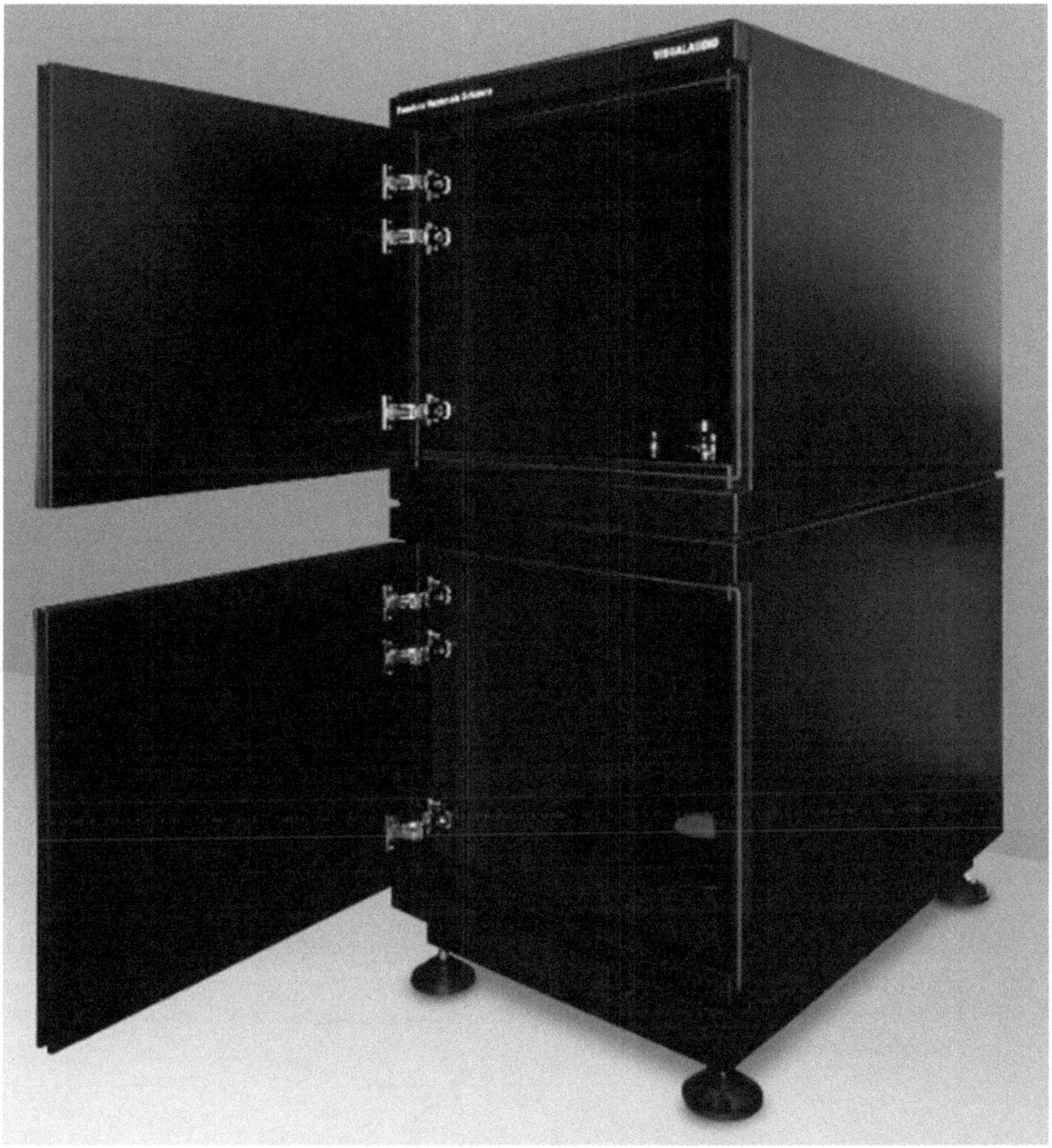

Figure 3.

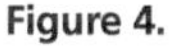

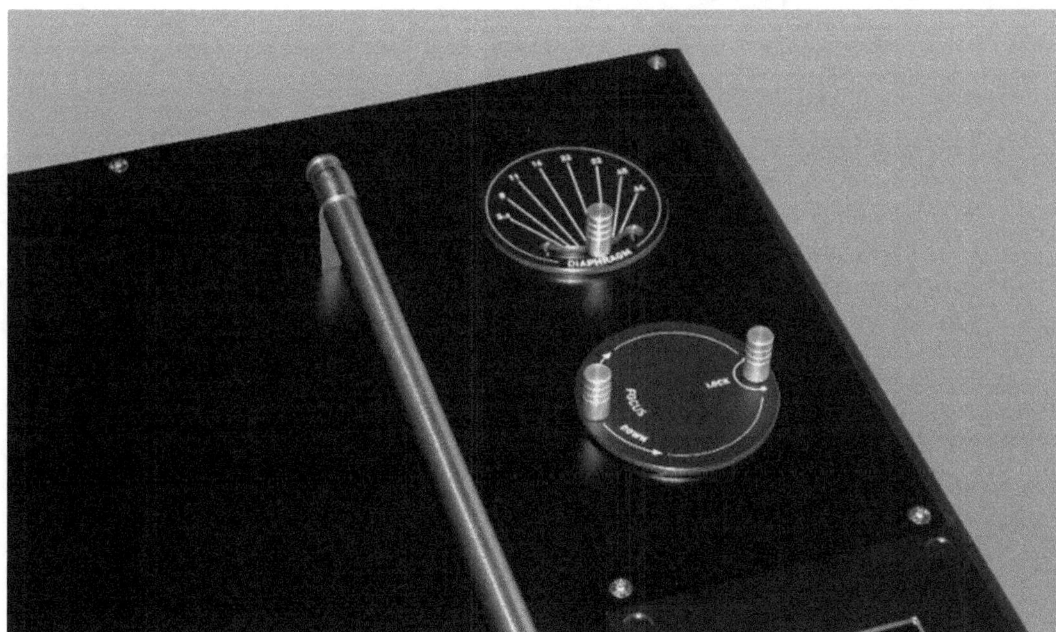


Figure 4.

Figure 5.

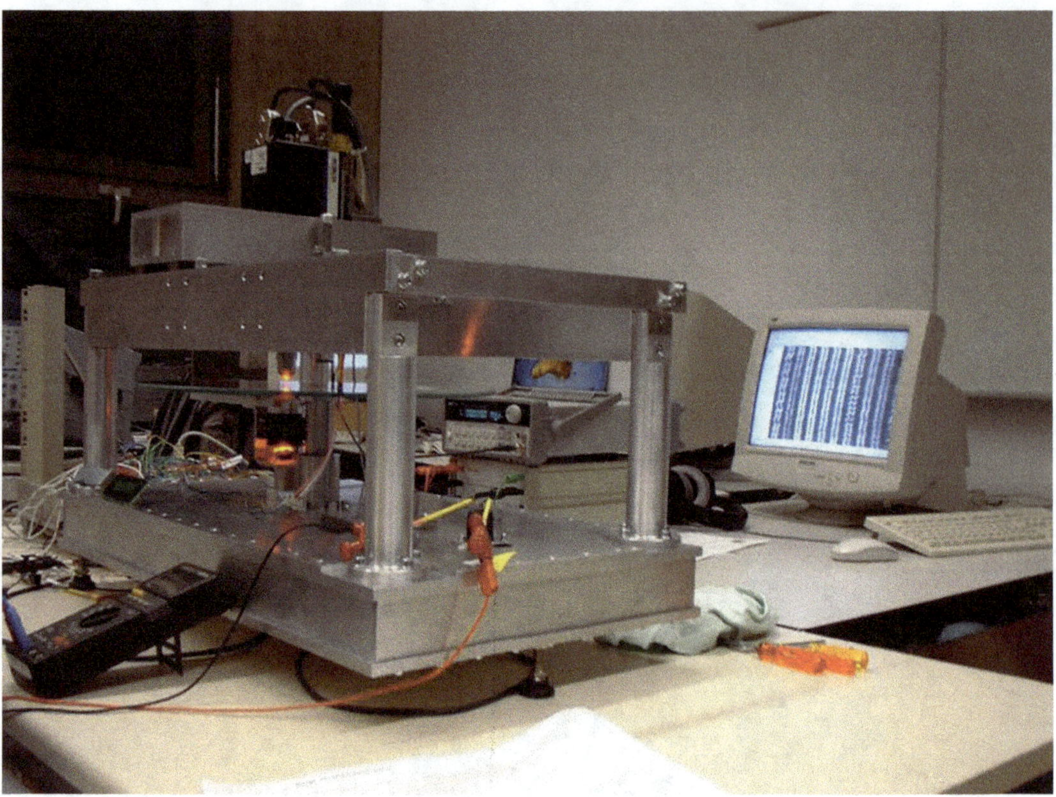

Pathé disc. We were able to look at the groove and to extract the information, despite the two-dimensional system, because the width of the groove changes in function of the depth.

- Image processing is very well established. It is relatively easy to make corrections to the physical incoherencies of the disc.
- Film is a quite stable, small, and cheap carrier for storing sound information. We may consider it a long-term storage format.

## Disadvantages

Is analog film disappearing? If so, by when?

## Performance

The average timings for the points outlined in the workflow are:

- Photography: 10′
- (disc positioning, picture shooting, film development)
- Film scanning: 30′
- (film positioning, ring-by-ring scanning and merge)
- Image processing and image-to-sound transduction: 2h 30′
- (groove alignment and reconstruction, image-to-sound transduction, de-emphasis)

These processes are independent. They may be carried out by various people, in various locations, on a different schedule. If for instance you have two operators in the same room where the picture is shot, you can cut the time by two because one shoots while the other develops, so you can really make it much quicker. The most important step is to get the photographs; later on you can decide to go further.

The timing for steps 2 and 3 is just a guidance, it relies very much on the shape of the disc. These values are typical for processing records that are badly delaminated and cannot be read on a conventional turntable.

## Room for Improvements

The VisualAudio system, as for every known imaging system, has its limits, in terms of reproduced audio quality, for instance. There is certainly room for improvement in the following areas:

- The current image sampling frequency is of 64 or 128k samples/ring, while standard audio sampling frequencies are of 44.1, 48, or 96 kHz. How do these different figures correlate?
- On an image, the radial position of the groove can be estimated by detecting the edges of the groove (2 or 4). On a turntable it is determined mechanically by the pivot and the inertia of the arm, as well as the stylus tracking the groove. What is the impact on the audio quality?
- Image processing extracts the position (i.e., the amplitude) of the groove, while a stylus gets the velocity. Is the derivative (i.e., the signal) the same for both methods? If so, can we apply the same de-emphasis, such as the RIAA or any other less known curves?
- Is it possible to get a better digital image by using a (semi-)automated imaging tool for improving sharpness and contrast and reducing noise?
- Or, thinking outside the box, what about developing a tracing system instead of scanning, that is, something like a laser beam the follows the groove on the image?
- Are any of the other optical retrieval systems, such as IRENE or ELP, suitable for processing our analog pictures?

## Brainstorming

The concept of VisualAudio itself and all the above questions lead to an expansion of our view. Assuming that we summarize the business of audio archiving as:

- To provide broad sonic access to our cultural heritage as it has been captured and preserved in sound
- To provide the faithful reproduction of the intended signal source—"Preserve history, not rewrite it"
- To collect and preserve recordings as a means to provide sonic access

And that there is currently no existing global solution:

- Investment in engineers, technologies, and research not proportional to the mission
- Millions of recordings with grossly insufficient staffing, inadequate tools
- Need for a strategic plan to assess and implement evolving technical advances to address mass transfer and global access

And that today's self-assessment, best-practices model delivers:

- No enforceable mechanism for adherence
- No universal quality control or assurance
- Not supportive of an education degree
- History of incorrect practices

Which possibly lead to permanently corrupted files:

- "Record everything" re-recordings comingle all signal and noise sources and assumes that someone in the future will be better able to address issues
- But there is neither evidence that comingled noises will ever be able to be separated, nor that anyone will ever have time to go back
- Pragmatism can lead to stagnation not innovation

## The Ultimate Goal

The G•MARC initiative, meaning Global Media Archive Research Consortium, is being launched *to support research, develop applications, and design and produce standards-based systems and procedures specific to the needs of media archiving.*

How does VisualAudio fit into G•MARC? Imaging is an objective means for transferring the physical representation of a sound recording (i.e., the groove) to another media while retaining full authenticity.

## Conclusion

Optical retrieval technology for reproducing audio documents is there. A couple of things for making it fly are still missing; however, thanks to such initiatives as G•MARC, the future looks bright.

Stefano S. Cavaglieri is the Chief Technology Officer of the Swiss National Sound Archives in Lugano, Switzerland. His career started back in the late 70s in the audio engineering field. In the late 80s, in parallel to audio, Stefano broadened his interests to computer science and very soon became involved in software design and all things digital storage. His expertise and analytical skills led him to be now recognized as one of the leading technical authorities in the multimedia archives community. In 2011 he was awarded the James A. Lindner prize for his contributions to research in the field of the technology of preservation of recorded sound. Stefano holds a degree both in electroacoustics and in computer science. He serves as an active member of IASA, ALA, and AES.

# Sound Reproduction of the First Speaking Films

15

**Thierry Delannoy**

Abstract

The preservation of the early sound film is a major issue for a curator. Fortunately, over the last few years new scanners have been appearing on the market, which allow us to digitalise optical sound as never before. With the greatest respect for the work of these pioneers of cinema, we will discuss in this article the workflow from scan after mechanical restoration to the movie theater in operation.

Keywords

restoration, optical sound, scanner, sound negative, density, focus.

Digimage Classics is a laboratory which perpetuates the tradition of photochemical fabrication, while at the same time, utilizes the cutting edge of digital technology. We are dedicated to film restoration. Our premises are in Joinville-le-Pont, just outside Paris, on the historic site built by Charles Pathé in 1906. Looking after analogue film treasures is what we do every day with passion.

When restoring a film, the sound is one of our major concerns. Fortunately, over the last few years, new scanners have been appearing on the market which allows us to digitalise optical sound as never before. The invention of new high-definition captors, along with LED lighting, are among the technological advances which have made these new scanners possible. The makers have also taken into account the shrinkage of films, so that entire reels can be scanned with no risk of distortion or damage.

Our first concern when we start a new restoration of a 1930s archive is being able to access the original sound negative which was used for making the positive prints. It is the final element, as validated by the director, with the most precise sound information. It is sometimes the case, however, that the sound negative has been either partially or entirely destroyed. We then seek out the sound positive, fine grain, or optical prints which are the closest or most faithful to the original negative. We often ask the International Federation of Film Archives [FIAF] network for help, and we want to thank the FIAF team for its crucial role.

In the early days of the talkies, several competing processes were patented, the best known of these coming from Western Electric and Tobis Klangfilm. These processes called on the talents of the best engineers of that era. We are often surprised by the richness of the sounds we are able to scan on the negatives, in view of the technical means available for recording at the time. Despite the carbon microphones and the voluminous material which had to be carted around in a truck, the recordings, often of very high quality, testify to the care taken by the sound people during shooting.

In figure 1 and figure 2, we see an engraving of the Radio-Cinéma recording truck, which was used in France. In the early days of the talkies, a stagecoach on the move or a chase on horseback could not, of course, be recorded as the material was too cumbersome, and directors had to take this new constraint into account. From the documentation we have found, we have learned that sound postproduction was in an embryonic state. For the most part, the sound negative was recorded live, with the mixing of noises, voices, music and effects being done in the recording truck during filming.

# LA ROULOTTE AUTOMOBILE *du cinéma sonore*

Un film cinématographique idéal devrait reproduire avec fidélité, dans la salle de projection, toutes les impressions sonores et lumineuses nécessaires pour donner au spectateur l'illusion parfaite de la réalité. Cette tâche est extrêmement vaste et les divers problèmes ainsi posés n'ont, pour la plupart, reçus jusqu'à présent que des solutions encore incomplètes, certains même, comme la restitution des couleurs et celle du relief, n'ont encore fait l'objet d'aucune réalisation vraiment satisfaisante.

En ce qui concerne la reproduction des sons, les tendances actuelles sont nettement orientées, même pour les scènes les plus simples, vers un « truquage » à outrance (voir *Science et Monde*, n° 33) qui donne, il est vrai, dans certains cas, des résultats incontestablement intéressants, mais n'en devient pas moins critiquable en raison de l'abus qu'on en fait. C'est ainsi que la technique des prises de vues sonores au studio a fait, ces derniers temps, des progrès considérables qui ont évidemment pour conséquence que, suivant la loi si naturelle du moindre effort les metteurs en scène font « tourner » au studio la presque totalité des scènes du plein air.

Et pourtant, de l'avis de tous les techniciens qualifiés, les conditions acoustiques et optiques sont de beaucoup préférables à l'extérieur, et les difficultés particulières ne surgissent que lorsque la mise en scène vient à se compliquer exagérément.

Du seul point de vue technique, la prise d'un film en plein air s'effectue exactement de la même manière, mais plus simplement qu'à l'intérieur d'un

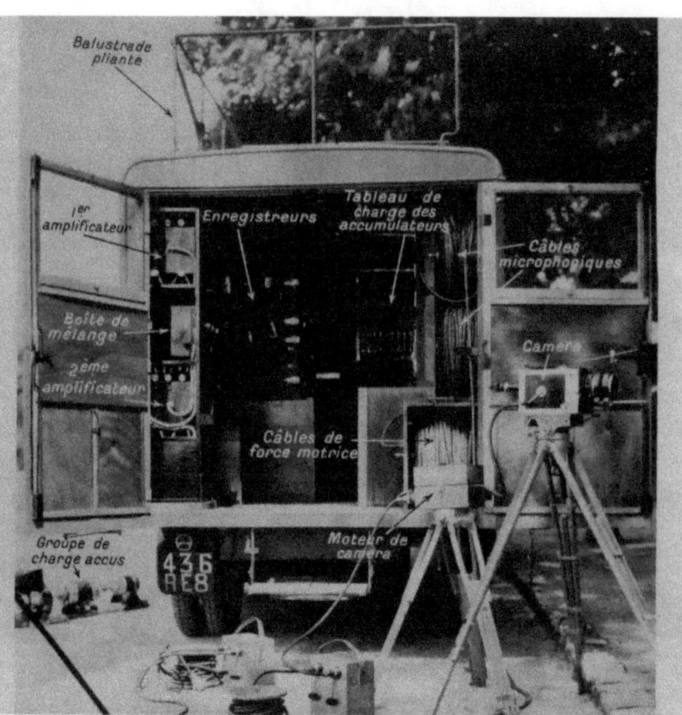


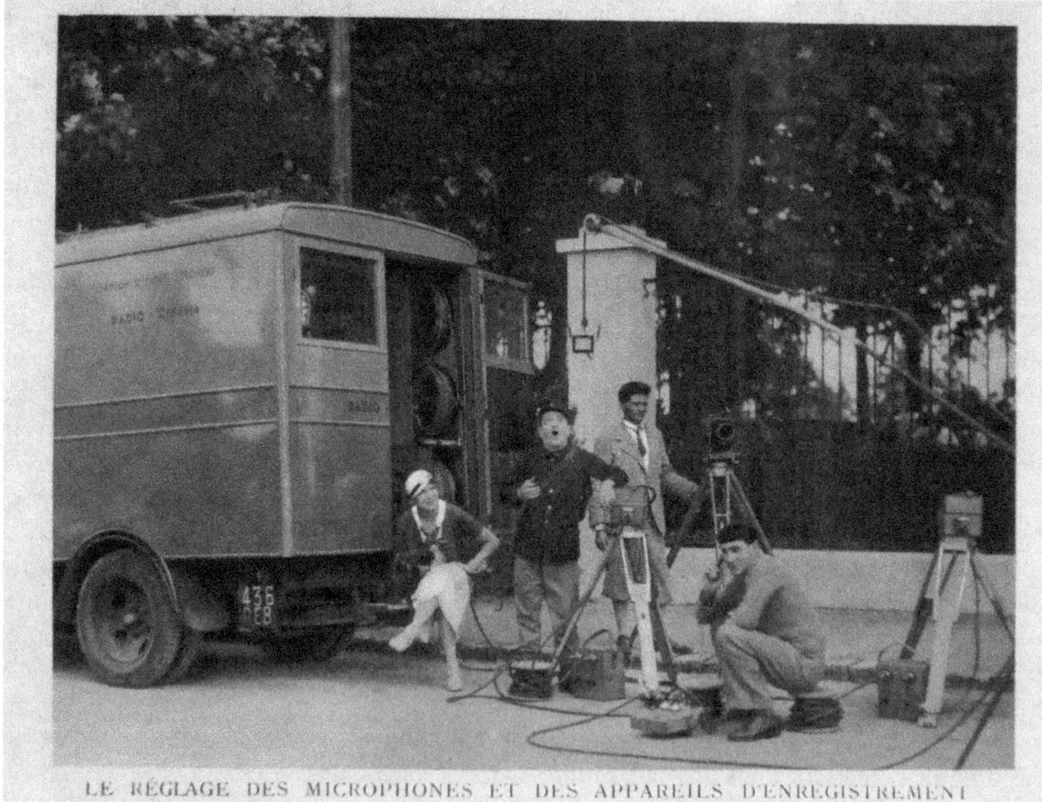

LE RÉGLAGE DES MICROPHONES ET DES APPAREILS D'ENREGISTREMENT

Figure 3 is our Resonance machine, with a toothed wheel that adapts to shrinkage. The 1k camera captures 48,000 lines per second and reconstitutes the entire range of the sound spectrum. With a precision of a few microns, it can read variable density, as well as variable area.

Figure 4 is a screen capture of our software. On the left side of the image we see the result of the sound capture, and the right side shows the corrections made by the software.

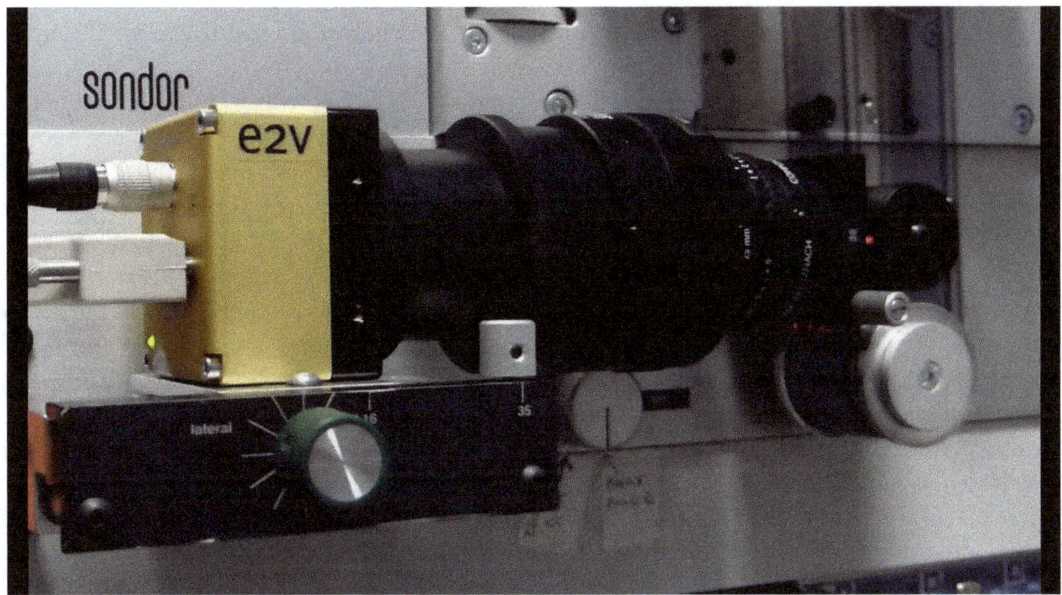


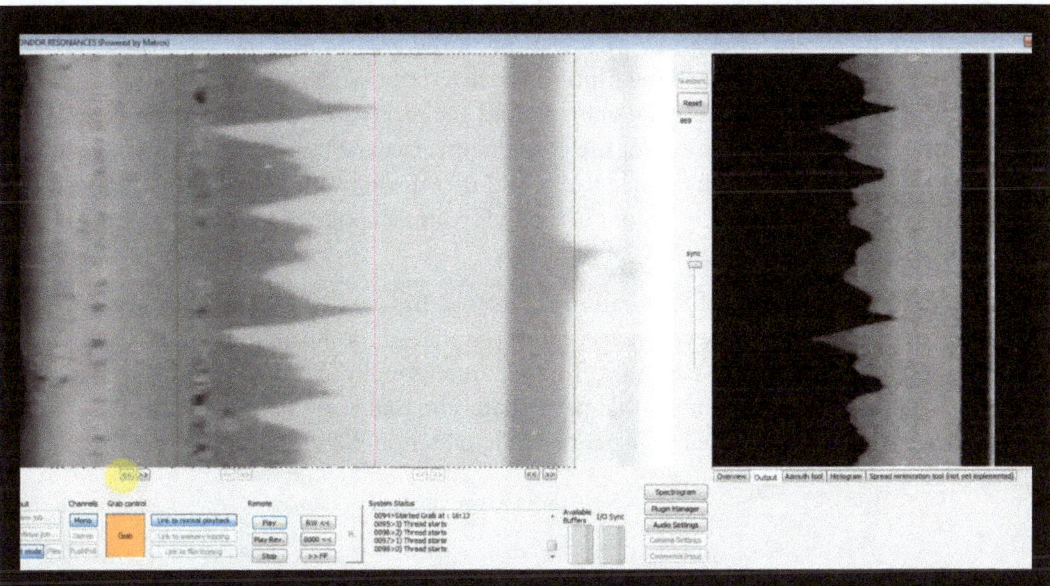

We must first define a capture zone if the elongation is not in the right place, and we move the cursors to capture the useful part of the support. Then the software enables us to intervene as regards density and contrast, and to simulate the printing of a positive sound. If the optical sound is not homogenous, we have to do several captures in order to extract the best from a sequence.

We also have a tool with which we can rectify dust, as well as wear and tear during capture. It is a tool we have to use with moderation because it can distort the modulation if used with too heavy a hand.

It is essential that focus is done at the moment of capture, because a loss of definition will immediately result in a loss in high frequencies.

We are perpetuating our photochemical know-how because it is evident that there will be no point to this wonderful machine if we cannot repair films so that the splices and perforations can pass through the player without damage. There is no wet gate system for the capture of sounds, yet it is of vital important for the film to be cleaned and for all stains and mould to be removed. It is not possible to obtain a decent result if the film is stained with moistures and dust.

Optimising the capture is the guarantee of a quality final result. When we are satisfied with the digitalization, we proceed to a first stage, called "de-clicking," which consists of removing all the disturbing elements in the modulation, such as the clicks and pops, the muffled sounds generated by the splices, the parasite frequencies, and so forth.

Next, we have to sort out the colour of the sound as well as its texture. Sound reproduction systems in cinemas, but also in people's homes, have made huge strides forward. For people watching these films, we want to restore the sound to find it as close as possible to how it was when the films came out in the 1930s. However, we cannot expect people to use photoelectric cells and valve amplifiers, to abandon their 5.1 or Dolby Atmos equipment, or to reduce the bandwidth by half in order to recreate the conditions of the 1930s. We must, therefore, adapt these sounds to current reproduction technologies, but without betraying them. We must also respect the audio mix in its mono artistic conception. That which was conceived mono must remain mono. Of course, it would be too dangerous and risky to project a nitrate print, but when a safety print exists, we project it, because it is a good starting point: the results obtained by digital means must be compatible with those obtained in photochemistry. In a calibrated cinema auditorium, our task is to make the sound comprehensible and pleasant to the ear; the voices of the actors are a reference, and we know we are moving in the right direction when human voices sound natural. So, needless to say, we strive to preserve every detail present in the sound.

The sound from the 1930s testifies to the lack of possibilities available in its final fabrication. The talkies created new professions, such as the sound mixer, sound-effects engineer, and re-recording operator. We preserve the faithful testimony of the past.

One final anecdote, reported by Marcel Pagnol, the grandson of the novelist, playwright, and one of the most successful talking-films filmmaker, Nicolas Pagnol. After a sound engineer criticised the timbre of his voice, the actor Raimu took his revenge by throwing olive stones violently on the floor—very painful for the poor engineer's eardrums!

The beginnings of sound in cinema can sometimes make us smile today, but they also continue to move us, and it is an honour for our laboratory in 2016 to reconstitute these early sounds recorded by the pioneering engineers of the 1930s.

Thierry Delannoy, Head of Restoration at Hiventy, has worked since 1988 in scanning 35 mm feature film and for seven years in film restoration for theaters and festivals, such as Cannes Classics, Imagine Ritrovata, Toute la mémoire du monde. Hiventy (formerly Digimage Classics) is a laboratory that perpetuates the tradition of photochemical fabrication while being at the cutting edge of digital technology dedicated to film restoration.

# Marginal Analysis of Digital Video Archives Restoration Project

16

**Yang Haisheng and Jiang Huijun**

## Abstract

The research on the optimization of digital video archives restoration is conducted through marginal analysis. Based on the interaction among three production factors (the contents, the techniques, and manpower in the restoration projects), an optimal scheme is formed for reference.

## Keywords

digital restoration, restoration principles, technological process, marginal analysis.

## Introduction

The passage of time is increasingly aging the historic video archives. The restoration and utilization of these archives has, therefore, become a major issue for current archives management. The digital restoration proposed in this paper uses the frame information (i.e., HSV) to fill and repair the missing and damaged parts of digitized video archives, in particular those recorded on magnetic tapes. It aims to restore images and restore them close to the original condition.

The frequently used technology of video restoration mostly relies on the film postproduction and restoration equipment. However, there is a lack of available equipment to restore the types of damage that particularly affect broadcast magnetic tapes, as shown in figure 1. At present, the restoration work is often performed manually with the consequent low efficiency and high cost of investment in equipment and labor. These problems directly restrict any improvement of the efficiency of restoration.

With the rapid development of Internet applications in multimedia, the demand for the reexploitation and reutilization of precious video archives grows. In order to balance cost and value, the authors, from the perspective of marginal analysis, try to optimize the production process of restoration to maximize the benefits.

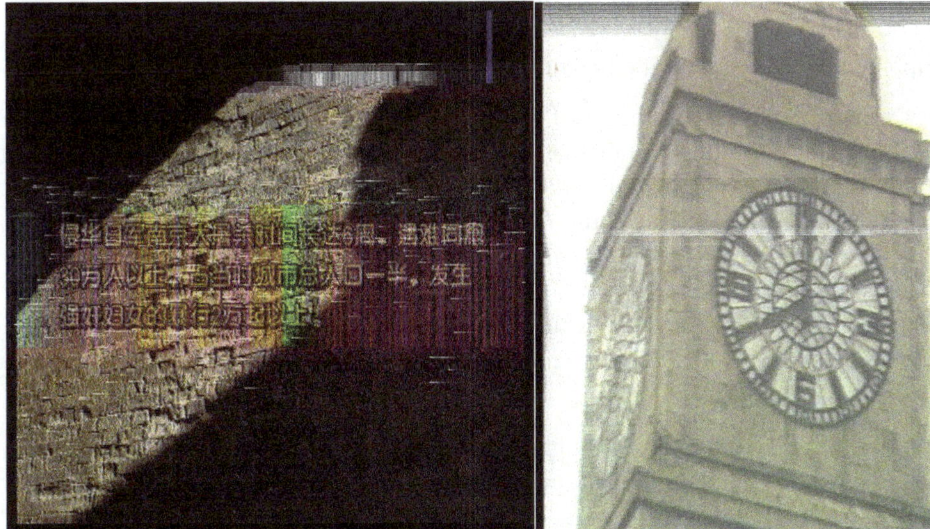

**Figure 1.** Types of magnetic tape damage.

## Production Issues on the Digital Restoration

The digital restoration of video archives is a long-term process during which the following issues occur frequently.

### Low Use Rate after Restoration

Taking actual data (see table 1) of the restoration and reuse in Shanghai Audio-Visual Archives, the annual use rate of the restored video in the archives increases at first, and then decreases with the progressively increasing capacity of restoration.

At the beginning, the use rate increases with the restoration amount, but as the restoration amount increases to a knee point, the use rate stops increasing and a decreasing trend shows up (see fig. 2).

**Table 1.** Annual restoration and use

| Year | Annual restoration (min.) | Use after restoration (min.) | Use rate |
|---|---|---|---|
| 2010 | 544 | 13 | 2.39% |
| 2011 | 450 | 20 | 4.44% |
| 2012 | 302 | 22 | 7.28% |
| 2013 | 550 | 51 | 9.27% |
| 2014 | 606 | 37 | 6.11% |

### High Restoration Costs

So far, the easily available standard products which are widely used in restoring film damage (i.e., the technical equipment can be selected and purchased directly from the market) cannot fully meet the restoration requirements of damaged magnetic tapes. That leads to high costs both in manpower and equipment for the tape restoration.

- High cost of manpower. Because of the lack of available restoration equipment for magnetic tapes, more manpower has to be allocated to restore magnetic tapes than is required for the restoration of damaged films. That leads to high labor costs.
- High cost of equipment. In addition, the standard products selected and purchased directly from the market for use in the restoration of magnetic tapes often require purchasing both hardware and software equipment. That leads to a high cost of equipment but poor compatibility with the surrounding system.

### Slow Improvement of Restoration Efficiency

The slow improvement of restoration efficiency is reflected as follows:

- Heavy workload required by manual restoration. The features of the current system using the standard products show that more manual restoration is needed to keep the machines operating. The manual operation a six-month training period. Therefore, simply increasing the available equipment does not raise restoration efficiency.
- Lack of skilled and experienced personnel. Video archives digital restoration demands high levels of competence (excellent painting skills, image quality appreciation and computer equipment control, etc.) from the operational staff. Hence, professionals are in urgent need.

## The Three Production Factors for Digital Restoration

We discovered that three production factors affect the efficiency of video archives digital restoration. They are (1) contents, (2) techniques, and (3) skilled manpower.

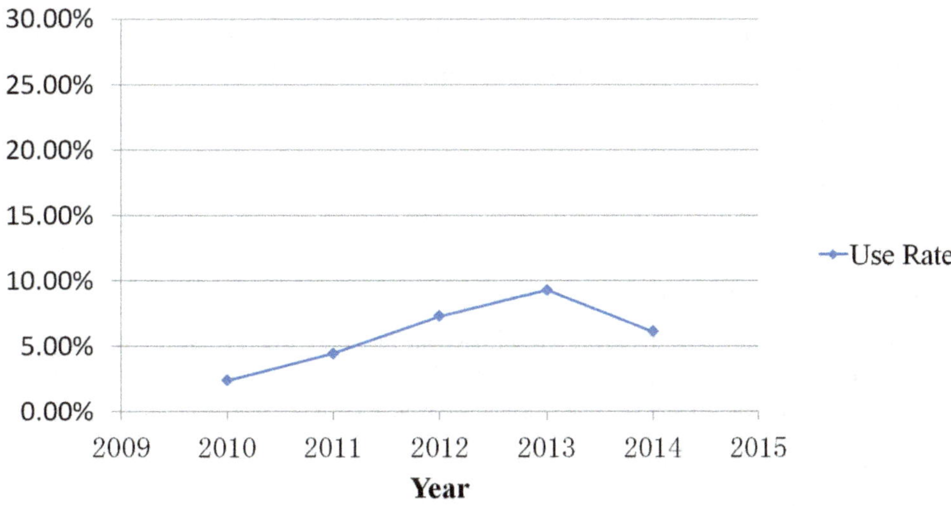


**Figure 2.** Curve for use rate after restoration.

Experience has shown that the efficiency of restoration follows the law of diminishing marginal returns. That is, the gains made through improving one productive factor while maintaining the other factors will, sooner or later, progressively decrease.[1]

- Supposing the content to be restored is fixed, an increase in production will not directly increase the utilization of the restored content.
- If the restoration technology and equipment is unchanged while the strategy of restoring content remains constant, the initial rate of restoration will increase if manpower levels are increased. However, beyond a certain level of manpower increases, the growth rate of production is going to decrease.
- In addition, more restoration equipment encourages new demands for the existing restoration technology and equipment environment until a bottleneck is reached.

From this it is clear that blindly increasing the labor force or the available equipment does not always enhance the marginal returns of archival restoration.

When the marginal benefits of restoration surpass the marginal costs, the restoration project will be in a state of high value; when costs surpass benefits, the project will be in a state of low value.

Hence, in order to maximize the marginal returns, the input amount and proportion of the most economical factors of production should be set, in the light of the quantity of the restoration. In order to make the greatest gains from the work to improve the efficiency of the restoration processes, the quantity of material to be restored using the most economic methods must be controlled. From the perspective of production factors, the following is going to analyze the interaction among them.

### Analysis of the Contents to Be Restored

The restored content is analyzed using the following four factors:

1. Value Classification

   The archives can be divided into three grades according to their value:

   - Important: the archives (1980s) reflect most recent social development
   - Very Important: the archives (1950s–1980s) present social changes
   - Highly Important: the archives (-1950s) show the history of the society

2. Amount to Be Restored

Shanghai Audio-Visual Archives, at the moment, holds a total of about 510,000 hours of digitized video archives with about 123,700 hours of them requiring some level of restoration. Listed below is the ratio of the content requiring restoration from each of the three value grades:

- Important: 70.5%
- Very Important: 29.2%
- Highly Important: 0.3%

3. Use Rate after Restoration

The recordings to be restored are chosen at random, but generally speaking, the larger collection has a greater probability of being used. Therefore, the estimated use rate of restored video archives is ranked by value-grade as

Important > Very Important > Highly Important

4. Degree of Quality Damages

Materials from different periods suffer different types and degrees of damages:

- Important: damage include spots, flickers, scratches, etc.
- Very Important: most damage is irregular scratches which specifically belong to magnetic tapes
- Highly Important: most damage consists of vertical scratches, mildew stains, and so forth, which usually arise on the tapes transferred from films.

To raise the use rate of the restored archives, the production plan should be arranged intelligently by the selection of content to be restored by a combination of the estimated use rate and the value distribution. Meanwhile, to improve the restoration efficiency, restoration techniques appropriate to the damage should be adopted (see fig. 3).

## Analysis of the Restoring Techniques

Alternatives to the restoration techniques for digital video archives can be provided by

- purchasing the standard products (mentioned before as topological standard products, mainly suitable for film carrier); and
- developing in-house techniques and systems (on the basis of the types of magnetic tape damage of the holdings).

As for the video archives on magnetic tapes, we recommend the self-developed software system to conduct the restoration.

For instance, the irregular scratches, as a type of damage of magnetic tape (see fig. 1) are caused by magnetic particles shedding or head clogging of the playback machine. The scratches often appear in thick horizontal stripes with black on the left and white on the right. This varies with time sequences but the position of scratches remained basically unchanged. This kind of damage can be restored by using a damage detection algorithm[2] based on perceptual code. Extreme points can be labeled through a gray morphology processing method, so that the scratches can be automatically detected using similarity and connectivity rules of perception.

This restoring algorithm brings about a clear improvement in the efficiency of restoring this kind of damage. In addition, improving the level of intelligent restoration software is also helpful for its efficiency.

The feature analysis of the self-developed system and the standard commercial products are shown in table 2, which indicates that the self-developed system and the standard products have

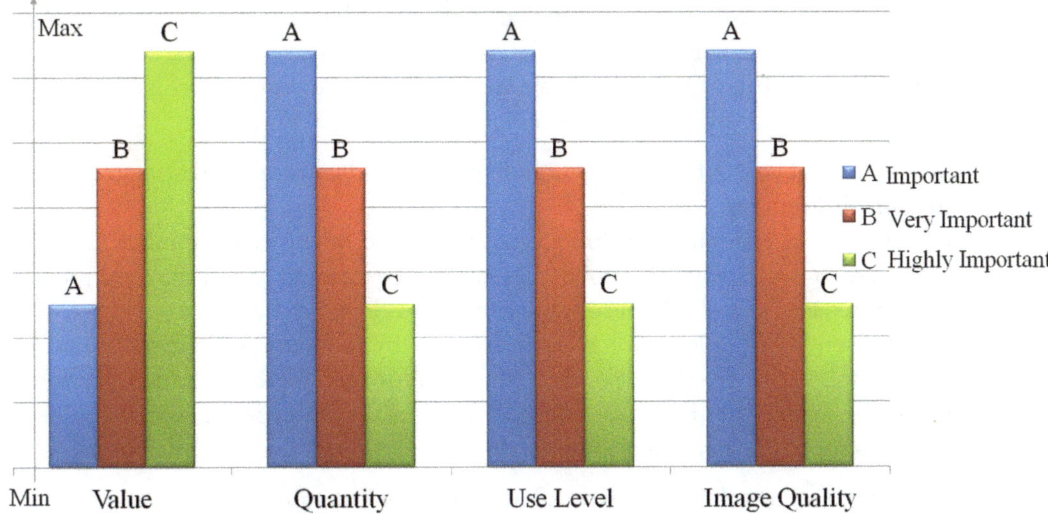


**Figure 3.** The feature analysis of the holdings.

their own strengths in restoration. The self-developed system has lower topological cost, higher restoration efficiency and better compatibility.

**Table 2.** The feature analysis of the standard products and the self-developed system

| Equipment name | Percentage of topological cost in the original single unit cost | Upgrade cycle | Restoration techniques | Average restoration efficiency (see note below) | Compatibility with the existing system | Format of input and output |
|---|---|---|---|---|---|---|
| Standard product system | 100% | Waiting for new version or alternative product | Color effect is obvious; for thin vertical scratches, noise reduce restoration without any traces; but for irregular scratches, manual operation is needed | 1:50 | Need to develop relevant interface | Support mainstream high-standard format |
| Self-developed system | 5% | 1 ~ 2 years | Can automatically restore magnetic tapes with different damaged types, especially for restoring big blotches, irregular scratches | 1:40 | Fully compatible | Support mainstream high-standard format |

**Note:** Average restoration efficiency means ratio of the playing length of the contents to be restored to the real time spent in restoration.

## Analysis of the Manpower

The third important production factor of digital video archives restoration project is the manpower.

1. Total Investment in Manpower

The total investment in manpower depends on the cost of the restoring equipment and the environment of the restoring hardware.

2. Specialized Skills of Individuals

Restoring digital video archives requires more operational staff with a higher comprehensive level of training and experience. Without the relevant experience guiding the restoration and operation, it takes a longer time to train the skilled operators. What's more, the specific restoring effects and efficiency rely heavily on operators' personal experience.

Summarily, how to strike a balance among these three production factors is the key issue the restoration project of massive video archives faces.

- The selection of content for the restoration plan should consider the estimated use rate and value distribution.
- The selecting of restoration techniques and the investment in equipment should be appropriate to the damage types of the archives to be restored. Then standard products can be purchased or restoration software can be developed in-house.
- The distribution of the labor force complies with the total amount of restoration to be undertaken and the investment in the training in the techniques to be used. Personnel training, especially the transmission of restoring skills from experienced staff to newer colleagues should be paid great attention to improve the production efficiency.

The following discusses the solutions used to create more marginal restoring returns in the Shanghai Audio-Visual Archives.

## Optimizing the Restoration Workflow

The digital restoration of video archives should adhere to the mode of project management, that is, be operated and maintained. The restoration workflow should be optimised by managing the following procedures:

- Making an annual restoration plan
- Perfecting the working process
- Improving the restoring quality evaluation system
- Establishing a restoration database
- Updating the equipment and techniques

In the light of the three production factors, the best scheme with the best investment ratio has to be devised to maximize the marginal benefits.

### Optimizing the Content Selection

There exists a certain connection between the selection of the contents to be restored and its use rate after restoration. The use rate tends not to be ideal if we only consider the value determined by age when selecting the content to be restored. Neither is the restoration efficiency at the highest. According to the feature analysis of the archives' value grades in 3.1, it is impossible to maximize the marginal benefits while blindly selecting the contents to be restored. We should:

- Distribute the restoration ratio of archives in the different value grades by the use ratios over the years.
- Estimate the future use rate in light of the market demand and then make pertinent arrangements for production.

Table 3 shows the proportions of content to be restored that we put forward for an annual plan.

**Table 3.** Proportioning of contents to be restored each year

| Value grades of the holdings to be restored | Annual proportion in the total amount of restoration |
|---|---|
| Important (1980s–) | 45% |
| Very important (1950s–1980s) | 35% |
| Highly important (–1950s) | 20% |

## Optimizing the Technical Line

1. Different Technique for Different Damage Type

Table 4 explains the different restoration conditions for different value-graded archives:

- The important archives (1980s–): have higher image quality and a real-time restoration with simple noise reduction algorithm could be adopted.
- The very important archives (1950s–1980s): have various types of damage and can be restored mainly by real-time restoration supplemented with various algorithms.
- The highly important archives (–1950s): have a higher estimated use rate and can be restored frame-by-frame to restore the images to their original quality.

**Table 4.** The contents to be restored and technical requirements

| Value grades of the holdings to be restored | Technical requirements for restoration |
|---|---|
| Important (1980s) | Simple and real-time restoration by use of automatic noise reduction |
| Very important (1950s–1980s) | Special restoration software algorithms |
| Highly important (1950s) | Frame-by-frame manual restoration |

2. Adopt the Self-developed Techniques

Magnetic tapes, because of the shedding of magnetic particles, are likely to produce large quantities of irregular horizontal scratches. The effect of the existing home made products, however, is limited when faced with this kind of damage. It is considered, therefore, that the independent research and development of restoring software system to improve horizontal scratches on magnetic tapes, is the best technical line.

Shanghai Audio-Visual Archives, considering the characteristics of the types of damage, has developed a digital video restoration system for dealing with the following 10 typical damage types:

- Color distortion correction
- Contrast and brightness correction
- Noise reduction
- Flicker elimination
- Random spots removal
- Big blotches removal
- Definition improvement
- Small scratches removal
- Irregular scratches removal(the restoration effect see Figure 4)
- Large lost images check and repair, etc.

The algorithm for handling the pictures' fundamental attributes (i.e. the correction of color distortion, contrast and brightness and improving resolution) can adjust the parameters to improve the picture quality by employing individual experience. The rest of the restoring algorithm has two main steps: automatic detection and automatic repairing. Automatic detection is used to locate and estimate noise by computer vision model in both the spatial and temporal domains. The results of the automatic detection are used for interpolation based on domain correlation by motion estimation and motion compensation at the stage of automatic repairing. Our system has functions of task allocation and process operation, which are suitable for large-scale industrial application.

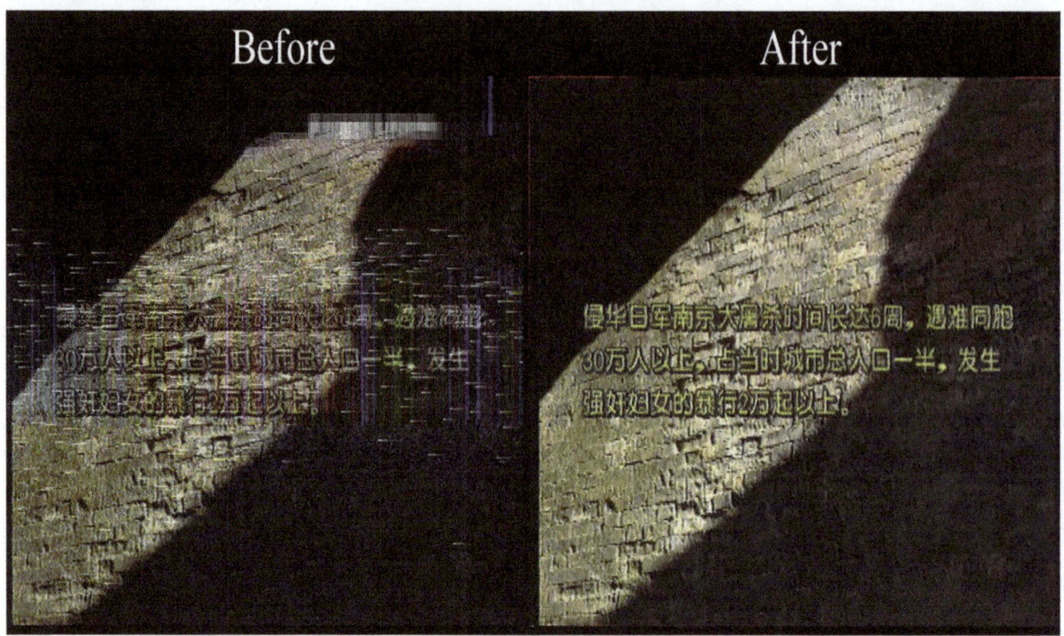


**Figure 4.** Restoration effect of the irregular scratches.

## Optimizing the Human Resources

The human resources optimizing can be achieved by these two suggested methods:

- Enhance the professional restoring skills of personnel by standardizing the restoration principles and procedures and by strengthening knowledge training.
- Reduce the burden of professional demands on the operators by upgrading the restoration system with more intelligent functions based on the experience and knowledge gained from operating the restoration system.

Here we have two questions raised to explain further about the above methods.
Q1: What are the restoration principles?

- Select and preserve the best edition

Before setting about the restoration, it is advantageous to search for the copy of the material with the highest definition and the least damage from the collection. If necessary, the material can be redigitised and the more distinct fragments can be edited in to replace damaged sequences, by which basic information (i.e., colors, brightness, etc.) and adjustment parameters can be provided to the follow-up restoration. As to those archives which cannot be restored by means of the existing techniques, a relatively untouched edition should be kept for future technological innovations.

- Maintain the Original Untouched

The main principle of restoring historical video archives, "maintain the original untouched", tells us that altering the original material to "improve it" using subjective decisions is not allowed. We should try to recover the original features, keep the brightness and tonality of the initial videos, repair damage caused by extrinsic factors (i.e., physical damages, humidity, mustiness, etc.), rather than painstakingly try to beautify the damage.

- Balance Quality and Noise Reduction

In the process of digital restoration, reducing noise always brings about the reduction of image quality. Under such circumstance, noise reduction must be based on the premise that normal recognition and identification of the contents won't be disturbed, instead of focusing too much on its effects.

Q2: What is the Guiding Process of Restoration?

This following guidance is proposed. It is offered as a result of repeated verification and correction by practical restoration experience, and will keep being optimized and supplemented in the future operations.

(a) Browse the entire video archives, and section them in accordance with still/motion, black and white/color, single damage/composite damage;
(b) Record the basic parameters (i.e., brightness, contrast, colors), and unify the restoration targets;
(c) Observe the defects using the relevant algorithms, and adjust the parameters to improve the restoration effect;
(d) Add the corresponding algorithm for different sections, and record the section to be restored again;
(e) Record the parameters of the algorithm, and when the optimal restoration effect is achieved, try to apply them to other sections;
(f) Because the sequence of the algorithms affects the restoration result, try to determine the best operating sequence of the algorithms if there is more than one algorithm for one section;
(g) Restore the relevant sections two or three times;
(h) Examine and revise the image in coherence caused by adding different algorithms in sections;
(i) Carry out manual restoration on parts of the frames for fine repair.

Overall, the optimization scheme for digital video archives restoration is summarized as follows:

- Optimize the content selection: Figure out a reasonable proportion of contents from each of the different value-grades for an annual restoration plan. We advise an inverse ratio between the value-grade and the planned restoration volume.
- Optimize the technical lines: Adopt the software and system developed in-house for magnetic tape restoration to improve the efficiency; choose different algorithms for different types of damage.
- Optimize the human resources: Reduce the dependence on professional skills to cut the high cost of labor force, by carrying out the management of experience and knowledge, upgrading the equipment and increasing the intelligence of the systems.

## Prediction of the Optimized Scheme

### Comparison: The Optimized and the Non-Optimized

According to marginal benefits theory, the above concrete optimization scheme was proposed after deep analysis of the following three production factors:

- The contents to be restored
- The technical line
- The human resources

In order to maximize the marginal benefits and promote the development of industrialized restoration, we make a comparison between the non-optimized schemes and the optimized one based on a set-up restoration project model.

Now taking the example of Shanghai Audio-Visual Archives, a restoration project model is set up with:

- 3 restoration workstations (PC)
- 3 restoration operators
- 264 working days annually

The comparison is illustrated as follows between the non-optimized scheme and the optimized one.

**Table 5.** The annual plan of restoration project non-optimized

| Type to be restored | Proportion of annual restoration | Efficiency of single device | Time consuming (day)** | Effect | Benefits | | Costs | |
|---|---|---|---|---|---|---|---|---|
| | | | | | Annual output (min.) | Use rate | Manpower (rmb) | Equipment (rmb) |
| Important | 33.3% | 1:30 | 52.8 | Significant | 739.2 | 3% | | |
| Very important | 33.3% | 1:60 | 105.6 | Significant except for the irregular scratches | 739.2 | 1% | | |
| Highly important | 33.3% | 1:60 | 105.6 | Significant | 739.2 | 2% | 6,000×12 ×3 = 216,000 | 580000×3 = 1,740,000 |
| Total | 100% | | 264 | | 2217.6 | 6% | 1,956,000 | |

**Table 6.** The annual plan of restoration project optimized

| Type to be restored | Proportion of annual restoration | Efficiency of single device | Time consuming (day)** | Effect | Benefits | | Costs | |
|---|---|---|---|---|---|---|---|---|
| | | | | | Annual output (min.) | Use rate | Manpower (rmb) | Equipment (rmb) |
| Important | 45% | 1:30 | 98.6 | Significant | 1380.4 | 8.5% | 5000×12×3 =180,000 | 640,000+ 30,000×2 =700,000 |
| Very important | 35% | 1:30 | 76.7 | Significant | 1073.8 | 3% | | |
| Highly important | 20% | 1:60 | 88.7 | Significant | 620.9 | 1.5% | | |
| Total | 100% | | 264 | | 3075.1 | 13% | 880,000 | |

*(** 7 hours of per working day in the tables)*

As the comparison shows, the optimized annual restoration scheme (see table 6) has archived higher marginal benefits, which means higher *outputs* and *use rate after restoration* with lower marginal costs in both manpower and equipment. The specific optimizing measures are as follows:

- The contents to be restored: the equal distribution has turned into different proportions adjusted according to the use demands
- Techniques and equipment: Independent developed techniques and equipment help to make great improvement in the restoring efficiency of the *very important* archives

## Actual Data of the Optimized Scheme

We consider the use rate after restoration as the highly important factor for evaluating the restoration benefits; hereby especially analyze and compare the actual use rate after restoration between the non-optimized situations and the optimized one.

The actual data of yearly restoration projects recorded by Shanghai Audio-Visual Archives in the past 6 years shows that the use rate after restoration has been improved in 2015 after optimization (see Table 7).

Figure 5 illustrates the trend of the annual use rate after restoration from 2010 to 2015. The dotted line indicates its trend if the optimization had not been carried out in 2015.

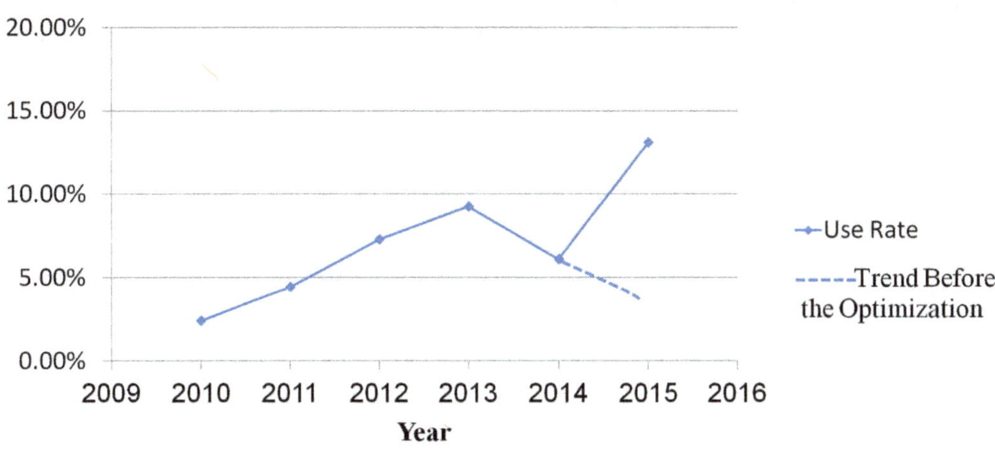


**Figure 5.** Trend of use rate after restoration.

**Table 7:** Annual Use Rate after Restoration

| Year | Optimized/ Non-optimized | Annual restoration output (min.) | Use amount after restoration (min.) | Use rate |
|---|---|---|---|---|
| 2010 | | 0 | 11 | 3.04% |
| 2011 | | 450 | 16 | 3.56% |
| 2012 | | 302 | 22 | 4.50% |
| 2013 | | 554 | 37 | 6.74% |
| 2014 | Non-optimized | 606 | 23 | 3.92% |
| 2015 | Optimized | 702 | 92 | 13.11% |

## Conclusion

Digital restoration of video archives involves many factors. Through marginal analysis, archive institutes can put forward methods to increase outputs and improve the use value by researching the interactive relationship among the three main production factors: the contents to be restored, the techniques, and the manpower.

- Allocate a reasonable proportion of those archives to be restored according to the data analysis and market demands prediction, to improve the use rate after restoration.
- Restore the archives with the mode of project management, form a reasonable management mechanism, and keep to perfect techniques.
- Follow the three restoration principles, and accumulate and correct repeatedly the knowledge of restoration, to raise the restoration efficiency.

Considering the cost and benefit, the exploration of the restoration techniques and maximizing the marginal benefits of large-scale production will be our eternal goal.

Yang Haisheng, Senior Engineer, has long worked in the field of broadcast information technology management, and is director of Copyright Assets Centre of Shanghai Media Group (SMG) and Shanghai Audio-Visual Archives, former vice director of the Information Centre of Shanghai Media and Entertainment Group (SMEG), former director of General Engineer Department of Shanghai Media and Entertainment Group (SMEG).

Jiang Huijun, works as an engineer engaging in broadcast media assets management in the Technology Department, Copyright Assets Centre of Shanghai Media Group (SMG).

## Notes

1. Tao, D. (2003). Marginal utility analysis of transportation production of transportation enterprise[J]. *Journal of Wuhan University of Technology*. (2)
2. Yang, Z. (2012). Automatic detection method for line scratches in old film and video [J]. *Ideo Engineering*. (7).

# Digital Video Damage in Archives: Detect, Repair, and Prevent—Results from the DAVID Project

17

**Peter Schallauer and Franz Hoeller**


## Abstract

The DAVID project[1] studies how to keep digital audio-visual content usable in the face of adversity: obsolescence, media degradation, and indeed failures in the very people, processes, and systems designed to keep digital content safe. For file- and tape-based digital video DAVID analyses the origin of potential damage and its consequences on the usability of content, detects and restores damage that has already happened, and develops strategies for avoiding future damage in a way that balances long-term costs, risks of loss, and content quality.

The presentation gives an overview of the major findings of the two-and-a-half-year research project, it will present results on audiovisual preservation metadata standardisation (MPEG MP-AF) and will especially focus on the detection and restoration of damage in digitised and born-digital audiovisual content. We present solutions to detect and repair errors of file-based audiovisual objects in the baseband/essence/content level; that is, we will show how digital tape dropouts (Digital Betacam, IMX and others), field issues, and other baseband errors can be detected and restored.



## Keywords

archive, video, damage, detect, repair.


## Introduction

DAVID is a European Commission Framework Program 7–funded research project that aims at keeping audiovisual content (video) usable in the face of adversity: format obsolescence, media degradation, and failures in the very people, processes, and systems designed to keep digital video content safe. The aim of the DAVID project is to address following questions:

- How does damage occur in digital file and digital video tape-based systems used for preservation and access? What are the consequences of this damage on the ability to make use of audiovisual content?
- How can this damage be efficiently monitored and detected?
- Accepting that damage will occur, how can content be repaired to enable reuse?
- Are there better ways to structure media files that make them more resilient?
- How can the technical quality of content be improved beyond the original state to satisfy requirements of new use channels and to ensure efficient storage utilisation?
- How can all this be done at scale and at speed for large audiovisual collections?
- How can effective risk management and quality assurance techniques be built into preservation systems so that the systems themselves become more robust and resilient?
- How can better preservation techniques be incorporated directly into the devices and systems that produce born digital content?

The project consortium includes the broadcaster Österreichischer Rundfunk (ORF) and the national archive Institut National de l'Audiovisuel (INA), both with experience of research and development in digital preservation; the two industrials HS-ART Digital Service GmbH (HSA) and Cube-Tec International GmbH (CTI) on the supply-side providing media migration, digital restoration, and quality control; and the two research partners Joanneum Research

(JRS) and University of Southampton—IT Innovation Centre (ITInnov) with long histories in digital audiovisual content analysis and restoration, risk management, and storage technologies and services.

DAVID has produced following main project results:

- Report on Data Damage and its Consequences on Usability (Deliverable D2.1)
- Report on Analysis of Loss Modes in Preservation Systems (Deliverable D2.2)
- Digital BETACAM Dropout Detection Tool
- Block Dropout Detection Tool
- Advanced Field Error Repair Tool
- Noise Repair Tool
- Video Echo and Overshoot Correction Tool
- MXF D10 File Repair Tools
- BPRisk: Risk-Aware Preservation Workflow Planning and Optimisation Tools
- Preservation Metadata Model and Library
- Report on Recommendations for Born Robust AV Content (Deliverable D3.5)

More information on othe tools developed can be found at the website spotlight section,[2] and public reports (including those mentioned above) are available at the website deliverable section.[3]

## Selected DAVID Project Results

Selected results are provided for the project research areas damage detection, damage repair and damage prevention.

### Damage Detection

#### DIGITAL BETACAM DROPOUT DETECTION

The Digital Betacam tape format is a major digital, high-quality archiving format. First mass migration projects (from tape to file) started recently. Due to the high market acceptance, the migration of all Digital Betacam tapes is expected to be continued for many years. A major class of errors which may occur is digital tape dropout. They need to be found during migration of content into IT-based storage systems, as later detection and repair causes higher costs due to the need of re-ingesting tapes or is even impossible when tapes are further degraded.

Within the DAVID project, JRS developed a content-based (essence-based) algorithm for the detection and repair of Digital Betacam tape dropouts. We have developed initial detector prototypes for two specific dropout classes, as there are *luminance dropouts* and *chrominance dropouts*, first, by utilizing specific spatial properties of single blocks affected and second, by using also the spatiotemporal distribution of multiple affected blocks within the frames.

The detector supports two modes. The *basic mode* provides a decision about which frames within a video are damaged to what degree, and the *detailed mode* provides the exact position of all damaged blocks within a single frame. The basic mode prototype of the Digital Betacam tape dropout detector can be incorporated in essence QC systems like VidiCert; the detailed mode prototype can be utilized within AV media repair systems like DIAMANT.

#### BLOCK DROPOUT DETECTION

For detecting a broad range of digital tape dropouts, originated from tape formats different to Digital Betacam, a more general detection algorithm was needed . Similarly to the previously mentioned type, these dropouts may also occur during the migration process, but have a different appearance. Instead of a chessboard structure, these dropouts appear as blocks or horizontal stripes within a constant block size. They need to be found during migration of content into

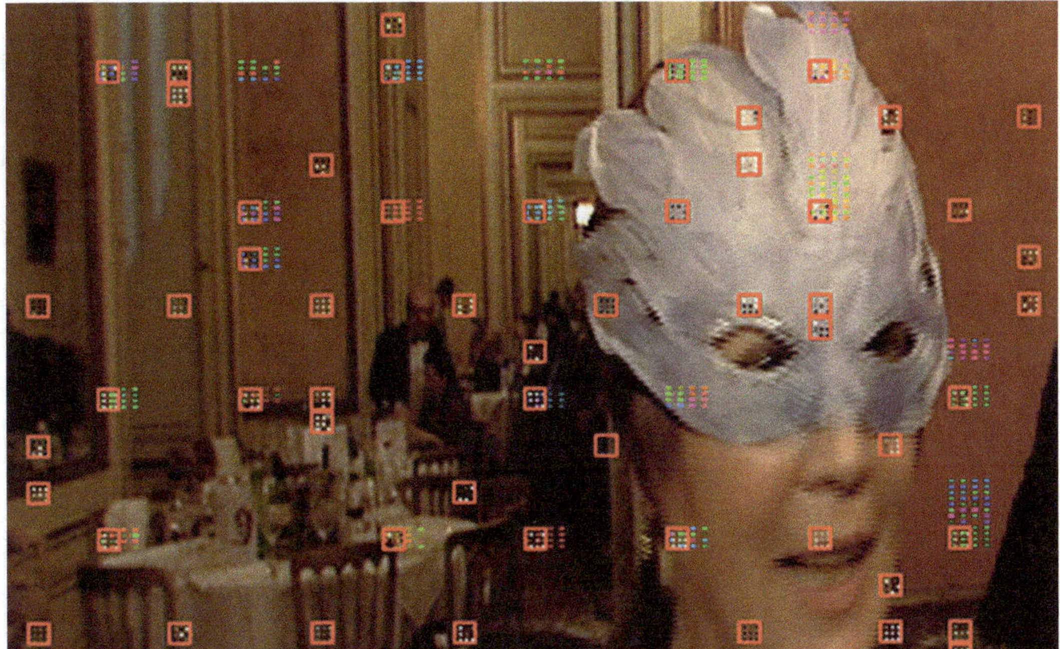

**Figure 1.** Digital Betacam luminance dropouts found by the JRS dropout detector prototype. © ORF, JRS.

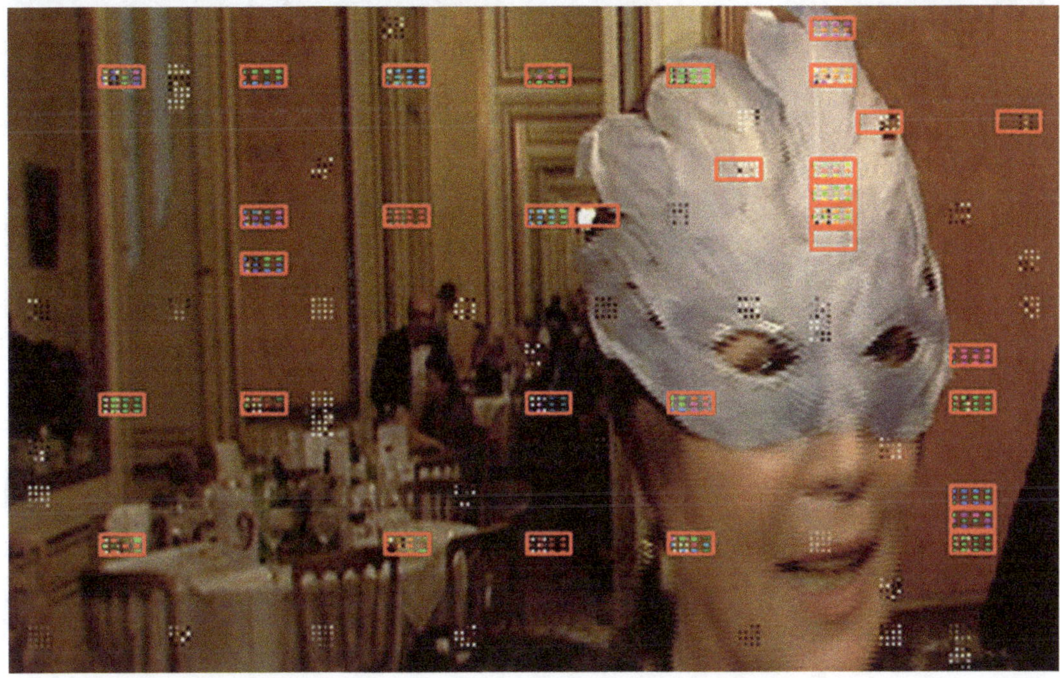

**Figure 2.** Digital Betacam chrominance dropouts found by the JRS dropout detector prototype. © ORF, JRS.

IT-based storage systems, as later detection and repair causes higher costs due to the need of re-ingesting tapes or is even impossible when tapes are further degraded.

Within the DAVID project, Joanneum Research developed a Block Dropout detection algorithm which is able to find block dropouts in one or multiple frames of the video. An automatic grid detection algorithm allows for the detection of the block size and its corresponding regular block grid location.

## ADVANCED FIELD ANALYSER

The Advanced Field Analyser (AFA) is a tool which is able to automatically detect various field issues which may be found in digital AV files. The AFA was designed as a core library and can easily be integrated into different workflows.

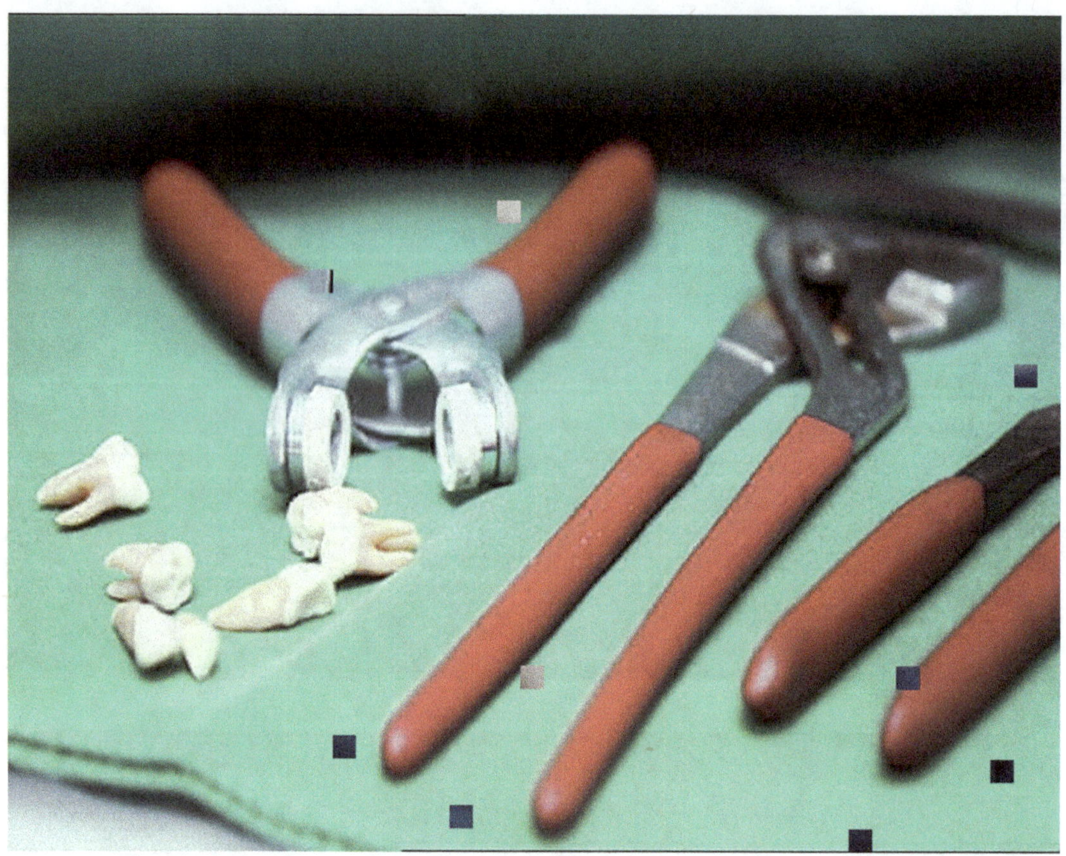

**Figure 3.** Sample frame affected by block dropouts. © ORF.

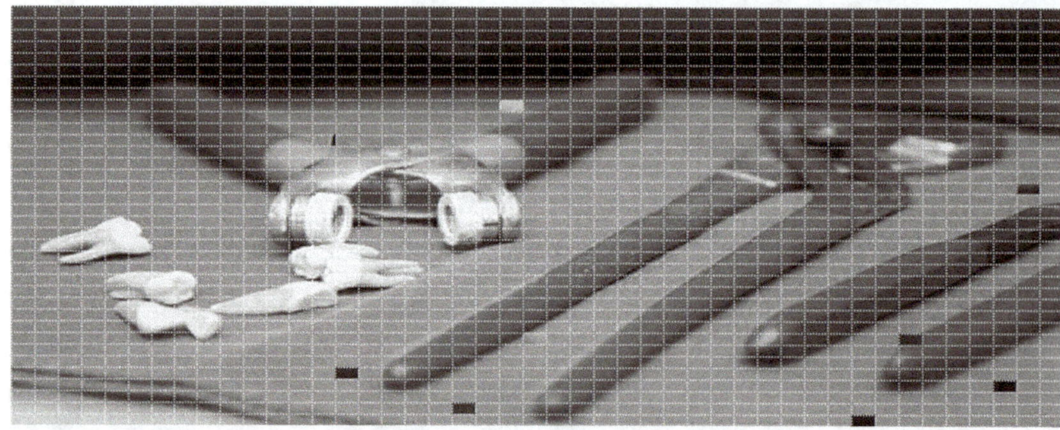

**Figure 4.** Block grid found by the JRS block dropout detector prototype. © JRS.

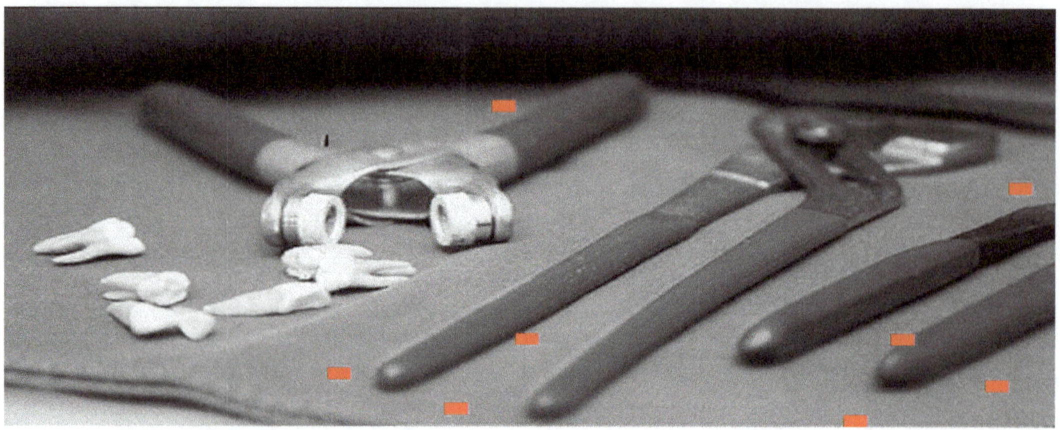

**Figure 5.** Block dropouts found by the JRS block dropout detector prototype. © JRS.

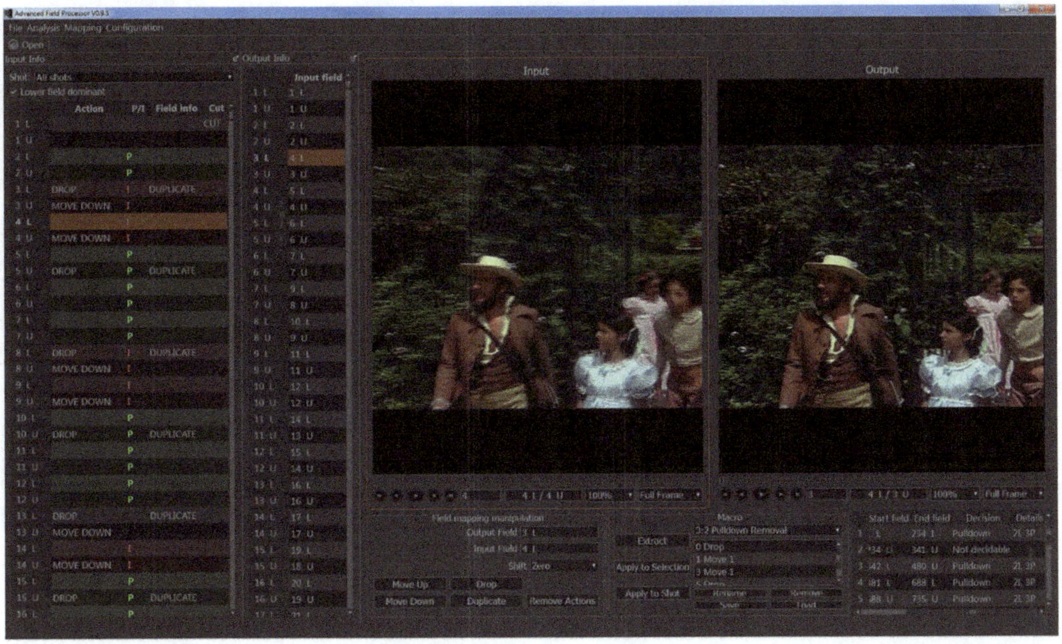

Figure 6. Screenshot of the Advanced Field Processor. © HSA.

## Damage Repair

### ADVANCED FIELD ERROR REPAIR

The Advanced Field Processor (AFP) developed by HS-ART Digital Service uses the results of the Advanced Field Analyser and is able to correct various field issues. Some corrections can be done quite simply; for example, if the fields are only in the wrong order, we just need to exchange upper and lower field. A key functionality is to remove a pull-down generated by the telecine process. After the pull-down removal (reverse telecine) we should have progressive images again. The AFP is able to handle scene changes and pull-down pattern changes automatically if the AFA is delivering the right patterns.

But there are a lot more field issues out there which cannot be handled automatically by any software. And there is no solution on the market which allows an interactive fix by a user using "manual" methods in an easy way. So the other strength of the AFP is that it will allow to manually fix a large variety of field problems.

### NOISE REPAIR

The occurrence of noise, digital sensor noise as well as film grain noise, reduces the perceived quality of video and film significantly and lowers the viewing experience of a consumer. In times where Full HD TV (1920 x 1080) is mainstream and Ultra HD TV (3840 × 2160) is upcoming, this becomes even more evident. Furthermore, noise has an adverse influence on efficient storage utilization for long-term preservation as the high-frequency noise components require encoding with a higher bitrate, or when the bitrate is limited (e.g., in a Blu-Ray production or for satellite delivery) noise causes encoding defects (e.g., blocking).

JRS developed within the DAVID project a highly automated, highly scalable noise repair algorithm which allows archives to exploit their content properly—for example, for TV or DVD/Blu-Ray release. Due to the high degree of automation and the good scalability, the method is expected to work for a broad range of archive content and the costs for content exploitation are expected to decrease. We plan to achieve a high degree of automation by adapting the noise repair algorithm automatically to the noise characteristics (noise magnitude, coarseness, signal dependency) occurring in the content.

An initial noise repair algorithm prototype was developed within the first year of DAVID; it utilizes the information from the current frame (or field) and its temporally neighboring frames

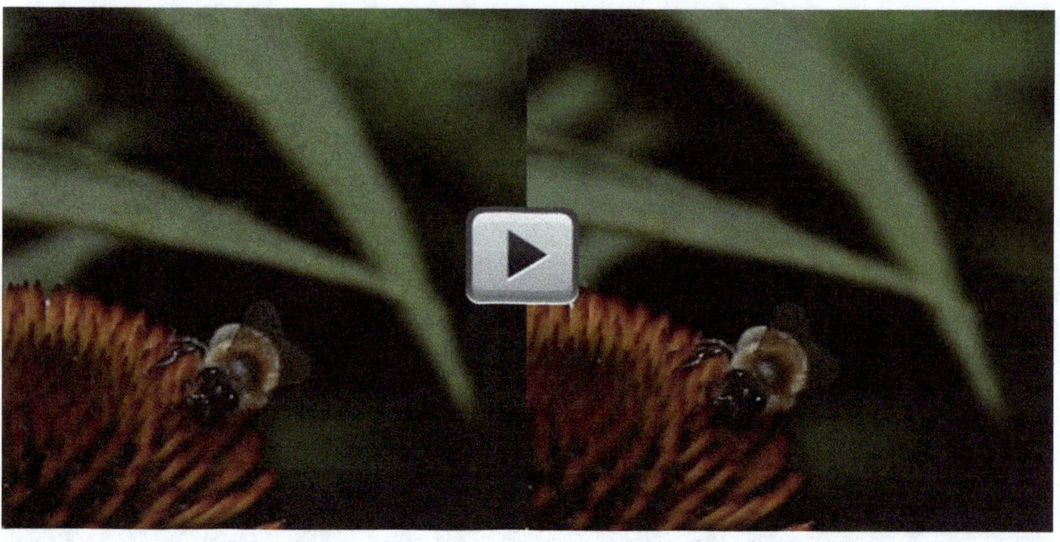

**Figure 7.** DAVID noise repair prototype. Left: original, right: noise repaired. © Peter Schallauer, JRS.

in order to reduce noise in the current frame. Novel methods have been researched which are applied within the initial noise repair algorithm in order to keep the introduction of artifacts at an absolute minimum. A sample noise repair video is available at the DAVID website.

### MXF D10 FILE REPAIR

In 2013 ORF detected in its archives a defective collection of MXF files, which originated from an earlier mass migration project of SD video tapes. In total, about eight thousand hours of video material were affected to a degree that no further usage was possible.

Re-ingestion of the original video tapes was not an option because of cost and time constraints. ORF was looking for a software solution that is capable to repair the damaged files. Because there was none available it was decided to solve that problem within the DAVID project.

ORF sent a representative subset of damaged files to DAVID partner Cube-Tec International for pre-investigation. Cube-Tecs engineers were able to analyse the origin and symptoms of the occurring errors. As a result, a customized repair tool has been developed. This version can now fully automatically detect the occurring errors in different combinations, in the MXF container as well as in the MPEG bitstream. With this new procedure, errors are fixed selectively, and at the same time the bitstream is wrapped into a fully standard-compliant MXF file. Neither reencoding nor rewrapping would have solved these problems. Transcoding was no option; because of the quality reasons, re-ingest would have been the only alternative.

Additionally, an MD5-checksum is created to allow easy independent checks of the file integrity at any time. The progress of the repair process as well as results of the file checks are automatically monitored and reported monthly in consolidated form directly to the ORF. The Cube-Tec team provide the operation and maintenance of this repair service via remote supervision.

## Damage Prevention

### PRESERVATION METADATA MODEL AND LIBRARY

DAVID has developed a preservation metadata model, which has been contributed to standardisation of the MPEG Multimedia Preservation Application Format (MP-AF).

The scope of the preservation metadata model is to document the history of creation and processing steps applied, as well as their parameters. The model serves as interface between various components that produce preservation-related metadata in different (often proprietary) formats and consuming applications, such as risk management application.

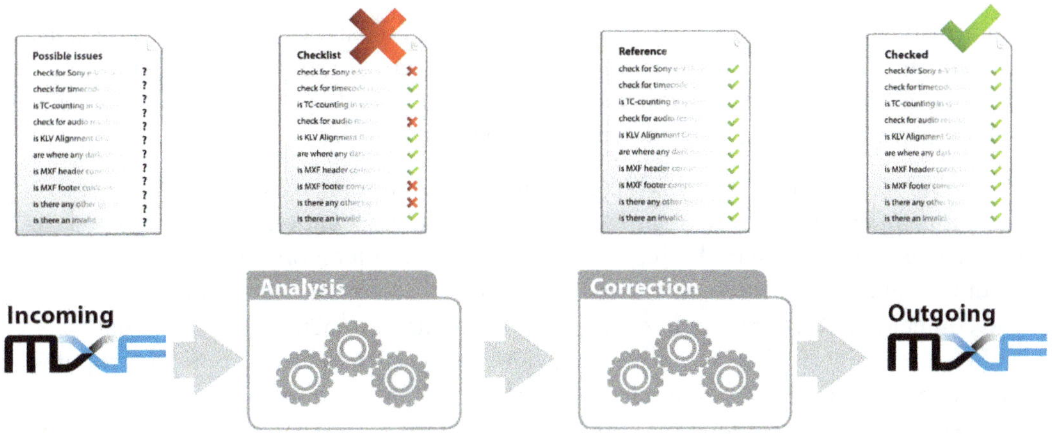

Figure 8. MXF D10 file repair workflow.

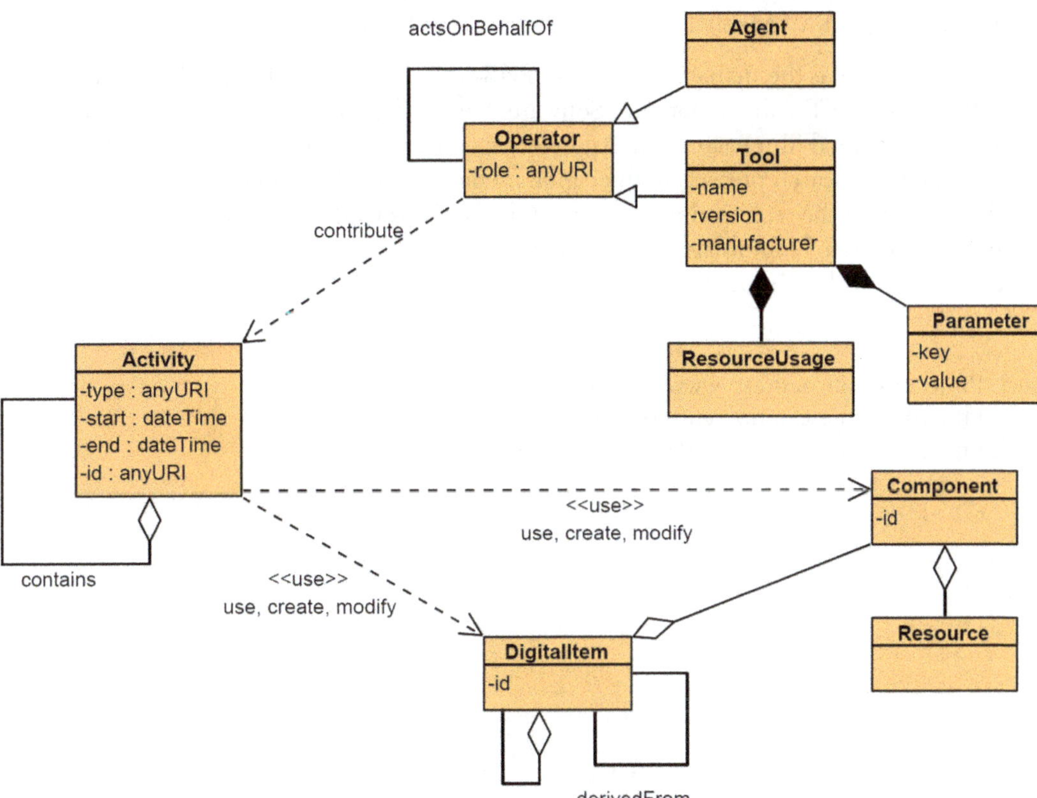


Figure 9. DAVID Preservation Metadata Model.

The model represents the preservation actions that were actually applied. The model supports a set of specific types of activities in the model (e.g., digitisation, with possible further specialisations, such as film scan), in order to improve interoperability between preservation systems. It also describes the parameters of these activities.

The model is designed around three main groups of entities: content entities (DigitalItems, their components, and related resources), activities, and operators (agent, tool) and their properties. The content entities are created, used or modified in an activity, which involves operators that contribute to performing the activity. The basic entities of the model and their relations are shown the figure below.

The DAVID preservation metadata model has been contributed to the standardisation process for the MPEG Multimedia Preservation Application Format (MP-AF), expected to be finalised in 2016. More details about the data model can be found in this publication.

In order to handle documents conforming to MP-AF, JRS has implemented a C++ library. With this library application developers are able to create preservation metadata descriptions, manipulate them, serialize to XML, and deserialize—with validation—from XML. Target operating systems are Windows, Linux/Unix, and Mac OS X systems, supporting the 32- and 64-bit versions of the systems respectively. The library has been published under the open-source license LGPL v3, and is available at https://bitbucket.org/wbailer/mpaflib.

Peter Schallauer has worked with Joanneum Research since 1995 as scientific and development coordinator for creating numerous digital video/movie technologies and productive systems. Systems for high-quality digital film restoration (DIAMANT-Film), automatic movie and video content analysis, content description, information mining and content-based retrieval, efficient digitisation and documentation of audiovisual archives, semantic analysis of video, traffic video analysis, and efficient human computer interaction. In recent years he has focused his research on signal-based video and movie quality assessment tools for improving the efficiency of archive digitisation and production processes (VidiCert). He is actively involved in relevant standardisation activities (EBU QC, EBU/AMWA FIMS QA). He coordinated the EC FP7 project DAVID—Digital AV Media Damage Prevention and Repair.

Franz Hoeller is the managing director of HS-ART Digital, and the product manager for the DIAMANT-Film Restoration Software. He works as trainer and consultant in the fields of digital film restoration. As project manager he was involved in several international research projects in the digital media area. He has a master's degree in telematics from the technical university in Graz and has worked as R & D software engineer in the fields of image restoration and processing at Joanneum Research in Austria and Pandora-International in the UK.

## Notes

1. Project website address: www.david-preservation.eu.
2. http://david-preservation.eu/spotlights/.
3. http://david-preservation.eu/publications/public-deliverables/.

# PREFORMA and the MediaConch Project: Open-Source Tools for Open Standards

18

**Erwin Verbruggen, Dave Rice, Bert Lemmens, Jérôme Martinez, Ashley Blewer, Emanuel Lorrain, Antonella Fresa, and Claudio Prandoni**

## Abstract

In the PREFORMA project, collection holders pool their resources to work with experts at small- and medium-sized companies. This collaboration is made possible through a "pre-commercial procurement" approach, funded by the European Commission and memory institutions across the continent. After a selection and early design process, the project awarded MediaArea, who previously built the widely used MediaInfo application, the contract to: (1) do standardization work on an open-source format for video, and (2) develop a toolset that performs policy checks and corrects remaining errors in the build-up of incoming or existing files. This paper gives an overview of the format selection process, the development work that has gone into building the MediaConch toolset, and the standardization activity of the selected preservation format for audiovisual assets.

## Keywords

digital preservation strategy, OAIS model, conformance checking, policy checking, normalization, file format selection, open file formats, audiovisual archives, open-source software, standardization process.

## Introduction

In the PREFORMA project, collection holders pool their resources to work with experts at small and medium-sized companies (or SMEs). This collaboration is made possible through a "pre-commercial procurement" approach, cofunded by the European Commission and memory institutions across the continent. The project seeks to develop solutions for three file types: documents, still images, and audiovisual materials. After a selection and early design process, it awarded MediaArea, who previously built the widely used MediaInfo application,[1] the contract to: (1) do standardization work on an open-source format for video, and (2) develop a toolset that performs policy checks and corrects remaining errors in the build-up of incoming or existing files. This paper gives an overview of the format selection process, the development work that has gone into the building of the MediaConch toolset, and the standardization activity of the selected audiovisual preservation format.

## The PREFORMA Challenge

A file format is a standardized way of encoding information for storage. Pragmatically, different software applications and versions can vary in the exact ways they implement or apply a certain standard. Regarding long-term preservation efforts, memory institutions should have full control of the process for testing the conformity of files to these standards before they are ingested into their archives.

The conformance checker software developed in the PREFORMA project is intended for use within the Open Archival Information System (OAIS) Reference Framework. It focuses in particular on the OAIS ingest function, which represents the first step in the digital curation and preservation workflow. PREFORMA aims to work on one specific step in the OAIS process, that is, file validation. The tools it is tendered for are developed in an iterative process, with multiple releases, and with a number of experiments with 'real' data sets (files) from memory institutions.

One of the most important technical challenges institutions and organizations that focus on long-term storage face, is the tactic of normalizing the files within their collections. When an organization decides to limit the number of file types it takes responsibility for, it makes managing these files a less haphazard task. Homogeneous collections allow for bulk monitoring and bulk solutions. A conformance checker can help by narrowing down the variety of files for ingest. For the PREFORMA project, a conformance checker should:

1. verify whether a file has been produced according to the specifications of a standard file format;

2. verify whether a file matches the acceptance criteria for long-term preservation by the memory institution;

3. report, in human and machine readable format, which properties deviate from the standard specification and acceptance criteria; and

4. perform automated fixes for simple deviations in the metadata of the preservation file.

A memory institution needs to know the files they create or receive are healthy. Validation tools help control whether composition is correct. If a file is malformed upon arrival, this must be known upon ingest. Whether the institution's policies say that the error should be corrected (and thus change the original), or note the flaw in the metadata, a memory institution needs tools to aid this purpose. The main objective of the PREFORMA project is to give memory institutions these types of tools—by developing a toolset that enables the testing process to happen within an iteration fully under the memory institution's control.

PREFORMA's research and development activities aim to empower memory institutions to gain full control over the technical properties of preservation files. This is achieved through the development of an open-source conformance checker and the establishment of a healthy ecosystem around an open-source 'reference' implementation of three specific file formats.

## Selecting an Audiovisual File Format

The audiovisual files that memory institutions receive need to be highly adapted to the (post) production and distribution workflow of the domain in which they are produced. Files from broadcasters are made for streaming and efficient editing. Files created for film productions have extensive functionality for encrypted access to the content. These properties often complicate and weaken the long-term preservation of the content. Workflows in audiovisual collections mostly rely on professional broadcast and film production software for efficient and reliable processing of audiovisual files. Consequently, collections prefer using the corresponding proprietary formats for managing these files.

For PREFORMA, fitness for long-term preservation depended on the following four criteria:

1. A format that is lossless. The format should be able to capture content in an uncompressed or mathematically lossless encoding, and retain as many original properties as possible (i.e., bit-depth, resolution, etc.). Not losing information in compression is a requirement for implementing an effective preservation strategy. This condition meant ruling out well-adopted but lossy codecs.

Based on experience from digitization projects, PREFORMA considered the advantages of lossless compression for storage cost and self-description. While storage cost is likely a short-term concern, in the project's start-up phase there was still a clear financial concern on the part of decision-makers. Uncompressed would complicate adoption for a lot of collections where storage costs often represent a big argument in favor of choosing a lossy format. Beyond storage, lossless compression gives advantages for self-description and fixity (frame checksums, error concealment, etc.). FFV1's version 3 has, amongst others features, integrity validation via CRC checksums, which is highly beneficial for long-term preservation.

2. A format that is Free/Libre. This requirement was a key issue for the PREFORMA project. Software developed within the scope of the project must be licensed under a specific copyleft license (i.e., "GPLv3 or later, and MPLv2 or later" [Lemmens, 2014]) to ensure that the tools for checking archive files will be available over very long periods. This requirement ruled out the MXF wrapper since the current licensing of the required MXF specifications do not allow for implementing a validator under the given license. Moreover, the specifications for MXF are behind a paywall and thus limit their collaborative use. The cost for acquiring necessary specifications and access to the standardization process of MXF was too high for an open-source project, in particular in comparison with MKV. Furthermore, PREFORMA could not tender for MXF because of Swedish Law that obliges public services to tender for open formats as defined in the European Interoperability Framework (European Communities, 2004).

3. A format that is well documented. There needed to be a specification available, which was additionally accessible and well maintained. Without it, writing an implementation or creating test files becomes a challenge. PREFORMA considered that working on the documentation and standardization during the course of the project would be more feasible with the MKV community than with SMPTE for MXF. Given that there was already a validator available for MKV, the project expected that the investment in this container would have a higher payoff.

4. A format that has been adopted. Some formats have very promising specifications, but the project needed a degree of adoption that proved that the file format is viable and usable in real life situations.

In the end, the project opted for standards where it could imagine that the existing shortcomings could be solved within the scope of the project. It evaluated the tenders in two stages and chose the project that offered the best strategy for solving the existing shortcomings. The result of this exercise for the audiovisual format ended up in a set of two containers (MKV and Ogg) and three video/image codecs (JPEG2000, FFV1, and Dirac). Tenderers were invited to make an R&D project proposal for a combination of a container and codec from this list. For long-term preservation of digital video, choosing both a sustainable container format as well as audio/video codecs are necessary. There is no consensus to date among the archival community as to which file format or codecs should be used for preservation purposes for digital video. The previously proclaimed encodings were JPEG 2000 (lossless) and uncompressed video. FFV1 turned out to be a viable addition to that choice and was, therefore, recently added as a suitable option for preservation encoding.

Professional archives are already using FFV1, with compression ratios comparable to JPEG 2000 lossless and its lower computing requirements, as their long-term storage codec.[2] Especially, archives whose collections do not feature extensive broadcast materials, but rather oral history- or ethnographic-recordings and the likes, "favored the lossless FFV1 encoding" in communications with the "Federal Agencies Digitization Guidelines Initiative" (FADGI) team (Fleischhauer, 2014). FFVI is also listed as a format option for long-term preservation of moving images on sites of the US Library of Congress, State Records NSW, and others. The Society of American Archivists published a paper in August 2014 suggesting only FFV1 as preservation codec for video. The Digital Preservation project at the US Library of Congress identified AVI and Matroska as common container formats for FFV1.[3]

## The MediaConch Application

The first design phase lasted four months. Six suppliers were selected (two for each media type), and the suppliers of the three best designs were requested to proceed to the current prototyping phase. The MediaArea team has worked on several software tools used in preservation data conformance, including MediaInfo, a tool to extract metadata from audio and video files, and Bay Area Video Coalition's QCTools project, a tool that performs quality control checks and analysis on digitized analog video.

MediaArea is one of three teams that have moved forward from Phase 1 (design) into Phase 2 (software prototyping). This second phase will last twenty-two months. In Phase 1, MediaArea was tasked with researching community standards and developing file conformance checks for FFV1, Matroska, and LPCM to support efforts of long-term preservation in memory institutions. In Phase 2, MediaArea has been developing MediaConch, an extensible, open-source software project consisting of an implementation checker, policy checker, reporter, and fixer that target preservation-level audiovisual files. It provides detailed and batch-level file conformance checking via an adaptable and flexible application program interface that is accessible by the command line, a graphical user interface, or a web-based shell. MediaConch, furthermore, makes use of a new reporting feature for documenting the structure and contents of digital files with a particular concentration on audiovisual data: MediaTrace. It is a complementary tool to MediaInfo that summarizes a file's significant characteristics and offers comprehensive documentation of file information in a powerful XML format for precision identification and conformance checking.

## The CELLAR Working Group

The goal of the PREFORMA project is to address the challenge of implementing good quality standardized file formats for preserving data content in the long term. Its objective in regards to standardization FFV1 and Matroska is to improve the sustainability factors for both formats—including disclosure, credibility, and transparency—while also creating a mechanism to authoritatively clarify the intent of the specifications. The MediaArea team is dedicated to the further development of the standardization of the Matroska and FFV1 formats to ensure their longevity as a recommended digital preservation file format.

After presenting on FFV1 and Matroska at IETF 94 in 2015, they have incorporated feedback and input from IETF members to draft a new charter for a working group that includes FFV1, Matroska, and FLAC under the name CELLAR: Codec Encoding for LossLess Archiving and Real-Time Transmission. Like all the Task Force's working groups, it works in an open sense—by means of mailing lists and open gatherings.

FFV1 is a lossless video codec, and Matroska is an extensible media container based on EBML (Extensible Binary Meta Language), a binary XML format. There are open-source implementations of both formats, and an increasing interest in and support for the use of FFV1 and Matroska. However, there are concerns about the sustainability and credibility of existing specifications for the long-term use of these formats. These existing specifications require a broader review and formalization in order to encourage widespread adoption.

There is also a need for a lossless audio format to complement the lossless video codec and container format. FLAC is a lossless audio codec that has seen widespread adoption in a number of different applications, including archival applications. While there are open-source implementations of the codec, no formal standards for either the codec itself or its use in container formats currently exist. Review and formalization of the FLAC codec standard and its use in Matroska container formats are needed for wider adoption.

Using existing work done by the development communities of Matroska, FFV1, and FLAC, the Working Group will formalize specifications for these open and lossless formats. In order to provide authoritative, standardized specifications for users and developers, the Working Group will seek consensus throughout the process of refining and formalizing these standards. The Working Group seeks consensus and refinements for specifications for both FFV1 and Matroska in order to provide authoritative, standardized specifications for users and developers.

Erwin Verbruggen is project lead at the Research & Development department of the Netherlands Institute for Sound and Vision where he works on research projects related to preservation and access in audiovisual archives.

Dave Rice is an audiovisual archivist and technologist, whose work focuses on independent media, open-source technology in preservation applications, and quality control analytics. He is the project lead for the MediaConch team.

Bert Lemmens works at the Belgian Centre of Expertise PACKED, where he is a specialist in preservation tools and semantic applications for cultural heritage. He led the task of gathering the project requirements for the PREFORMA tender specification.

Jérôme Martinez is the Founder and President of MediaArea.net, the lead developer of MediaInfo, and a technical consultant to a variety of projects within the fields of broadcast video, audiovisual archiving, and web video.

Ashley Blewer is a developer, archivist, moving image specialist, applications developer at the New York Public Library, and open-source enthusiast, and has worked on BAVC's QC Tools and the MediaConch Project.

Emanuel Lorrain works for PACKED, a Centre of Expertise in Digital Heritage created in 2005, based in Brussels. He works as a researcher developing and disseminating knowledge about the preservation of audiovisual heritage and media artworks.

Antonella Fresa is an ICT expert, and Director and General Manager at Promoter SRL. She is Technical Coordinator of PREFORMA and Communication Manager of national and European projects in the domains of digital cultural heritage, creativity, and cocreation, citizen science, smart cities, digital preservation and e-Infrastructures.

Claudio Prandoni works at Promoter SRL, where he is involved in several projects supported by the European Commission, especially targeted at the tourism and cultural heritage sectors. He is the assistant to the Communication Manager of PREFORMA.

## Notes

1. MediaInfo. Retrieved July 4, 2016, from https://mediaarea.net/en/MediaInfo.
2. An up-to-date list of institutions can be found on the FFV1 Wikipedia page: https://en.wikipedia.org/wiki/FFV1#List_of_institutions_known_to_use_FFV1 (accessed 2016/10/07).
3. http://www.digitalpreservation.gov/formats/fdd/fdd000349.shtml; http://www.digitalpreservation.gov/formats/fdd/fdd000343.shtml.

## Bibliography


European Commission. (2013, June 25). Communication from the commission to the European parliament, the council, the European economic and social committee and the committee of the regions. Against lock-in: building open ICT systems by making better use of standards in public procurement. *European Commission*. Brussels, BE. Retrieved from https:/ec.europa.eu/digital-single-market/en/news/against-lock-building-open-ict-systems-making-better-use-standards-public.

European Communities. (2004). European interoperability framework for pan-European eGovernment services [internet]. *European Commission*. Luxembourg: Office for Official Publications of the European Communities. Retrieved from http://ec.europa.eu/idabc/servlets/Docd552.pdf?id=19529.

Fleischhauer, C. (2014, December 3). Comparing formats for video digitization [webpage]. *The Signal Digital Preservation*. Retrieved from https://blogs.loc.gov/digitalpreservation/2014/12/comparing-formats-for-video-digitization/.

Fresa, A., Justrell, B., & Prandoni, C. (2015). Digital curation and quality standards for memory institutions: PREFORMA research project. *Archival Science, 15*(2), 191–216. Retrieved from http://doi.org/10.1007/s10502-015-9242-8.

Lemmens, B. (2014). *Challenge brief* (artefact document) (p. 15). Retrieved from http://www.digitalmeetsculture.net/wp-content/uploads/2014/06/PREFORMA_Challenge-Brief_v1.0.pdf.

Murray, K. (2015, September 23). Improving technical options for audiovisual collections through the PREFORMA project [web page]. *The Signal Digital Preservation.* Retrieved from https://blogs.loc.gov/digitalpreservation/2015/09/improving-technical-options-for-audiovisual-collections-through-the-preforma-project/.

Society of American Archivists. (2014). Museum archives section standards and best practices working group electronic records project. Retrieved from http://www2.archivists.org/sites/all/files/MAS%20E-rec%20project.pdf.

# From Tape to File: Solutions for a Data-Centric Migration Workflow in the Haus des Dokumentarfilms for the Magnetic Tape Collection of the Landesfilmsammlung Baden-Württemberg

19

**Michelle Carlos**

**Abstract**

This conservation project aimed to develop a digitisation workflow for the magnetic tape collection of the Landesfilmsammlung Baden-Württemberg (LFS) in the Haus des Dokumentarfilms (HDF) to assist them in transitioning from a tape-based video-production workflow into a file-based one.

The empirical part of this study was conducted in HDF in October 2013 using data gathered primarily from the reports of the film archive and interviews with film archivist Anna Leippe. Supporting technical information was obtained through recommendations from product specialists in the postproduction and broadcasting industry.

A comprehensive investigation of the current workflow as well as the present condition of the LFS collection of the film archive was conducted in order to understand the need of a data-centric workflow in a film archive. The focal point of this project was the design of a transitional tape-to-file migration architecture to demonstrate its key steps, which also featured the necessary hardware and software solutions that best fit the technical requirement and at the same time the financial capacity of HDF.

**Keywords**

digitisation, small film archives, migration, workflow, magnetic tapes, documentary films.

## The Challenges of a Film Archive in the Digital Age

The Haus des Dokumentarfilms is responsible for about 14,600 hours of various media and content that include three film collections in the state of Baden-Württemberg. About 8,000 historical film documentaries, 22% of the content, belongs to the collection of the Landesfilmsammlung Baden-Württemberg, and the collection has grown continually since its inception in 2000. From the LFS collection, more than 4,500 titles are already digitised and are recorded in Digital Betacam, IMX, DVCPro or HDCAM tapes, with some more titles still in analogue tape formats waiting to be digitised (see fig. 1). Due to the increased awareness of the existence of the HDF and LFS, the number of film acquisitions through donations over the years has steadily increased. The earliest documentary in the collection is dated as far back as 1904.

The growth of the collection, however, poses two major problems to the archive: public access of the content in high-definition digital format and a centralised repository of the physical and digital media.

Digitisation plays a vital role in the conservation and archiving of historical and cultural video. Outsourcing the digitisation slices a huge portion from an archive's annual budget. Assembling a digitisation workspace in-house likewise requires investment in equipment, staff training, and maintenance. Since 2012, HDF has been using a tape-based video ingest assembly that can only output to DigiBeta tapes or standard definition H.264 digital videos. But standard definition format is no longer an option. The inability to deliver in HD from a centralised location not only inhibits HDF from complying to the current broadcast and film standards but

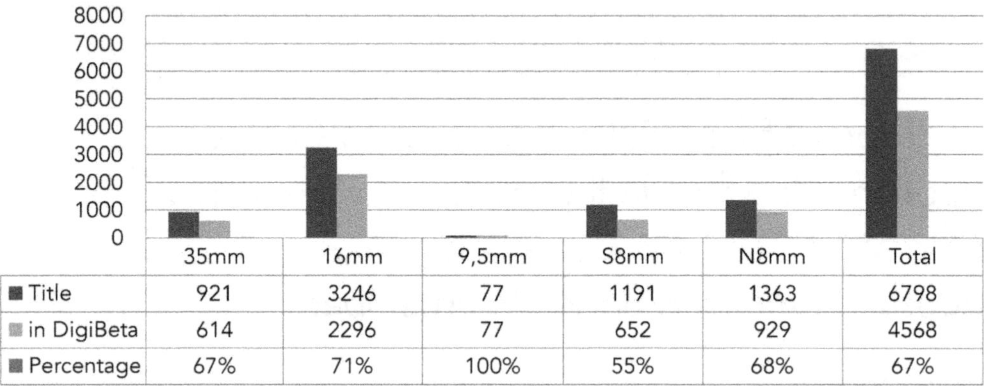


**Figure 1.** Total number of Digital Betacam cassette tapes for every film format as of October 2013.

**Table 1.** The LFS video collection excluding celluloid film, CD, DVD, and audio media as of October 2013

| Media Container Type | Number of Film Titles | Number of AV Media Containers | Total Minutes of AV Media |
|---|---|---|---|
| Betacam | 4 | 5 | 60.43 |
| Betacam SP | 322 | 311 | 4,948.35 |
| Betamax | 1 | 1 | 12 |
| DVC Pro | 557 | 126 | 4,548.12 |
| DVC Pro 25 | 200 | 45 | 2,806.72 |
| Digital Betacam | 4,422 | 2,335 | 55,766.48 |
| HDCAM SR | 75 | 21 | 1,001.20 |
| IMX-Sony 1/2 Z | 53 | 35 | 754.8 |
| Professional Disc 23,3GB | 111 | 52 | 1,509.85 |
| Professional Disc 50GB Dual Layer | 61 | 14 | 993.25 |
| Super VHS | 61 | 60 | 404.22 |
| U-matic | 41 | 44 | 622.53 |
| VCR | 2 | 2 | 15.6 |
| VHS | 810 | 709 | 16,204.20 |
| VHS Long-Play | 1 | 1 | 2 |
| Video 2000 | 1 | 1 | |
| Video 8 | 2 | 2 | 61.48 |
| Video High 8 | 31 | 31 | 63 |
| Mini Digital Video | 133 | 100 | 975.52 |
| TOTAL | 19,259 | 16,557 | 189,899.92 |

also prevents them from responding to the public's demands to instantly access the content in streaming high-resolution file format.

Even though the LFS is supported by the Ministerium für Wirtschaft, Forschung und Kunst Baden-Württemberg (MWFK) and the Medien- und Filmgesellschaft mbH Baden-Württemberg (MFG), digitisation of analogue film material can be only funded through self-financing of the copyright owner or a project-related external funding. HDF's income through the sale of film rights is too menial to support digitisation.

A central shared storage for data is non-existent. Magnetic tapes are still the main media carrier plus a handful of external hard drives stored in a climate-controlled room maintained at 42% relative humidity and 19°–20° C in the basement of the archive. All are properly labelled with barcode numbers generated from the FESAD database for identification and are encased in original manufacturer plastic housing (see fig. 2).

With the archive's intention of acquiring more files in time for the 2014 launch of the online video portal project, the amount of data should not be underestimated. Assuming that 900 hours

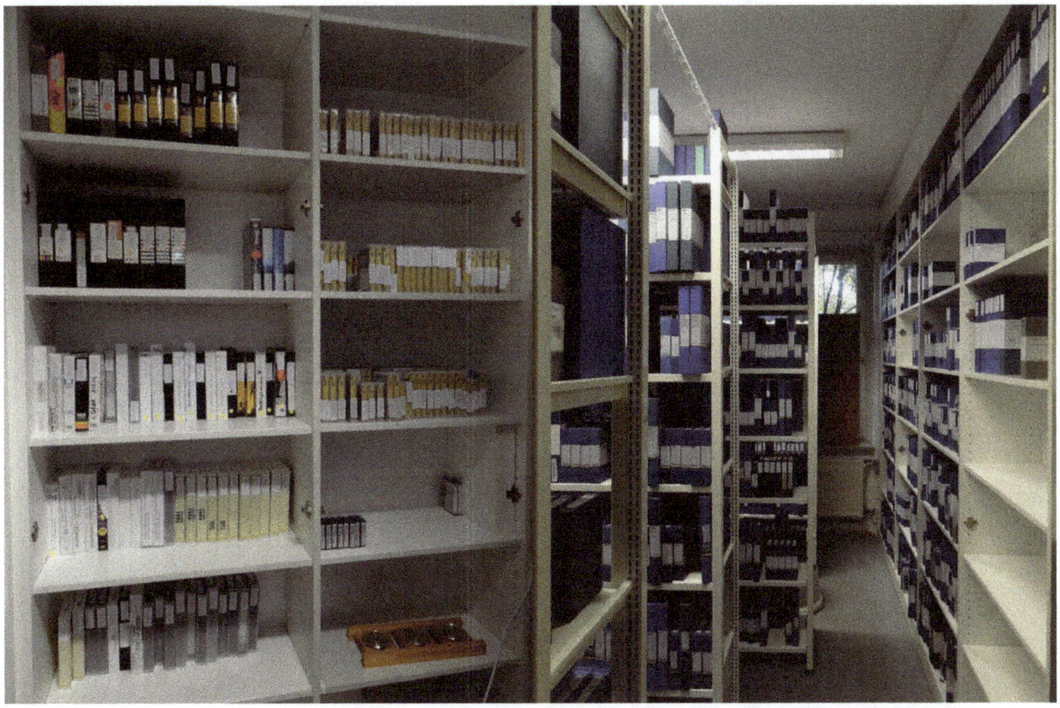

Figure 2. LFS tape library containing mixed format videotapes.

of SD material are to be converted to uncompressed HD video at 10 bit, 1920 × 1080 p, 25 fps, this alone will be equivalent to approximately 90.5 TB[1] of storage space. Moreover, video data must be organised, stored, and secured. In case of disasters, an off-site back-up storage must also be considered.

HDF outlined their media preservation goals for the succeeding years:

- Produce more video files in HD quality to meet client requirements
- Present LFS to a larger audience through the video portal
- Increase income of the house through selling video clips from the collection
- Capability to edit and process content
- Have a unified workflow to be able to accommodate the files from digitising laboratories
- Maintain a centralised data storage for the growing collection
- Back-up the original analogue video tapes and store them in the Südwestrundfunk (SWR) storage facility in Endersbach
- Back-up the video files

## An Outdated Infrastructure

A tape-based workflow means that the source material comes from a tape medium and then recorded back onto another tape medium. HDF follows the same primitive linear process. In this case, the input material is either an analogue or a digital tape (VHS, U-matic, Betacam, DigiBeta or IMX). The analogue video signal is then digitised and is simply dubbed onto a blank Digital Betacam (see fig. 3). The step-by-step procedure of the current workflow is as follows:

Step 1. Once HDF receives an order, they produce a DVD of the requested clip from the tape library with burned-in timecode that serves as reference and copy-protection and sends it to the client via mail.

Step 2. When the client confirms the order using the clip timecode as reference, HDF processes order and prepares the Digital Betacam source tape for capture.

Step 3. Tape is ingested into VTR (video tape recorder) deck.

Step 4. After manually encoding the given timecode into the deck, the VTR captures video in SD PAL format.

Figure 3. Current tape-based workflow in HDF.

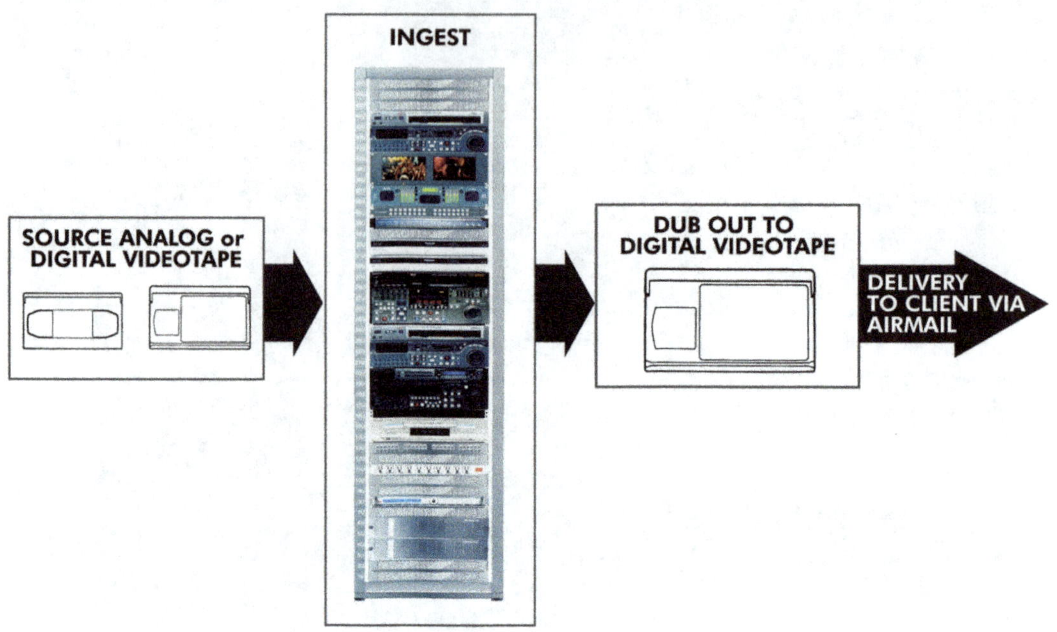


Step 5. The captured video is dubbed out to Digibeta with at least 2-second in- and outpoints.

Step 6. The DigiBeta is sent to the client by post.

This system is no longer effective as the media becomes relatively inaccessible to the end user, who has to capture the clips to convert into more accessible files. In more cases finding a facility that offers the extraction of the data from a DigiBeta is becoming more difficult unless the users have their own capturing device. Likewise, the SD content is no longer accepted by broadcasters since their conversion to HD broadcasting. Even streaming videos are in HD and moving towards to Ultra-HD resolutions.

## The Need for a Data-Centric Video Workflow

Digitising audiovisual media can be very complicated because of the many variations in the formats, equipment, and processes. In addition, there is the issue of format and equipment obsolescence, which is becoming increasingly prevalent, but preserving the original content of the media is important in tape and film collections conservation. Digitisation consequently allows access of the content without repeatedly using the analogue media. Scanning once, for example, allows the original film to be stored properly in a suitable climate-controlled environment. Migrating the content of videotape to a digital format will probably extend the shelf life of a carrier media that was never intended for archiving purposes. But once the media is digitised the next big question is storage and the data overflow. Developing technology has answers for that.

Unlike a full-service postproduction house that is required to have quick turnover of materials, HDF receives orders for clips, on average, once a week and with minimum of 1.5 minutes running time. Nevertheless, there is consistent demand for clips from all over the country and even outside Germany. The Internet alone is a great source of such videos but rarely displays acceptable quality. Users need material that is usable for HD broadcasting while 4K is becoming the norm in cinema releases. There is no escaping the UHD digital route. Everyone who wishes to present their works in this platform should only follow the technical requirements dictated by standards.

HDF needs to address this demand through its distribution of video clips. But HDF is not only concerned in presenting their film collection to the public but also is primarily tasked to preserve the contents and its representations as close to the original source as possible. Digitisation is the logical solution to this challenge.

## The Benefits of a File-Based Workflow

Many industries, specifically broadcasting and postproduction, have already converted their video workflow into a centralised file-based infrastructure. Several film archives all over the world have also followed suit. This all happened within the span of a decade since HD digital broadcasting took off. Migrating from tape to file and overhauling an analogue system into a data-centric one will benefit a film archive in many ways:

Accessibility. The film archive would be able to access the media without sacrificing the original source, which is ideally kept in proper climate-controlled storage. All media will be in file formats and stored in a centralised storage that can be accessed by anyone in the network.

Consolidation. With a film archive such as HDF that holds four large film collections of the state, not only LFS but also the other collections in the house will benefit from this file-based workflow since all of these will be able to use the same digitisation workflow.

Flexibility. There will be the ability to move the video files around the network—from file transferring to non-linear editing and non-destructive processing of the media.

Self-reliance. A film archive will depend much less on commercial digitisation labs to have their videos digitised, which normally takes a period of time and sum of money. Therefore, having an in-house digitisation system provides savings in cost and time. In this manner, the archive has total control of their media, whereas when digitisation is outsourced, the objects are removed from the facility.

Profit. Income is generated from a faster and increased output. Apart from sales of the clips, the archive may also look into offering digitisation services to smaller local communities with film collections, private collectors, or amateur filmmakers who cannot afford the higher rates imposed by bigger digitisation labs.

Investment. The initial steps for the system upgrade may incur expenses, but this can only be seen as a profitable investment for the consequential growth of the collections, of which rights for distribution and use can be sold.

Broader audience reception. The convenience of being able to upload the video files in a web portal will give the possibility of presenting the collection to a much wider audience.

Personnel skill development. Staff can be trained to operate the equipment and understand the technical operations of the workflow even with the lack of in-house IT or digital intermediate specialist.

## Transitional Tape-to-File Migration Workflow

At this point, HDF is not yet ready for a purely file-based architecture, therefore a transitional video-migration workflow that allows them to convert their analogue and digital videos to files is more feasible. Their existing set-up and equipment can still be utilised. A system upgrade rather than a complete overhaul is more practical. After all, they have the basic equipment necessary for ingesting the magnetic tapes (see figs. 4 and 5).

A workflow is necessary to be able to organise the tasks, designate responsibilities, and monitor the progress of the project. Basically the analogue media is ingested as digital files into storage for access and long-term archiving. The transitional workflow will be the crucial stage to complete this project. The workflow ushers the passage from a tape-based workflow into a data-centric one. The magnetic tapes will be the source material in this process and thus will need proper handling as they undergo digitisation and format conversion. The general tasks involved in digitisation are as follows:

Preparation and Inspection. The tape is prepared for capture. This means that it is checked for any sign of damage or deterioration. The equipment to be used is also cleaned, set-up, and tested. A test tape is used to check the operation ability of the equipment. The source tape is tested. Repair and cleaning of both tape and equipment is done, if necessary. Labels and documentation are also compared to the FESAD database to match file naming and metadata recording upon capture.

Capture. The source tape is ingested and digitised into the required format and specifications and then transferred to the network storage for future access. Metadata is collected.

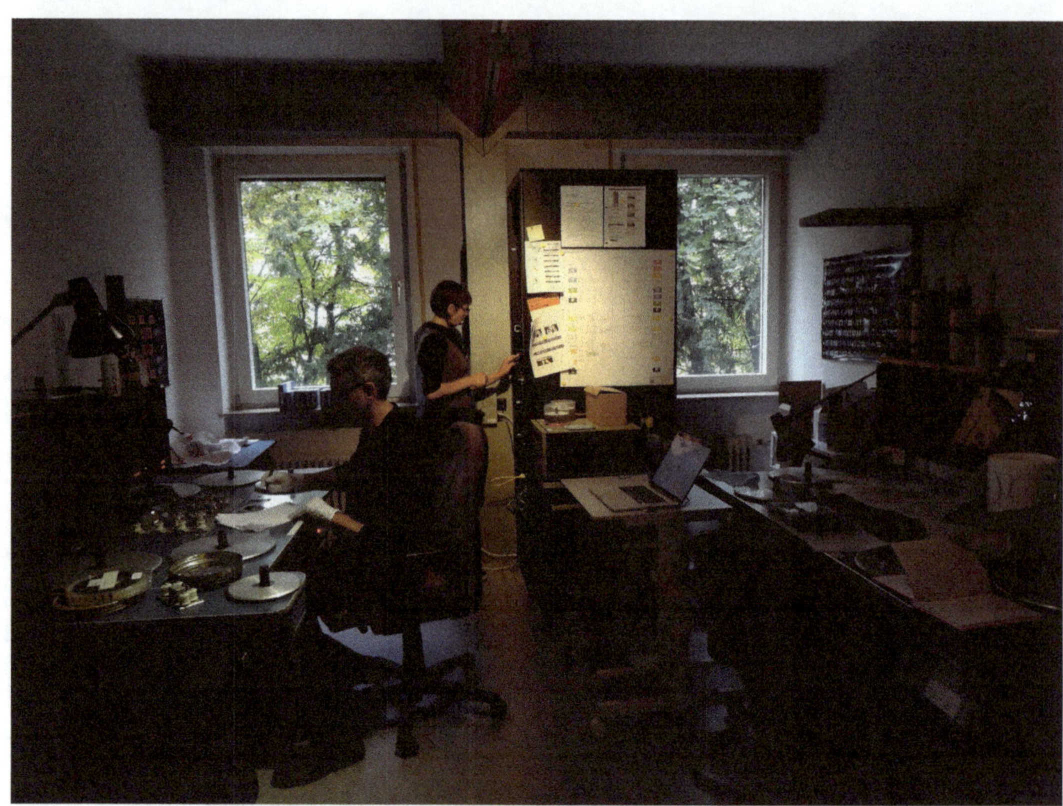

**Figure 4.** HDF's working area for film viewing and video ingest and dub-out.

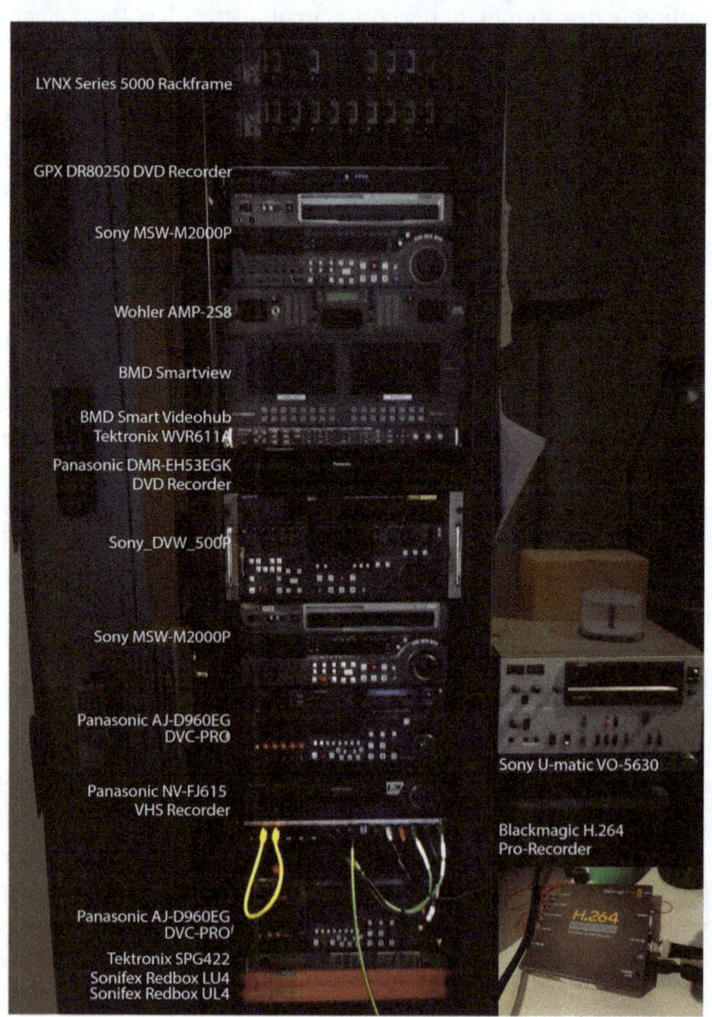


**Figure 5.** Tape deck donated by SWR in 2012.

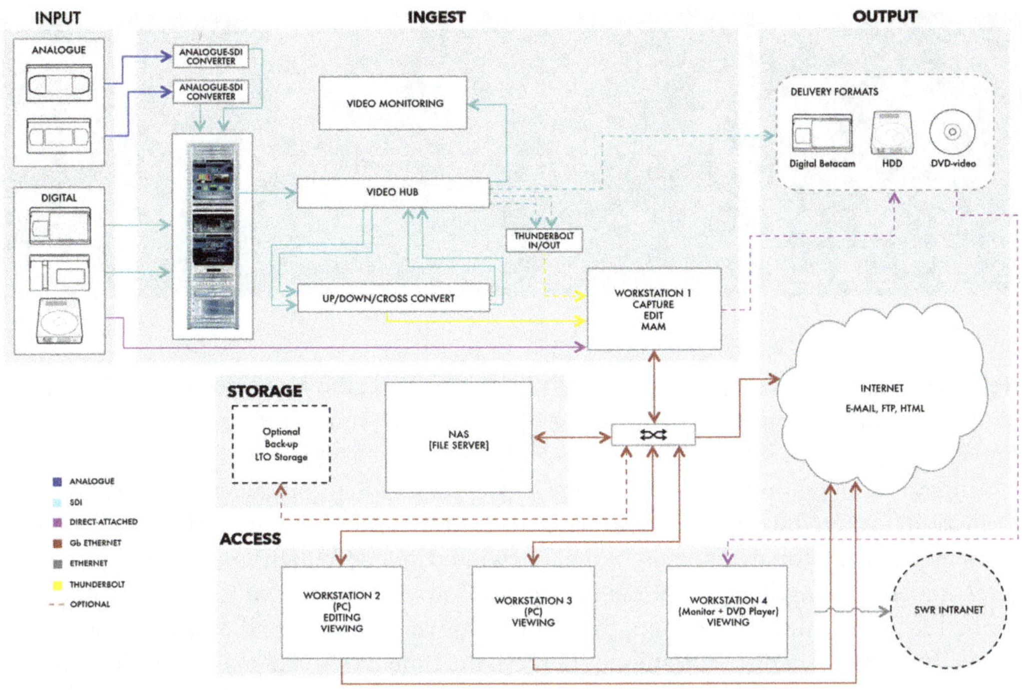

**Figure 6.** Transitional workflow for digitisation and conversion.

Processing and remastering. The digitised media is edited, in some cases, digitally processed (removed of noise and drop-outs, colour correction, audio syncing, etc.), and converted to different formats and prepared for delivery or archiving. Metadata is collected.

Storage. The digitised media is stored into the network-shared storage (NAS). The media is also managed for archiving. Allowance for backup storage must also be considered.

Delivery. The digitised media is outputted to various formats for access over the Internet, optical discs, mobile devices, digital magnetic tapes, etc.

Figure 6 illustrates the principles of the new architecture as described below:

Step 1. All analogue sources (VHS, SVHS, Betacam, etc.) are converted to digital signals through an analogue to SDI converter and then fed through the existing Blackmagic Design (BMD) Smart Videohub via SDI connection. The digital sources are directly fed through the videohub.

Step 2. The digital output can now be viewed through the BMD Smartview monitors and at the same time can be processed using a hardware-based video processor (i.e., BMD Teranex 2D processor) for high-quality up/down/cross conversion from SD to HD, PAL to NTSC, or interlaced to progressive. The video processor can be directly connected to the workstation for remote control using a Thunderbolt cable.

Step 3. The processed digital signals will return to the Videohub for distribution.

Step 4. Optionally, the processed digital video passes through an SDI to an I/O interface that is connected to Workstation 1 that will do the capturing, metadata gathering, and/or editing (i.e., BMD Ultrastudio 3D SDI input to Thunderbolt output connected to an iMac). This is necessary when capturing using NLE Programs such as AVID MC or FCPX.

Step 5. Workstation 1 also functions as the network administrator. It is connected to the network switch that will connect to the storage and the other workstations all via Gigabit Ethernet.

Step 6. The files in are transferred to the 16TB NAS shared storage, which also functions as a file server.

Step 7. For backup storage an optional LTO appliance can also be connected to the server through fibre channel, mini SAS, or Gigabit Ethernet.

Step 8. The workstations will be able to access the media and do editing or previewing.

Step 9. Final output of video files is through a faster Internet connection through cloud, email, or FTP file sharing for delivery to clients and for web portal uploading. Additionally, dub-out to Digital Betacam or recording to other media is still possible.

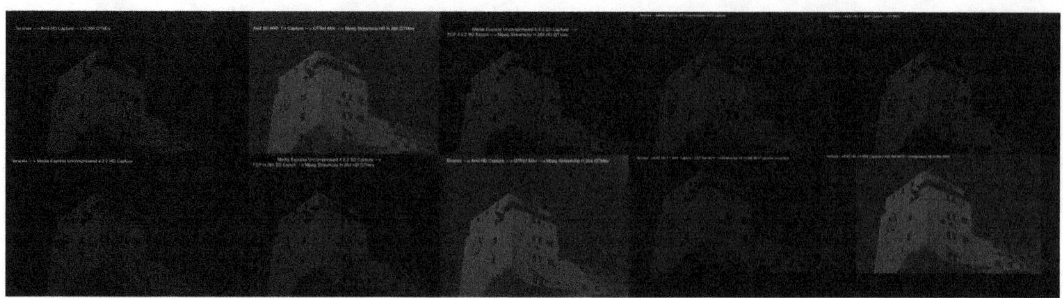

**Figure 7.** Visual comparison of the many Quicktime Codec variants.

## Compromise to Deliver

After a series of tests to compare the end results of various digital HD video output formats, the one that best fit the storage capacity and at the same time, usage and visually acceptability in terms of image quality, is the Apple ProRes HD 4:2:2 25p (see fig. 7).

It may not be an archival format, but it is a widely used format in postproduction and broadcasting, where the video clips produced by HDF are mostly used. The reasons are that clients request this format, that most of the files will be uploaded to the web portal, and that the source material, a DigiBeta, is not the best quality anyway, so no need to go uncompressed. If they had to, HDF must go to the original source film and transfer it all over again, which is of course, very costly and time consuming. At the same time, HDF had to be realistic in utilising the capacity of their 16 TB NAS RAID storage and the recording capability of the workstation. HDF's decision to use this format is for practical and technical reasons—a compromising decision that most archives typically face.

These HD videos are to be uploaded into HDF's own web-based video portal, DOKSITE (still a beta at the time of writing), which is a major project of the archive that allows wider public access to their film collection. HD video web uploading is done automatically using FFMpeg,[2] whereas metadata gathering for the portal is automated using a script program.

## Preserving Small Film Archives

Success stories of big digitisation, restoration, and migration projects of big audiovisual archives are commonplace despite the big challenges they have encountered. In reality though, there are several smaller archives in the world who are struggling not only financially but also technically. They can only dream of what larger and well-supported institutions can accomplish. They are in dire need of digitisation and migration solutions that balance the financial and technical capacity of the archive.

One may argue that the film collections in HDF are only documentaries done by amateur filmmakers, which may not have commercial value—so why digitise?

Documentary films are the personal narratives of individuals who were witnesses to historical events that had direct impact to their lives in that time and, as the viewers now, we are privileged to witness the events through their shaky lenses. Through them we see evidences of the lives they lived, follow a continuing tradition, or realise a disappearing way of life—their histories are learned so as to avoid the same mistakes in the future.

But are the efforts in digitising these films worth it? The images are raw, grainy, unsteady, and generally degraded. Digital reconstruction or processing will be too intensive, time-consuming, and costly, and yet it should also be argued that such films are supposed to be raw and that every millimetre of that frame tell a story on how the filmmaker dedicatedly worked on his home movie. The real value of a documentary film is the story in front and behind the camera.

A film archive is tasked to preserve these extracts from a historical timeline so that future generations will never forget their heritage. HDF is doing this job just as well but they need all the assistance they can get to improve their operations to provide better services to the public. They are faced with the challenges of a rapidly changing technology worsen by the debilitating and fluctuating economy and must learn to adapt for the sake of upholding their vital role as custodians of national visual treasures. They need to compromise between the longevity of the digitised media and storage capacity and easier accessibility. An uncompressed media may be the best archival format, but in some cases an alternative format fits a certain workflow. Their main objective is to be able to access and work with the digital media.

The solution they need is simple, available, and affordable. An effective digitisation workflow while utilising the appropriate tools makes it easier for a film archive to be adaptable to the evolution of moving images and at the same time capable of adhering to industry standards.

MICHELLE CARLOS is a freelance digital colourist and restoration artist and has worked on commercial and full-length feature film jobs in Manila and Germany as well as digital restoration work of archival films in Singapore. She graduated cum laude with a bachelor of fine arts degree from Tarlac State University. Since completing her master studies in new media preservation management at the Staatliche Akademie der Bildende Künst-Stuttgart (ABK). She has been involved in conservation and digitisation projects for audiovisual collections at the ABK Hochschularchiv and the Haus des Dokumentarfilms in Stuttgart.

## Notes

1. Calculation is based from estimated number of hours of the LFS collection (see table 1).
2. FFMpeg is an open-source command line tool used to record, convert, and stream audio and video.

# 20

# Transfer Quality–Controlled Archive Digitization Approaches for Large Tape-Based Repositories

**Jean-Christophe Kummer**

Abstract

Typically archive stakeholders have a one-time possibility to finance the digitization of an archive and might spent millions in budgets on people and systems or for service providers to get their archives transited from a carrier-based archive to an information-based repository. As everyone wants to avoid errors in the process, yet be enough efficient to be able to finance the work, parallelization in digitization has become the way to go. However, parallelization does introduce many errors which may pass by unnoticed if not taken care of at the time.

An overview is given on state-of-the-art methods used in the transfer of video collections to digital repositories, specifically outlining innovative methods to secure transcription integrity by monitoring the channel code parameters of the replay machines involved.

The collected parameters are provided as process-generated metadata, and may be collected using standardised interfaces. Thus they may be used to help with process optimisation not only during an individual transfer, but also for planning of maintenance, balancing pro-active and re-active policies of wearing parts, or choosing the best use of tape cleaning procedures.

Keywords

digitization, ISR, RF control, quality control, transfer quality, mass transfer.

## Parallel Transfers Have Arrived in the World of Archives

### The Background of Parallelity

The way to tackle *degralescency*[1] has been addressed in the beginning of the 21st century by 1:1 transfers. Archive digitisation was coupled with an idea about the status whether a digitised item is broadcast ready or not. Some approaches even asked for a parallel restoration of each item. One could consider the late '90s as a paradise for archive safeguarding given the resources which were thought to be available in the following years. But soon it became clear that 1:1 monitored transfers is a never-ending work for which budgets do not exist to tackle the typical 30.000–100.000 hours of a broadcast archive.

Nowadays it becomes clear that the remaining large repositories do request a differentiated approach introducing parallelisation. As 80%–90% of the repositories are in a fairly good condition, preservation managers cannot afford to spend above-average budgets per hour of digitised content for the pure digitisation transfer.

Millions of hours of recordings have a finite time window left to get digitised at a reasonable price (a typical estimate of the remaining period is 7–10 years). From then on, the cost of digitisation will be ruled by the number of machines that remain and the remaining spare parts for these machines.

Whereas vendor locking fortunately does not exist in the field of audio (different replayers from different vendors still exist on the market, and it is still technically possible to rebuild analog audio ¼″ tape players, given the transparency of technology), vendor locking is a fact for late digital-born formats such as IMX and DigiBeta, and, of course, the huge number of analog videotapes recorded on BetaCam. Furthermore Sony has (around October 2015) announced that support for DVW-2000 and MSW-2000 machines will cease (the early Beta family was discontinued years ago) by the year 2023.[2]



*Sustainable Audiovisual Collections* (2017): 146–152. DOI: 10.2979/jts2016.0.0.22

Luckily—especially with broadcasters—the Betacam family (Betacam, DigiBeta, IMX) has been used so widely that usually enough machines exist in-house to set up a decent scenario with 16 parallel machines to digitise even an archive with 100.000 items.

### Insecurity of Parallel VTR Transfer Needs to Be Addressed

One-to-one transfers can be done against an adequate quality standard, even with the previously mentioned cost overhead. That, however, restricts them to a comparatively small-scale operation. The most obvious challenge for any industrialized approach is quality management.

As acceleration potential is close to nonexistent for videotape transfers, only automation and parallelization promise relevant efficiency yield. When aiming at significant cost savings, there are two competing strategies:

- using robotics
- manual parallelism

The opinion of the author is quite clearly in favor of manual parallelism, simply because recent experience has shown that robotics cannot prevail in many industry-scale preservation projects because of their relatively high cost and limited flexibility.[3] Another frequently underestimated cost factor is the repackaging of the carriers after digitization. It is namely a typical process requirement to handle concordant package throughout the transfer process. That is self-evident when the physical carrier remains in preservation after digitization, but even when destroying tapes, incoherent carrier boxes may cause process mayhem.

Another key factor in industry-scale transcriptions is process automation. Workflow systems targeted at archive preservation support operators by process segmentation, leading to a strictly distributed workflow. This allows for standardization of each process step and raises the potential to fully automate some time-consuming tasks such as retranscoding and packaging. Moreover, workflow automation aims at reducing human error by restricting operation parameters to a predefined set. When integrating systems, a pain-point NOA has become aware of in the last fifteen years in close work with its customers is the question of whether process steps can be made repeatable, or if a trivial failure downstream breaks the whole process. NOA addresses this and other questions by centralized logging of the process data life cycle management, aspects that often make the difference between hit and miss with generic or purpose-built solutions. This is a result of more than fifteen years market presence in audiovisual digitization.

For preservation transfers, it is important to emphasize the importance of quality assurance as a key means of producing authentic information, and the main scope of quality control here is to detect if any errors have been added in during the actual preservation transfer. Practically, for transferring videotapes, this means a good understanding of which parameters in the process chain are critical to the reproduction and digitisation is necessary to providing accurate preservation copies.

The most common user story in digitization is something like the following: I may be able to finance the work of 100.000 hours of digitization once, so which parameters do I have to concentrate on in the process of digitization so that I am not accused in ten years' time of gross negligence?

When dealing with archival collections of video material, it is not always clear whether the actual video carrier is the first manifestation of the content. Very often you may find film which has been previously copied via TeleCine to SD material. U-matic material might have been migrated in the '90s to Digibeta, and hopefully 1" and 2" has been copied to newer formats. Now comes the big question: How should we address the migration of this content?

Even if any defect may be unwanted for later reuse, for the preservation process itself it is unambiguously necessary to have a clear view between defects sourcing from the preservation transfer and those that already existed in the signal from an earlier manifestation.

## VTR Dropout Detection

To make quality control more efficient in archival transfers, from the very beginning NOA has developed a concept of algorithmic and electrical analysis of the transfer quality of audio tapes which has resulted in a method called Traces Aided Spot Checking (TAS).[4] In a graphical overview, replayer conditions such as Azimuth, ISR BLER, or C2-Errors are aligned in a diagnostics window with the extracted essence. This automatically produced analysis metadata helps then the operator to assess within seconds a sixty-minute file without the need for analyzing the complete transfer in a separate 1:1 quality check task. This methodology has now been extended to VTRs for the relevant parameters necessary to semiautomatically assess the quality of the pure transfer—not the content. Error pointers can, therefore, be provided to the user with a high probability of a transfer-related issue, rather than an essence-based guess which is prone to having a high false-positive rate. Moreover, the concept considerably lowers the entry barrier to utilize quality-controlled archival transfer procedures. This is because error pointers provide metrics that are simple to evaluate, including automated decision-making. The specific NOA approach is, however, to provide an integrated hardware and software solution, as described below.

"Dropouts" have been defined by the EBU QC group[5] in different ways such as analogue frame synchronization or digital tape dropouts.[6] On analogue VTRs, these usually manifest as line-based artefacts while digital streams usually exhibit block-based deformations. In extreme cases the result is complete break-up of the picture.

Playback problems, such as dirt, misalignment, clogging, and wear of the reproduction heads, or decreased information quality in the magnetic layer, do have an impact on the carrier signal level.

Detection on that layer in opposite have the advantage to specifically inform about dropouts that occur during an extraction by an analysis of RF levels for analog VTR, or on read-out of channel conditions for their digital counterpart. These methods work independently of the actual error pattern in the essence, on a higher protocol layer than essence-based detection. This also means that they will be able to discriminate between actual transfer errors and burnt-in defects.

In the file-based domain, dropout detection uses an essence-based analysis that hints at a problem with the need for considerable computing resources without showing whether the error has happened at the actual transfer or was already within the existing file. The drop out detection pattern will also need to detect all error patterns, unlike existing baseband analysis tools which have been extensively tested on the market. Here the results will either not detect the error at all or create too many false positives.

## Dropout Detection on Beta SP

NOA has developed specific hardware to be attached directly on the VTR's reproduction circuit board (sensor plate), and to connect to a processing device (VTRi) that also includes VTR remote control and QC metadata to NOA's video-capturing software.

After buffering the RF signal, the logarithmic, rectified envelope is generated. As illustrated in figure 1, the relevant characteristics are already obvious with an analogue measurement, using a standard vector scope. Whereas the left example exhibits a typical signal envelope for an intact luminance signal, in the right example we can see enormous momentary fluctuations.

Using a simple analog-to-digital converter, the RF envelope is sampled and evaluated. The evaluation is passed to a mathematical weighting model and allows for an easy assessment of preexisting versus actual transfer errors.[7]

Figure 2 illustrates how a defect is presented to the user in the capturing software. The active frame shows a multiline dropout, in place with a highlighted error event marker.

On the other hand, when validating the problem shown in figure 3, the RF trace clearly identifies the dropout as a preexistent part of the signal. Quality assurance thus allows for the decision that a retransfer of this content is unnecessary.

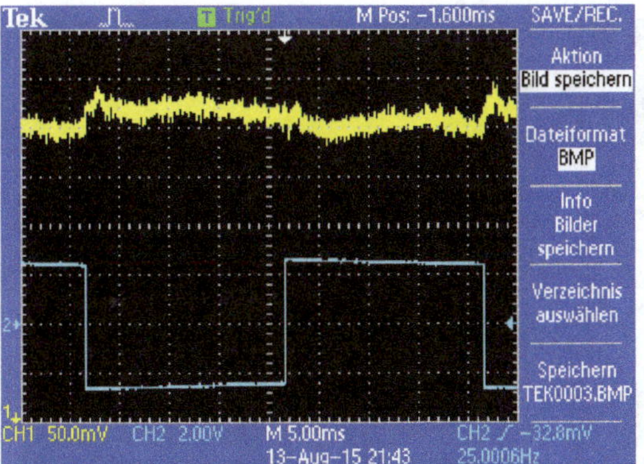


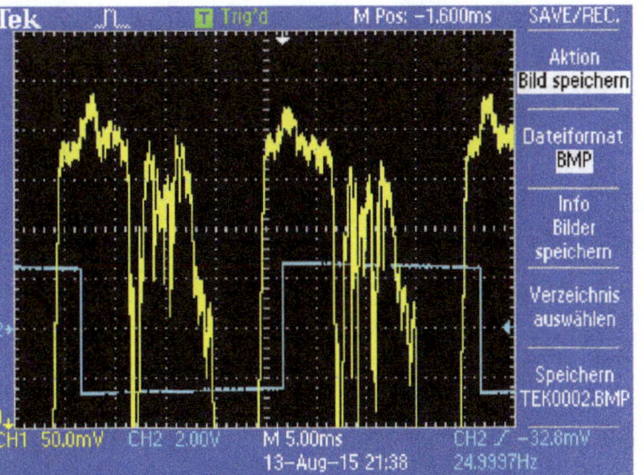


**Figure 1.** Normal RF envelope vs. dropout pattern.

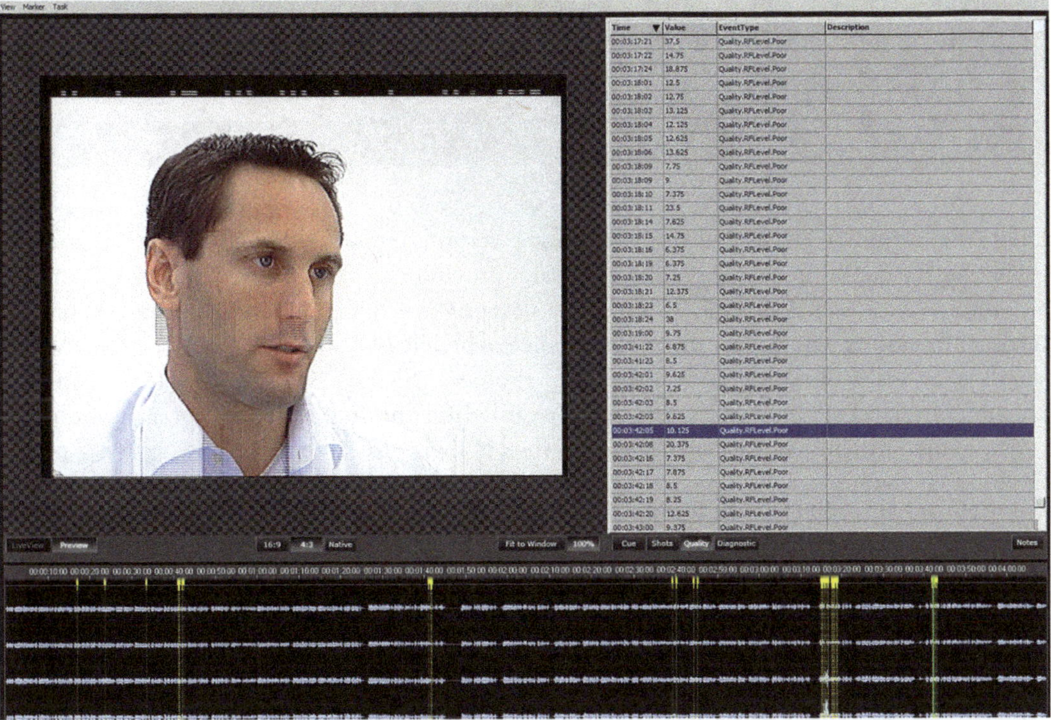

**Figure 2.** Beta SP line artefact.

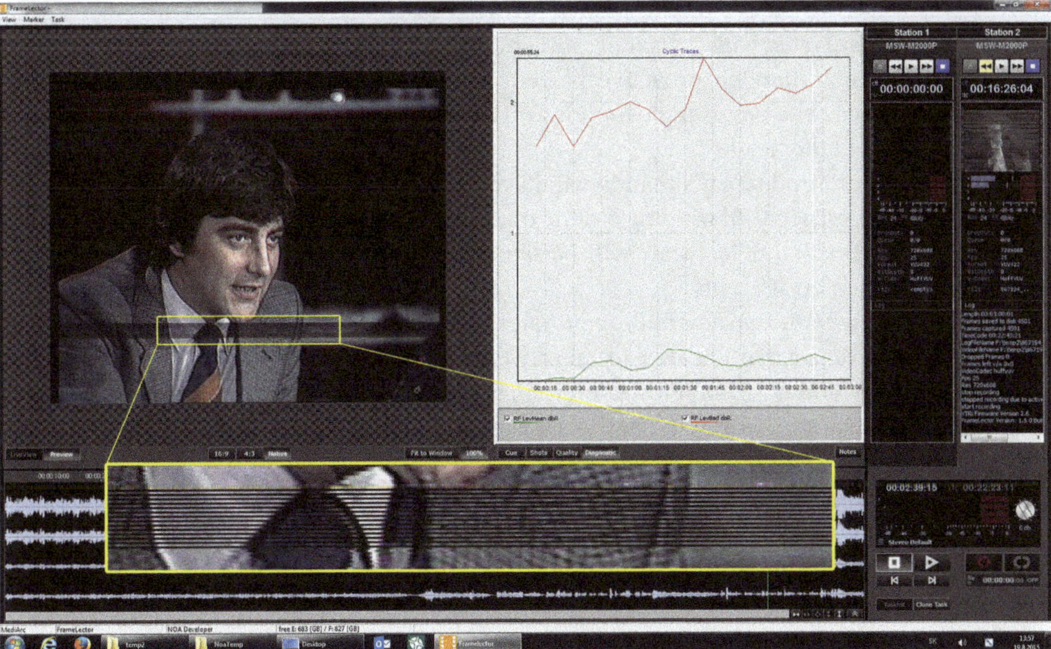


**Figure 3.** Burned-in defect.

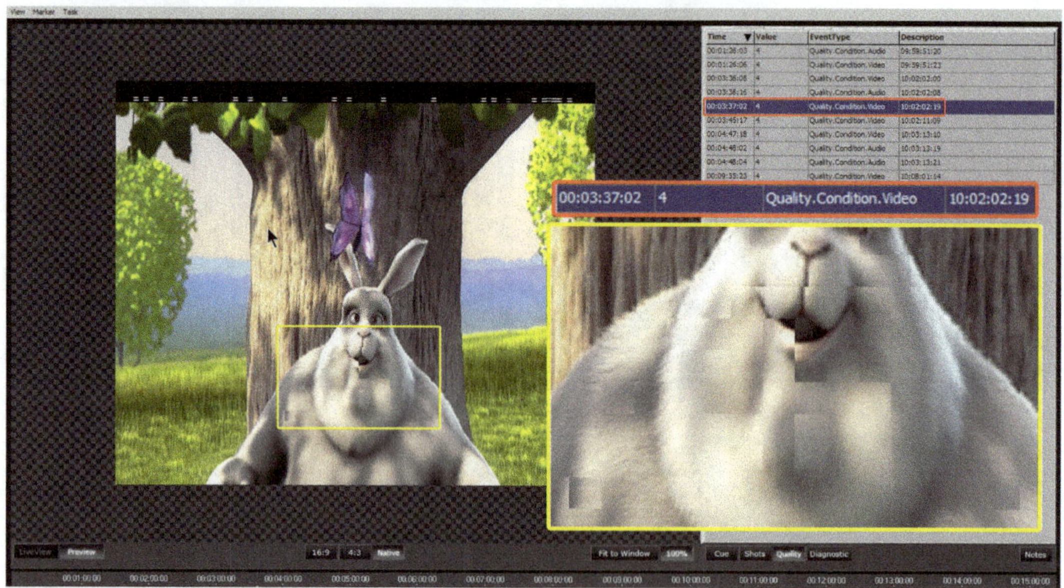


**Figure 4.** Digital dropout on IMX.

## Drop-Out Control on Digital VTRs

Digital Beta family VTRs include inbuilt systems for status reporting. These systems can be made usable for the quality analysis of archival transfer processes.

Interactive Status Reporting (ISR) is Sony's proprietary implementation that aims to provide remote monitoring, diagnostics, and maintenance of broadcast equipment. Based on the SMPTE standard Status Monitoring and Diagnostics Protocol (SMDP, SMPTE 273M), it features a private command set that includes functions suited for runtime signal monitoring. Sony has implemented the protocol in several generations of their professional VTRs, including professional DAT machines, DigiBeta and IMX families.

To make the ISR data usable for the capturing software, NOA provides the same *VTR-i* hardware as for RF measurements.

Figure 4 exemplifies break-up resulting from a tape-coating damage. For demonstration purpose, the picture defect and the error pointer are presented here in line. However, when dealing with large-scale digitization projects, these error pointers can even be assessed automatically.

## Replayer Maintenance

IMX VTR heads are rated with 5.000 operating hours in a heavy postproduction shuttle-editing environment. Recommended proactive playout maintenance is requesting 1000/3000/5000 hours maintenance. The cost is pretty much 1,- EUR per hour, especially when it comes to the replacement part of the head.

However, an archival replay situation will have much less impact on head wear than in post-production usage, especially if winding is done on a separate machine. As with any mechanically wearable part, the actual defect state will be signaled by an exponential growth of the logged Channel Condition error events.

Using the long-term statistics of dropout rates, in a setup with 16++ parallel machines, one can switch the proactive maintenance to a reactive scenario, which might bring the cost down to 0,2 EUR per hour. This does not release you from regular cleaning of the machines—depending on the material played, IMX and DigiBeta have much less abrasive tape coatings than, for example, Beta SP.

The fear of large archive holders of sending their collection to service providers for digitization is very often driven by the supply of spare parts by manufacturers. However, typically both larger and smaller broadcasters still have hundreds of machines in their machine park each with probably less than 4000 hours of drum time.

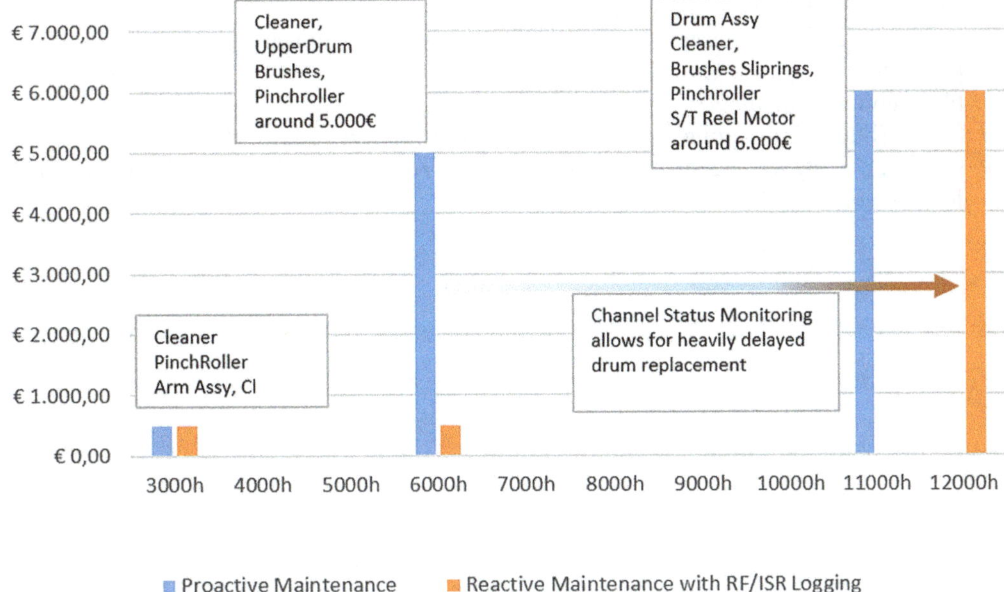


The usage of ISR and RF traces makes those machines usable again for a transfer process with significantly reduced maintenance costs. Setting up 16 machines, each with a remaining time wear of 8000 hours, gives useable replay machinery at practically no cost for a 130.000 hours archive.

## Conclusion

Parallelised transfer approaches take the efficiency lead when it comes to videotape digitisation. Specific process-management technology will allow the owner of such a system to scale out the throughput and minimise operational overheads. Quality management is a key requirement and an operational driver for any large-scale transfer process, as systematic errors would scale with the throughput and thus must never go undetected. Quality control is, however, required as process centric, not essence centric, as in contrast to production operations.

The proposed solutions allow operation with the market-dominant Sony Beta formats from the last four decades, and not only allow the production of accurate content transcription with minimal operational overhead, but also open new opportunities when it comes to the efficient use of the remaining VTR consumables for the remaining life cycle of half-inch Sony VTRS, and the optimized use of maintenance manpower.

Jean-Christophe Kummer is managing director and co-founder of NOA Archive. He successfully brought the company from a technical niche solution provider of audio archive digitisation and preservation workflows to a large-scale operating archive system specialist delivering CAPEX systems for digitization and management for all kind of AV media. He has successfully set up archive digitization and management systems at clients such as Swedish National Broadcaster (SRF), Belgium national broadcaster (VRT), Austrian Archive and National Broadcaster (ORF and Mediathek), Fonoteca Mexico, Croatian Radio Television, Slovenian Radio Television, Hungarian National Radio & Television MTVA and many others. The estimated total value of AV material which has been digitised with NOA Technology is more than 3 mio hours worldwide (2016).

## Notes

1. Casey, IASA journal no. 44, January 2015: degralescence: the combination of obsolence of replayers with degradation of carriers.

2. See: http://www.sony.co.uk/pro/article/broadcast-products-vtr-announcement, 6.2.2016.
3. Kummer, FKT journal 2016/03, p 73.
4. Gabler, in 24th Tonmeistertagung—VDT International Convention, November 2006, p. 527 ff, 3.3.
5. http://ebu.io/qc/items/.
6. 0002B (http://ebu.io/qc/items/0002B) and 0039B (http://ebu.io/qc/items/0039B).
7. Gabler, Quality Management for preservation of Analogue and Digital Video Tape, IASA Journal 46.

# Review and Comparison of FFV1 versus Other Lossless Video Codecs for Long-Term Preservation

21

**Peter Bubestinger-Steindl**

**Abstract**

For audio preservation, the codec question is resolved, but for video which lossless encoding to use is still in discussion. This paper shall give insight based on real-life practical experiences about what it is like to use FFV1, compared to other lossless codecs. Most of it is based on the work at the Austrian Mediathek, mainly due to its role as early adopter of FFV1.

Topics addressed are performance comparison (speed/compression), accessibility, interoperability, sustainability, standardization, transcoding and nonlinear editing, as well as current and future application/vendor support.

**Keywords**

lossless, video, encoding, codecs, compression ratio, FFV1, JPEG2000, Dirac, H.264, uncompressed, NLE, transcoding.

## Introduction

At the end of 2009, the Austrian Mediathek (national audio/video archive)[1] was planning to start digitization of their tape-based video collection, consisting mainly of VHS and DigiBeta. The demand was not to use any lossy compression for the digital archival copy.[2]

At that time, the only two valid candidates for storing video in such a way were either uncompressed or JPEG2000 lossless. Uncompressed was not an option because the size of uncompressed material—even for PAL SD material (720 × 76, 8 bits-per-component)—has a noticeable impact on the requirements on hard-disk space and network-throughput on all machines that work with the material. This would have greatly exceeded the available budget.

We asked other institutions that were already using JPEG2000-lossless for preservation about their experiences. None of them were working with the JPEG2000-lossless (in MXF container) files directly—mainly because this format combination was supported by few applications or because there were severe interoperability issues.

Since eternal migration should be considered when choosing a format for long-term preservation, the effort of getting in and out of a format plays an important role. We continued searching, therefore, for alternatives and found FFV1 in a lossless-codec comparison from the Graphics and Media Lab at MSU.[3] FFV1 was originally written by Michael Niedermayer as part of the FFmpeg project, leading to its name: FFmpeg Video codec 1.

The Mediathek then contacted Niedermayer, and hired him for implementing improvements such as multithreading and CRC checksums in the bitstream for additional error resilience. Dave Rice's contributions were also very vital to the success of this undertaking.

The result was FFV1 version 3 (FFV1.3), which was extensively tested[4] and officially released in August 2013.

## Performance Comparison

In order to compare the performance of FFV1 in terms of speed and compression ratio, four lossless codecs were selected for a test setup[5]:

- JPEG2000-lossless
- H.264-lossless

- Dirac-lossless
- FFV1

Although more than these lossless codecs exist, these four were chosen due to their possible suitability for long-term preservation. Other codecs were omitted, due to certain properties:

- Proprietary licensing
- Limited colorspace options
- Limited subsampling options
- Insufficient compression
- Insufficient speed

The test-setup was to encode an uncompressed YCbCr video source to these lossless codecs, and then decode back. In order to confirm the mathematically losslessness of the encoding/decoding procedure, FFmpeg's "framemd5"[6] functionality was used.

The three codecs—JPEG2000, H.264, and Dirac—only have lossless as an option. The main use-case for these formats in practice is lossy. Attention must be paid to avoid accidentally running them in lossy mode; many applications that support these formats are usually set and tested for lossy mode. Due to the popularity of lossy encoding, many applications do not even implement the lossless mode, do it incorrectly, or are not tested, as well, as some of our other tests have shown.

### JPEG2000-Lossless

The implementation used was "libopenjpeg."[7] At the time of testing, it did not support multithreading. There is also a JPEG2000 implementation available directly in FFmpeg, but it did not implement lossless mode correctly and could therefore not be used. In previous tests, Morgan "M-JPEG2000" codec package[8] was used to create the JPEG2000 lossless files. With these files, the framemd5 validation was negative. Due to the fact that Morgan's implementation is proprietary, we were unable to investigate what caused this mismatch. All we can say is that losslessness could not be verified. Therefore we chose libopenjpeg, which allows us to inspect and adapt the code if necessary.

### H.264-Lossless

Nowadays, H.264 is omnipresent as well as widely supported by many applications and embedded devices. Yet, even though the H.264 standard contains a lossless mode, it is rarely implemented. The FFmpeg documentation explicitly states:

"Most non-FFmpeg based players will not be able to decode lossless . . . , so if compatibility is an issue you should not use lossless."[9]

The reliability of this source can be assumed, because one of the developers of FFmpeg was Jason Garret-Glaser,[10] the lead developer of "libx264,"[11] the Free Software implementation of H.264/MPEG-4 AVC. Most H.264 files currently existing are produced using "libx264".

### Dirac-Lossless

The BBC developed the wavelet codec "Dirac"[12] as open source from the beginning and standardized it as "VC-2" (SMPTE 2042–1:2009). The implementation used for these tests was "libschroedinger."[13] At the time of testing, it did not support multithreading. Although BBC did a great job with Dirac, its performance regarding speed as well as compression ratio is inferior to FFV1 and Dirac is less widely adopted than JPEG2000—both lossy as well as lossless.

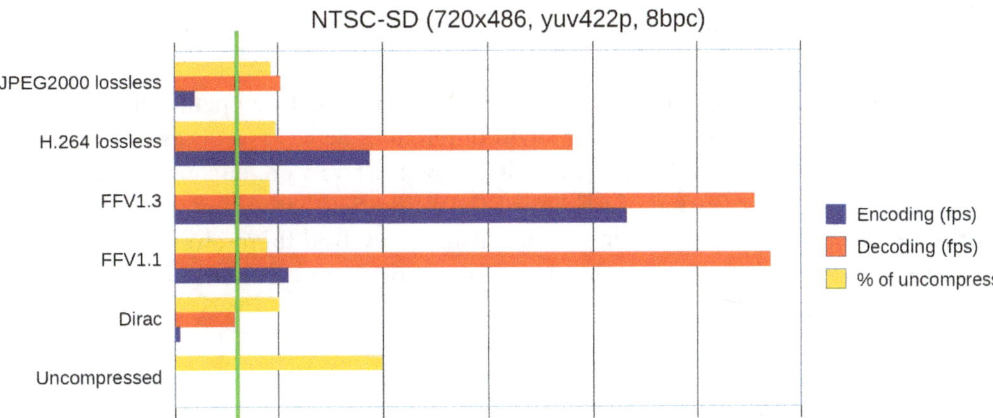


**Figure 1.** Codec speed / size comparison chart.

## Test Results

The environment these tests were run on was as follows:

- CPU: Intel(R) QuadCore(TM) i7–2600K CPU @ 3.40 GHz
- RAM: 8 GB DDR3 (1333 MHz)
- Disk: Intel SSDSA2CW080G3 (SSD)
- OS: GNU/Linux (Xubuntu 12.04.1, 64 bit)
- Tool: FFmpeg (version git N-59183-g3e62654)

The results of these tests show that the compression of FFV1 is almost equal to that ofJPEG2000-lossless, and noticeably smaller than H.264-lossless and Dirac-lossless. Here are two examples for common compression rates of FFV1 as observed in real-life usage andcompared to uncompressed. The size includes video (SD-PAL, 4:2:2, 8 bpc) and audio (PCM, 16 bit, stereo):

- Uncompressed: 1197,51 MB/min
- VHS: ca. 370 MB/min
- DigiBeta: ca. 650 MB/min

The speed improvements for encoding with FFV1.3 over FFV1.1 are also clearly visible in figure 1. On the ingest machines used at the Austrian Mediathek, FFV1.1 used around 70% CPU load, while the same material on the same machine had more than 90% CPU load on all four cores when running JPEG2000-lossless encoding.

Additional information, as well as the detailed parameters used for encoding/decoding of each codec can be found in the logfiles online.[14] Impact of different FFV1 encoding parameters on size and speed can be seen in the results of the tests we ran for the development of FFV1.3.[15]

## Accessibility and Interoperability

At this writing, the majority of applications and devices supporting FFV1 natively do so by using the FFmpeg/LibAV program libraries in their applications. Other applications that support system-codecs can handle FFV1 too, with appropriate codec-packages, such as ffdshow-tryouts[16] or LAVFilters[17] on Windows operating systems. Since FFV1 originated as part of the FFmpeg project, it has been available under a Free Software (open-source) license since the beginning.

The fact that the FFmpeg/LibAV libraries are very popular and used by a large number ofapplications, poses a different scenario that one usually encounters: with FFV1, any private developer, as well as companies, can use the exact same implementation of that codec. There is no necessity of writing one's own.

With other formats, the paper-standard specifications might be open, but implementations are proprietary, possibly containing slight differences between vendors or program versions. The only times where interoperability issues with FFV1 were encountered, were if an application used an older version of FFmpeg/LibAV libraries that was written before August 2013 (the release date of FFV1.3). These issues usually resolved themselves automatically as soon as a new version of the application built for a more recent version of FFmpeg/LibAV libraries was released.

## Sustainability

When first choosing FFV1, other institutions asked about sustainability concerns. The cases to be considered are:

- Decoding FFV1 in the future
- Different versions of FFV1

FFV1's Free Software (open-source) license, guarantees that it is allowed to "use, study, share & improve" the code now and in the future. Given these rights, archiving the source code of FFmpeg/LibAV is the digital equivalent of archiving the schematics—including building-components—of an analogue record/replay machine. So even if FFV1 might become unsupported by applications in the future, any institution or private individual that wants to access or transcode files encoded with FFV1 can do so without artificial restrictions. This means that anyone could then hire a developer to adapt the code to run under the then current circumstances—including any technology not yet developed or known.

Basically, this applies to any format where the proper implementation is available under a Free Software license. Additional concerns regarding licensing or patenting issues were also raised by some. These were addressed as part of the PREFORMA project (see "Standardization" below). The conclusion was that there are no patents known that might be related to FFV1. Even if there were, they would only apply to distributed application binaries—not the source code. The situation is the same that applies to the popular player VLC, for example.

So even in such a worst case scenario, an institution could legally build and use FFmpeg, for example, to then transcode from FFV1 to any other format. As the speed comparison charts above show, the times and computing resources needed for such a process are considerably less than using any other comparable lossless codec.

## Standardization

In 2014 the PREFORMA Project[18] started. Its goal is to have conformance-checking tools for long-term preservation file formats implemented. A result is "MediaConch,"[19] a tool for checking specification conformance of FFV1 and Matroska (MKV), as well as validating given format property policies (resolution, subsampling, etc.) of audiovisual files. MediaConch is being developed by "MediaArea,"[20] who are well known for "MediaInfo,"[21] a tool commonly used in audiovisual archives. As part of MediaConch, efforts are currently underway for standardizing FFV1 over the "Internet Engineering Task Force" (IETF).

IETF was chosen as standardization entity for several reasons:

- The discussion process is completely transparent, and mailing lists are archived for public review later on.
- Anyone can be invited to join the process.
- Only individuals, no companies, are allowed within the standardization process, which removes negative influence due to any commercial conflict of interest.
- The resulting standards paper is then available to anyone free of charge.

In order to provide a full package for audiovisual preservation, the IETF standardization roadmap currently includes the following:

- Video: FFmpeg Video Codec 1 (FFV1)
- Audio: Free Lossless Audio Compression (FLAC)
- Container: Matroska (MKV)

The intention is to have standardization for every one of these three components, but without users being required to use them in that combination. Since the standardization is work in progress right now, interested parties are invited to join the "CELLAR" working group.[22]

"CELLAR" stands for "Codec Encoding for LossLess Archiving and Real-Time Transmission" and was founded by MediaArea as part of the PREFORMA project.

## Transcoding and Nonlinear Editing

The current status quo is that applications that support system-codecs, as well as any application that uses FFmpeg/LibAV libraries, can handle FFV1. The Austrian Mediathek is using "Kdenlive"[23] (Linux) and "VirtualDub"[24] (Windows) for minor editing purposes. This has shown that direct editing of several tracks of SD material over a 1 GBit ethernet can be done without problems.

Given a 1-GBit ethernet, assuming 80 MB/s data transfer rate and video material with around 650 MB/min, this allows at least seven concurrent streams. With FFV1 from analogue VHS (370 MB/min), twelve concurrent streams would be possible before saturating the network bandwidth. Although popular editing suites such as AVID or FinalCut do not support FFV1 yet, these experiences show that it is technically absolutely possible to do nonlinear editing on FFV1 over a local network with moderate hardware requirements.

## Current and Future Application/ Vendor Support

There is no technical restriction preventing professional vendors from including FFV1 support if they want to. For example, if AVID, FinalCut or Premiere included FFV1 support, one would be able to have a seamlessly lossless production workflow. It would omit the necessity for requiring a separate lossy copy for editing.

FFmpeg/LibAV program libraries are commonly used in hundreds of programs, open source, as well as proprietary ones. This can be seen as a proof of concept, showing that if programmers can implement FFV1 support so easily that they do it in their spare time, it can be assumed that it is easily possible for other vendors, too.

With FFV1 gaining more momentum in the video preservation domain, interest for vendor's support may be increased. In terms of future improvements and additional features to FFV1, the intention is apply the basic principle of a minimalistic standard: "As complicated as necessary, but as simple as possible."[25] This should make future support easier and keep interoperability issues down to a minimum, although most of them are only temporary by nature—as explained above.

## Lossless Workflows

The Austrian Mediathek has used FFV1 productively as preservation format since mid-2011. The relevant steps in their workflow in terms of experience with lossless FFV1 encoded files are as follow:

- Ingest directly to FFV1
- Quality control (QC) on archive copy directly
- Automated mass transcodings for access copies, web, etc.
- Nonlinear video editing directly on FFV1

Except for ingest and QC, most of the automated transcodings are done using FFmpeg binaries on the command-line on GNU/Linux servers. For managing the whole workflow from tape-ingest to archive, the Mediathek uses "DVA-Profession"[26]—an ingest workflow management and automation tool, designed mainly for preservation archive use cases, and released under a Free Software license (GPLv3). Although there is room for improvement, this system makes use of FFV1 from beginning to end—with very satisfying results.

For other use cases or institutions, it might be desirable to have more vendors supporting FFV1, as well as joining resources to have more end-user applications with graphical user interfaces created, or improving existing ones. It can be said, that the example of the Austrian Mediathek choosing and improving FFV1 in collaboration with other archives and companies has shown that open-source licenses allow users to influence and shape their software landscape in a very effective and cost-efficient way.

## Conclusions

The experiences of more than five years of actively working with FFV1 on a daily basis confirms that using FFV1 was a good choice. It also allowed other institutions already to start digitization of their analogue material in a way that is accessible and highly interoperable. The properties of FFV1 also facilitate collaboration of institutions, as all improvements and experiences can be shared without artificial restrictions. The fact that the number of institutions choosing FFV1 as preservation codec, as well as their positive feedback when working with it, confirm the usefulness of this format.

Summing up the most important factors:

- FFV1 is more than four times faster than most J2K-lossless implementations.
- There is a wider choice of applications supporting FFV1 than J2K-lossless.
- Direct editing is currently not yet possible in most proprietary NLEs.
- There is increasing demand for GUI applications to handle FFV1.
- Sustainability of every version in existence is guaranteed by its Free Software license.
- There are no artificial restrictions getting in and out of FFV1.

Peter Bubestinger-Steindl is an independent consultant and developer, specializing in professional open-source solutions for long-term preservation needs and lossless audiovisual archiving workflows. He studied Media Computer Science at the Technical University in Vienna and has worked as project leader and developer in the field of digital preservation since 2002. As employee of "NOA Archiving Solutions," he set up and developed solutions for different broadcasting archives around the globe.

## Notes

1. http://www.mediathek.at/.
2. http://dva-profession.mediathek.at/fileadmin/MEDIASERVER/dva-profession html /documentation/projekt-motivation/index.html.
3. http://compression.ru/video/codec_comparison/lossless_codecs_en.html.
4. http://download.das-werkstatt.com/pb/mthk/ffv1_stats/latest/.
5. http://download.daswerkstatt.com/pb/mthk/info/video/comparison_video_codecs _containers.html#codec_tests.
6. http://dericed.com/2012/reconsidering-checksums-published-in-iasa-journal/.
7. http://www.openjpeg.org/.
8. http://www.morgan-multimedia.com/morgan/php/products.php?sProductId=5.
9. https://trac.ffmpeg.org/wiki/Encode/H.264#LosslessH.264.
10. http://www.x264.nl/developers/Dark_Shikari/CV.pdf.
11. http://www.videolan.org/developers/x264.html.
12. http://www.bbc.co.uk/opensource/projects/dirac/.
13. http://diracvideo.org/.
14. http://download.daswerkstatt.com/pb/mthk/info/video/comparison_video_codecs _containers.html#codec_tests.
15. http://download.das-werkstatt.com/pb/mthk/ffv1_stats/latest/.

16. http://ffdshow-tryout.sourceforge.net/.
17. https://github.com/Nevcairiel/LAVFilters/releases.
18. http://preforma-project.eu/.
19. https://mediaarea.net/MediaConch/.
20. https://mediaarea.net/.
21. https://mediaarea.net/en/MediaInfo.
22. https://datatracker.ietf.org/wg/cellar/charter/.
23. https://kdenlive.org/.
24. http://virtualdub.org/.
25. https://fsfe.org/activities/os/minimalisticstandards.html.
26. http://dva-profession.mediathek.at/.

# 22

# Hierarchical Storage and Managing Digital Media Assets for the Libraries and Archives of the Future

**Kia Siang Hock and Adrian Chan**


## Abstract

The National Library Board of Singapore (NLB) manages the National Library, the National Archives of Singapore (NAS), and the network of twenty-six public libraries in Singapore. It holds a collection of oral history interviews, music tracks/scores/lyrics, audiovisual and sound recordings which are valuable to Singapore as a nation.

The technical issues affecting the long term survival and accessibility of the audiovisual collections require the careful management of these materials which can pose significant challenges to libraries and archives.

The risk of media obsolescence, particularly for the analogue formats and media, requires urgent migration and digitization. This is managed by the Sound and Moving Image Laboratory (SMIL) of NAS. SMIL is the centre of excellence within NLB which conserves, digitises and preserves audiovisual recordings for NLB.

Collaborating with NLB's Technology and Innovation (TNI) team, SMIL's hierarchical storage strategy was implemented to effectively and efficiently manage the huge storage required for the audiovisual contents. Ingest systems were set up to ingest new formats in high-definition (HD), 2K, and eventually 4K resolutions. The constant need to migrate digital files into newer formats is systematically done to ensure that nothing is lost to technological obsolescence.

This paper shares NLB's experience in the end-to-end management of its growing audiovisual collections for access and preservation.



## Keywords

audiovisual, preservation, digitisation, conservation, hierarchical storage, media asset management.


## The NL-NAS Story

The National Archives of Singapore (NAS) joined the National Library Board (NLB) in November 2012. Both NAS and the National Library have been actively digitising Singapore content for many years. This coming together created a catalyst to synergize a NL-NAS Digital Preservation and Delivery Strategy to serve as a critical pillar for its digital collections and services. This strategy provides comprehensive digitisation and digital acquisition plans to enrich our National Collection. It hopes to ensure that current and future generations of Singaporeans will have access to Singapore's past, are inspired by such historical moments. They can also cherish the parts they played in creating such shared memories, and weaving the fabric of the nation.

We looked at how best to utilise our limited resources and knowledge expertise within our archival eco-system to provide access to uniquely Singapore content for future Singapore in a sustainable manner. A future-oriented and future-ready NLB needs to be a custodian of Singapore-related audiovisual content to inspire Singaporeans to participate in the nation's past, present and future.

The audiovisual collections play an increasingly important role in libraries and archives. Audiovisual experience is a useful tool to create a vibrant reading culture in Singapore and develop a nation of active readers of all ages.

Our strategies using multimedia contents on social media started with the Singapore Memories Project and Read@School (Early Read and kidsREAD) where we immersed different



*Sustainable Audiovisual Collections* (2017): 160–169. DOI: 10.2979/jts2016.0.0.24

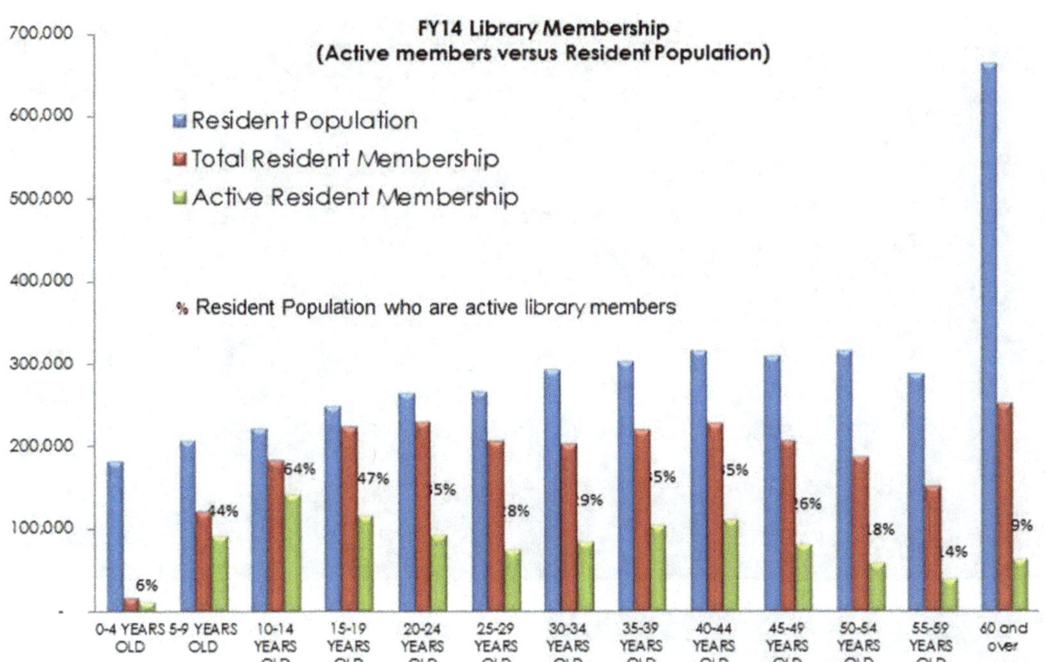


**Figure 1.** FY14 Library membership.[1]

spaces for young readers with inspiring collections and arts and culture programs where collaborations and mentoring created opportunities for the communities.

## Sustainable Workflow and Quality Digitization

Preserving and enhancing discovery for our audiovisual collections in a digital era require an IT infrastructure for end-to-end archival management with the ability to view, ingest, perform quality checks, and generate access copies while managing classified or restricted access in the most seamless integration possible.

Over the last three years, digitization work has evolved rapidly. As a policy, we still keep the analogue tapes after digitization. The tapes are kept in repositories and the digitized master files now become the master copy. It is therefore critical that the digitized master files are at the best quality possible. Comprehensive quality checks (QCs) are integral to this regime.

Today, NAS manages about 20 TB of in-house AV digitization and 40 TB of outsourced AV digitization every month. The digitized files include a preservation copy (in lossless compression JPEG2000[2] OP1a codec wrapped in MXF format for video and BWF for audio), a working copy (in XDCAM or IMX30 lossy file wrapped in MXF format for video and BWF for audio) and access copy (in H.264 wrapped in MP4 format for video and MP3 for audio).

The records which are digitized into these files go through the QC process where our QC system uses tools for video and audio compliance to our in-house policy formats, checks for drop-outs of the generated content, updates our digital audiovisual preservation (DAP) system with timecodes and technical metadata, and checks for baseband quality in audio and video. Most importantly, it checks for encoding/transcoding errors in files which will end up as our master files for the original records. Checksums and file integrity can then be included at this stage as a reference when transferring files to different media to keep the integrity of the file in check.[3]

We handle quality checks of about 1,000 hours of AV records every month at 24 hours and 7 days a week. This is achieved through a combination of file-based automated QCs and selective manual QCs.

These QCed files are then archived into a LTO tape library into two preservation copies and one working copy which are externalized and placed into repositories with controlled humidity and temperatures. Checksum is done once the LTO tape is placed in the tape library. Our staging SAN-storage servers has been 75% utilized since it was commissioned on 1 October 2014.

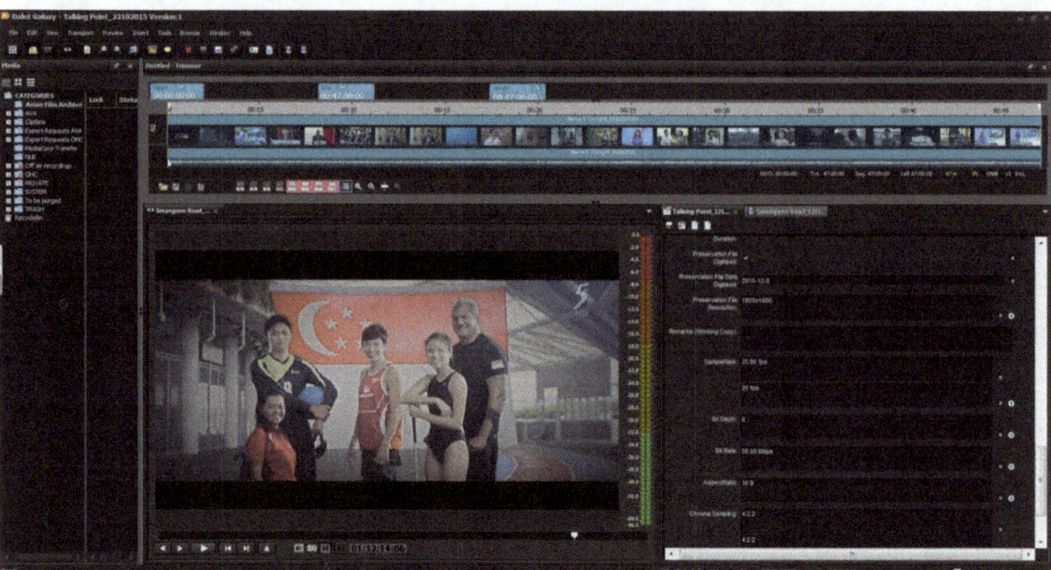
Figure 2. Broadcast archive.

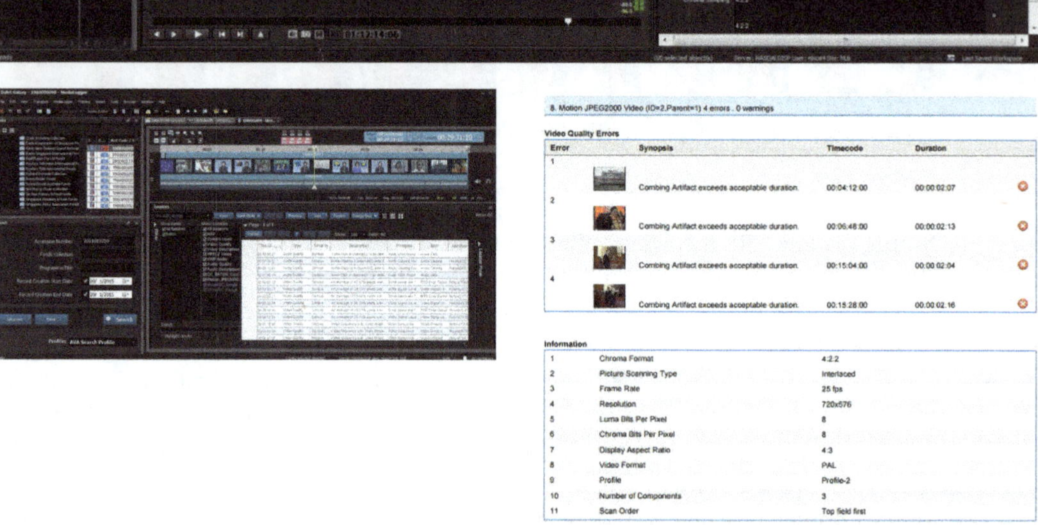

Figure 3 and 4. File base quality check system.

That averages 500–700 TB of digital contents every year which is set to double in the next one to two years as we race to digitize the obsolete AV formats.

For this reason, we made enhancements to our DAP system that allows AV records created by these public offices to be viewed, tracked, and archived into various storage media. This was set up to mitigate the risk of obsolesce for these high volume of digital files. Our hierarchical risk-management strategy is to have placeholders for different levels of files for the same record at different storage point and our DAP system tracks and indexes these records.

## Changing Needs and Flexible Requirements

Today's collaborative workflows need a faster turnaround for content digitisation, creation, and distribution. Faster throughput (bandwidth) means more works can be accomplished by the same number of producers, artists, archivists, and other professionals, allowing them to be more productive. Greater flexibility and capability will allow these professionals a greater field of expression within the modern digital workflows which are capable of delivering these different services by utilizing faster connectivity, processing power and digital storage.

This requires a digital storage platform that can both adapt to quickly changing requirements, whether for higher performance, higher density, greater cost efficiency, or long-term asset protection, while greatly enhancing the control and capability of the primary content creation, finishing, deployment, and management solutions. The hierarchical storage with this combination of digital storage can adapt to changing needs, while enhancing the value of the content creation and management solutions. This requires a workflow optimized storage platform which only a hierarchical storage[4] can achieve.

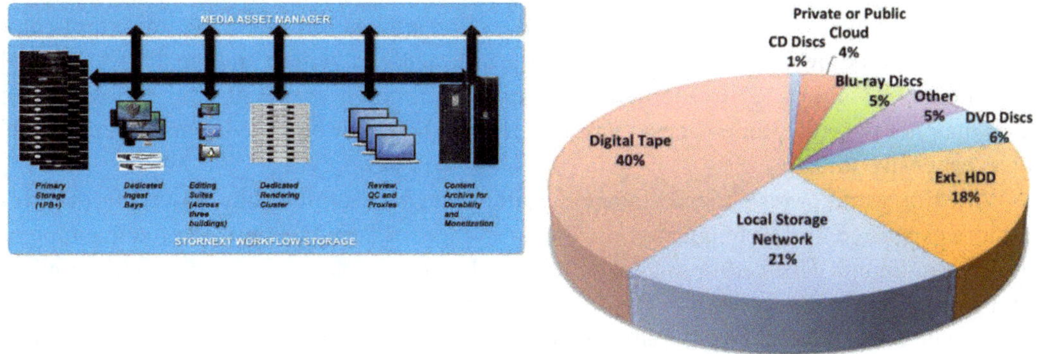


**Figure 5 and 6.** Hierarchical workflow and percentage of digital long-term archives on various media.

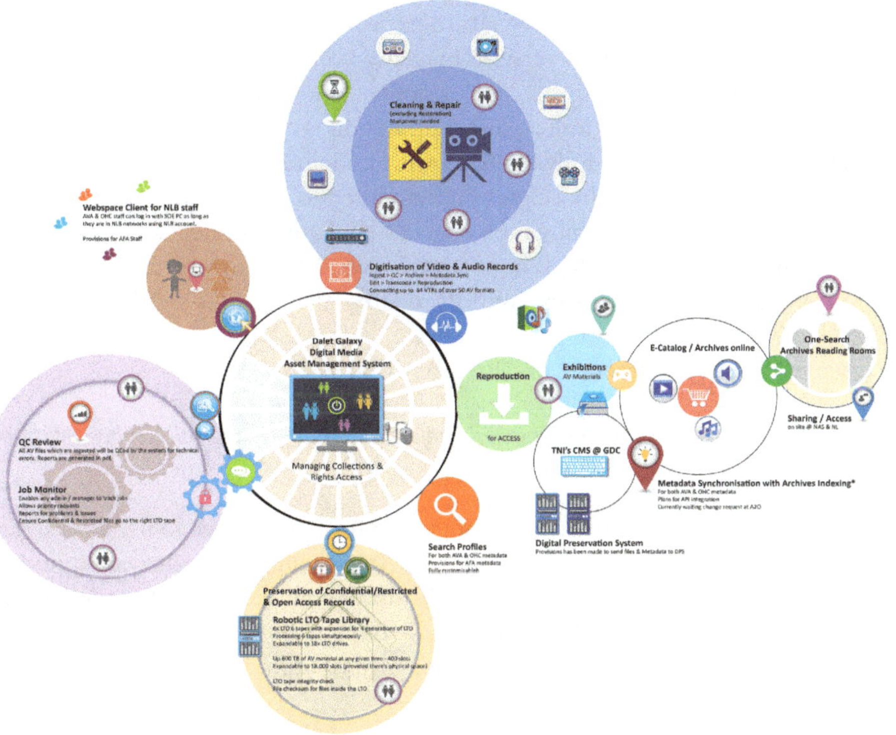


**Figure 7.** NL-NAS end-to-end workflow overview.

Digital storage optimized[5] for video workflows is different from general-purpose IT files. This is because the demands of moving and streaming large, high-resolution media files are quite different from the demands of storing and accessing photos, database records, or documents. Similarly, the file movement demands of a general business or IT environment are very different from the needs of AV content movement throughout AV production workflow.

Files in a general business or IT environment are quickly moved from a primary, active storage to a more static archive. AV records or content-centric workflows require content to move from primary storage to different storage archives, and back several times within the ingest, QC, reproduction, distribution, and archiving workflow. An intelligent hierarchical storage platform allows asset management or workflow automation solutions to address the entire end-to-end workflow[6].

## Value in Hierarchical Storage for Different Needs

The key difference is its ability to customise the type of the storage to be used depending on the application's needs, in terms of speed, performance, and cost. The needs of one workflow may be very different from the next, and great efficiencies can be gained by segregating workflow by using different types of storage, rather than using the same class of storage for all workflows or content.

This adds value to various technologies for the same application where the important component of the workflow-optimized storage is in the automatic migration and recall of AV record and content from one storage to another, based upon the lifecycle of that AV file. As this content ages it may not have the same access requirements and thus can be stored more economically on less expensive storage.

With this workflow-optimized storage,[7] content can be automatically moved from faster but more expensive storage to cheaper secondary storage, or even back to cost-effective tape or optical-base storage. This can dramatically reduce the costs to store the content. This application manages, optimizes, and unites the different tiers of storage that we have and uses the same interface and tools for managing the storage to automatically restore older content for immediate reuse.

With generic IT network storage there is often only a single storage and it may require third-party data management applications and even third-party storage systems to enable a multitiered storage which may not work when new versions of software or hardware emerge.

NL-NAS is currently considering the use of optical disc archival library. We are in the infancy of the digital preservation. Time is, however, not on our side, and the entire collection of audiovisual materials needs to be fully digitized within the next few years.

This hierarchical capability of the system implemented to manage and preserve both SD/HD AV records and 2K/4K film content which is of national and historical significance to mitigate the risk of loss of contents. What NLB hopes to achieve is our mandate to fulfill our national patrimonial role of making our content accessible through 4-ABLES: PreservABLE*, FindABLE, ExpandABLE, DeliverABLE.

(*The essence of this paper focuses on "PreservABLE")

## Making Memories Accessible and PreservABLE for Future Singapore

*"I can rest assured that everything in the National Collection that is precious will last beyond this generation."*

Preservation of the National Collection is of paramount importance to us. We see digitization as the key to both preserving the National Collection digitally and also enabling NLB to provide access to current and future generations. Whilst digital files can offer quick onsite and offsite access to our content, digital file formats also require specific needs to preserve them as they can become obsolescent even faster than paper materials, due to technological evolution and physical deterioration.

The digital content stored in a digital archive is subject to a number of threats that endanger the ability to preserve this content for the future. These threats relate to various types of technology obsolescence. The media itself can become obsolete and you can no longer find a machine to read the file. Digital materials are machine dependent in order to be accessed. The speed of change in technology means that the timeframe available to take action to preserve the digital materials is very much shorter. An analogue audiovisual record stored in an office environment or storage space lacking appropriate environmental controls will need to be migrated regularly or there will be the possibility of catastrophic loss through deterioration over time.

The phasing out of old analogue audiovisual players is certain. Many players are either already extinct, or they will shortly be. So digitization from such formats would need to be completed within our generation. Accessibility to the content may be totally lost if we do not make it preservABLE now.

Part of our preservation works include the migration of our collection of audiovisual records created by public offices and private organizations covering sixty years of our broadcasting history that captures defining moments such as the momentous self-government victory rally speech of 1959. The past will continue to inspire us but as Singapore continues to develop, new events become part of the memory of the nation.

The Singapore broadcast industry has moved into full HD digital transmission in 2015 and there is a corresponding rapid phasing out of analogue equipment. NAS has to step up the

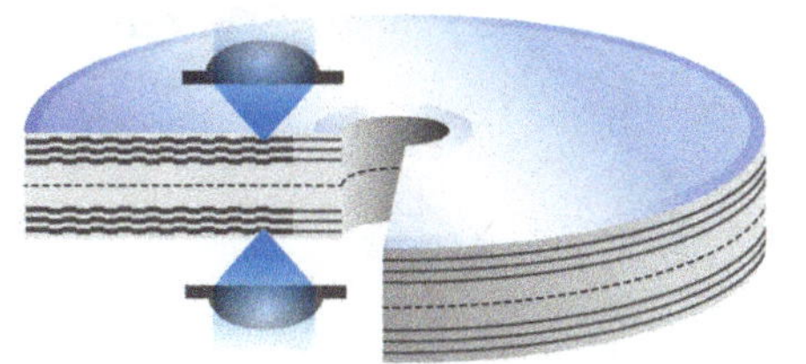

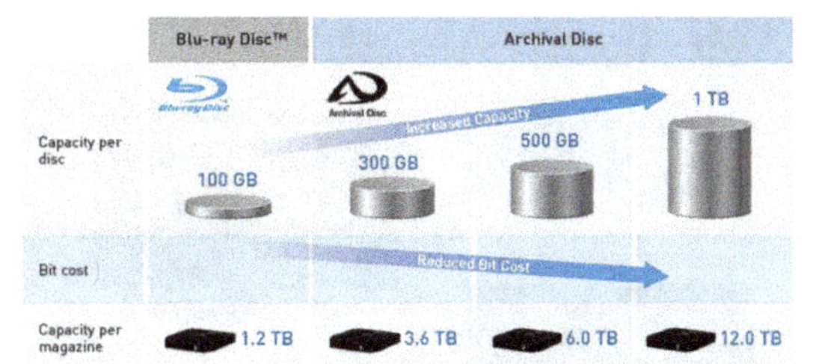


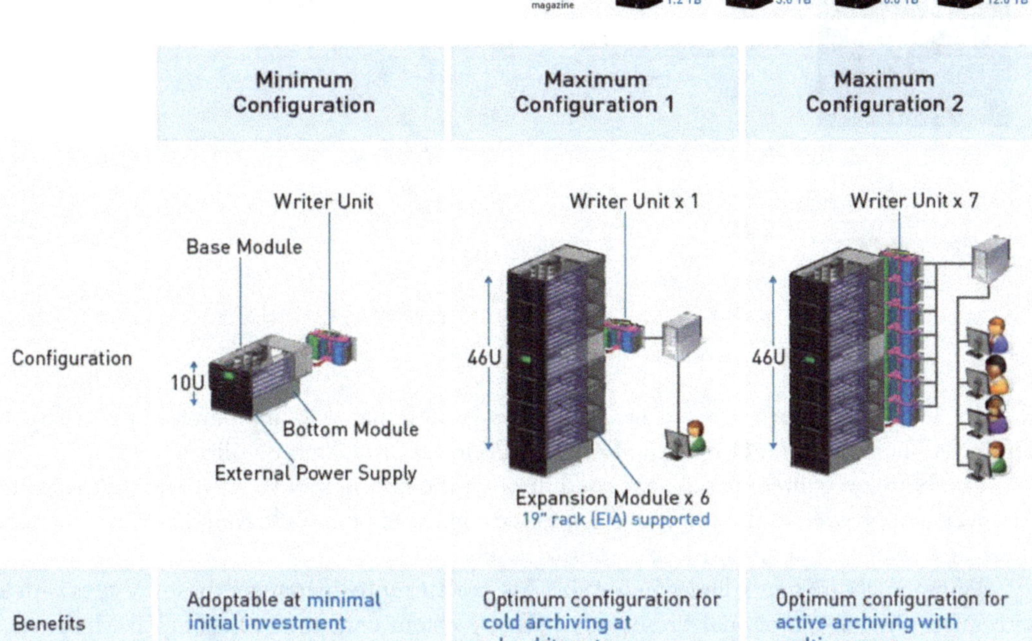


**Figure 8–10.** Archival disc from Panasonic and Sony.[8]

pace of migration and digitization of AV records so as to reduce the risk of loss due to format obsolescence. This migration and digitization of about 64,000 analogue AV recordings currently preserved at NAS and a projected 10,000 recordings yet to be transferred to NAS by public agencies will be our focus for the next three to five years[9].

The conversion to digital file-base AV records will facilitate and allow for the simultaneous access of recordings through all NLB libraries and not just at the Archives Reading Room. The current plan is for digitized AV recordings to have immediate access at NAS and extended to all the libraries across Singapore for viewing where copyrights permit.

NAS has also been transcribing and translating oral history interviews after digitization to facilitate greater and easier use of the contents. Transcribing and translation work is vital as it provides easier access to the oral history recordings through enabling easy searches and shorter research time. Transcripts are also useful when quotes need to be extracted quickly for use in publications and exhibitions. Therefore, there will be a corresponding wider usage of rich oral history contents for programming and exhibitions. With more translated interviews, language will no longer be a barrier to the dissemination of stories and information in the oral history collection.

## How the Story Ends?

With so much valuable memories, NL-NAS can no longer depend on just a one-size, one-storage-fits-all solution. The intelligent hierarchical storage platform provides us the cost-effective and scalable solution to meet the blazing pace of AV digitization. Our story should NOT end, but memories must continue into future generations. And for this to happen, NLB has architected and put in place a comprehensive suite of well-integrated systems.

One of which is the DAP system for AV which handles over 500 TB of preservation materials annually. The other key system is the Ex Libris Rosetta Digital Preservation System (DPS). Rosetta is one of the leading digital preservation solutions used by libraries and archives in the

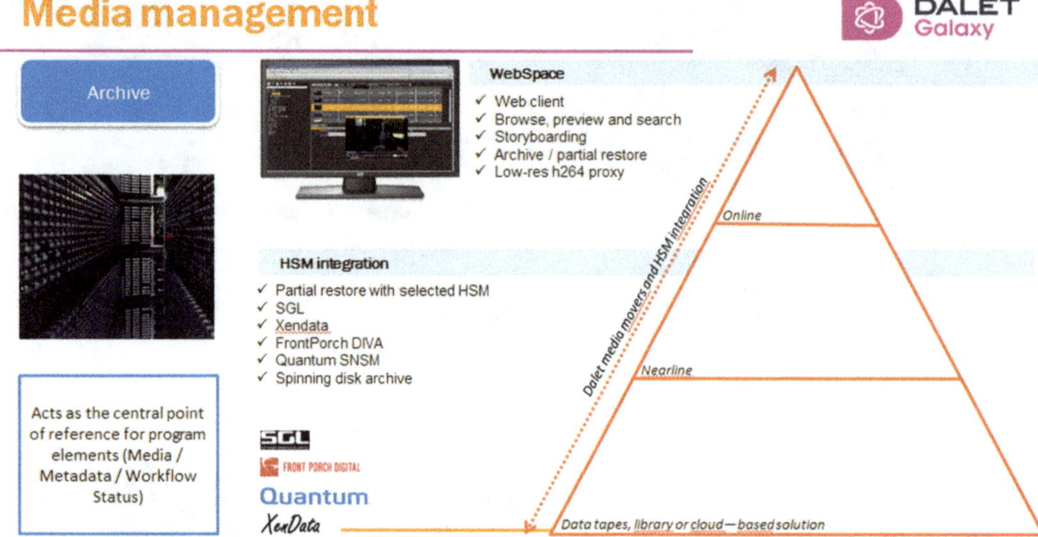


**Figure 11.** Integration to digital media asset management.

world.[10] As of December 2015, over 140 TB of preservation materials are managed in the Rosetta DPS. NAS has also started to use the Rosetta DPS for its photographs collection.

The NAS AV content can be accessed through the one-stop NAS Archives Online portal. Archives Online streams the AV content, and is designed to be mobile-friendly. It also manages the access levels, including onsite and offsite access.

AV materials are much larger in file size. We are currently managing these AV files with an integrated Digital Audiovisual Preservation (DAP) system consisting of a Digital Media Asset Management System from Dalet (which includes Brio and Amberfin ingest servers), Baton file base QC system from InterraSystems, and Quantum Hierarchical StorNext. The beauty of the hierarchical storage system is that once it is populated, we can externalize and put in new storage at lower cost so we will not run out of storage space.

This hierarchical concept[11] uses an "object storage" which fundamentally is a different approach by presenting a namespace of simple key and value pairs in contrast to traditional storage systems that organize files in folders and files mapped to blocks on disk. By using a flat namespace and abstracting the data addressing from the physical storage, object storage-based systems offer more flexibility in how and where content is stored and preserved. Because object storage leverages the scale-out capabilities of IP networks, this addressing allows digital data sets to scale indefinitely. Object storage controller breaks data into data objects and distributes them over multiple independent nodes, disks, and sites according to policy. If one of the data objects is lost because of a disk failure, the object storage will rebuild that data object on another storage node.

This purpose-built workflow-optimized storage saves time. It eliminates costly human errors and allows the creative users to focus their valuable time on core creative pursuits that yield more for the organization rather than spending their time on manual and unpredictable content workflow steps. It delivers values throughout the entire archival and production workflow. Purpose-built workflow storage extracts more values in the processes, creating values from content with the same staff and facility and over the entire managed lifecycle of the content produced to yield long-term benefits.

Professional media also has been dependent upon a variety of digital storage technologies to carry on the various operations. It starts from content capture, through post-production, content distribution, and finally archiving. The shift to digital technologies has highlighted the role of digital storage in every aspect of video production and use. Its characteristics of various storage technologies have led to their use in different applications.

Flash memory has become the dominant storage technology in modern professional video cameras, and it is playing an increasing role in content distribution and perhaps, as the price declines, post-production, due to its high performance.[12] Reflecting the move to information

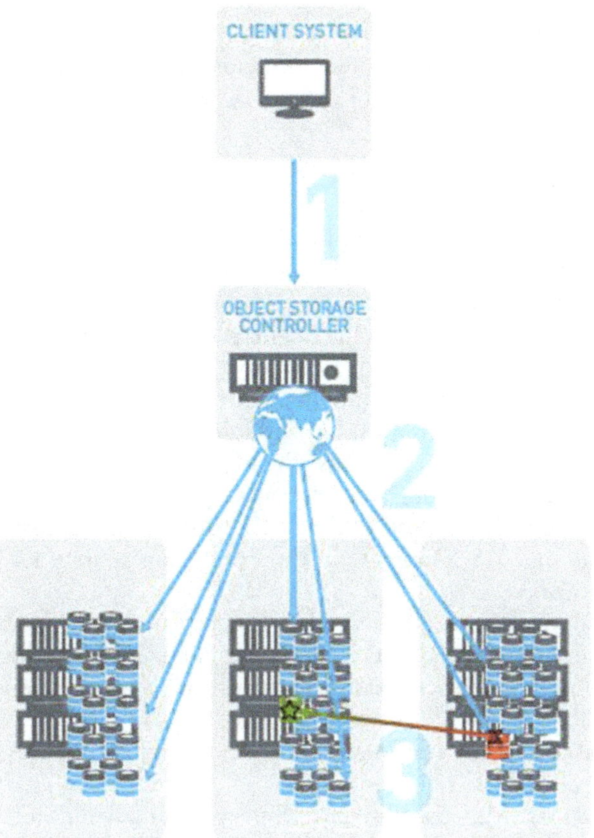


**Figure 12.** Object storage technology for scalability and flexibility.

1. Client system writes data to object storage.
2. Object storage controller breaks data into data objects and distributes them over multiple independent nodes, disks, and sites according to policy
3. If one of the data objects is lost because of a disk failure, the object storage will rebuild that data object on another storage node.

technology networking in many production facilities, network storage and even cloud-based storage is assuming an important and growing role in post-production, content distribution, and even archiving. These cloud storage systems uses HDDs, flash memory, optical discs, and magnetic tape to allow for trade-offs of cost and performance.

By implementing a hierarchical storage workflow together with a digital media asset management, we are able to scale out our high-performance primary storage system to enable specialized ingest stations, editing bays across multiple buildings, and simultaneously dedicate high performance to any rendering bays or transcoders, which can help in speed up priority records within the comprehensive workflow while focusing on the archival and production process all at the same time. This allows NLB to have higher efficiencies from our limited resources to preserve and provide access to future Singaporeans our memories, our stories and our legacies.

Kia Siang Hock is currently the Deputy Director overseeing IT Architecture and Innovation at the National Library Board of Singapore (NLB). He and his teams are heavily involved in the conceptualisation, prototyping, design, and development of various innovative services at NLB.

Adrian Chan is currently the Assistant Director overseeing the Sound and Moving Image Lab (SMIL) at the National Archives of Singapore (NAS). He and his team manage the conservation, preservation, migration and archival of analogue and digital AV records for Audio Visual Archives, Oral History Centre, and the National Library. This involves identifying, organizing, and preserving the audiovisual records according to medium, carrier type, format and media by a system of migration and exploring new audiovisual technologies. SMIL also recommends and implements appropriate technologies relating to the preservation of audiovisual records and its condition via a risk management strategy.

## Notes

1. 2015 Nation of Readers National Library Board.
2. Heiko Sparenberg and Siegfried Foessel, 2016, A Concept for File-Based Content Exchange Using Scalable Media.
3. Interra Systems, Inc, 2015 Auto QC in the Digitization Workflow, Digital Media Group.
4. SMPTE 124–08: 2015 T. M. Coughlin, 2014 Survey of Storage in Media and Entertainment, Coughlin Associates, http://tomcoughlin.com/techpapers.htm.
5. T. M. Coughlin, 2011 Making a Robust Media Archive, Coughlin Associates.
6. T. M. Coughlin, 2011 Maximizing Process, Creative and Content Lifecycle Value with Workflow-Optimized Storage, Coughlin Associates.
7. T. M. Coughlin, 2011 Making a Robust Media Archive, Coughlin Associates.
8. Panasonic Corporation, 2015 A Long-Term Data Archiving Strategy for More Sustainable Business, AVC Networks.
9. National Archives of Singapore, 2015 NL-NAS Masterplan,National Library Board.
10. Siang Hock Kia, Adrian Chan, Peter Pak and Jasper Phang, 2015 End-to-end management of audiovisual and multimedia content and services—the NLB experience, National Library Board.
11. Quantum Corporation, 2014 Reinventing Large-Scale Digital Libraries With Object Storage Technology.
12. SMPTE 124–08: 2015 T. M. Coughlin, 2014 Survey Summary for Storage in Professional Media and Entertainment, http://tomcoughlin.com/techpapers.htm.

## Reference List


Coughlin, T. M. (2011). Making a robust media archive. Coughlin Associates.

——. (2011). Maximizing process, creative and content lifecycle value with workflow-optimized storage. *Coughlin Associates.*

——. (2012). 2010 Survey of Digital Storage in Professional Media and Entertainment, SMPTE Mot. Imag. J., 121:27–31, Jan.-Feb. 2012.

——. (2014). Survey of digital storage in professional media and entertainment. *Coughlin Associates*. Atascadero, CA.

——. (2014). 2014 Digital Storage in Professional Media and Entertainment Report. *Coughlin Associates*. Atascadero, CA.

——. (2014). Survey summary for storage in professional media and entertainment. SMPTE 124–08: 2015. Retrieved from http://tomcoughlin.com/techpapers.htm

International Telecommunications Union. (2014, February). Advanced video coding for generic audiovisual services. ITU-T Recommendation H.264. Geneva.

International Telecommunications Union. (2015, April) High Efficiency Video Coding. TU-T Recommendation H.265. Geneva.

Interra Systems, Inc. (2015). Auto QC in the Digitization Workflow, *Digital Media Group*.

Kia, S.H., Chan, A., Pak, P. and Phang, J. (2015) End-to-end management of audiovisual and multimedia content and services—the NLB experience. *Singapore National Library Board*.

National Archives of Singapore, (2015). NL-NAS Masterplan. National Library Board.

Pallett, J. (2014, April). Bitrate requirements for HEVC: Comparing H.265, H.264 and MPEG-2. Proc. Proceedings from NAB: *NAB Broadcast Engineering Conference*. Las Vegas.

Panasonic Corporation. (2015). A long-term data archiving strategy for more sustainable business. AVC Networks Company.

Quantum Corporation. (2014). Reinventing large-scale digital libraries with object storage technology.

Singapore National Library Board. (2015). Nation of Readers.

(2014). Interoperable Master Format—Application #2 Extended. SMPTE ST 2067–21:2014. Retrieved from https://www.smpte.org/standards.

Society of Motion Picture and Television Engineers. (2012.) Material exchange format (MXF) file format specification. SMPTE ST 377–1:2012.

Sparenberg, H., and Foessel, S. (2012, October) Real time file system for content distribution. Proceedings from SMPTE 2012: *SMPTE 2012 Annual Technical Conference*. Hollywood, CA.

Sparenberg, H. and Foessel, S. (2013, October). Advanced storage techniques using scalable media. Proceedings from SMPTE 2013: *SMPTE 2013 Annual Technical Conference*. Hollywood, CA.

Sparenberg, H. and Foessel, S. (2016). A concept for file-based content exchange using scalable media.

Sullivan, G. J., Schwarz, H., Keng Tan, T., and Wiegand, T. (Dec. 2012). Comparison of the coding efficiency of video coding standards—Including high efficiency video coding (HEVC). IEEE Trans. Circ. Syst. Video. Tech., 22(12):1669–1684.

Taubman, D. and Marcellin, M.W. (2002). JPEG2000: Image compression fundamentals, standards and practice. Boston: Kluwer Academic Publishers, p. 513ff.

# 23

# The Role of Optical Storage Technologies in Future Digital Archives

**Morgan David and Yuji Sekiguchi**


## Abstract

Digital archive storage especially for the storage of sound and moving images continues to present significant challenges in finding the best solutions for long-term preservation of valuable assets at reasonable cost and performance. This paper sets the choice of storage technology in the wider context of risk management for digital archives in general and develops key requirements to be considered for different types of archive. The paper discusses media reliability, lifetime, and failure scenarios and then goes on to consider the longer term issues of technology obsolescence and content migration strategies.



## Keywords

optical disc, storage, archive, environment, lifetime reliability.


## Introduction

All observers of data storage and archive trends agree that the strong growth in size will continue for the foreseeable future potentially reaching 9,000 exabytes by the end of this decade (fig. 1).

This is driven by many factors, but a continuing trend of falling storage cost (per byte) and rapid increases in the amount and size of content being created, especially audio-video content, are two of the biggest. As digital storage technology has developed media archives have benefitted greatly in terms of size, cost, and performance because these are priorities shared with the IT industry in general. However, other requirements, such as long-term cost of operation, have been less well served because rapid technology renewal and hence obsolescence presents a significant problem when affordable, reliable preservation are your highest priority; these are not goals shared with the main-stream IT world. It is therefore important to understand the longer-term operational implications when different types of media such as tape, optical disc, hard disc, and solid-state memory are to be adopted. It is also important to consider the way economies of scale as applied to established technologies can act as a barrier to change and how that affects the perception of risk by those who have the duty to ensure the long-term preservation of irreplaceable assets.

## Digital Archive Storage Requirements

There are several different applications for storage technologies even in the world of digital media archive. One example is that of the many archives that focus exclusively on the long-term preservation of assets for access by many different users. The focus is on the need to preserve large amounts of content with the best possible quality for the longest possible time at the lowest cost.

In other cases, archives are required to be integrated with fast-moving production systems providing an efficient way to migrate content in to and out of archive storage efficiently. In this case, as with the first group, the archive needs to preserve large amounts of content with the best possible quality for the longest possible time at the lowest cost. But in this case there is an additional need to automate the handling of archive media to provide near-line storage and this in turn is integrated with high-performance storage architectures for production and hierarchical storage management software to automate the process of migrating content in and out of online storage. This online/near-line/offline architecture allows us to specify the optimum archive technology for cost and lifetime while minimising the compromises for operational responsiveness.



*Sustainable Audiovisual Collections* (2017): 170–176. DOI: 10.2979/jts2016.0.0.25

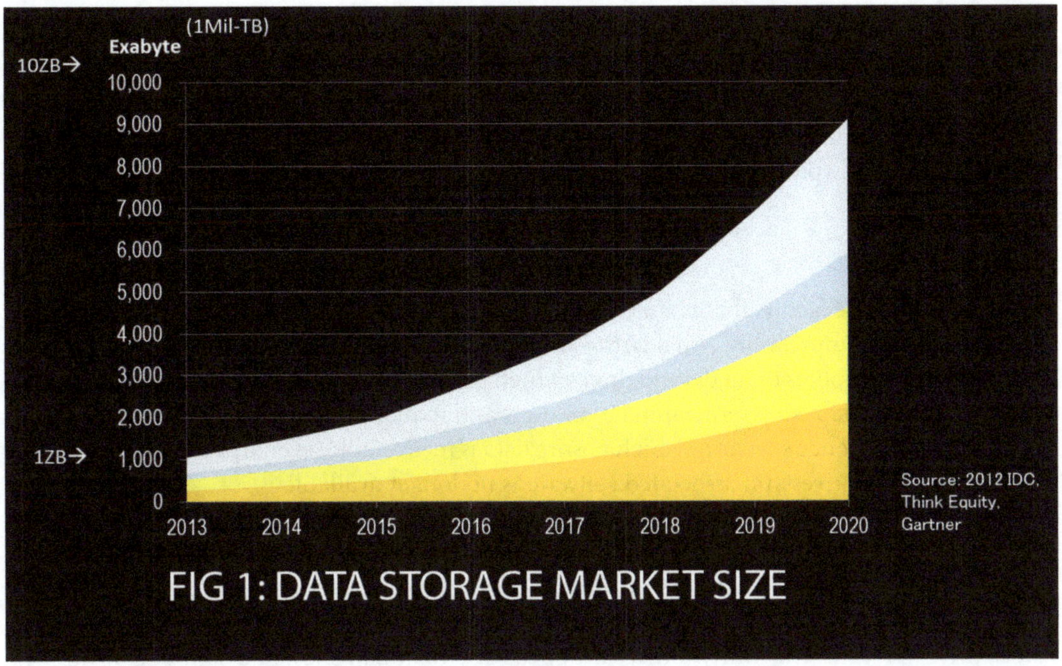

**Figure 1.** Data storage market.

## Environmental Requirements

In recent years regulators have become very aware of the rapid growth in the number and size of "data centres" and the environmental impact they have in terms of energy usage which is believed to be growing at a rate of 16% annually. The European Union (EU) for example is looking at Power Usage Effectiveness (PUE) and also considering whole life cycle usage including manufacturing and disposal of IT equipment and infrastructure. Today just 50% of that energy is used to power the IT hardware in data centres with the rest consumed by power distribution and cooling. Not only is this a major operating cost for the IT industry but it is expected to become a target for environmental legislation and, therefore, many ideas are being tried including air and water cooling with Microsoft recently trialling under-sea locations.

Looking specifically at data storage, moving data from spinning hard discs to removable media that can be stored for long periods without needing power offers a considerable energy and cost saving, but cooling and air conditioning are still a concern if there is a requirement for temperature and humidity to be permanently maintained within tight tolerances to maintain acceptable lifetime. As we shall see in more detail below, this is an issue for tape but not optical disc which can be safely stored without special air conditioning in a wide range of indoor environments, even in the humidity and heat of the tropics.

## Key Factors for Choosing Storage Technology and Media for Archive

There are three main factors when choosing archival storage that we will consider in turn: data integrity, future security, and cost.

Data integrity issues include

- data written to media but later cannot be read due to some failure
- files on media are erased, overwritten or corrupted
- through age, physical handling or mechanical wear media becomes un-readable

Data integrity is influenced by three factors:

1. The availability and use of professional read/write drives, which offer write-verify capability where all data that has been written to media is read back to automatically verify the write was successful. This is managed by the device and ensures high reliability is achieved. This function is enabled by default on Sony Optical Disc Archive drives.

2. Media for professional applications is designed to be handled, with the critical media contained within a shell to protect the data carrier from finger-marking, dust, etc. Sony media

for Optical Disc Archives are contained within a 12-disc cartridge. Furthermore, the design of this disc handling system means that the read-write heads never touch the surface of the disc in operation thus ensuring that the disc does not suffer from surface wear with repeated use.

3. The availability of write once-read multiple media for professional archive makes it possible to permanently protect data from erasure.

### Future Security

There are also three factors that characterise the future security of a storage technology:

1. Backward compatibility—that is, the ability to read old media in new generations of drives

2. Multiple suppliers of media and drives which promote a commercially competitive market place helping to establish a "critical mass" of users and reduce the risk of early end-of-life issues

3. Postobsolescence scenarios which ensure data is recoverable, even in a worst-case scenario where a supply of drives and associated software is no longer available

Optical disc has an excellent record on backward compatibility with the latest generation of multi-format drives capable of reading discs all the way back to the original introduction of the audio CD in 1982. This also points to very good post-obsolescence options as the Optical Disc Archive discs will continue to be readable by standard BD XL drives and, therefore, in future drives as well. This thirty-four year optical disc roadmap shows no sign of slowing with the announcement last year of the archival disc development agreement between Sony and Panasonic to jointly develop and trademark archive disc media, starting with the introduction of a 300-GB disc and with plans for a 1-TB disc in the future.

Of course it is important to know that data recovered from a (set of) discs can readily be exported in an open form for use elsewhere and, in the case of ODA, Sony is preparing an Optical Disc Archive Salvage Tool which allows individual discs from a cartridge to be read and assembled into a virtual disk which can be mounted on a Linux or Windows host. This provides a good mechanism for disaster recovery (e.g., due to mechanical failure) and also an insurance against future obsolescence.

Cost is possibly the biggest factor in choosing suitable technologies, but is more complex to analyse than it may at first appear. Digital Archive assets are a source of revenue but the archives they come from are often justified for cultural or operational reasons rather than commercial ones. As we would expect investment decisions are influenced by factors such as efficiency and reliability, but the media cost per byte is often the dominating factor. However, media purchase price is not the only cost associated with long-term storage, especially where media has a finite life and, therefore, requires periodic migration. The cost of maintaining the storage environment should also be factored in here, as should the cost of planned migrations where media lifetime and/or device obsolescence can be foreseen. These "on-costs" reflect the unusually long-term commitments that an archive typically has and are, therefore, very real. However, those responsible for investment decision-making can find it difficult to support the long-term argument when the horizon for planning in other areas of business and government are generally limited to just a few years. Archive optical disc has excellent long-term storage characteristics when compared with currently available alternatives, but the cost benefits are accrued over a longer period. The decision to adopt optical storage needs to be factored into the discussions with stakeholders and decision makers at an early stage to ensure that the longer term benefits can be taken in to account.

## Understanding Optical Disc Technologies

To many people optical disc is an ubiquitous technology and its standard 12-cm physical format and extensive backward compatibility creates the impression that the technology is common to all optical drives and media. This is not the case and in thirty-four years several recording mechanisms have been developed (fig. 2) starting with the pressing system originally developed for audio CDs.

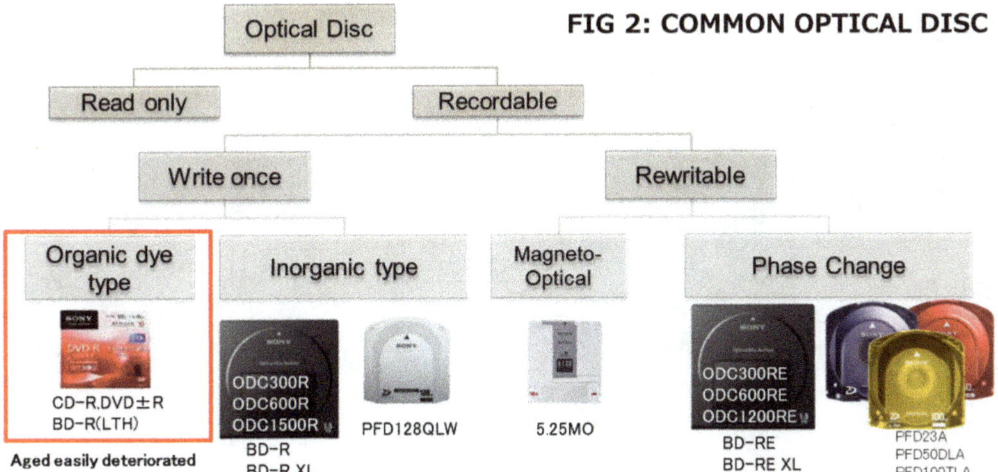


Figure 2.

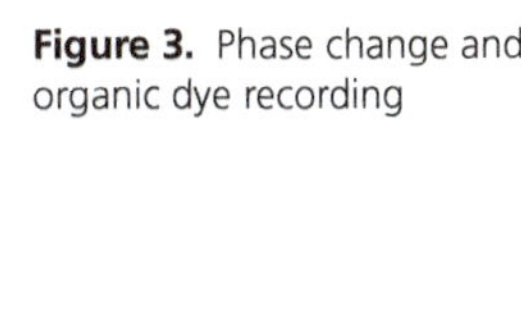

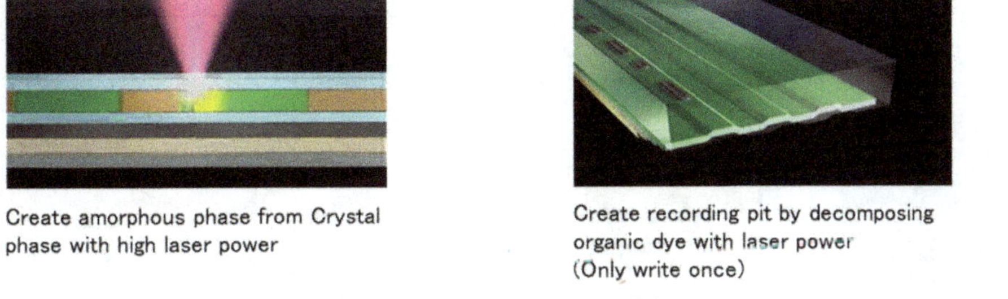


**Figure 3.** Phase change and organic dye recording

For writeable and rewritable discs the system relies on using heat from the laser write head to change the physical state of an internal recording layer. The use of organic dye for writable discs became popular because it cost less to manufacture and was readable by CD players (fig. 3).

However, the organic dyes degrade after extensive exposure to UV light and this has caused reliability issues that make them unsuitable for archival. An alternative system uses an inorganic layer which changes physical phase rapidly from reflective crystalline to a non-reflective amorphous state in the presence of heat in excess of 400°C from the write-head laser and will return to a crystalline phase with a longer period of heating at around 200°C. This phase change recording system is not affected by UV light or by temperatures found in habitable environments and is generally considered suitable for archive applications.

## Next-Generation Archive Optical Disc

The next generation of Archival Optical Discs will bring progressively larger capacities up to 1 TB per disc, lower cost per bit, and faster data transfer rates. The core parameters of 3-layer BD discs will be retained for compatibility reasons with the same 405nm laser and NA 0.85 optical specification (fig. 5).

Increased recording densities will be achieved using land and groove recording, and advanced signal processing to cancel crosstalk between tracks to achieve higher lateral densities,

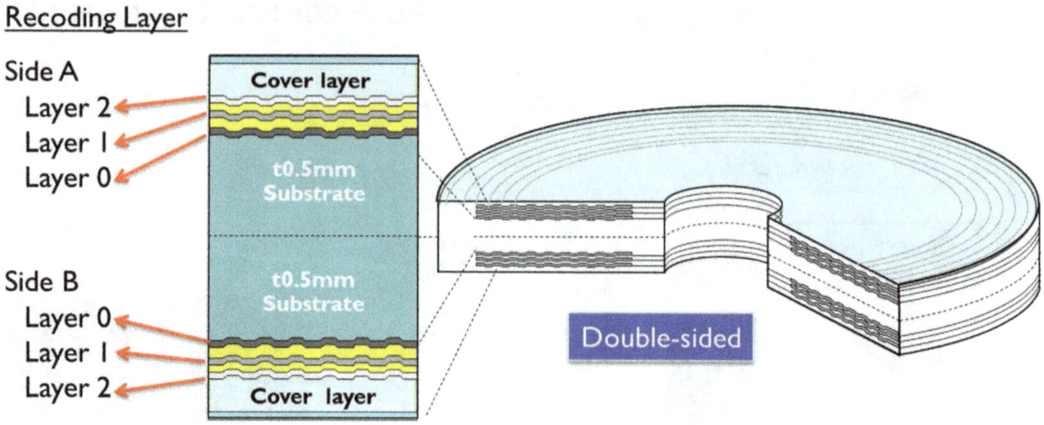

Figure 4a. 3-layer/side double-sided structure

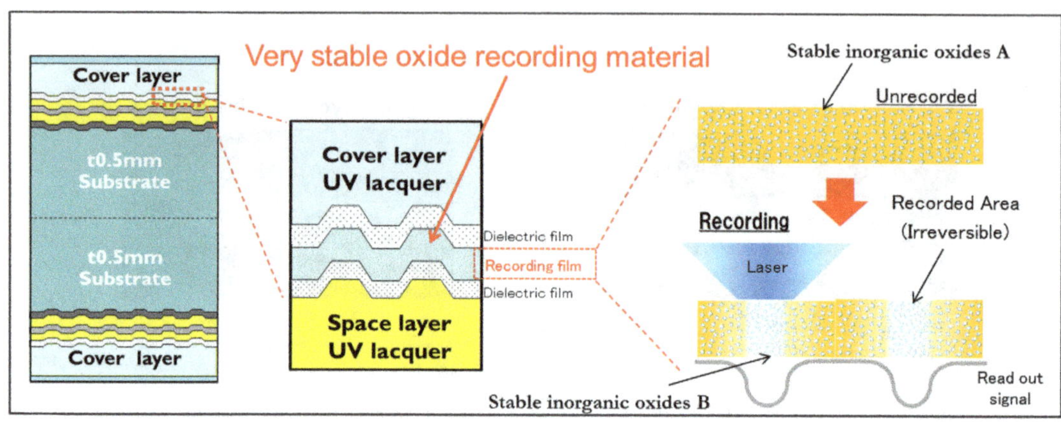


Figure 4b. Triple stacking of oxide materials

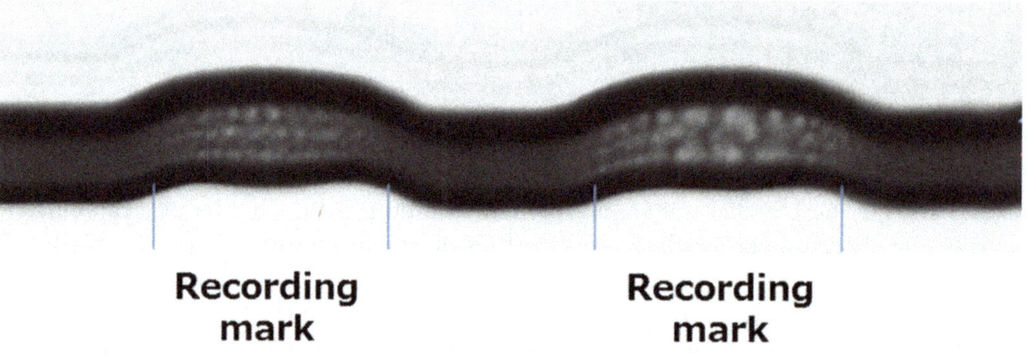


Figure 4c. SEM image of recording media section

and intersymbol interference cancellation and ultimately multilevel recording to achieve higher linear densities.

Also, a significant change will be the adoption of a very stable oxide-based recording layer featuring a nonreversible recording process providing even greater data security than that afforded by phase change recording (figs. 4a, b, and c). Ageing tests also indicate that this new recording system will provide even greater media lifetime, exceeding 50 years at 50°C and well in excess of 1000 years at 25°C.

These drives will implement 3-layer double-sided recording with a total of 8 channels increasing transfer speeds to 360 MB/s.

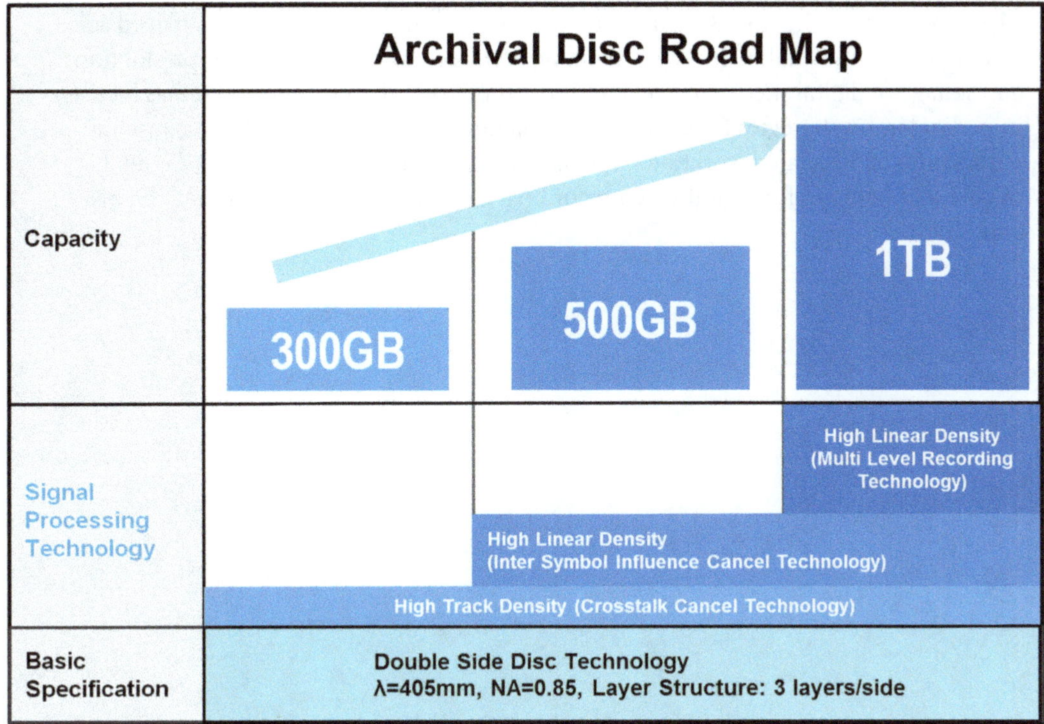


**Figure 5.** Archival disc road map

## Conclusion

We have set out the key technical and commercial requirements that relate to long-term data storage for archive application and how they are liable to change in the future due to market trends and legislative factors. We have taken these requirements and evaluated the suitability of optical storage technology developed specifically for professional archive applications and shown that it not only meets these requirements but also exceeds the capabilities of alternative technologies in most areas too. In the last section of the paper we have introduced the road map for the next generation of archival optical discs that clearly shows how we will increase storage density, speed and lifetime while continuing to reduce the cost per bit for media.

Archives have one unique requirement in that they typically have a duty to preserve valuable content in perpetuity, and this is a big and potentially expensive responsibility. While it would be naive to claim any storage technology will last more than a few decades before even in the best case it becomes desirable to replace it, optical discs do have an exceptional record for backward compatibility and long media life. Therefore, they deliver lower costs and higher reliability in the long term. Our expectation is that the next generation of optical archive disc technology will very much help to shorten that time-frame and simplify the technology choice.

Yuji Sekiguchi (General Manager, Content Creation Solution Business Division, Professional Solution Group) joined Sony in 1983 and gained extensive experience developing strategic OEM relationships with Apple, Sun Micro and SGI, including a number of years based in the USA establishing a cable modem business. In Japan he worked on the development of advanced QoS algorithms for network device designs, then the PSX digital HDD recorder with PlayStation game, before joining the Blu-ray Disk introduction program. Following a further period with PlayStation network in the US, he returned to Japan to take charge of the business development of Optical Disc technology for archive applications.

Morgan David (Director, Research and Development, Sony Europe) has played a leading role in the challenges of systemizing architectures for acquisition, production, and storage of digital media and metadata for professional applications. He has focused, in particular, on strategies for acquiring, managing and exploiting metadata and the automation of associated workflows. He has also been involved in the development of core technologies for digital video recording, networking, high definition, 3D, 4K and HDR.

# The (Carbon-) Black Ops of Recording Tape: Sticky-Shed Syndrome Exposed

24

**Charles A. Richardson and Martin Atias**

Abstract

There are many "authoritative" papers and presentations on the topic of sticky-shed magnetic tape deterioration. However, few are based on adequate or original scientific research, relying instead on physical observation, casual interpretation of prior works, convenient theories, and practices justified by temporary results without an examination of the chemical reactions.

The famous Ampex baking patent is one such work that abandoned the scientific method of investigation. It was never published as a scientific paper subject to peer review; it ignores chemical basics and superior prior research; it was never subject to the scrutiny of a chemical laboratory; it contains contradictory statements, gaps in theory, and process; and thus its conclusions do not follow the evidence.

This paper is based on rigorous chemical scientific study that has been published in numerous journals and presented at several conferences. Along with an analysis of earlier research by others in the field, this research work was analyzed, performed, and reviewed by multiple teams within a premiere independent forensic laboratory using state-of-the-art equipment and processes. This work conclusively identifies the chemical component reaction that causes sticky shed, as well as the resulting reactions and their behavioral effects. It then shows that magnetic recording tapes suffering from sticky-shed syndrome are fully recoverable and safely restorable to their original sonic and physical performance, with their oxide layer intact, and can remain so for decades or more with no further processing. The results are proven with actual tapes being restored and preserved by using a process invented over 12 years ago.

Paper readers will benefit from the chemical basics tutorials listed via YouTube videos and Internet articles.

Keywords

sticky-shed syndrome, carbon black, carbon-black particles, magnetic tape, recording tape, moisture, carbon-black back coating, back coating, chemical equilibrium, reverse reaction, hydrolysis, hydrolysis reaction, shedding, oxide, oxide coating, chemistry, binder, Cuddihy, Bertram, Richardson, tape storage, Ampex patent, deterioration, degradation, decomposition, baking, sticktion, polymer, preservation, restoration, chemical lab analysis.

Recording tape can and originally used to be a relatively simple product of necessary chemical components. It has a plastic base film layer and magnetic particles suspended in a binder chemical that adheres the particles to the base film. These early tapes have never exhibited sticky shedding.[1]

When evaluating the cause of magnetic recording tape malfunctions, one must consider that of the five components of modern recording tape (oxide, binder, base film, back coating, and a different binder), only one is functionally critical to recording audio or data. That one—the inorganic magnetic particle—comprises only 20% of the total weight. Two of the remaining components are synthetic organic chemical products and are employed entirely to physically support the magnetic component. The remaining two optional components, carbon black and its (different) binder, are also organic and were employed beginning in 1970 as a back coating to mitigate certain physical performance issues under certain use conditions.

Given this perspective, magnetic tape must be viewed as a chemical product. Any changes in physical or performance attributes from its original state must be the result of either physical abuse or a chemical reaction. We will explore this in some depth following a historical review.

## The History

In the 1950s and 60s, NASA was a large consumer of magnetic recording tape, using very high-speed transports for computer and mission data storage. Professional music and broadcast production studios were also collectively large consumers. To maximize cost efficiencies, tape manufacturers utilized many of the same manufacturing machines, processes, and chemicals for both markets.

During the same time period, Europe was storing tape on (AEG type) hubs that did not allow flanges. These pancakes required precise tape winding and packing. AGFA & BASF, two European manufacturers, started adding plastic particle back coatings to increase friction. These have not suffered from sticky shedding.

However, by the late 1960s, NASA was experiencing problems with uneven tape packing and static discharge on their high-speed data transports. Beginning in 1970, American tape manufacturers added a carbon-black back coating to add friction and dissipate static. Again to maximize plant efficiency, they also added this back coating to audio and video recording tapes and heavily marketed them as a "superior" product.

Not long after, another troubling anomaly emerged. After being stored for some months, certain tapes would not play back properly. They would squeal on the transport, tape layers would stick together, and sticky brown/black debris collected on tape guides and heads. Many people concluded that because this debris appeared on oxide contact surfaces that this debris must be the oxide shedding or being pulled off the tape. A common causal hypothesis was oxide binder failure due to tape decomposition or deterioration. It was further speculated that post-1970 oxide binder formulas were inferior to pre-1970 formulas. Curiously, the addition of the carbon-black back coatings, which occurred around 1970, was not considered suspect.

Typically, each studio and data center favored one tape formula, brand, or model for a variety of technical or personal reasons, so a single studio had little basis for comparing different tapes after so many months or years. Not until the 1980s did it became apparent that different tape models behaved differently. Some behaved better or worse than others, some had no problems at all, while some were simply unplayable.

## Chem Talk, In Context

As we studied the past research and many papers written on this subject, we noted certain key words frequently used to describe the aged sticky condition of magnetic tape. Since the key words we assign to form an understanding matter greatly, a misuse in context can lead readers to misconstrue their meaning and the topic. According to Merriam-Webster,

- Deteriorate(d): to become worse as time passes; to make (something) worse; to make inferior in quality or value
- Degrade(d): to treat (someone or something) poorly and without respect: to make the quality of (something) worse
- Decay: to be slowly destroyed by natural processes: to be slowly broken down by the natural processes that destroy a dead plant or body: to slowly lose strength, health, etc.

These popular terms are typically attributed to sticky tapes because we relate them best to living organisms biologically aging and dying. Carbon-based organic living and nonliving materials are subject to aging, decay, or death, especially for plants and animals. However, where infection, disease, and extreme environmental conditions cause premature biological deterioration, a medical treatment may be developed to slow, stop, or reverse the process. In one sense, decay is a gradual process by which something breaks down or falls apart as a result of natural causes. Bones become brittle, skin loses its elasticity, hair grays.

In another sense, decay is a natural reaction that results over time when a substance is exposed to a reactive environment and/or other substances with which the substance will chemically react.

These reactions occur at a particular rate, depending on the nature of the substances involved. It could take anywhere from fractions of a second to millennia. Environmental conditions such as temperature and humidity can significantly affect the rate of change. Freezing foods slows the reaction rate to extend their useful shelf life. Pasteurizing kills certain contaminants and vacuum packing removes oxygen and moisture, both reactants that cause decay.

On the other hand, there are also many special carbon-based materials found in living things, such as DNA, genes, and chromosomes that can last for millions of years and are passed from one generation to another. Indeed, some organic chemicals, and some inorganic chemicals, such as many pure base metals, can exist for centuries or more if the environmental conditions are favorable. Unfavorable environmental conditions can lead to oxidation, evaporation, compound chemical breakdown, or compound chemical creation—where two or more elements combine to form a new product, such as water from oxygen and hydrogen. The most favorable condition creates a chemical equilibrium, where the chemical elements in the substance and the environment they are surrounded by are balanced so that no additional reactions occur.

The life span of almost any chemical can be increased from short to long or decreased from long to short depending upon the materials, the environment, and the way the materials are stored and treated. The chemicals used on recording tape, including the binders, are synthesized from organic materials, but are not biological. Most parties believe that the binder chemicals used in tapes can only last a few decades. In fact, they can be quite stable for many centuries if equilibrium stability conditions are maintained.

The condition known as sticky-shed tape is caused by a preventable chemical reaction due to an outside influence. We will show how this reaction can be reversed and stabilized to restore and preserve a tape. When that is done, long-term archival preservation can be achieved.

Merriam-Webster offers one more on-point definition for *degrade(d)* for our chemical application: to cause (something complex) to break down into simple substances or parts.

Reading further, we will show that during a chemical reaction known as hydrolysis, polymer binder compounds breaks down to component chemicals that are referred to as "new byproducts." This semantic label is really a matter of perspective, based on which side of the reaction equation one starts from, because a polymer is made by combining these same chemicals. "Synthesis" and "hydrolysis" are opposite, or reversible reactions caused by a change in environmental conditions. However, there is a balance that can be achieved such that under certain environmental conditions, no chemical change will occur. This is called chemical equilibrium and is essential to media preservation.

Our very existence depends on a variety of physical and chemical equilibria, defined as a state of rest or balance due to the equal action of opposing forces. Those forces can be dynamic, continuing to push against each other. When one begins to dominate, a reaction change occurs. If the other pushes back hard enough, the reaction is reversed and a balance is restored. See the sections on Reverse Reactions and Chemical Equilibrium.

## The Science: Historical & Practical

Dr. Edward F. Cuddihy, a materials chemist at NASA's Jet Propulsion Laboratories, did extensive chemical analysis on this problem from 1976 to 1982 and published three major lab articles in the IEEE *Journal of Magnetics*. He analyzed the chemical composition of affected tapes and unaffected tapes and the differences between new unaffected tapes and affected aged tapes. Cuddihy identified that hydrolysis of the binders (explained below) is solely responsible for mechanical malfunctions and that utilizing a well-known chemical process, the reverse chemical reaction—specifically, reverse hydrolysis—can restore a tape naturally and safely (Cuddihy, 1976; Cuddihy, 1980; Bertram and Cuddihy, 1982). This process required only climate-controlled storage conditions of low humidity and low temperature. After a time, these tapes reverted to a perfectly playable condition and revealed that the magnetic oxide on the affected tapes was indeed unaffected.

From 1982 to 1989 Cuddihy's method of moderate storage climate conditions was the only known way to restore a tape. However, it was not popular because it can take months to years for the reverse reaction to complete, and it required a specially built, environmentally controlled storage locker. This new understanding afforded some relief, but Cuddihy's work was not widely known. The production studios and record companies were panicking about their precious master tapes, and NASA wanted a quicker fix.

Ampex, having supplied NASA with much of their malfunctioning data tape, contracted a research team. This research team was aware of Cuddihy's earlier work and that of his later research associate Dr. Neil Bertram. Dr. Bertram's 1980 paper researched and described the "print-through phenomenon" which revealed that above the recommended 21°C (70°F) storage temperature, print through level increases by .14 dB per degree centigrade, thus documenting one type of permanent magnetic damage done by elevated temperatures (Bertram, Stafford, and Mills). The researchers were also aware of a 1982 paper coauthored by Cuddihy and Bertram entitled "Kinetics of the Humid Aging of Magnetic Recording Tape," in which the authors state "the purpose of a kinetic analysis is to allow the prediction of the effect of various environments on tape hydrolysis," which included variations in temperature and humidity. They did extensive research on the ideal conditions for tape storage (35°–70°F; 35%–40% RH) to prevent hydrolysis from either occurring or to reverse it if it does occur, with the aim of preserving the tape's chemical, magnetic, and physical properties.

They were employing the scientific principle of equilibrium, where the conditions exist that no physical or chemical changes occur. They understood that equilibrium is critical to archivists and engineers desiring to preserve physical media for long periods of time.

You may remember from science class that "for every action there is a reaction." A hot-air balloon, for example, can float motionless in air provided that there is no change in air temperature or humidity either inside or outside of the balloon, that the air around it is perfectly still, and that nothing in the cargo basket moves. Any imbalance in this "system" represents an action for which the reaction will cause the balloon to move. This physical example directly correlates to how environmental changes can cause chemical reactions.

On a deeper level however, we must recognize that, while on a macroscopic or visual level, a glass of water in equilibrium on a countertop may seem perfectly still, but on a microscopic level, the molecules and atoms in the water, the glass, and the countertop are always moving around in their orbits and in relation to those around them. The rate of their molecular activity can easily change as a reaction to any disturbance in the environment such as inertia, temperature, humidity, air pressure, gravity, etc. Any change or imbalance in these conditions can cause the materials to expand, contract, move, or change temperature or even physical state (solid, liquid, gas).

For a better understanding of chemical equilibrium, watch these excellent YouTube videos: Equilibrium Crash Course Chemistry 28- https://youtu.be/g5wNg_dKsYY, Le Chateliers Principle Part 1 - https://youtu.be/7zuUV455zFs, Le Chateliers Principle Part 2 - https://youtu.be/XhQ02egUs5Y. Also, on Wikipedia: Chemical Eqilibrium - https://en.wikipedia.org/wiki/Chemical_equilibrium. For a more in-depth study of chemical equilibrium, reverse reactions, and more, visit http://www.chem1.com/acad/webtext/chemeq/index.html.

By 1989, Desmond Medeiros, John Curtis, and Robert Perry of Ampex invented a heat-treatment remedy, which Ampex then patented. In the patent, they declared that tapes had "become unusable due to age and deterioration of the magnetic coating on the base film ... and that ... magnetic tapes deteriorate slowly over a number of years, and eventually exhibit the undesirable properties of stickiness and excessive shed of the magnetic oxide coating layer (Medeiros, 1993)."

Curiously, the Ampex patent makes several contradictory claims, such as that a "deteriorated" tape can be "restore(d) ... to playable and excellent quality media by heat treatment ... usable for recording and playback as intended." The patent later states, "It has been observed that restoring magnetic tapes according to the present invention produces a restored tape that remains in a usable condition for a number of weeks or months. However, it can be expected that an aged magnetic recording media, even after restoring according to the present invention, is likely to revert back to its deteriorated condition over time" (Medeiros, 1993).

The patent called for baking temperatures ranging from 122° to 130°F for 3–24 hours. The fact that this violated Ampex's (and many other tape manufacturers') safe-temperature-exposure warranty limit of 90°F was never commented on or explained. The safe-temperature range of any product is established and limited by the component chemical with the most restrictive temperature tolerance, which in this case is 90°F.

As can be seen, there is little demonstrated evidence that the team that researched and developed the Ampex patent heeded this earlier scientific and factual chemical information. They sought only a method of quickly drying out the absorbed moisture, even if the results were limited in scope, and without testing for adverse side effects of the chemical components caused by applying heat. All of the cited references in this document were also other patents. No scientific studies or publications were cited.

However, Ampex never set out to perform their process as a service, and, to our knowledge, never defended it against patent violations.

It is important to note here that patents are a registration of intellectual property for legal protection against commercial competition. In contrast to scientific journal papers, patents do not establish, nor do they require scientific evidence that they actually work or have any positive or negative side effects. Patents establish property rights and are only evaluated against prior art or prior claims of invention.

Permanent thermal decomposition is a chemical reaction that occurs when the safe temperature limit is exceeded. To demonstrate, imagine wearing a pair of uncoated leather work gloves in the rain. When new and dry, they have certain unique properties. If they get wet, they become softer, they stretch, and can even change shape. Set them down in an air-conditioned room and they will return to their original condition. This is an example of a chemical process or forward reaction known as hydrolysis, when absorbing water changes something's properties, and also of a reverse reaction, in this case when the water evaporates slowly and naturally.

However, let those wet leather gloves dry under a very hot sun or, worse, in the clothes dryer, and they will shrink and harden like a stale biscuit. This is because the application of excessive heat energy will evaporate the water but also acts on the leather's other chemicals, changing them permanently. Once this heat damage is done, the leather will never regain its original properties.

Heat is raw energy that accelerates chemical activity and can change and destroy chemical compositions (fig. 1). One cannot selectively control the heat's general effect, to make it act on just one thing and not another, such as just the water and not the molecules in the leather. It is an equal opportunity agent of change, with the result that the leather fibers and oils, the tape binder chemical, base film, magnetic materials, and content are all affected by (will react to) the inherently destructive heat energy. It is an absolute chemical principle and accepted fact that one does not ever heat up or bake heat-sensitive organic materials if one's aim is to restore and preserve them. Just as one does not bake films, photographs, vinyl records, hard drives, books, paintings, or other organic plastic- or paper-based media to preserve them! Using elevated heat levels on magnetic tape violates archival "do not harm" standards. Preservation requires an environment that balances the material's chemical composition with its surroundings to provide for a state of chemical equilibrium where no change in composition will occur as long as the system is left undisturbed.

For a brief tutorial on energy and thermal decomposition, watch these excellent YouTube videos: Enthalpy Crash Course Chemistry 18 - https://youtu.be/SV7U4yAXL5I, and Thermal Decomposition - https://youtu.be/BQymwRKKTTM. Also, on Wikipedia: Thermal degradation of polymers - https://en.wikipedia.org/wiki/Thermal_degradation_of_polymers.

Figure 1.

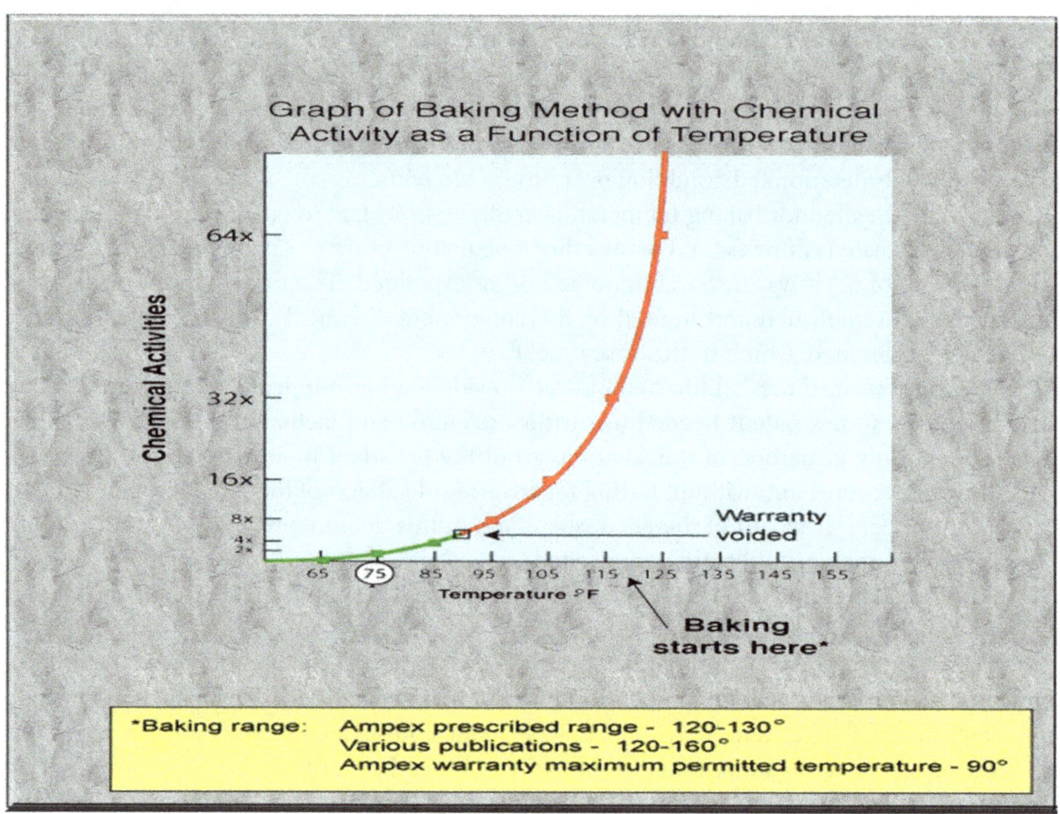


## The Historic Science in Perspective

While Cuddihy had the advantage of access to the Jet Propulsion Laboratory forensic materials laboratory and analysis equipment, and Bertram was a physicist/mathematician, their available analytical capabilities pale by today's technology. They all missed several critical diagnoses.

Cuddihy, Bertram, and the patent inventors focused their attention solely on the oxide binder. While Cuddihy did notice and made special mention in his 1976 paper that the carbon-black back coating was more vulnerable to hydrolysis than any other component of the tape (he actually called it a "sponge"), they failed to realize that the oxide and back coat binders were not the same and did not test them separately. They failed to make a connection between the gooey back coating and the debris found on the oxide surface, and they failed to realize only carbon-black back-coated tapes suffered from hydrolysis under normal conditions.

For an understanding of chemical hydrolysis of polymers, view these excellent YouTube videos: What is Hydrolysis + Examples - https://www.youtube.com/watch?v=G_mT9JI_jxE, Hydrolysis and Dehydration Synthesis - https://www.youtube.com/watch?v=ZMTeqZLXBSo, and Hydrolysis of Esters - https://youtu.be/iMHRf83TZTo. Also, on Wikipedia: Hydrolysis - https://en.wikipedia.org/wiki/Hydrolysis.

So what is really going on then? Let us go back to chemistry for answers. All things are made of chemicals, and many can combine to form compounds. For our area of study, we are particularly interested in polymers such as polyether and polyester, which are used for the binder chemicals and the base film.

As Cuddihy discovered and documented in his '76, '80, and '82 papers, the back-coating binder is relatively weak and absorbs a lot of moisture when the ambient humidity is high. When moisture (water) mixes with the carbon-black particles and its weak binder, a chemical hydrolysis reaction occurs that produces three new by-product chemicals:

1. Carboxylic fatty acid (a sticky, gooey solvent)
2. Alcohol (a solvent)
3. A base chemical that contains compound fragments and debris

However, Cuddihy, Bertram, and many others after dismissed the back coating as a factor, and attributed this only to the oxide binder. Had they not, they would have discovered that this new soft and sticky chemical goo on the back of the tape attracts and grows mold, mildew, and other debris from the atmosphere. It also transfers itself, mechanically and chemically, onto the oxide surface of the tape layer above it, which can then rub off on tape guides and heads. Once on the oxide's surface, the CFA and the alcohol solvents can also react with the oxide's binder. This reaction is why both carbon black and (often brown) oxide can often be detected on heads and guides.

There are many chemical structure changes that take place with moisture absorption and heat application. The polymer binder chemical is a linear molecular chain 32 links long. When the relative humidity is high, it creates a chemical imbalance, with the reaction being the absorption of moisture, which then breaks down the chemical into the three smaller components mentioned above by breaking the chain at specific links. The long molecular chain link is now reduced to three new by-product molecules with only about ten links per new molecule (fig. 2). These smaller molecules are not as strong or as hard as the original long binder chemical. They are now soft and sticky with much higher surface friction, and the tape therefore squeals. The problem can be fixed by the use of the reverse reaction, by placing the tape in a low-humidity, low-temperature environment, allowing the moisture to evaporate naturally. That joins the three small molecules back together again to form the original large hard binder molecule. In fact, this process is similar to how polymers are made or synthesized in the lab. Synthesis and hydrolysis are opposite and reversible reactions.

However, this is only the case where moisture alone, not heat, is involved. The introduction of added heat energy has multiple effects. The alcohol byproduct evaporates, which precludes the reverse process from working, and the increased heat energy activity can break the chains but at different heat sensitive links that can never be repaired (fig. 3). Heat can also form new cross-links that are not wanted because added-cross-links (vs. linear chain links) make the polymer structure brittle and inflexible. Chemistry, therefore, rules out applying heat as a remedy if the desired results are to restore the tape's original properties.

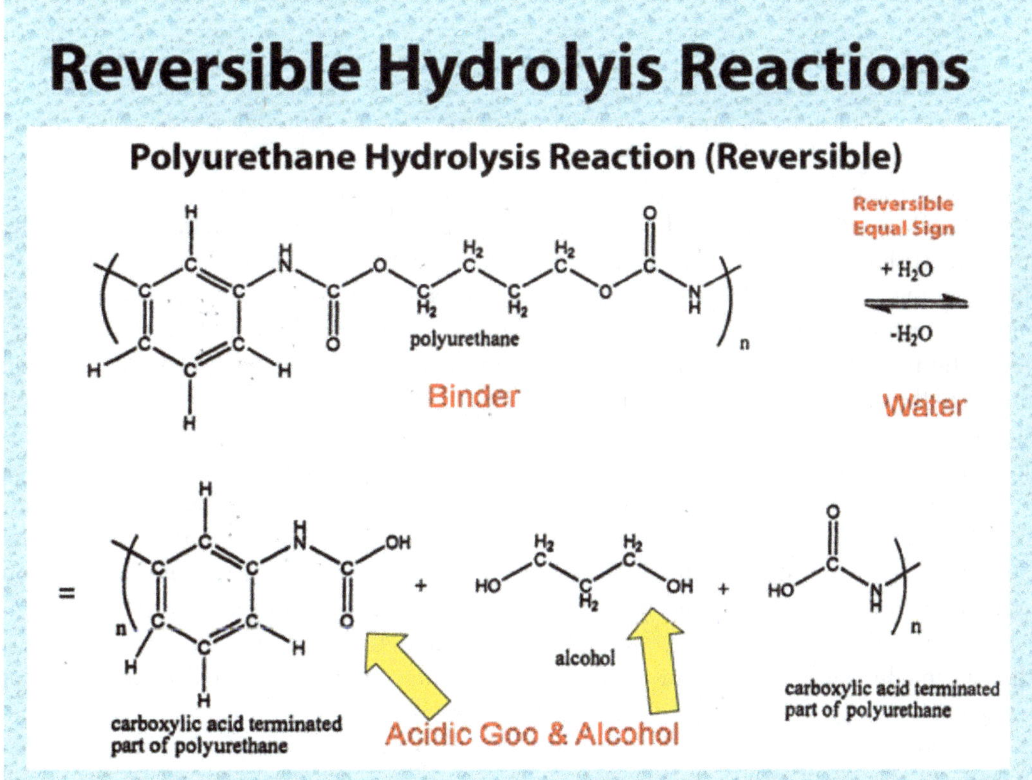


**Figure 2.** Reversible reaction—one which can be caused to proceed in either direction by suitable variations in the conditions of temperature, volume, pressure, or of the quantities of reacting substances. (*Handbook of Chemistry and Physics*, 41st ed., 1960, p. 3120, Chemical Rubber Publishing)

Figure 3.

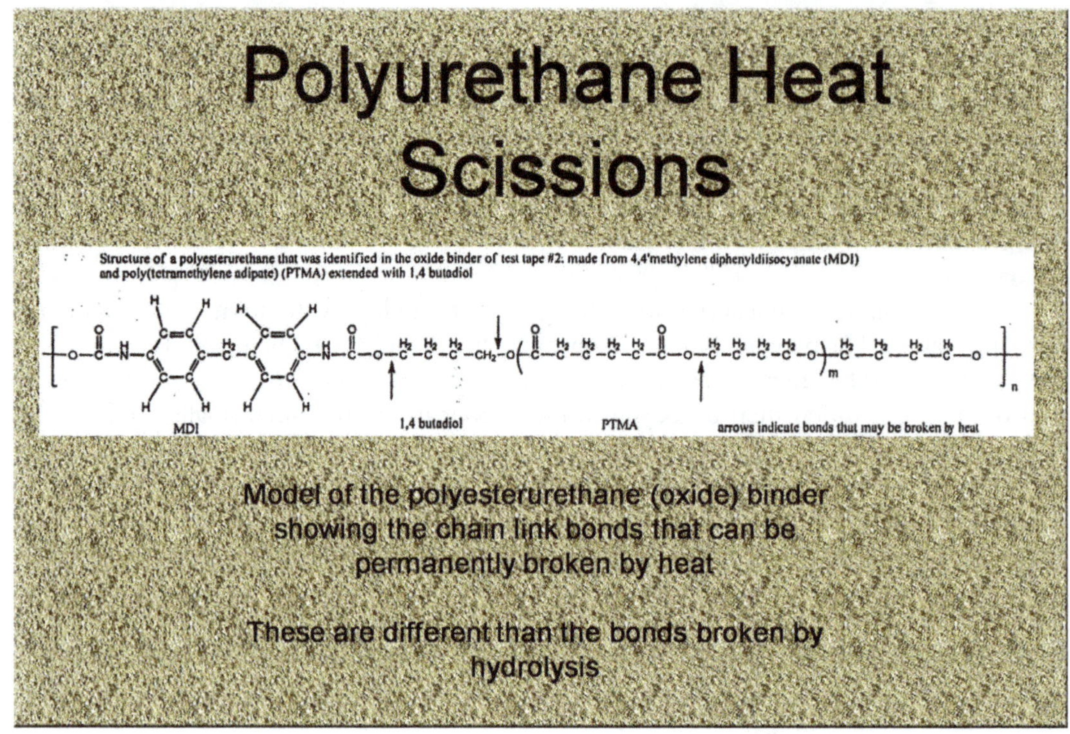


### Reversible Hydrolysis Reaction

Forward reaction: Polyurethane + Water (> 40% Humidity) = Carboxylic Acid + Alcohol + Fragment

Reverse reaction: Carboxylic Acid + Alcohol + Fragment – Water (< 30% Humidity) = Polyurethane

Equilibrium Stability (optimum conditions for storage): The hydrolysis equation is equalized in an environment of 35% humidity and 65°–70°F where no chemical reaction will occur.

## New Theories and Lab Findings

In 2002, Charles Richardson was attempting to remaster some 30-year-old recordings he had done on Ampex tape that suffered from sticky-shed syndrome. Upon a thorough review of the earlier research by Cuddihy, Bertram, and others, as well as the Ampex patent, he noticed several logical disconnects and was curious why the researchers had not followed certain evidentiary leads.

In 1992 Mr. Richardson started to examine the empirical research on sticky-shed syndrome during the first attempts to remaster his pre-1992 tape records for CD. In 2002, while trying to remaster some 30-year-old Ampex tape recordings that suffered from sticky-shed syndrome, he conducted further, more extensive reviews of the earlier research by Cuddihy, Bertram, and others who researched the topic from 1970 to 1990, including the Ampex patent. Richardson concluded that there were still questions that had not been addressed, such as the contribution of the back coating. He identified chemical facts that had not been applied and had theories that had not been tested. He realized that the last research conducted in a chemical lab was published in 1982. After documenting his own research from 2002 to 2006, he enlisted the services of Chemir Labs, a highly regarded independent chemical forensics laboratory, to verify his research by using modern methodology and equipment, such as the scanning electron microscope, to look deep into and under the surface of both sides of the tape. The research tested the chemistry of affected tapes and the stability and absorption rates of the two binders and analyzed the debris on the oxide surface as well as the condition of the oxide and its binder (figs. 4 and 5).

It was found that the two coating binders exhibited different hygroscopic properties and that the oxide binder was relatively resistant to hydrolysis compared to the easily hydrolyzed back

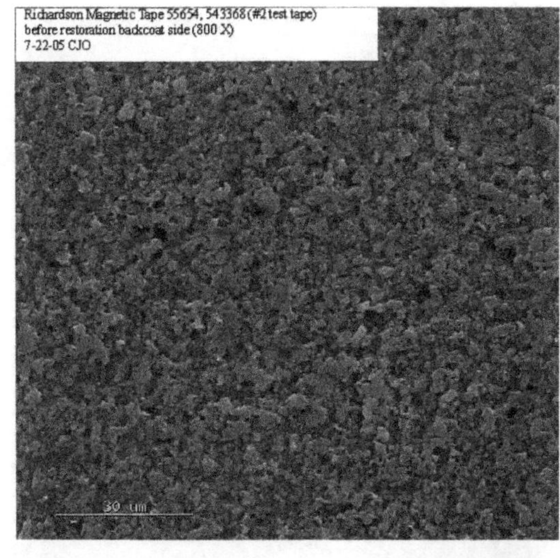


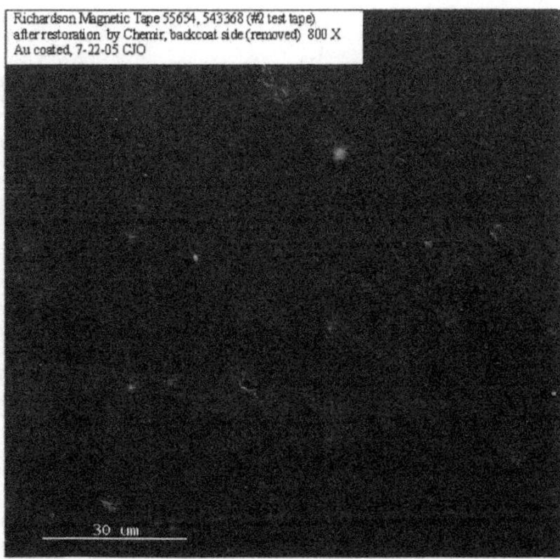


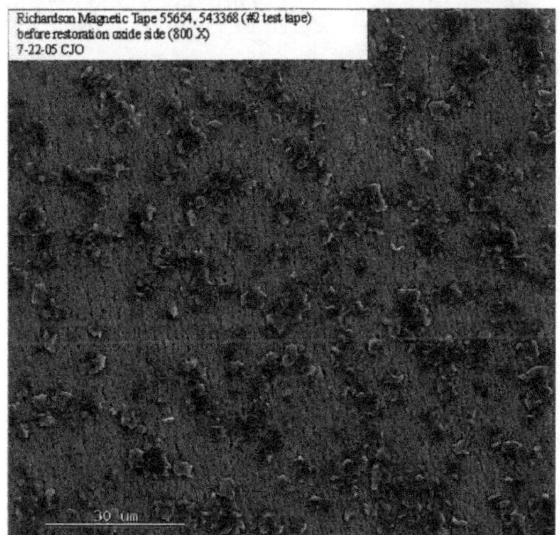


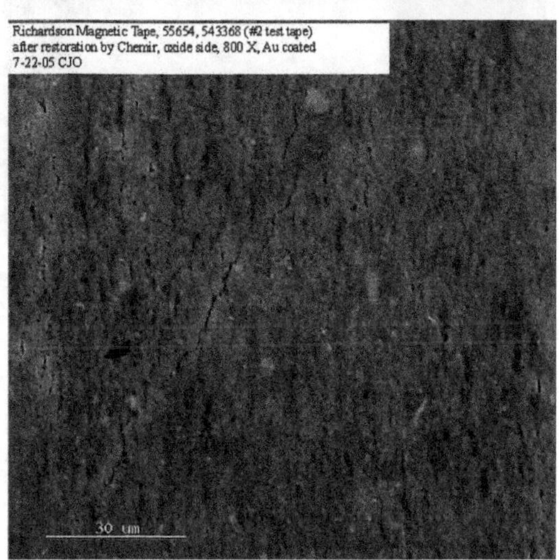


Scanning electron microscope images, all ×800 mag. Figure 4, top left, back coating before removal. Figure 5, top right, back of base film after back coting removal. Figure 6, lower left, oxide before restoration. Figure 7, lower right, oxide after restoration.

coating binder. The rate of absorption is much higher for the carbon-black back coating. They found deposits of hydrolyzed carbon-black back coating binder by-products on the oxide surface along with collected mold and other debris. These sticky deposits were mechanically transferred on the reel from the adjacent back-side layers.

With this new information, the lab then went on to prove that the back coating could be safely removed from the base tape without adversely affecting the base, the oxide binder, the oxide, or its magnetic properties. In addition, they proved that the debris can be safely removed from the oxide surface without the application of chemicals (figs. 6 and 7). Richardson patented a new tape restoration process in 2004 that was deemed safe and effective by the chemists and has been proven so in the twelve years since he restored his first few reels of Ampex 406 tape (Richardson, 2004).

This work was first presented in 2006 and published as a convention paper for the Audio Engineering Society's 121st convention (Richardson). Subsequent presentations were given at the IASA convention in 2010, the ARSC convention in 2012, and at the 139th AES convention in NYC in 2015 (Richardson and Atias, 2015, October 31) (Ramsey, 2016, January/February).

Tapes restored by removing the carbon-black back coating and cleaning the oxide exhibit several remarkable properties:

1. The entirety of the tape's chemistry is simplified by reducing the number of materials used. This greatly reduces the opportunity for unintended chemical reactions.

2. The oxide surface is actually and visibly cleaner, with a bright shiny appearance (figs. 7 and 8).

3. Mechanical surface friction is greatly reduced which stops the squealing problems.

Figure 8.

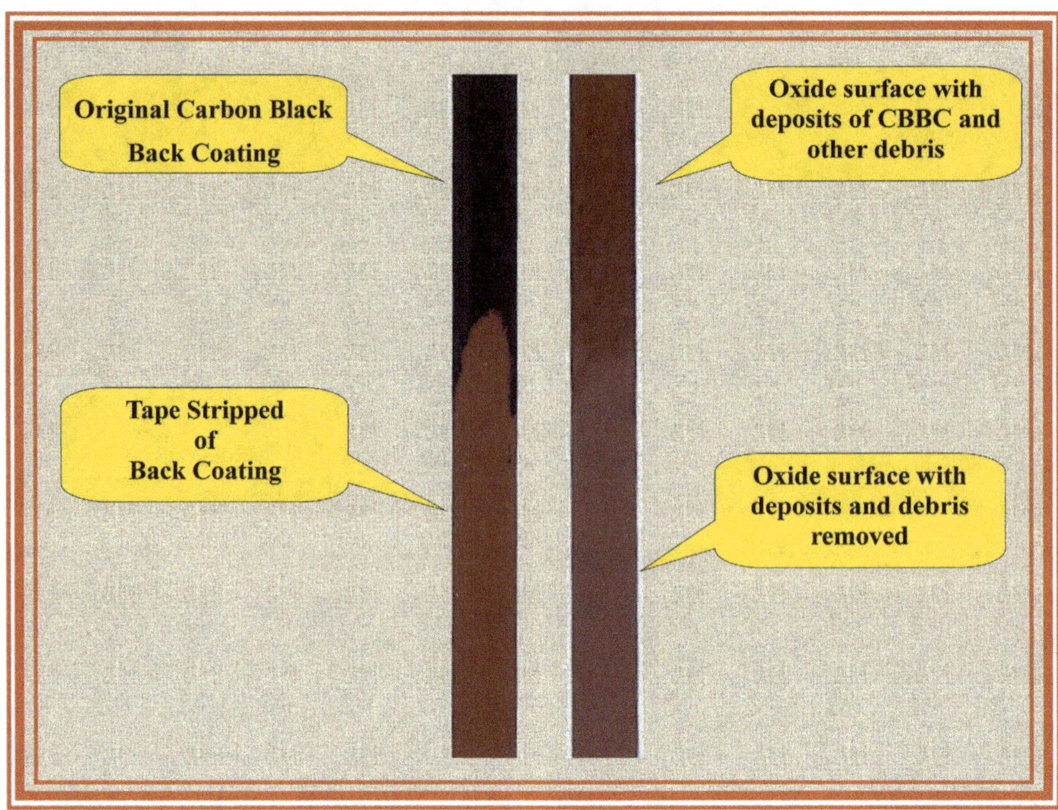


4. The tape's traverse across a Nagra deck with its floating feed and exit guide rollers is rock solid and without a hint of sticktion instability from end to end of the tape.

5. The tape recording's high-frequency response and depth of musical detail are audibly restored by eliminating collected debris that causes tape-to-head spacing losses. These restored high-frequency characteristics are thereby extended to any digital transcription.

6. Twelve years later, these restored tapes can be simply taken out of their box and played with no evidence of degradation, low friction, effortless tape payoff, excellent frequency response, and excellent musical detail.

## Conclusions

According to the IASA's Ethical Principles for Sound and Audiovisual Archives:

> Any kind of preservation, restoration, transfer and migration of sound and audiovisual content should be done in such a way as to avoid or minimize the loss of data and other relevant information on the original recording. . . . The original carriers should be preserved in usable condition for as long as is feasible. . . . Any kind of physical restoration process on the original carrier should be performed with utmost care to balance the possible improvement of restoration against possible further deterioration or subsequent damage in the long time preservation (Assmann et al., 2010, 2011).

Given this ethos, the scientific evidence that using elevated temperatures does both physical and chemical damage, that adding any kind of chemical (such as lubricants, solvents, etc.) to the oxide serves only to complicate the chemistry with untested reaction results, and that the scientifically recommended option is to restore, preserve, and chemically simplify the original carrier without damage, then there would be little ethical or logical choice.

With the actual cause of sticky-shed syndrome now defined, the restoration solution developed by Richardson follows and carefully implements the above IASA principles to the highest degree—far exceeding other practices and views.

We have heard from many processors that owner's priorities have been digitization, placing minimal importance on the content's original carrier. We propose that due to misinformation in the industry (or the suppression of it) regarding restoration options, owners have simply resigned themselves to the notion that tapes suffering from sticky-shed syndrome cannot be restored without damage, and that further deterioration is inevitable, hence the urgency to digitize. We further propose that as digital recording technology advances, going back to the original analog carrier for content poses the best opportunity for taking advantage of those advances for new digital copies. In addition, as an archival storage media, analog tape has far fewer vulnerabilities than, and can outlast, any digital media provided that it is handled and stored properly.

Charles A. Richardson has been a member of ARSC, SMPTE, and AES for thirty-five years, and a recording engineer for nearly fifty years. His recordings on many labels are praised for their sonic quality. Presentations on tape topics have been made to these organizations. His interests in chemistry, physics, mechanics, electronics, acoustics, scientific methodology, and practical problem solving are unique skills and have been used to solve a number of recording tape related problems.

Martin Atias started working with magnetic recording tape around 1973 and has over forty years in the pro audio industry with production and engineering experience in studio and remote music recording, network television and radio, systems design and integration, and equipment servicing. He opened ATS Communications in 1989 to serve the equipment, systems, and production needs of the Washington, DC, television production community, while maintaining a strong interest and ties to the music industry where he has rededicated his interest.

## Note

1. Non-back coated acetate film based tapes sometimes exhibit similar and/or different symptoms with very different moisture caused problems such as vinegar syndrome. Mylar or PET film–based tapes without any carbon-black back coating are very stable and normally do not have moisture caused sticky-shed problems

## Bibliography


Assman, I., Bradley, K., Chaudhuri, S., Davies, M., Deggeller, K., Fennesz-Juhasz, C., Flam, G., Flynn, A., Gallenmiller, C. P., Gaustad, L., Giannattasio, I., Gray, J., Humbert, D., Hubert, R., Jönsson, G., Koch, G., Schüller, D., Seeger, A., Fargion, J. T., and Walaszkovits, N. (2010, Rev 2011). *Ethical Principles for Sound and Audiovisual Archives.* International Association of Sound and Audiovisual Archives (IASA).

Bertram, H. N., and Cuddihy, E. F. (1982, September). "Kinetics of the Humid Aging of Magnetic Recording Tape." *IEEE Transactions on Magnetics*, 18, no. 5:993–999.

Bertram, H. N., Stafford, M. K., and Mills, D. R. (1980, October). "The Print-Through Phenomenon." *Journal of the Audio Engineering Society*, 28, no. 10:690–705.

Cuddihy, E. F. (1976, March). "Hygroscopic Properties of Magnetic Recording Tape". *IEEE Transactions on Magnetics*, 12, no. 2:126–135.

Cuddihy, E. F. (1980, July). "Aging of Magnetic Recording Tape." *IEEE Transactions on Magnetics* 16, no. 4:558–568.

Medeiros, E. A. (1993, Aug 17). *Patent No. 5,236,790.* USA.

Ramsey, F. (2016, January/February). "Magnetic Tape and Tomatoes." *AES Journal*, 64, no. 1/2:96–97.

Richardson, C. A. (2004, September 28). *Patent No. 6,797,072.* USA.

Richardson, C. A. (2006). "Solving the Sticky Shed Problem in Magnetic Recording Tapes: New Laboratory Research and Analysis Provides a Safe and Effective Remedy." *AES Convention 121 Paper. Paper # 6969*: 1–17. San Francisco, CA: AES.

Richardson, C. A. (2013). "The New 'Non-Baking' Cure for Sticky Shed Tapes." *ARSC*, 44, no.2:217–248.

Richardson, C. A. & Atias, M. (2015, October 31). "Magnetic Tape and Tomatoes (Oral Version)." *AES Convention. New York, NY: AES.*

25

# Neutralizing the Sulfate of Nitrate: An Opportunity for Restoration

**Alfonso Espinosa and Cesar De La Rosa Anaya**

**Abstract**

Degradation of film material composed of cellulose nitrate is endogenously self-degenerating, relentlessly consuming many nitrate films within collections around the world. One of the main problems of degradation in most advanced states is the formation of a hard oxide layer on the celluloid: sulfating. It prevents any kind of preservation or restoration treatment to the materials, not to mention the toxicity of the resulting compounds and the instability of its components which make it a flammable risk. However, it may be possible to stabilize the sulfation of nitrates using a method developed by Alfonso Espinosa in the Laboratory of Film Restoration, at Cineteca Nacional, in Mexico City. This procedure is the neutralization of sulfation of cellulose nitrate, which will allow the removal of hard oxide coating, typical in the sulfation, in order to handle the film safely, and apply all possible processes for the physical rescue of most of the frames and soundtrack that still exist within each film reel.

**Keywords**

cellulose nitrate, sulphating, neutralization, degradation, nitrate film.

## The Dilemma

The degradation of film material that is composed of cellulose nitrate[1] is endogenously self-degenerating, making it an unstable deterioration that consumes many nitrate films within archives around the world. This form of filmic destruction may be caused, not only by the instability of the material but also by the environment and conservation methods used to protect the film throughout the years. Those procedures and their subsequent consequences determine the scope of restoration and preservation possibilities. One of the main problems of degradation in advanced states is the formation of a hard layer of oxide on the celluloid–sulfating–that prevents any kind of preservation or restoration treatment to the material, not to mention the toxicity of the resulting compounds, and the instability of its components which always make it a flammable risk.

Like other institutions and film heritages, the Cineteca Nacional of Mexico has had many problems handling nitrates in critical stages of degradation within their collections. Because the volatile chemicals can cause multiple health risks for the staff, as well as risk the safety of the facilities, it is not safe to work with materials in this condition.

The remission of the stages of degradation of cellulose nitrate[2] is virtually impossible to achieve since the self-degenerating degradation of its components cannot be reversed with any chemical process known so far. However, there is the potential to stabilize the sulfation during critical stages using a method developed by Alfonso Espinosa of the Laboratory of Digital Restoration of the Cineteca Nacional in Mexico City. This procedure is the sulfating of cellulose nitrate neutralization.[3] The process removes the hard oxide coating typical in the sulfating and makes it safe to handle the film while applying all possible methods to rescue the majority of the physical frames and the soundtrack that are still salvageable for a digital restoration.

## Sulfating

What is the sulfating of cellulose nitrate? It is a chemical reaction that happens between the silver of the photosensitive emulsion and the hydrogen sulfate ($H_2S$), which are composited within itself. Hydrogen sulfate is formed when the thiosulfate ($S_2O_3^{2-}$) used in film material fixatives is in an acid environment like the one generated during the degradation of the cellulose nitrate. This degradation could happen because of bad preservation conditions, such as any external agent, like water, dirty chemicals, or other elements that the film has been exposed to, or through the natural consequence of time. As a result, the silver sulfide ($Ag_2S$), reacts to the nitrous acid (a consequence of degradation), generates nitric oxide (NO) and water, provoking this cyclic and self-degenerating decomposition (Selwitz, 1988:15–16). This is how the hard oxide layer forms over the film material and makes chemical intervention or treatment difficult.

**Sulfation Reaction (silver sulfide formation)**

$$2\,Ag^+ + H_2S \longrightarrow Ag_2S + 2H^+$$

**Silver Sulfation Reaction to Nitric Acid to Form Nitrogen Monoxide**

$$3\,Ag_2S + 2\,NO_3^- + 8\,H^+ \longrightarrow 6\,Ag^+ + 2\,NO + 3\,S + 4\,H_2O$$

## The Method

The first tests were applied to a film corroded with cellulose nitrate. Focusing on reel one out of five, this 35mm film negative, the black and white feature, *Pasaporte a Rio* (Tinayre, D. and Saslavsky, L. [Producers], and Tinayre, D. [Director], 1948), was in a stage 3 to 4 degradation, and contained the presence of rust over the whole picture.

The main problem with sulfation is the formation of acids (as a result of degradation) that promotes oxidation on the nitrate film stock. In order to stop this oxidation, we generated more acidity from the same oxides. The result was a simultaneous neutralization, transforming toxic components and solids into non-toxic gasses and aqueous states that were now possible to remove. This was a kind of "Trojan horse" reaction, removing oxidation from the inside so that both oxides and its own acids were capable of self-neutralization.

We began preparing a 10% aqueous sodium bicarbonate-based[4] solution, which was applied on the entire layer of oxide with a sprinkler. Being an aqueous solution and coming into contact with oxides, it induced the formation of nitric acid,[5] whereas, simultaneously, sodium bicarbonate was neutralizing these acids, resulting in gas, water, and neutral salt as end products. All

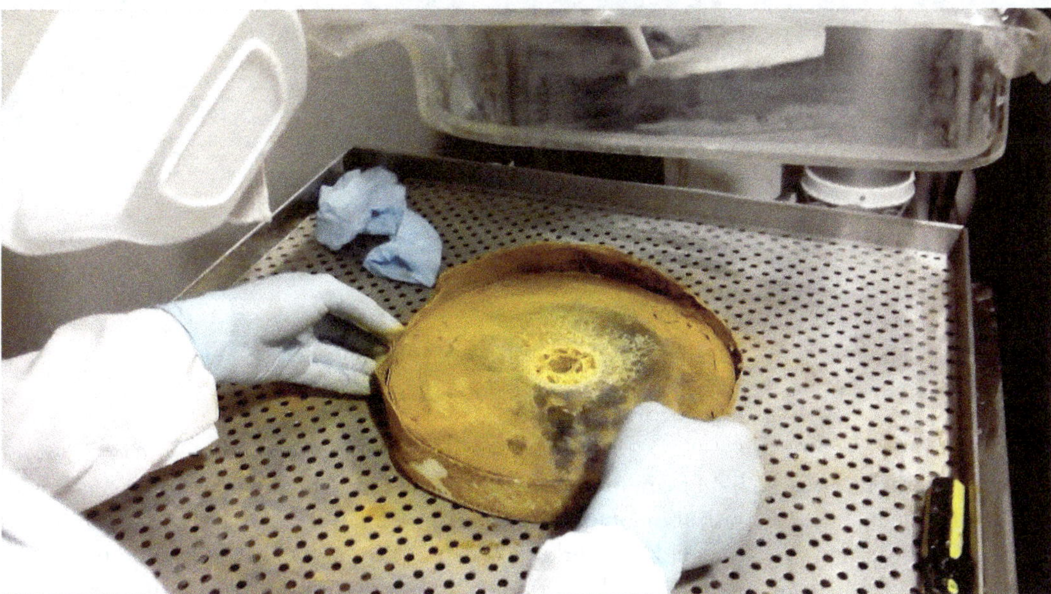

**Figure 1.** Nitrate film with presence of sulfating.

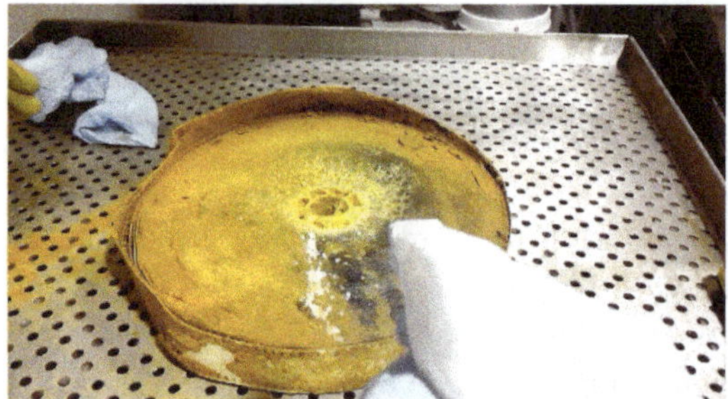
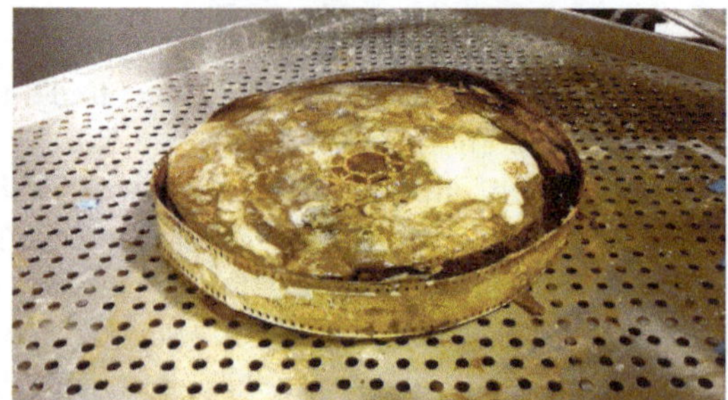

**Figure 2 and 3.** Application of the basic solution to transform solid compounds into gaseous and aqueous nontoxic states.

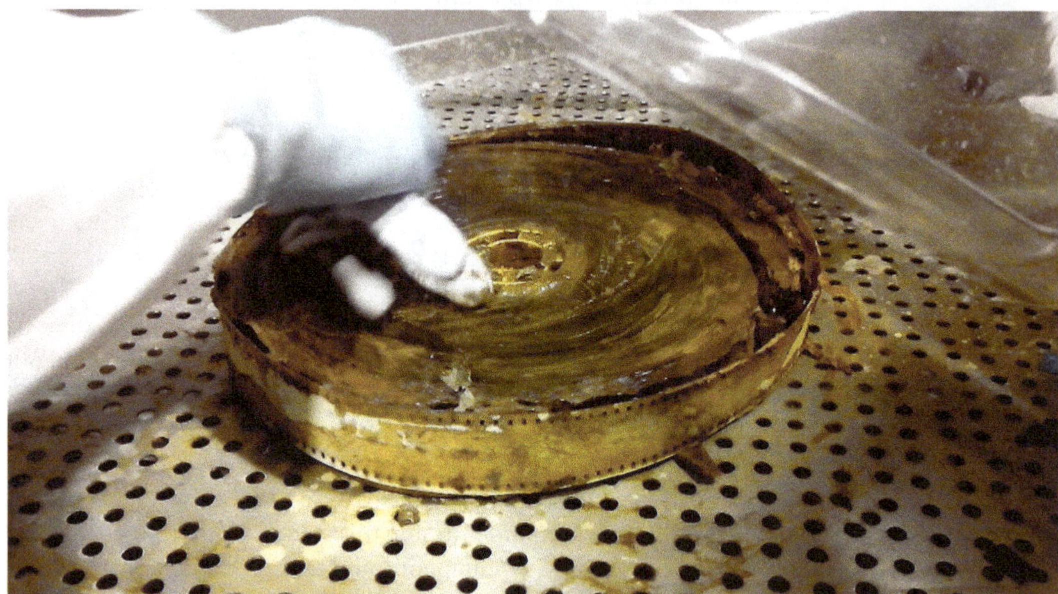

**Figure 4.** Easily removable with a cloth.

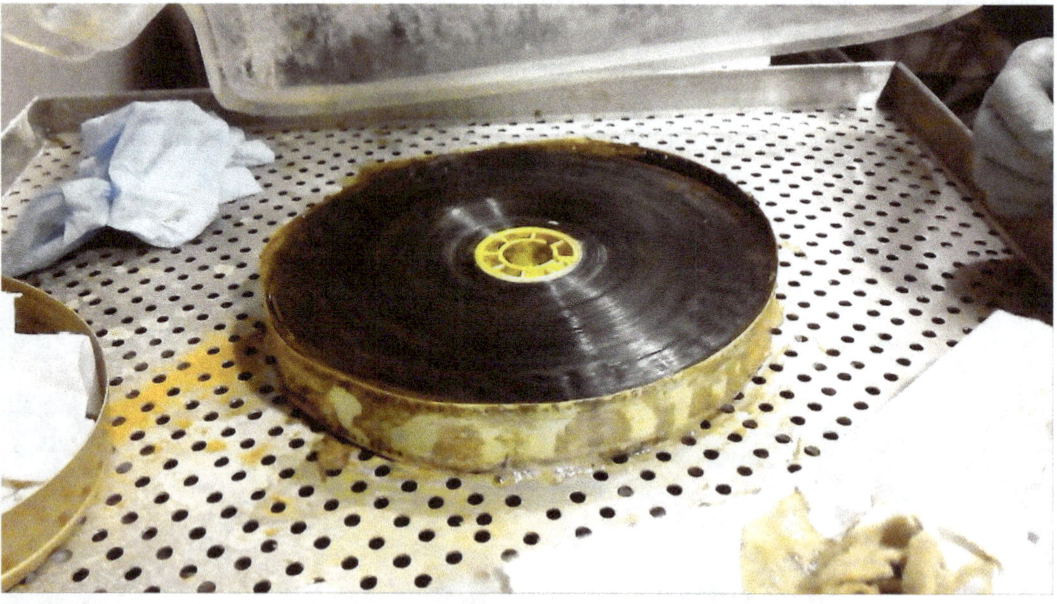

**Figure 5.** Easily removable with a cloth.

these compounds formed a light foam on the surface of the film which was easy to remove with a cloth. To check if the neutralization of the acid had been effective, some tests were conducted to determine the new levels of acidity and degradation of the material through the use of pH indicator strips[6] (a-d strips) that give a shift of color depending on the pH[7] of the material or

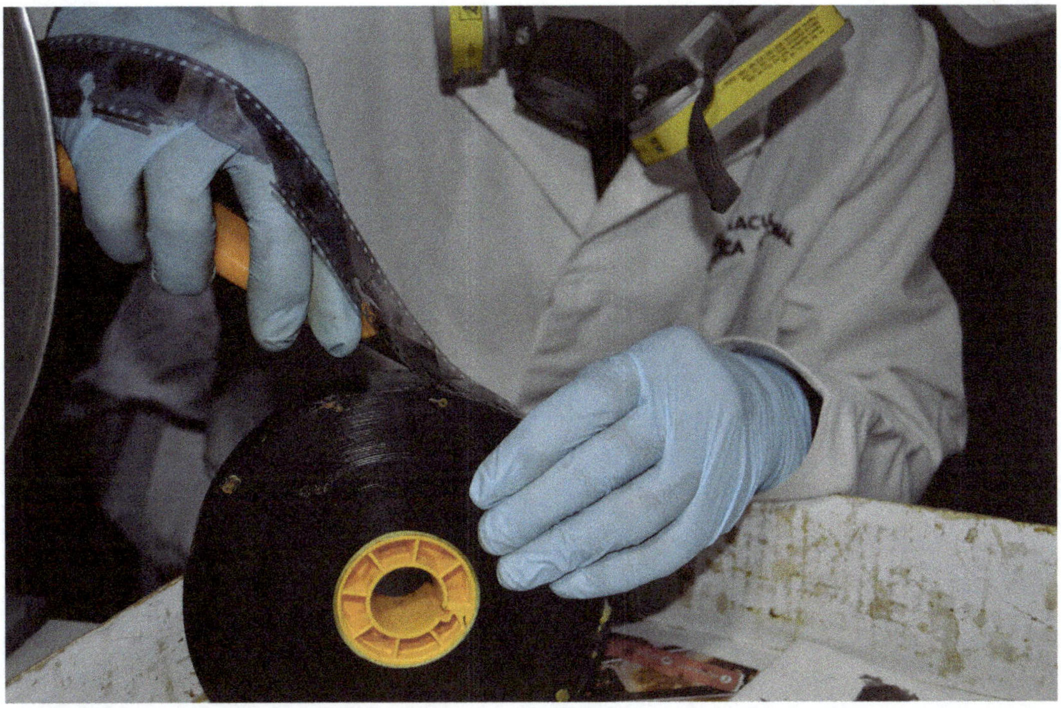

**Figure 6.** Treatment and physical repair at the work table.

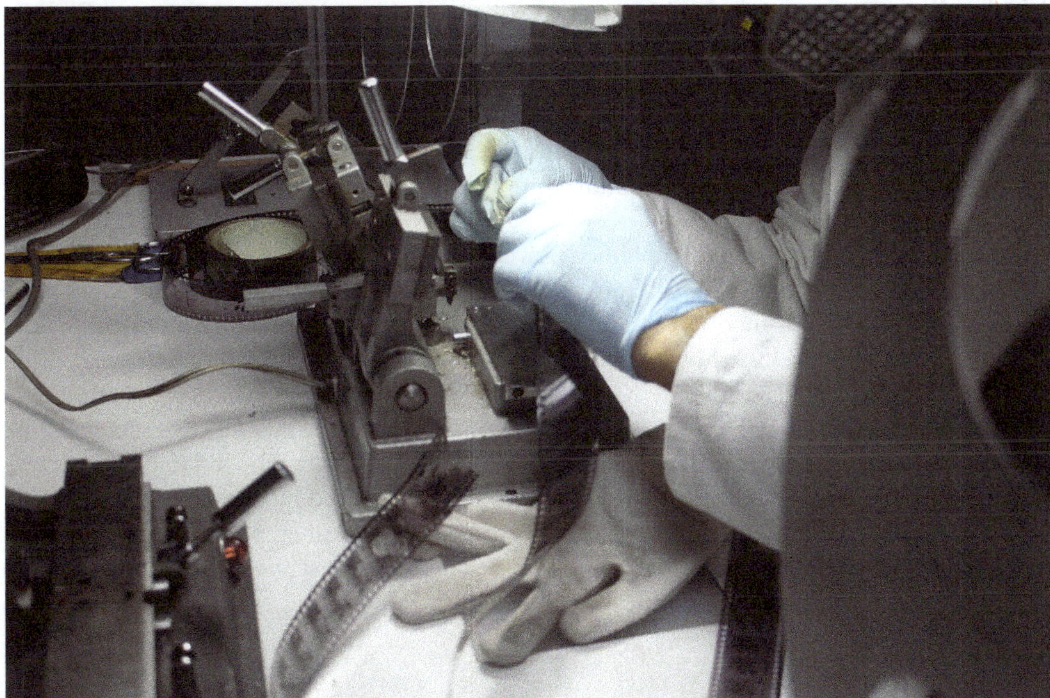

**Figure 7.** Treatment and physical repair at the work table.

examined compounds. In this case, when they came in contact with the newly processed film strip, they tacked to a neutral pH, which means it was safe to handle the waste.

After removing the resulting compounds, using another cloth, we immediately absorbed as much of the moisture as possible that remained on the film surface. Since one of the neutralization products is water, if it is not removed entirely it will produce oxidative reactions that will accelerate the degradation of the already damaged material. After the elimination of contaminants, a layer of natural eucalyptus essential oil was applied to the edges of the film strips, providing a degree of flexibility and moisture. It is this flexibility that allows the film to be rewound.

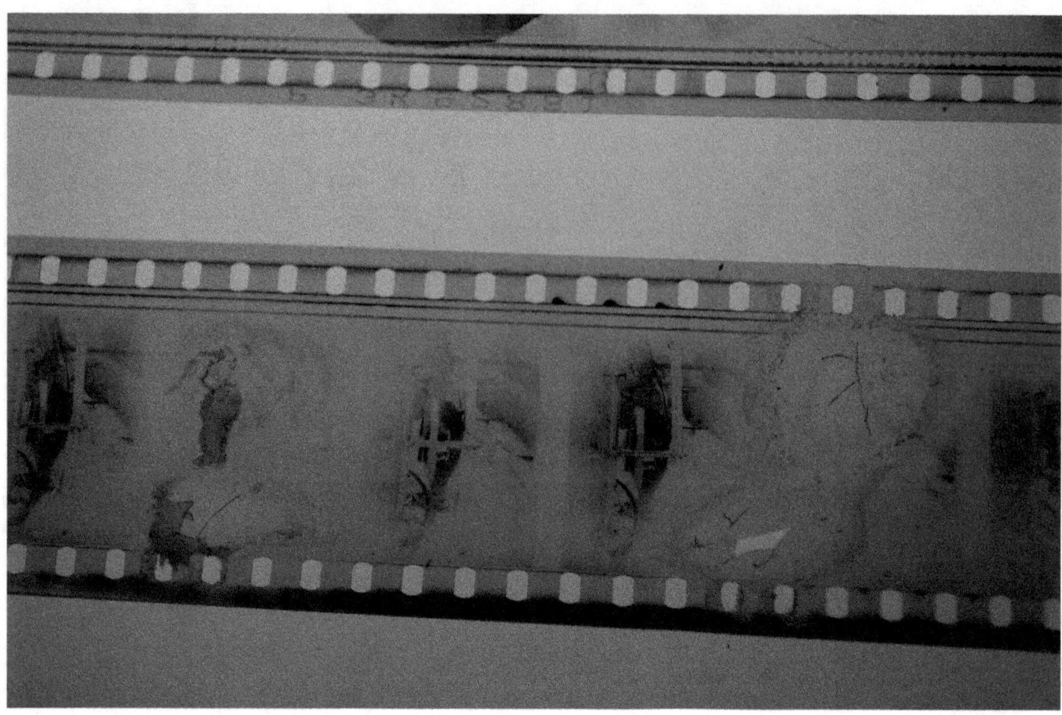

**Figure 8.** Treatment and physical repair at the work table.

Additionally, environmental conditions, such as the right weather, equipment, and facilities designed to handle nitrate films, all play a crucial part in the final outcome of this procedure.

In reassembly, many frames and fragments were lost since, as mentioned earlier, the material was in a stage of degradation so advanced that it precluded the total rescue of all the audiovisual information. To preserve some of the separated pieces of fragile film, more alkaline solution was applied to the fragments where degradation complicated the separation of existing tape, taking care not to use it in excess.

Finally, many of the fragments obtained proved to be strips of nitrate without any trace of the image. This is due, broadly speaking, from the nitric acid formed in the degradation of cellulose causing a drastic drop in the pH of the film, provoking a gradual and constant discoloration, fading of the image, and loss of physical characteristics. However, despite the loss of many film pieces due to this degradation, there were still long sections of this black-and-white feature, as well as the optical track, which was in very good condition and could still be rescued. Those multiple pieces and strips were cleaned of excessive waste arising from the treatment of neutralization. All of the rescued frames' rips and punctures were repaired manually on the worktable with heat and Mylar bonders. Additionally, the emulsion was cleaned of dirt, dust, stains, and mutilated fragments at the beginning of the film were recovered, while the rest of the picture was preserved as a single piece of film, approximately 600 feet.

## The Results

In general, aqueous sodium bicarbonate proved to have favorable effects on the outer layer of oxide that was formed by the sulfate contained within the critically deteriorated state of this film. By chemically manipulating their toxic compounds (solid products of the oxidation of nitrate), a transformation developed into more health friendly and easy-to-remove compounds (liquid and gaseous products with neutral pH). This neutralization also resulted in more flexibility and humidification to the film stock, making it more manageable for a subsequent reconstruction on the worktable, and viable to be included in a digital workflow (digitizing, digital restoration, color correction and sound correction, etc.). The neutralization of this sulfating method has also been applied to the other four reels of *Pasaporte a Río,* as well as, three reels of films in similar sulfatic degradation, Francisco Regueira's *Yo Soy Usted* (1943). All of them have shown promising results (figs. 9 and 10 show examples of frames before and after a digital restoration workflow.).

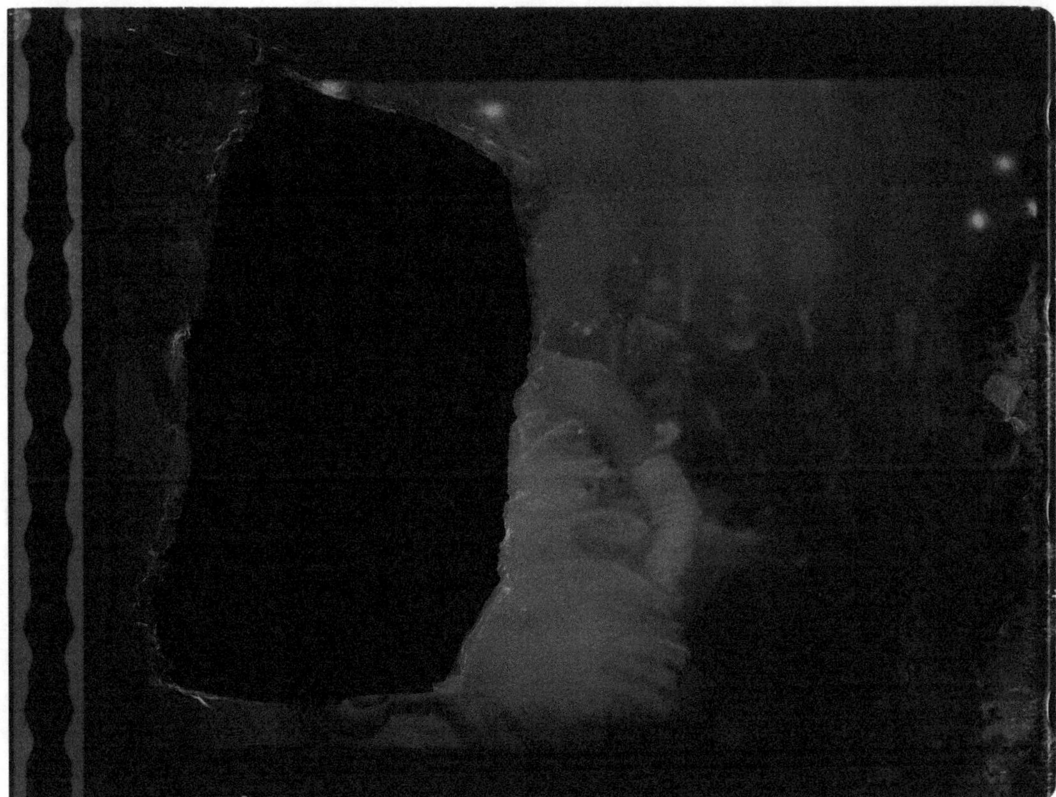

**Figure 9.** Before

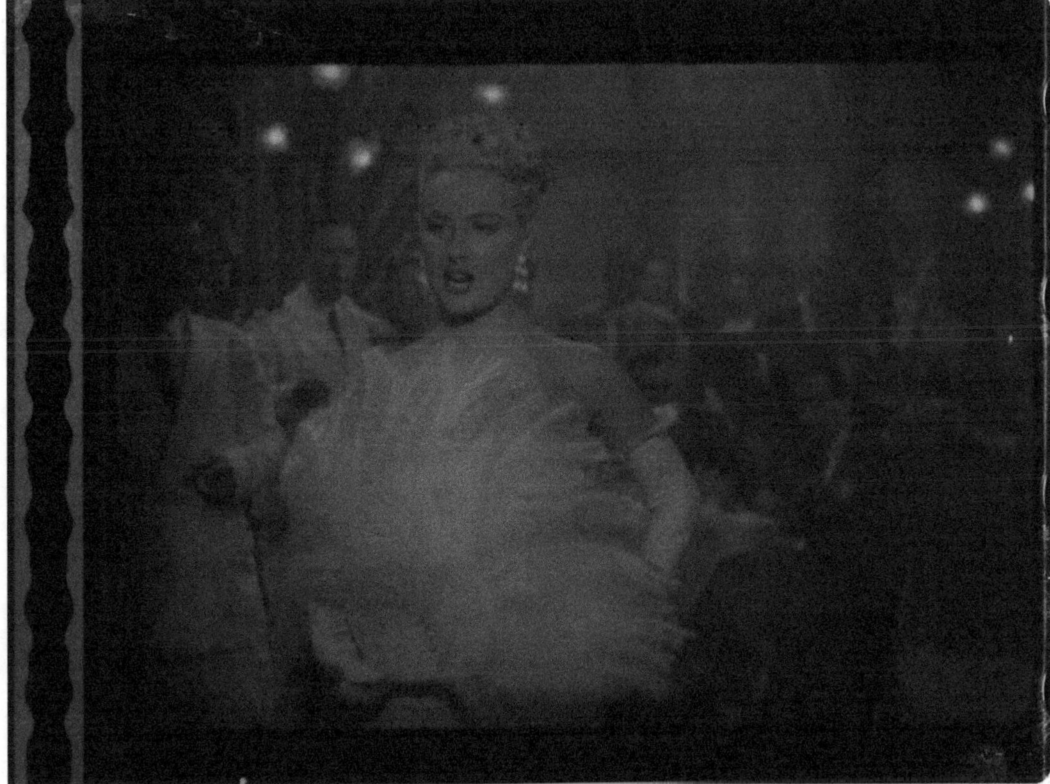

**Figure 10.** After

However, we will need to run more tests with additional films containing nitrates at this stage in order to compare the results and side effects. As for *Pasaporte a Rio* and *Yo Soy Usted,* it has been five months since we applied this method to these films and no negative results have been reported since. It will be necessary to continue to observe the film's degradation evolution for a longer time period to define the scope and limits of this process. We must clarify that we only can stop sulfating on some celluloid, but we can not stop the degradation of the material, which inevitably will continue.

## Perspectives

The results obtained by applying this method of neutralization of sulfating reflects the possibility that collectors and preservationists no longer need to be powerless witnesses to the loss of older films due to nitrates voracious stages of deterioration. Laboratories and film collections possessing materials in this condition will have a great opportunity to preserve and restore those films that would ordinarily be considered unsalvageable. Even in cases where reels of films are considered irreplaceable losses, we can rescue the information contained in its emulsion through digital methods (image and/or sound), then try to reprint it in celluloid in order to return the picture to its original format, and be preserved again in a film collection.

However, it is necessary to consider the value and limitations of the materials to be rescued in order to evaluate if it is worth the restoration challenge since this process does not work for all nitrate conditions. Consideration is advised, prior to each project, by the selection of materials according to their historical value, the degree of degradation, and the viability of the restoration. As mentioned previously in this article, this method is not a magical solution. Loss of emulsion and frames will be inevitable in any digital, physical and chemical process. Degradation of nitrates is never uniform, nor predictable, causing various modifications to each project's restoration.

## Conclusions

Like Paolo Usai Chechi says in his book *The Death of Cinema*, "Cinema is the art of destroying moving images" (Chechi, 2005). Indeed, the more a film is exhibited, the faster it deteriorates, regardless of its preservation and restoration care. A film's life is like a human life, it has a cycle of beginning and ending, of creation and destruction. After being exhibited to their physical limit, films will disappear, and new productions will arise in their place. That has been the raw history of cinema.

Conclusively, not all sulfating nitrate films have to be lost, not when there is a chance to extend their ephemeral existence on cellulose through transfer to a digital medium, thus safeguarding those films for new generations, evoking and reviving their aesthetic and historical records. If the method briefly proposed in this paper can do that, a small advance will be achieved facing the passage of time in celluloid.

Alfonso Espinosa is a chemist trained in the film restoration of archival collections and their senescent films. He specializes in the chemical stabilization and physical repair of severely degraded films for preservation and digital restoration purposes. Since 2013, he has been responsible for the chemical division of the laboratory of restoration in Cineteca Nacional Mexico.

Cesar De La Rosa Anaya is an audiovisual researcher and a film scanning specialist in digitizing film archival collections and senescent films, primarily for digital restoration projects. He is the supervisor and lead technician, using ARRISCAN, for the scanning division of the laboratory of restoration in Cineteca Nacional Mexico, as well as a hands-on collaborator with the laboratories' research department for the past four years.

## Acknowledgments

I want to thank Paolo Tosini (Italy), Sophie-Charlotte Poiré (ÉCLAIR, France), Dora Moreno, María del Carmen López, Edgar Torres, Mónica Ruiz Loyola, Carlos Filoteo, Manual Vegara, Paola Cornejo, Juan Pablo Roldan, Rafael Calderón, Marco Oswaldo Vargas, Alberto Macías, Rodrigo Moreno, Gustavo Ríos, Carmen Govea, Ana Cuellar, Omar Sánchez, Karla Ángeles, and Sofía Arévalo (Cineteca Nacional, Mexico).

## Notes

1. Cellulose nitrate is an organic polymer that can synthesize with the substitution of groups of hydroxyl (OH) of cellulose by groups of nitro ($NO_3$). This nitration and the addition of plasticizers give the polymer the unique feature of flexibility and transparency, but at the same time, makes it chemically unstable, highly flammable and explosive (Miessler, 1991).
2. Stages of degradation of cellulose nitrate:
   a. Initial degradation. At this stage the celluloid looks good, but there is a slight decrease of the pH and may feel slightly moist to the touch.
   b. Serious degradation. The film becomes slightly sticky and you can see the properties of the image fading.
   c. Very serious degradation. The material is very sticky, images are moved, and the loss of physical characteristics of the imagery is evident.
   d. Total loss. The celluloid has become a sticky solid mass with plenty of rust on it, and it is possible the images have been completely lost.
   e. Final degradation. The bracket is a solid block which splinters when trying to rewind it, the image is nonexistent and will eventually become oxide powder. (FIAF Preservation Commission, 1992.)
3. Neutralization: chemical reaction that occurs between a base and an acid, resulting in neutral salt and water; it is called neutralization reactions because it neutralized the properties of the acid and basic substance (Miessler, 1991).
4. Sodium bicarbonate: white crystalline solid compound ($NaHCO_3$); it has a basic pH and an alkaline taste. (National Library of Medicine, Medical Subject Headings, 2006).
5. Nitric acid: corrosive viscous liquid ($HNO_3$), which may cause severe burns. (Hollinshead, 1987:4).
6. PH indicator strips are used to determinate the acidity in film materials. They are impregnated with one or more qualitative indicators, which when coming into contact with the film will change color depending on its pH. The color change is due to a structural change induced by the protonation or deprotonating of the chemical species (Miessler, 1991).
7. pH: potential hydrogen (pH) is an indicator of acidity or basicity of a substance. In the field of preservation of film supports, it measures degradation of the tapes (Miessler, 1991).

## Bibliography


Cherchi Usai, P. (2005). *La Muerte del Cine*, Barcelona: Editorial Laertes.

Del Amo, A. (2006). Características físicas, químicas y funcionales de los materiales, *Clasificar para Preservar*, España, pp. 9–15.

FIAF preservation commission. (1992). FIAF Handling, Storage and Transport of the Cellulose Nitrate Film, FIAF.

Fuentes de Cía, M. and Robledano Arillo, J. (1994). *La identificación y preservación de los materiales fotográficos*, México.

Hollinshead, P. W., Wan Ert, M., Holland, S., and Velo, K. (1987). *Deteriorating Negatives, A Health Hazard*, Collection Management.

Image Permanence Institute. (1995). User's Guide for A-D Strips Film Base Deterioration Monitors, version 1.0 1/95.

Miessler, L. M., Tar, D. A. (1991). *Inorganic Chemistry*, 2nd ed., Pearson Prentice-Hall.

National Library of Medicine. (2006). *Medical Subject Headings*.

Selwitz, C. (1988). *Cellulose Nitrate in Conservation*, pp. 9–25.

Tapia Gonzáles, A. C. (2007). Cinética de la reacción de precipitación de plata complejada con tiosulfato, Tesis de ingeniería en Minería Metalúrgica, México, Universidad Autónoma del Estado de Hidalgo, Instituto de ciencias básicas e ingeniería, área académica de materiales y metalurgia, pp. 21, 22, 26.

Tinayre, D. and Saslavsky, L. (Producers), and Tinayre, D. (Director). (1948) *Pasaporte a Río* [Motion Picture] Argentina: Argentina Sono Film

Francisco R. (Director and Producer). (1948). *Yo Soy Usted* [Motion Picture] México: México Films.

Yúfera, E. P. (2007). *Química orgánica básica y aplicada: de la molécula a la industria*, México, Vol. 2.

# 26

# Fighting the Decay: Permanent Refreshment of Acetate Media

**Nadja Wallaszkovits**

## Abstract

One of the most urgent preservation issues in audiovisual archiving is the decay of material based on cellulose acetate, widely investigated and summarized as "vinegar syndrome." In this connection it seems that another chemical deterioration process of plasticizer loss has been so far underestimated in the world of audiovisual archiving.

Together with leading Austrian research institutions, a method to permanently refresh acetate media has been developed for audio tapes as well as cinematographic film material. The treatment is designed to refresh the material in the sense of playability and long-term storability: (re)gain material elasticity, and therefore playability, enhance the digitization process and quality due to higher physical flexibility of the material, and reduce acidity in the material. This will optimize storage conditions in the long term.

The paper briefly describes the mechanisms of plasticizer volatility and related parameters influencing this process. Possible solutions are discussed and the various methods to verify the restoration success of the chemical treatment are outlined.

## Keywords

chemical deterioration, cellulose acetate, vinegar syndrome, loss of plasticizer, restoration.

## Introduction

The chemical deterioration process referred to as "vinegar syndrome"[1] is a widely investigated topic that in fact hides a complexity of interactions that should be recognized by archivists, to allow proper identification of damage and to perform the necessary preservation and restoration activities—not necessarily limited to acetate-based media.

One reaction involved in acetate degradation processes has been monitored already very early in history, but seems to be a rather underestimated factor in A/V media-related research activities, namely the loss of plasticizer (also known as leakage or migration of plasticizer—migration is not the general term but a specific form of loss), as well as of other volatile substances.

While manufacturers, especially of cinematographic film materials, have always faced the problem of dimensional changes of cellulose acetate-base film and, therefore, have developed optimized production processes (e.g., Charriou and Valette 1936), in many scientific studies the phenomenon of plasticizer loss, although discussed in outline, was usually described as a side action of the vinegar syndrome and mainly found in acetate-based materials. Looking at the problem from a more general view it is clear that plasticizer loss is a phenomenon per se, being discussed also in various fields of medical and chemical research.

Loss of plasticizer and other volatile components from a chemical system is not necessarily caused by the vinegar syndrome, but usually by evaporation during long-term storage. This phenomenon can occur with any synthetic material containing plasticizer and does not necessarily depend on the vinegar syndrome reaction. A long list of polymers containing plasticizers can be found in Wypych (2012).



*Sustainable Audiovisual Collections* (2017): 196–204. DOI: 10.2979/jts2016.0.0.28

## The Role of Plasticizers in A/V Media

A plasticizer is a substance incorporated into a plastic or elastomer to increase its flexibility, workability or processability (ASTM D883-12, 2012). As outlined in detail by Reinecke, Navarro, and Pérez (2011), plasticizer separates the polymer chains, and with this the intermolecular bond strength decreases, making the plastic softer.

Plasticizers can be either internal or external. Internal plasticizers are actually part of the polymer molecule. They form integral parts of the polymer chain and are chemically reacted with the polymer (i.e., the process of copolymerization). Monomer units are built into the polymer chain, acting as irregularities in the otherwise regular chain structure and thus causing a decrease in the glass transition temperature compared to the unmodified polymer. The advantage of internally plasticized polymers is the fixed chemical linkage of the plasticizing unit with the polymer chain—they do not suffer from plasticizer loss or migration effects. However, this leads to relatively limited properties of the modified materials. Hence, internal plasticizers are used to a much smaller degree than external plasticizers, which can be more easily varied (Braun et al., 2012).

External plasticizers are materials that interact physically, but are not chemically reacted with the polymer. External plasticizer molecules are not attached to polymer chains by primary bonds and can therefore be lost by evaporation, migration, or extraction. The smaller the plasticizer molecules are, the better is the effect of plasticization that can be achieved. But due to the short-chained structure of these molecules and the resulting higher vapor pressure, volatility is increased.

The typical amount of plasticizer in audio tape and photographic film substrates is 15%–20% (wt), the typical value of plasticizers in binders is 3%–5% (wt).

A very good historic overview about the beginning of the use of plasticizers and dedicated chemicals is given in Rahman and Brazel (2004).

The physical-chemical causes of aging of plasticized polymers have been well described by Voigt (1967): The permanence of a plasticizer, that is, its tendency to remain in the plasticized material, depends on the size of the plasticizer molecule and on its rate of diffusion within the polymer. The larger the plasticizer molecule, the lower its vapor pressure or volatility and, therefore, the greater its permanence. Other factors, such as polarity and hydrogen bonding, will also affect the permanence of the plasticizer.

Diffusion of plasticizer is also dependent on the area of the material surface exposed to the atmosphere, the thickness of the diffusion zone, the diffusion coefficient and the saturation concentration and vapor pressure of the plasticizer in the material. Also the plasticizer concentration and vapor pressure of the surrounding atmosphere is influential, as well as temperature, atmospheric pressure (vacuum accelerates!), exposure to light, and involvement of adjacent media (so-called transport phenomenon).

For archival storage, this means that high temperature and humidity are the main influencing parameters triggering loss of plasticizer from audiovisual materials. Additionally, the storage container has an important function in preventing loss of plasticizer from the system.

## Problem-Solving Approach

The Phonogrammarchiv of the Austrian Academy of Sciences, Vienna, has together with the Austrian Institute for Chemistry and Technology, developed a method to permanently refresh acetate media, especially those affected by the chemical deterioration process referred to as "vinegar syndrome."

The method has been patented (Oesterreichische Akademie der Wissenschaften, 2011), and an exclusive licensing contract has been made with NOA. As part of a public-private-partnership, the restoration process is being further developed in cooperation with NOA Vienna for industrial applications.

The method is designed to reverse the effects of loss of plasticizers. It is based on a diffusion process in the liquid phase: The archive tape (e.g., magnetic audio tape, magnetic film or motion picture film material) is exposed to a treatment bath based on a chemically inert carrier liquid. The special properties of the inert liquid allows it to be mixed with plasticizer(s) with a suitable molecular structure, so that the plasticizer (or a mixture thereof) can diffuse into the material, while the inert liquid is inherently chemically inactive. Thus the plasticizer content of the tape can be refreshed and in most cases a replay without material breakup and time-consuming manual restoration processes (splicing) can be achieved. NOA Laboratory is investigating low-volatility plasticizing chemicals of sufficient strength to achieve an elasticity refreshment of high permanence.

At the same time, acidity content is reduced in the acetate carrier, as acidity is replaced by plasticizers during the extrusion process taking place during the liquid phase of the bath.

Our recent investigations have shown that this reduction of acidity can be carried out in the form of a very effective complementary treatment, so that at its best, a permanent reduction of acidity below the autocatalytic point within the material can be reached.

The restoration success has been verified for a defined range of materials, where it can be used without risk. Research to enlarge the applicability for a wider range of materials is ongoing.

## Verification Processes

Every restoration treatment should per se follow ethical guidelines. Therefore, it should be the aim "to restore and preserve artifacts without altering the original materials, whenever possible" (AMIA 2016, point 4).

This means, that the chemical treatment must not be harmful to the material, but should improve physical properties and chemical stability. However, it will not stay unaffected even if untouched and stored under optimum conditions. It will suffer concerning long-term changes in the long term and show signs of aging and deterioration. But it must be verified that the material will be enhanced and positively influenced by the chemical treatment, so that the playability and storability is extended for as long as possible.

The NOA Research Department and the Austrian Research Institute for Chemistry and Technology have started to develop best practices to verify the restoration process from various aspects. The procedures outlined will double-check the results and the long-term effects on the material by introducing methods to move from destructive chemical analyses to nondestructive and simply applicable verification and quality control processes. These include verification processes that use optical, mechanical, and chemical material properties.

## Optical Quality Control

The optical quality control routines are designed to verify that the chemical treatment does not negatively influence the image quality parameters, such as color accuracy, image sharpness and definition, etc. Therefore, one or more defined frames are digitized before and after the treatment, under a reference situation that has been tested and set up.

An industrial photographical microscope zoom lens (up to ×90 magnification) is mounted on a solid stand with a metal base and microscope stage. It is combined with a digital single-lens reflex camera with high-resolution sensor. A reference light situation is given by use of an LED daylight light box with defined color temperature. The whole setup is arranged in a closed box lined with molleton or a felted natural fibre, so that no reflections or other optical influences are produced:

As it is very important to compare exactly the same frame before and after treatment, the digitized frame is marked with a short piece of thread tied into the perforation that can be easily removed once the optical documentation is finished.

The setup was extensively tested for reproducibility. An IT8 colour target as well as a resolution test target are digitized under optimum conditions, documenting all parameters (white balance, color mode/display documentation, etc.) as well as the limits of the system. The mask image and the color target are documented as a reference every day the setup is

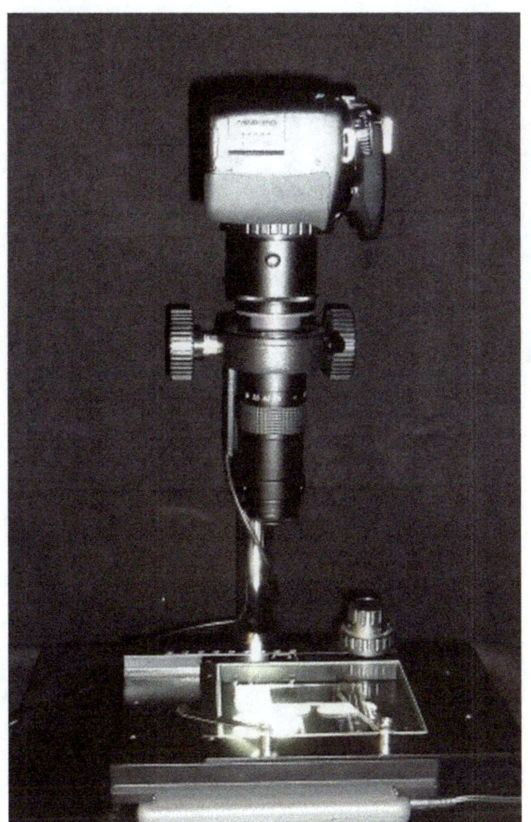

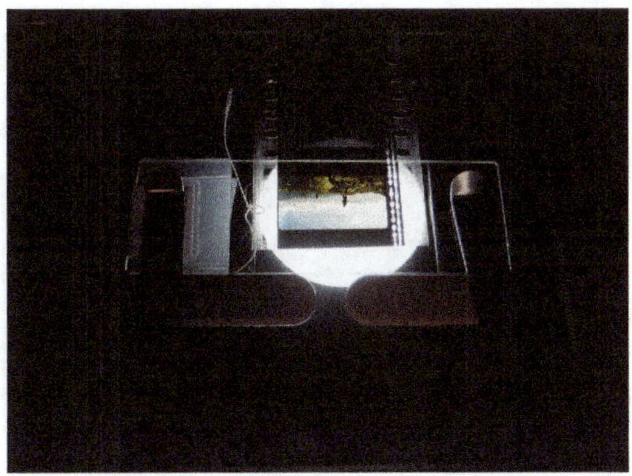

**Figure 1.** Setup for optical control (left) and detail of the optical control setup (right).

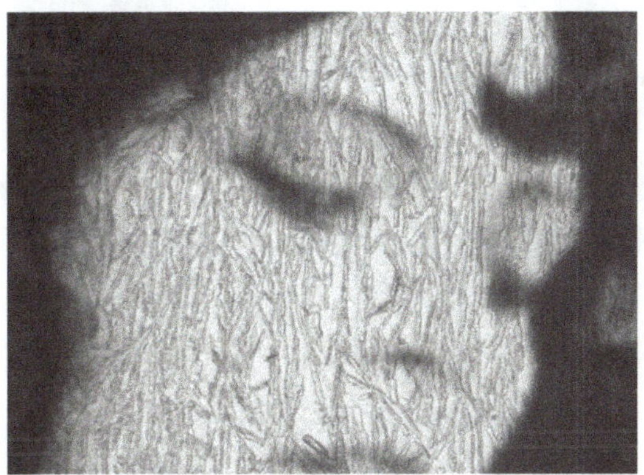

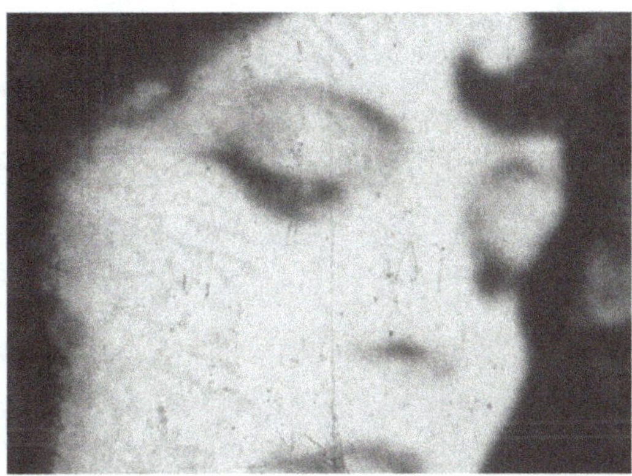

**Figure 2.** Image before (left) and after (right) treatment.

in use. This guarantees a continuous monitoring of the system performance and optimum reproducibility.

The sampled images are software analyzed for color accuracy, image sharpness, and geometrical distortion, before and after chemical treatment. Figure 2 shows a good example. In this case, during the chemical treatment, also deposits of crystallized plasticizer (e.g., triphenyl phosphate) were removed.

## Sound Quality Control for Magnetic Tapes/Tracks

A defined part of the tape/magnetic track(s) is digitized under optimum conditions, following actual recommendations (e.g., IASA TC04, 2009). The digitized file is spectrally analyzed using dedicated software tools.

## Mechanical Quality Control

A key feature to verify the restoration success is the improvement of the mechanical properties of the material as a result of the chemical treatment. Mechanical quality control is realized by

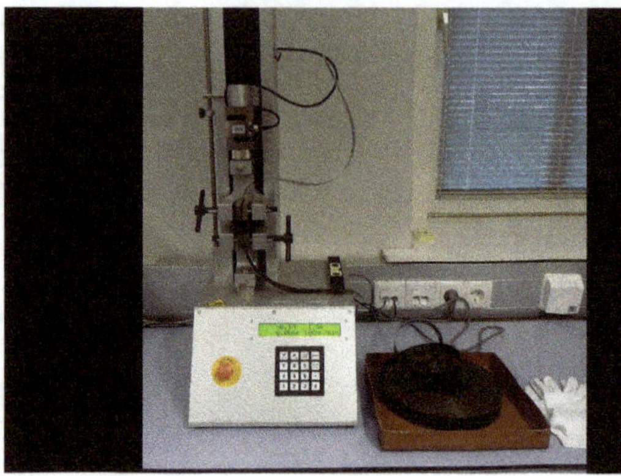

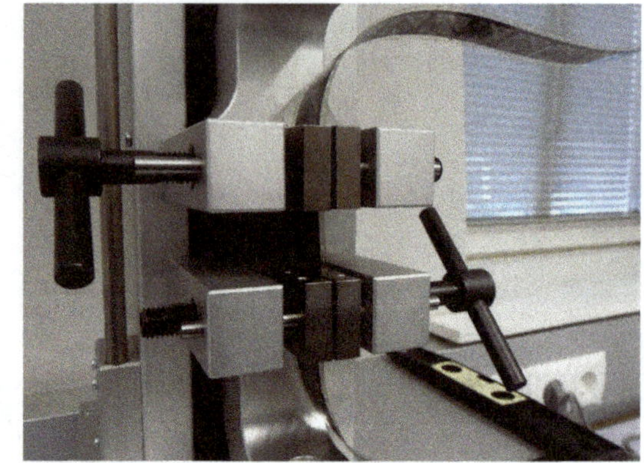

**Figure 3.** The tensile testing machine (left) and detail of the loaded film sample (right).

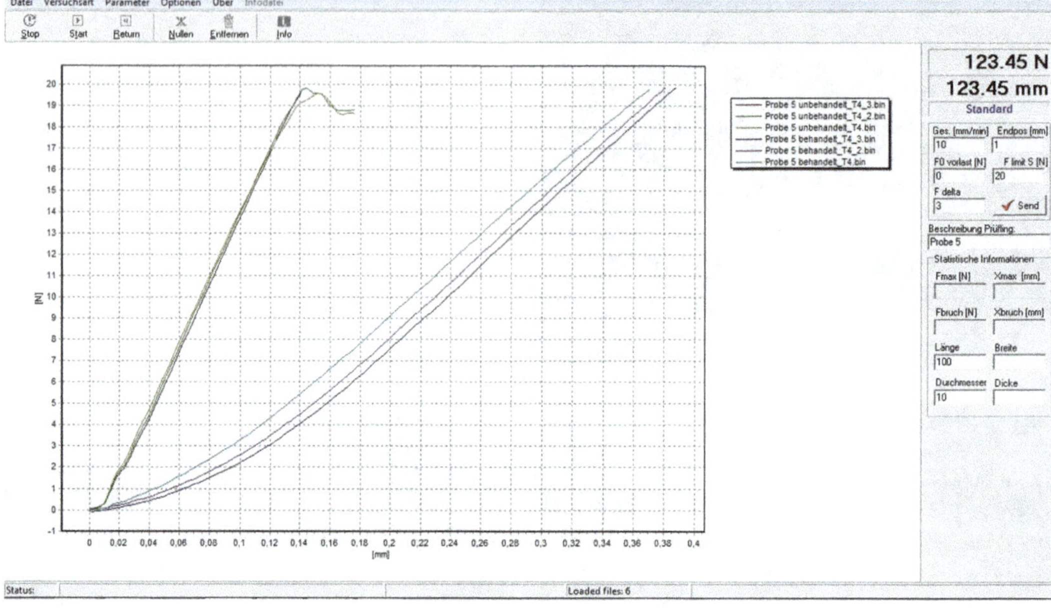


**Figure 4.** Stress-strain diagram of a sample before and after treatment.

nondestructive tensile testing within the reversible range of the individual film/tape before and after treatment.

Therefore, a software controlled tensile testing machine is used. The tensile tests are limited via several complementary parameters: stretching force, velocity, maximum elongation, as well as the breaking force detection.

The material tests are performed within a practical range of film operation in daily use, following the recommendations of SMPTE-Standard RP106-1994 in combination with the specifications of modern film scanning devices.

Figure 4 shows the stress-strain diagram of a sample before and after chemical treatment. To verify the values, every measuring procedure is repeated three times. The green curves on the left side show a steep increase with a maximum elongation up to 0.14 mm, where the material reaches the yield point (necking point, from where on the mechanical properties would further extend into a nonlinear region). This point is critical, as it shows the maximum force up to which deformations are completely recoverable upon removal of the load. A specimen loaded elastically in tension will elongate, but will return to its original shape and size again when unloaded. This is exactly the limit, within which nondestructive tensile testing is possible.

The curves at the right show that the material has become more ductile after treatment. The increase is less steep with a maximum elongation up to 0.38 mm, where the material reaches the given stretching force. Due to the chemical treatment the material has significantly

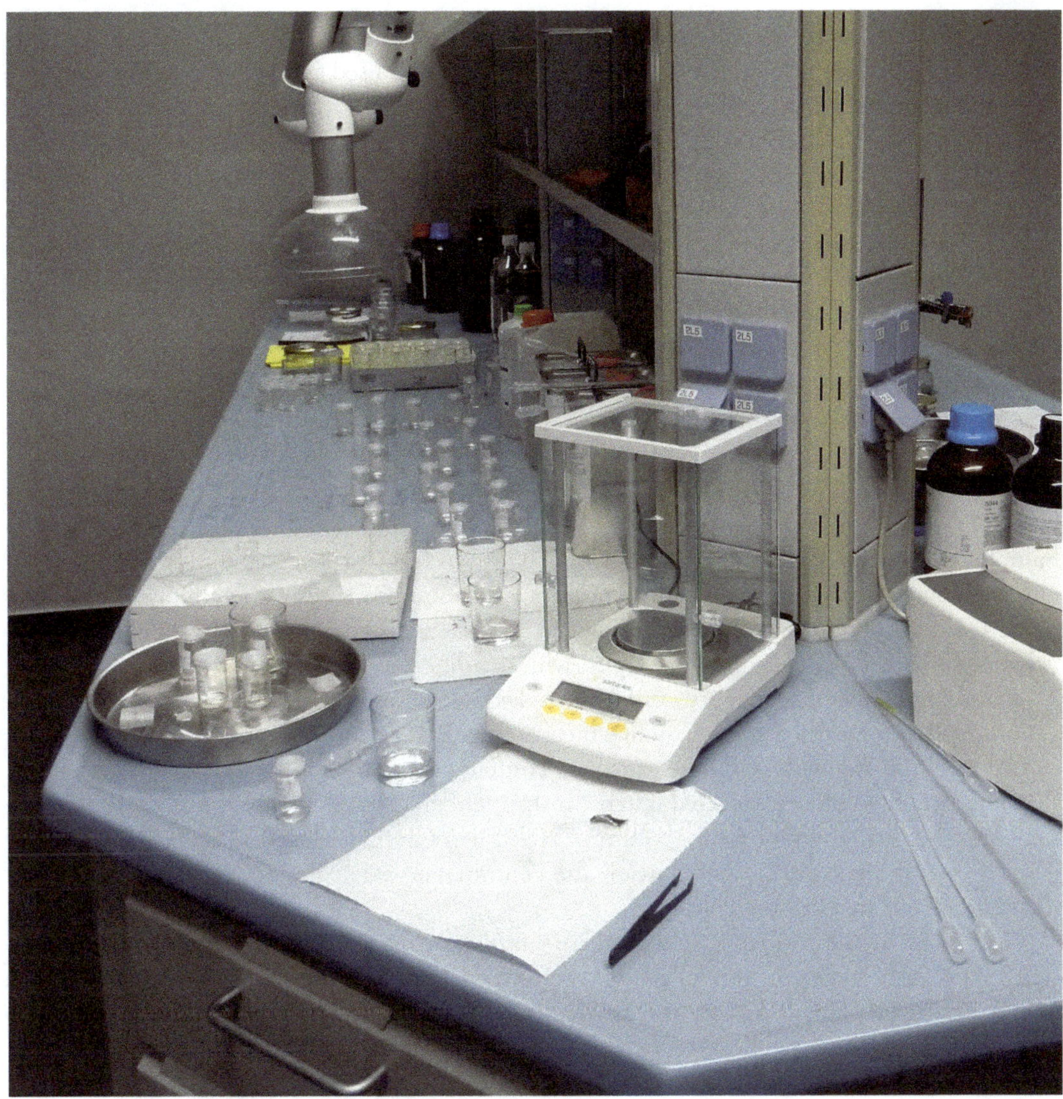

**Figure 5.** Analytical laboratory balance and test series.

improved in elasticity and mechanical properties, and the yield point is still far above these values. Details of mechanical testing and properties of plastics are outlined—for example, in Lampman, 2003.

The determination of the limits within nondestructive tensile testing is critical and requires extensive experience with highly deteriorated materials. The limits are depending on several factors, such as the dimension, degree of deterioration, brittleness, mechanical behavior in haptic test, etc. Tests should be carried out with utmost care, to avoid fracture. It requires dedicated know-how to load the samples correctly before and after treatment, with the same preload.

The moment the sample is loaded, the action of fixing it between the clamps creates a stressing force. This preload stress depends on factors such as how tight you fix the clamps, irregular elastic behavior/stiffness/elasticity of the individual sample, etc. This preload can (and should) be nulled before measuring; nevertheless, if the samples are fixed with different force between the clamps, you null different forces before measuring. This is particularly critical with shrunken and deformed materials. If the samples are not loaded accurately, the results will show a very high variance with significant measuring errors.

## Gravimetric Verification

Another possibility to measure the success of the process can be realized by weight analysis of a sample before and after chemical treatment. If the weight of a specific sample increases after being removed from the conditioning liquid and having dried off, this should be a main indication for plasticizer enrichment. Gravimetric verification is used as a first step in the sequence of more elaborated and complex chemical analysis methods. In the development phase of our research project, we started with the use of small samples of material that were available for destructive tests, as well as samples of uncoated, blank cellulose diacetate and triacetate film sheets, to optimally study the effects of various mixtures and concentrations.

The samples are prepared by punching/cutting out test specimen of similar size. To perform measurement with highest accuracy, an analytical laboratory balance is used.

The samples are weighed before and after treatment, directly after removal from the conditioning liquid, and then regularly monitored after given drying periods. All results are documented in a database.

Again this is the base data needed to transfer the results from destructive tests on small material samples into nondestructive verification procedures within the workflow.

## Chemical Verification: Analysis of Plasticizer Concentration

Samples that have permanently taken on weight are worth being selected for further advanced chemical analysis. One of the most important verification processes is the chemical detection and quantification of the plasticizer content in the refreshed material. A very accurate analytical analysis method is gas chromatography, with the disadvantage of being minimally invasive. Therefore, only materials that are available for destructive testing are used to create a quantification relation for further nondestructive measurements.

A gas chromatograph (GC) measures the content of various components in a sample.[2]

The sample solution is injected into the instrument enters a gas stream, which transports the sample into a separation tube, the "column." Helium or nitrogen is used as this so-called carrier gas. The components are separated inside the column, and a detector measures the quantity of the components that exit the column.

In a first step, the positive weight increase samples are prepared for GC analysis. This is carried out by plasticizer extraction following recommendations in literature, particularly Whitnack and Gantz (1952). The GC analysis is carried out at the laboratory of our project consultants-Erich R. Schmid, by his colleagues Josef Bailer and Wolfgang Werther, Institute for Analytical Chemistry, University of Vienna.

One method for the noninvasive characterization of the main components in the formulation of audiovisual materials is Attenuated Total Reflectance—Fourier Transform Infrared Spectroscopy (ATR-FTIR), as suggested in literature (e.g., Gómez-Sánchez et al., 2010). Infrared (IR) spectroscopy utilizes the fact that IR radiation can excite molecular structures to different frequencies of vibrations. This excitation leads to the absorption of characteristic bands of the irradiating IR light. The resulting IR spectrum makes it possible to identify compounds with detection limits between 0.1% and 1% volume concentration. Modern FTIR spectrometers irradiate the sample with a wide spectrum of IR radiation with wavelengths in the range of 2–50 µm. They enable analyses with a high time resolution and a good signal to noise ratio. The signal consists of the transmitted IR light or, in the case of samples that are nontransparent for IR, the reflected IR light (Boyd and Kirkwood, 2011).

Within our research, one main task is to correlate the results of GC analysis with the analysis of the IR results, so that a quantitative approximation to a plasticizer enrichment in percentage per weight (wt%) can be given, that will later be detected by noninvasive ATR analysis only.

## Acidity and pH Testing

Actual research is focused on acidity reduction and material neutralization. As a first step, the amount of acidity in a heavily affected film roll (acidity level 3 according to Image Permanence Institute A-D strip) was quantified. The result showed that 1 kg of 35mm film contained the huge amount of 2.8 g pure acetic acid. As a consequence, a method to filter acidity from the treatment bath has been developed. pH testing showed a reduction from pH 4.38 to 6.75[3] in the material within reasonable timespan, especially with the complementary treatment mentioned above. Further development is ongoing with the aim to obtain an internal buffer action within the material.

## Assessment of Long-Time Effects of the Treatment

In order to ensure that the long-time effects of the chemical restoration are not negatively influencing the future life span and quality of the treated materials, it is necessary to estimate the longevity and reliability of the treatment.

The following tests are proved to approximately represent the aging environment in archive environments: accelerated light aging tests according to EN ISO 4892-2, natural light aging tests in the window of NOA laboratory, as well as regular monitoring and verification of samples treated during the research phase (more than five years). Further tests are developed, according to Maxwell et al. (2005), to evaluate other effects—that is, possible influential effects of the storage container, permanence of material neutralization, etc.

Continuing development and verification processes are carried out to make the treatment a reliable and scientifically supported application. At the NOA laboratory, the highest efforts are made to reach top-level efficiency and validation of the restoration process.

## Conclusions

Our research has shown, that although the autocatalytic degradation of cellulose-based material cannot be cured, it is possible to largely revert the effects of loss of plasticizers and to substantially reduce the acidity content of the acetate carrier to a value below the autocatalytic point (the procedure has been registered under the name pHdetox). As a result, the storability of the material will be extended for many years, allowing archives worldwide to win considerable time for determining a migration and digitization strategy. Dedicated verification processes have been developed to verify the chemical treatment. By combining state of the art technology of many technological fields with the knowledge and experience of archiving and preservation, highest efforts are set to gain reliability with highest respect to the valuable originals.

Nadja Wallaszkovits manages the audio department of the Vienna Phonogrammarchiv as a specialist for audio restoration, rerecording, and digital archiving. She is consultant for archival technology for various institutions and is guest lecturer at the University of Vienna and at the Universities of Applied Sciences in Berlin and Berne. Recently she started managing the new research department of NOA, a public-private Partnership collaboration project dedicated to the restoration of acetate media.

## Notes

1. Wypych, G., (2012). Plasticizers: Use and selection for specific polymers. *Handbook of Plasticizers*. ChemTec Publishing. Toronto. Second Edition. Ch.11, p.274–379.1. The related extensive research activities around this topic to be found in dedicated literature are most respected and should be considered state of the art, as listing would by far exceed the scope of this publication.
2. The method of creating the sample (organic, solid, etc.) will depend on the parameter s that you want to measure. In many cases the samples are dissolved (e.g., the components you want to measure are prepared by liquid extraction). There are a range of methods that can be employed (see https://www.agilent.com/cs/library/primers/Public/5991-3326EN_SPHB.pdf ).
3. In this context it is important to know, that pH follows a logarithmic scale. It is defined as the negative logarithm of the hydrogen ion concentration in a solution. (http://chemistry.elmhurst.edu/vchembook/184ph.html.

## References


Association of Moving Image Archivists [AMIA]. (2016). Code of ethics. *AMIA*. Retrieved from http://www.amianet.org/about/code-of-ethics Access: 26.02.2016. (2012). ASTM D883-12, Standard terminology relating to plastics. *ASTM International*. West Conshohocken, PA. Retrieved from www.astm.org

Boyd, S., and Kirkwood, J. (2011). Quantitative analysis using ATR-FTIR spectroscopy. *Agilent Technologies, Inc.* Application Not. Publication Number si-01374.

Braun, D., Cherdron, H., Rehanhn, M., Ritter, H., and Voit, B. (2012). Polymer synthesis: theory and practice: fundamentals, methods, experiments. Fifth Edition. *Springer Science and Business Media*. p. 312.

Charriou, A., Valette, S. (1936, January). Realisation of undeformable cellulose acetate films for photography. *The Photographic Journal*. p. 27–31.

Gómez-Sánchez, E., Simon, S., Koch, L. Ch., Wiedmann, A., Weber, T., and Mengel, M. (2010). ATR-FTIR spectroscopy for the characterisation of magnetic tape materials. *e-Preservation Science Journal*. 8, p 2–9.

IASA Technical Committee. (2009). Guidelines on the production and preservation of digital audio objects. *IASA*. (Standards, Recommended Practices and Strategies, IASA-TC 04). Second edition.

Lampman, S. (2003). Mechanical testing and properties of plastics. *Characterization and Failure Analysis of Plastics*. *ASM International*. p185–196.

Maxwell, A. S., Broughton, W. R., Dean, G. D., and Sims, G. D. (2005). Review of accelerated aging methods and lifetime prediction techniques for polymeric materials. *NPL Report*. DEPC-MPR 016.

Oesterreichische Akademie der Wissenschaften. (2012). Method for Reconditioning Data Carriers. Inventors, P. Liepert, L. Spoljaric-Lukacic, N. Wallaszkovits. Appl. filed 23.12.2011, published 05.07.2012. IPC, G11B 23/50 (2006.01), G03D 15/00 (2006.01). Pub. No.WO/2012/088553.

Rahman, M., and Brazel C.S. (2004). The plasticizer market: an assessment of traditional plasticizers and research trends to meet new challenges. *Progress in Polymer Science*. Vol. 29, p. 1223–1248.

Reinecke, H., Navarro, R., and Pérez, M. (2011). Plasticizers. *Encyclopedia of Polymer Science and Technology*. Wiley and Sons. DOI: 10.1002/0471440264.pst245.pub2.

Society of Motion Picture and Television Engineers. (1994/2007). Film tension in 35-mm motion-picture systems operating under 0.9 M/s (180 Ft/min). *SMPTE*. RP106.

Truffa Giachet, M., Schilling, M., McCormick, K., Mazureka, J., Richardson, E., Khanjiana, H., and Learner, T. (2014, September). Assessment of the composition and condition of animation cels made from cellulose acetate. *Polymer Degradation and Stability*. Volume 107. p 223–230.

Voigt, J. (1967, November). Physikalisch-chemische Ursachen der Alterung von weichgemachten Kunststoffen. *Materials and Corrosion*. Vol. 18, Issue 11, p 969–977.

Whitnack, G.C., and Gantz, E. St. C. (1952). Extraction and determination of plasticizers from cellulose acetate plastics. *Anal. Chem.* 24 (6), p. 1060–1061.; access: 26.02.2016.

# The Sticking Point: Dealing With Blocked Motion Picture Films

27

**Mick Newnham**

## Abstract

Under prolonged storage, motion picture film may adhere within the reel, forming a solid mass; this is referred to as blocking. In response, the National Film and Sound Archive of Australia (NFSA) has developed conservation treatments to successfully deal with each of the mechanisms of blocking, and conducted several projects to treat large numbers of affected films.

## Keywords

film, blocking, gelatin, conservation, treatment.

## Background

For storage, motion picture film is wound onto reels or simple cores; also known as bobbins. The tension under which the film is wound has an impact on the chemical stability of cellulose ester-based films during long-term storage (Bigourdan, 1997). The more tightly wound the film, the lower the probable life expectancy.

However, as well as decomposition, tightly wound films may suffer from a strong adhesion between the layers of film. This is referred to as *blocking*. Blocking may be sufficiently strong enough to cause serious physical damage to the emulsion and base layer of the film. Additionally, blocking may occur in cellulose ester- and polyester-based films.

Before either a blocked cellulose ester- or polyester-based film may be safely unwound prior to projection, or duplication, the condition must be dealt with. There are several different mechanisms of blocking depending on not only the wind tension but also the chemical condition of the film. Broadly, we have found that there are three main types of blocking:

- Gelatin cross-linking between layers
- Exuded additive chemicals forming a cementing layer
- Decomposition by-products forming a cementing layer

External blocking or cementing agents, such as animal excrement, and structures, such as insect carton, are not considered in this paper, although blocking due to these reasons may also be occasionally encountered.

## The Role of Gelatin in Blocking

Since gelatin, both as the film emulsion and a major component of the backing layer, was the point of the adhesion between film layers, the majority of the research focused on the behaviour of gelatin.

Gelatin is a manufactured product formed by the combination of amino acids into a complex compound in long chains. Gelatin has many unique properties including significant response to changes in pH. Gelatin is a macromolecule that can be viewed, simplistically, as a combination of carboxylic and amino groups. Changes in pH alter the protonation of the groups. At the isoelectric point, ~pH 4.8, all the carboxyl groups are protonated, whereas the amino groups are not, giving the system a balanced charge (Kowalski, 1972). As the pH drops below the isoelectric point, the amino groups in the gelatin structure become protonated—that is, have a net positive (+) surface charge. Therefore, at the isoelectric point, there is a balance of small charges (+ and –) along the length of the chain. In this condition, the chains are tightly coiled. As the pH increases or decreases from this state, the balance of charge alters. Lowering the pH increases the prevalence of positive charges along the chain causing the gelatin chain to uncoil as the charges repel each other. Inversely, as the pH is increased there is an increase in the prevalence of negatively charged sites, and the chain once again progressively begins to uncurl.

## Interlayer Gelatin Cross-Linking

This is the most commonly encountered form of blocking and may be the result of:

- a disaster involving water
- improper drying after processing
- tight wind and storage under high, relative humidity
- natural shrinkage and subsequent increase in tension within the film reel
- exposure to extreme heat—for example, fire

The blocking mechanism is thought to be the cross-linking of the gelatin as the result of the gelatin chains being brought into close proximity and placed under pressure so that the charges on each surface may interact from one layer to the other.

The severity of the adhesion may be such that the bond between the layers of gelatin becomes stronger than the bond between the emulsion and the film base. Any attempt to unwind a film in this condition will tear the emulsion from the base, or even tear the base.

There is an additional caveat for polyester-based prints. While the longitudinal strength of polyester is high, the internal bonds holding the longitudinal polyester chains together is comparatively weak. If even a lightly blocked film is unwound, the polyester base will fracture and form voids inside the base polymer that permanently blemish the film.

The considered approach to this problem was to minimise the interlayer adhesion by raising the pH to promote a net negative charge on the adhering surfaces, causing the gelatin surfaces to slightly repel one another. Alkali processed gelatin, typical in photographic emulsions, shows an inflection point and significant reduction in the slope of the swelling curve around pH 8 (Sheppard, 1942). Kodak gave advice on two benign photographic solutions that worked in this region: Hypo Clearing Agent (HC-1) and Rewash (PB-6).

To identify any problems due to extended soaking in these solutions, test frames, colloquially known as "China Girls," were sought from as many different film emulsion types as possible. Additional test frames were printed on contemporary stocks. Each frame was measured using a Macbeth densitometer using the appropriate status filter. The test frames would provide information on density and colour balance changes due to the treatments. A pin register device was used to ensure that the same location was measured on the test frame for consistency.

After soaking in the solutions for time periods ranging from a few minutes to days at a time, the test frames were placed in an accelerated aging chamber for 49 days and the density measured.

The average density loss in each dye layer, in the negative test material, was in the order of 10%. It was noted that print stock typically had a lower dye loss with an average of 5%.

Further experimentation identified that sodium polymetaphosphate, a component of HC-1, was an effective swelling agent and caused the least dye loss when used by itself—that is, without the sulphite preservatives also found in HC-1. In solution, at a concentration of approximately 1.5%–2% w/v, the pH fell close to the 8–8.5 range. However, without the preservative, this solution required frequent changing, optimally on a daily basis. This protocol had the added advantage of preventing excessive bacterial action occurring on the films being treated.

It was noted that some films turned the solution slightly magenta. There were several possible reasons:

- Aged gelatin containing the upper magenta dye layer was dissolving
- Magenta leuco dye was being converted to a visible magenta form
- Residual cyanine sensitising dye

UV-visible spectrophotometry was used to determine the most likely underlying cause of the magenta colouration. Samples of image forming magenta dye exhibited a single peak absorbance at 530 nm, whereas, samples of the magenta water showed peaks at 499 and 547 nm, closely aligning to the absorbance spectrum of the sensitising dye. Kodak confirmed that while these dyes were mostly removed during processing, it was feasible that some may remain under some circumstances.

A further consideration was stabilising the film after treatment. Rewashing was required to remove the residual chemical from the film prior to returning to long-term storage.

Two problems became apparent:

- In the original processes, the dyes were stabilised by formaldehyde in the final bath
- The emulsion showed evidence of reticulation

There was no solution to the first problem, as formaldehyde is a now listed as a hazardous chemical, so the films were left unstabilised. The second problem was controlled with very careful attention to solution temperature.

## Exuded Additive Chemicals Forming a Cementing Layer

Additives are incorporated in the film base polymer for several reasons, such as to assist in the removal of other manufacturing additives and solvents, as a flame retardant, and as a plasticiser. Also, the additives are not chemically bonded within the base polymer.

Fourier transform infrared spectrophotometry (FT-IR) analysis of the crystal residues found on severely decomposed films identified triphenyl phosphate (TPP) as the dominant species. Kodak researcher, Dr. Tulsi Ram (1990) notes, "degradation of CTA polymer under ambient conditions is accompanied by its ability to pick up more water in the deacetylated regions which facilitates exudation of the solid TPP to the surface."

The positive charges on the gelatin surfaces provide bonding sites for the exuded TPP. The exuded TPP, firstly, bonds to the gelatin layers by hydrogen bonding. As the quantity of TPP increases, crystals form in situ via covalent bonds or van der Waal forces (Atkins, 1986), and thus create a linkage between the plasticizer coated surfaces, adhering the two layers firmly.

The increase in free acid, in the decomposing film, lowers the film pH below the isoelectric point. A pH-induced change was considered too risky to attempt due to the instability of the gelatin. The most feasible approach was to either remove the TPP cementing layer or break the crystalline structure.

TPP is highly soluble in lower alcohols such as ethanol and has a comparatively low melting point.

The first approach sought was to dissolve the TPP cementing layer without extracting the TPP remaining in the film base. A solution of 5%–10% ethanol in isopropyl alcohol (IPA) was dripped onto the point of adhesion as the film was unwound. TPP is only sparingly soluble in IPA. This is a slow process, as it takes a while for sufficient TPP to dissolve, and the residual acetic acid undergoes an ester reaction with the alcohol forming an acetate ester and water. The damp film requires drying before it can be safely rewound. This is a successful but slow treatment.

TPP has a comparatively low melting point (~50°C); however, there are risks to the film at this temperature. This temperature will possibly cause the deteriorated gelatin emulsion to pass through its $T_g$. Additionally, the rise in temperature may move the emulsion beyond the safe region for photographic materials and suffer plastic, or nonreversible, deformation (McCormick-Goodhart, 1996). This may lead to delamination of the emulsion during handling. Aware of the risks, severely decomposed and blocked films were placed in an incubator at slightly above the literature melting point and left for 100 minutes, sufficient to raise the internal temperature above 50°C. As expected, the TPP melted, and the films were very easy to unwind; unfortunately, the liquid TPP made handling the films awkward.

However, both methods occasionally struck persistent adhesions. Several mechanisms were hypothesised for this problem. The most feasible mechanism is that these adhesions are regions

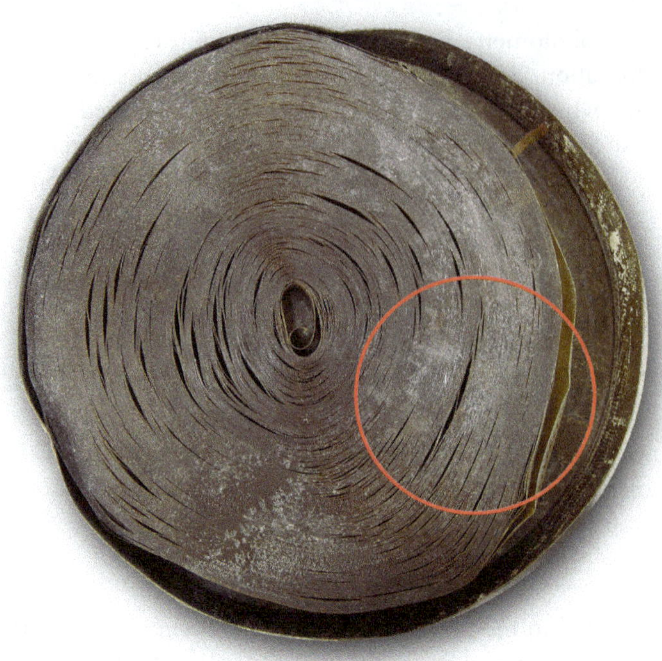

**Figure 1.** Decomposed film and area of compression through storage.

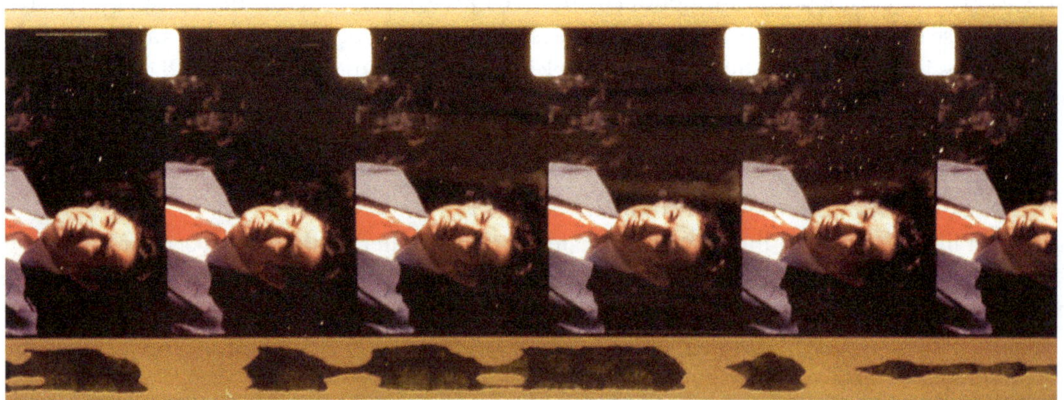

**Figure 2.** Damaged mag stripe.

of locally hardened gelatin that are strongly cross-linked and have hardened (Somasundaran, 2006, Bigni, 2004) prior to the onset of decomposition, and are not as affected by the pH change as other parts of the emulsion. This may be supported as the persistent adhesions appear to fall in regions of suspected greater compression caused by vertical storage orientation (fig. 1).

## Decomposition By-Products Forming a Cementing Layer

One method commonly used to synchronise sound to image in motion picture film, apart from optical tracks, was to apply a thin magnetic track, commonly called a *mag stripe*, to the film.

It is very common to find that the mag stripe has blocked the adjacent layer of film and unwinding the film will cause the stripe to become severely damaged (fig. 2).

There has been much research into the causes and treatments of blocking of magnetic media, such as audio and video tape. Where blocking occurs in magnetic media, the cause is often hydrolysis of the binder. However, the treatment for this problem, low relative humidity rejuvenation, is not successful with mag stripe on film.

The mag stripe was commonly made using cellulose nitrate as the binder (Kolb, 1961), unlike the PE/PU or PVC binders in magnetic tape. Analysis of the stripe by FT-IR and simple solubility tests confirmed that cellulose nitrate was the binder.

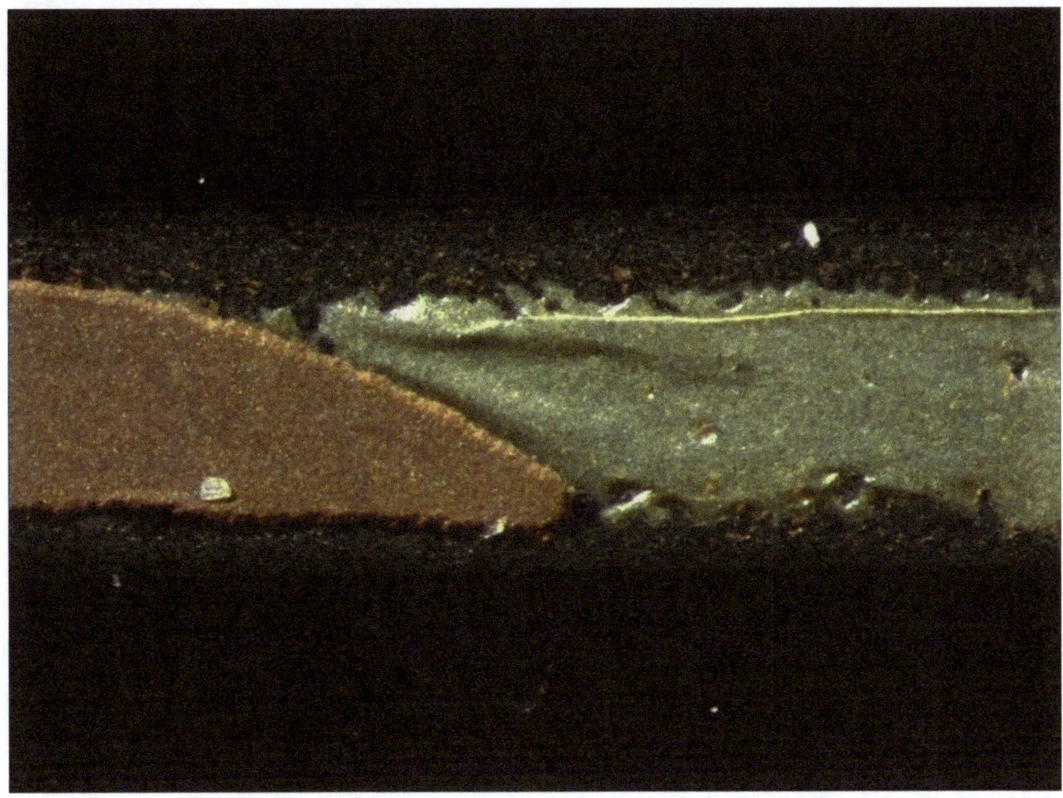

**Figure 3.** Deteriorated mag stripe cementing layer.

Examination of blocked areas under a microscope indicated that the adhesion was the result of a distinct layer that effectively cemented the two layers of film together (fig. 3). This layer was not present in nonblocked sections of stripe.

Samples of the cementing layer were analysed by FT-IR, melting point, and solubility. Analysis indicated that the cementing layer was primarily cellulose nitrate, silicon oils, and gelatin, but TPP was not involved in the adhesion. It was hypothesised that the cementing layer was formed by partial hydrolysis of the cellulose nitrate binder, and the acidic by-product was interacting with the adjacent gelatin layer.

Water was found to be successful in softening the cementing layer sufficiently to unwind the film, but the treatment is slow and laborious, with controlling the application and managing drying time. A solution of water, Photo-Flo, and isopropyl alcohol was formulated. This simple solution showed superior penetration of water into the adhesion and some improvement in the drying time; however, some persistent adhesions that could cause damage during handling remained.

FT-IR analysis had not given relative proportions of the two main constituent components of the adhesive layer, cellulose nitrate and gelatin. To specifically target these components two broad classes of enzymes were investigated:

1. amylases targeting the β1,4 glycosidic linkages found in cellulose, and
2. proteases targeting the peptide linkages within proteins.

It was hoped that targeting persistent adhesions with enzymes would enable unwinding without damage.

Since both components are found in the original film formulation, there is a risk involved in using enzymes to target the adhesive layer; however, it was felt that this avenue of research might discover a viable treatment on the proviso that a tightly controlled application method was developed.

Unfortunately, neither family of enzymes gave encouraging results within a reasonable time frame, and given the difficulty in controlling the application, and risks of enzymes nonspecifically attacking other components of the film, this appeared to be a dead end. Of the two enzymes, proteases showed the most promise, although this was also felt to be the riskiest, with severe damage to the emulsion possible.

## Conclusions

The balance of the charges on the gelatin chain is believed to be the key to understanding blocking.

While gelatin is at the core of each blocking mechanism, the treatment for each targets a different aspect of gelatin behaviour. Persistent adhesions may occur with all mechanisms of blocking, and these are most probably related to additional cross-linking and subsequent hardening as gelatin ages.

MICK NEWNHAM is currently the Manager of Conservation and Research, at the National Film and Sound Archive of Australia (NFSA) based in Canberra, Australia. For the past twenty years, Mick has been providing consultancies and training in audiovisual collection management and preservation on behalf of the NFSA and organisations such as UNESCO, SEAPAVAA, ASEAN and ICCROM for collections across the world. Mick is a lecturer with the Charles Sturt University's online audiovisual preservation course and a Visiting Fellow at the University of Melbourne, Grimwade Centre for Cultural Materials Conservation.

## References

Atkins, P. W. (1986). *Physical Chemistry, 3rd Ed.* Oxford University Press. pp. 10.

Bigi, A., Panzavolta, S., and Rubini, K. (2004). Relationship between triple-helix content and mechanical properties of gelatin films. *Biomaterials.* Nov. 25(25). pp. 5675.

Bigourdan, J. L., and Reilly, J. M. (1997). Environment and enclosures in film preservation. Final report to the Office of Preservation. *National Endowment for the Humanities, Grant #PS 20802–94.* pp. 15.

Kolb, F. J., Lovick, R. C., Peer, J. R., and Weigel, E. M. (1961). Precision striping of 8mm magnetic film. *Journal of the SMPTE.* Vol. 70. pp. 611–617.

Kowaliski, P. (1972). *Applied Photographic Theory.* J. Wiley and Sons.

McCormick-Goodhart, M. (1996). The allowable temperature and relative humidity range for the safe use and storage of photographic materials. *Journal of American Archivists.* Vol. 17(1).

Ram, A. T. (1990). Archival preservation of photographic films—A perspective. *Polymer Degradation and Stability.* Vol. 29. pp. 24.

Sheppard, S. E., Houck, R. C., and Dittmar, C. J. (1942). The sorption of soluble dyes by gelatin. *J. Phys Chem.* 46. pp. 158–176.

Somasundaran, P. (2006). *Encyclopedia of surface and colloid science, 2nd Ed.* Vol. 4. CRC Press.

# Biocontamination at the French Film Archives: Study of Its Origin and Its Remediation

28

**Bertrand Lavédrine, Daniel Borenstein, Marie Dubail, Benoit Furdygiel, Chantal Garnier, Martine Gillet, Geneviève Langlois, Thi-Phuong Nguyen, and Malalanirina S. Rakotonirainy**

## Abstract

This paper addresses the issue of mould development in a film archive. It encompasses a microbiological study, a test for different cleaning methods, and the study of the impact of the climatic condition of the room within the film can. Finally, the moisture absorption of movie films in good and bad conservation condition is assessed.

## Keywords

movie film archives, moulds, biocontamination, cleaning solvents, biocide, remediation.

## Introduction

The film archive service was established in 1969 as part of the CNC—*Centre national du cinéma et de l'image animée*—to look after the inventory of old films in France and conserve them. These archives represent one of the most significant collections of film production and distribution, from the beginnings of cinema to the present day. One million cans of film—about one hundred thousand films—are kept at sites in Bois D'Arcy and Saint-Cyr on the premises of a former military fort, located to the west of Paris. Most of the films were deposited in 1969. Storage vaults have been built to accommodate these collections under conditions of controlled temperature and humidity. However, sporadically when the film cans are opened, whether they are in a plastic or a metal can, moulds are found on the reel of the film. The CNC addresses this issue to the Research Center for Conservation in order to gain a better understanding of the origin of this fungal contamination and to remedy it. Firstly, a microbiological study was conducted to assess the health status of the premises and to identify the microorganisms. Then the efficiency and risks associated with the use of commercial cleaning solutions was estimated. Finally, the impact of the external climate on the temperature and humidity conditions inside the film can was investigated as well as the water content of some films.

## Microbiological Study

### Level of Contamination of the Air

The analysis of the contamination of the air by airborne spores was conducted in the months of March and May 2013, in the ambient air of the vaults in Saint-Cyr and Bois D'Arcy. Average spore concentrations are relatively low: almost three times lower than 170 cfu/m$^3$, defined as a low level of contamination in rooms (Reboux, 2009). As for external concentrations, they were low in March (outdoor temperature 3°–6°C) which was a relatively dry and cold winter with vegetation in dormancy. However, in May (outside temperature 12°–14°C) the outdoor concentration increased but levels within the stores had not changed. The indoor fungal concentration remained low regardless of the season and was not disturbed by external changes in contaminants. The storage areas, therefore, appear to be protected from external contamination. There was no difference between the stores on different floors of the same building.

## Level of Contamination of Surfaces

Surface analysis indicates levels of fungal contamination which may be four times higher than the recommended limit (50 cfu/dm$^2$) which is not surprising because the amount of dust. Dust promotes microorganisms in the form of spores or fragments of mycelium, which will quickly grow if conditions are favourable. However, despite fluctuations in climatic conditions, with sometimes significant increases in relative humidity, the metal shelves, with low levels of damp, and the mixing of air in the premises did not allow these fungal elements to develop. Sporadically, we observed mould on the damper walls and areas of condensation. These phenomena are accentuated near the air conditioning blowers. Comparing the levels of air and surface contamination, there is no correlation: there are contaminated surfaces in environments with low contamination rates and vice versa (Rakotonirainy, 2016).

## Identification of Fungal Species

The predominant species in the air are *Cladosporium* sp., *Penicillium chrysogenum,* and *Trametes versicolor*. Apart from the presence of *Cladosporium* sp. on surfaces and in the air, few common species have been identified. The mixing of the air by the air conditioning does, therefore, not cause the movement of dust and the mould spores contained in it. On the other hand, there are several species in the indoor air that are common with those in the outside air, in particular species of basidiomycetes, higher fungi that grow on trees.

On the reels of film, the species identified are different from those found on surfaces and in suspension in the air. Contamination probably took place prior to the films being deposited in the archives, and climatic conditions may have contributed to the growth of mould, having all their required nutrients in the film gelatin. It was noticed that the species isolated on the films are xerophilic, that is, adapted to low moisture environments. It is enough for humidity to increase slightly inside the cans for these species to grow. We noted that films with vinegar syndrome appeared to be less susceptible to a fungal development. These findings were confirmed by the study of the growth of *Penicillium corylophilum* and *Aspergillus versicolor* strains on a malt extract agar medium in the presence or absence of acetic acid.

## In Search of a Product to Clean Films

## Selection of Cleaning Products

On film, these moulds not only endanger the integrity of the document but also pose health or safety consequences for the health care workers. It is, therefore, important to clean contaminated films. Traditionally, perchloroethylene was used for film cleaning, which eliminates dirt, dust, and the mould spores they contain. It is now banned, and six industrial substitutes have been selected by the CNC's restoration laboratory (table 1) for testing. Their rough compositions were obtained either through the technical sheets, or by Fourier transform infrared spectroscopy. The chosen product must not pose environmental risks, and also not cause short-term and long-term changes to movie films, both the base, and the image layer. We, therefore, tested these products from the point of view of their impact on the image layer and the film base, and, if it is a fungicide, its inhibitory action on the development of mould.

## Evaluation of Antifungal Activity of Fonginet

Fonginet A20 is a fungicide, based on 3-iodo-2-propynyl butylcarbamate (IPBC) in (2-methoxymethylethoxy) propanol. Our preliminary tests have revealed an inhibitory action on moulds at a concentration greater than 0.4%. Six sequences of treatment (S1 to S6) and a control (reference) treatment were carried out on pieces of colour film on a cellulose triacetate base, seeded with the seven species of previously isolated fungi: *Penicillium corylophilum*, *Aspergillus versicolor*, *Cladosporium sphaerospermum*, *Penicillium crustosum*, *Penicillium citreonigrum*, *Alternaria*

**Table 1.** Products preselected for cleaning

| Product | Provider | Possible constituents |
|---|---|---|
| Arcane CNC3 | Arcane Industrie SA. ZI des Paluds. 73, avenue du Douard. 13685 Aubagne cedex. France | Methyl octadecadienoate? |
| Bioprint | Axe Diffusion. ZA Les Clottees. 72210 Voivres les le Mans. France | Hydrocarbons, C9, aromatics |
| Biosane T 218 | France Industrie SA. ZI. 28800 Bonneval. France | Ternary azeotropes, a substitute for HCFC 141 b |
| Biosolv2 | Axe Diffusion. ZA Les Clottes. 72210 Voivres les le Mans. France | hydrocarbons, C11-C12, isoalkanes, 2% aromatic |
| Fisolve E 200 | France Industrie SA. ZI. 28800 Bonneval. France | Methoxy propanol? |
| Fonginet A20 | MMCC. ZI La Massane. 13210 Saint Rémy de Provence. France | 3-iodo-2propynylbutyle (ipbc) in 2-(methoxymethylethoxy) propanol |

**Table 2:** Sequence of treatment of contaminated film in order to assess the effectiveness of Fonginet A20

| Film cleaning sequence | 1.5 g/L solution sodium carbonate for 3 minutes | 0.4% Fonginet A20 solution for 10 seconds | Rinsing with distilled water for a few seconds | Air drying | Mould growth on the film after 21 days' incubation at 26°C |
|---|---|---|---|---|---|
| Reference | no | no | no | yes | yes |
| Sequence 1 | yes | yes | yes | yes | no |
| Sequence 2 | yes | yes | no | yes | no |
| Sequence 3 | yes | no | no | yes | yes |
| Sequence 4 | no | yes | yes | yes | no |
| Sequence 5 | no | yes | no | yes | no |
| Sequence 6 | no | no | yes | yes | yes |

*brassicae* and *Leptosphaerulina chartarum*. These contaminated films were treated according to the various sequences (1–6) and were then deposited on a MA (malt agar) or DG18 (dichloran-glycerol) culture medium. The presence or absence of fungal growth was observed after 21 days of incubation at 26°C. The results (table 2) show the effectiveness of the Fonginet A20: moulds do not develop where the treatment includes Fonginet A20.

## Study of the Impact of Cleaning Products on Films

The impact of the cleaning on films was assessed in three ways:

- by measuring the image density on the black-and-white or colour films[1] right after 10 seconds immersion in the cleaning product, and after thermal aging (accelerated aging at 70°C and 86% relative humidity for 14 days.
- by applying the photographic activity test (ISO 18916, 2007) to a piece of Whatman filter paper soaked in the solution and dried.
- by measuring the shrinkage of the cellulose triacetate or polyester base after treatment and after aging.

Black-and-white films treated with Fonginet A20 exhibit noticeable density loss in high-density areas. After aging, Arcane CNC3 induced fading of one black-and-white film and Fisolve E200 had a harmful effect on two colour films (table 3). We did not notice any effect on shrinkage of cellulose triacetate or polyester base, either immediately after treatment, or after aging whatever the product was. Biosane T218, Biosolv2, and Bioprint solvents did not induce degradations on the black-and-white or colour films. These three solvents could possibly be used for cleaning movie films. It is still necessary to determine their composition and to evaluate physical properties such as their evaporation rate, their compatibility with film processing

**Table 3.** Results of compatibility tests between the cleaning product and the films

| Product | PAT | Base shrinkage of the film base | Impact on image density loss after soaking | Impact on image density loss after soaking and artificial aging | Results |
|---|---|---|---|---|---|
| Arcane CNC3 | rejected | no | no | yes | rejected |
| Bioprint | pass | no | no | no | pass |
| Biosane T 218 | pass | no | no | no | pass |
| Biosolv2 | pass | no | no | no | pass |
| Fisolve E200 | rejected | no | no | yes | rejected |
| Fonginet A20 | rejected | no | yes | no | rejected |

**Source:** http://www.sciencedirect.com/science/article/pii/S0360132314000614.

machines, and their refractive index for deciding which is more suited to the particular features of the film processing units.

## Monitoring Temperature and Humidity in Storage

The air conditioning in the vault is set to 10°C and 35% RH. Such conditions should not promote the growth of microorganisms. To assess the real conditions, we monitored temperature and humidity in the storage rooms using PEM2 data loggers[2] over three months.

Curves show that temperature stays around the 11°C, but relative humidity varies from 50 to over 80% RH (fig. 1). It was clear that the drying wheel of the air conditioner was not performing properly. Analysing such a condition with eClimatNotebook[3] software analysis indicates a good natural aging (time-weighted preservation index of 82) but a risk of mould growth (mould risk factor of 0.51). Although there is an issue with the level of relative humidity in the storage room that may explain some moulds development on the walls, the important factor to consider is the conditions inside the can of film itself. We placed hygro-boutons[4] in the centre of the reel of film in the can. After three months monitoring in different rooms, it shows that temperature in the cans follows the fluctuations of the room temperature. However, for relative humidity, even when there are wide fluctuations in the storage room, the relative humidity within the can does not fluctuate, only a slow shift may be sometimes observed over the weeks. We also note, significant differences (more than 20% RH) from one can to another (fig. 2). The relative humidity, over 70% levels in some cans, may be conducive to the proliferation of moulds and also explains the seemingly random nature of the presence of mould.

## Assessing the Microclimate in the Can

To understand the microclimate within the cans, we performed tests in a climatic oven by cycling temperature and humidity. We first put empty film cans in ovens with cycling conditions from (10°C, 60% RH) to (23°C, 70% RH) or from (10°C, 60% RH) to (23°C, 5% RH).

In the empty cans (metal or plastic) the temperature and humidity adjust almost immediately to external conditions. When we repeat this experiment on cans filled with film, the temperature follows external changes; however, the relative humidity stays almost unchanged whatever the external humidity is. It confirms that the relative humidity inside a full can is governed by the film—that is to say its moisture content—rather than by the outside conditions (Bigourdan, et al. 1997). In a can, the film acts as a buffer material by absorbing or desorbing moisture and stabilizing the humidity level. This fits the observation done in the film cans in storage over the months. If the can is not fully filled with film, the humidity fluctuates and may follow external changes. By repeating the same experiment on a film exhibiting a vinegar syndrome, we observed that the relative humidity increases slowly up to 55% RH while it stays around 40% RH in the can containing a film in good condition. To better assess the relationship between the film condition and the relative humidity we measured the water content of films in different conditions.

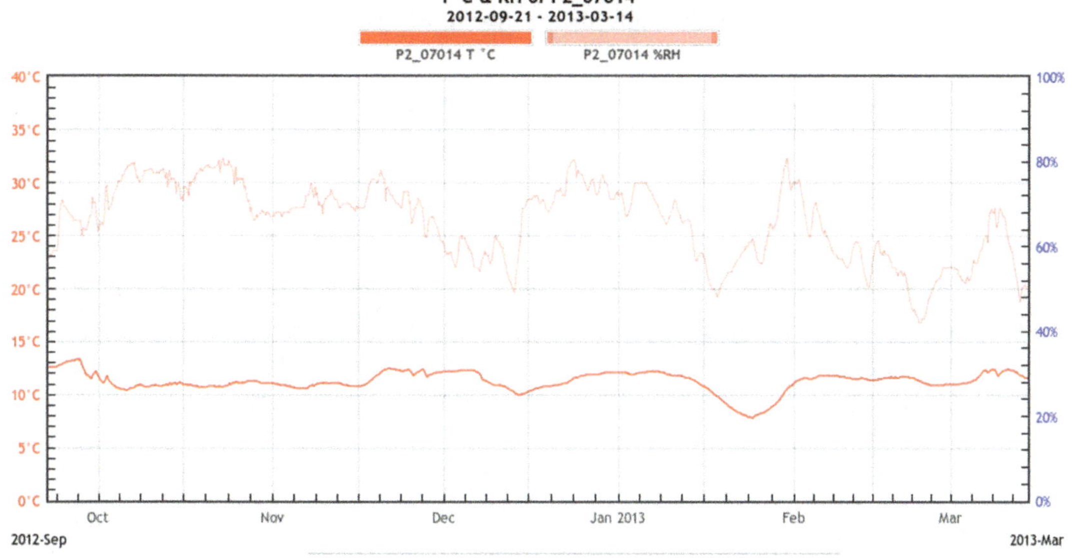


**P2_07014**

| Risk Summary | | Preservation Metrics | | Data Overview | |
|---|---|---|---|---|---|
| Natural Aging | GOOD | TWPI | 82 | Start | 2012-09-20 |
| Mold Risk | RISK | MRF | 0.51 | End | 2013-03-13 |
| Metal Corrosion | RISK | %EMC Max | 14.7 | T°C Mean | 11.3 |
| Mechanical Damage | RISK | %EMC Min | 10.3 | %RH Mean | 66 |
| | | %DC Max | 1.24 | DP°C Mean | 5 |

**Figure 1.** Example of temperature and humidity readings in vaults from September 2012 to March 2013 and the eClimatNotebook analysis indicating mould risk.

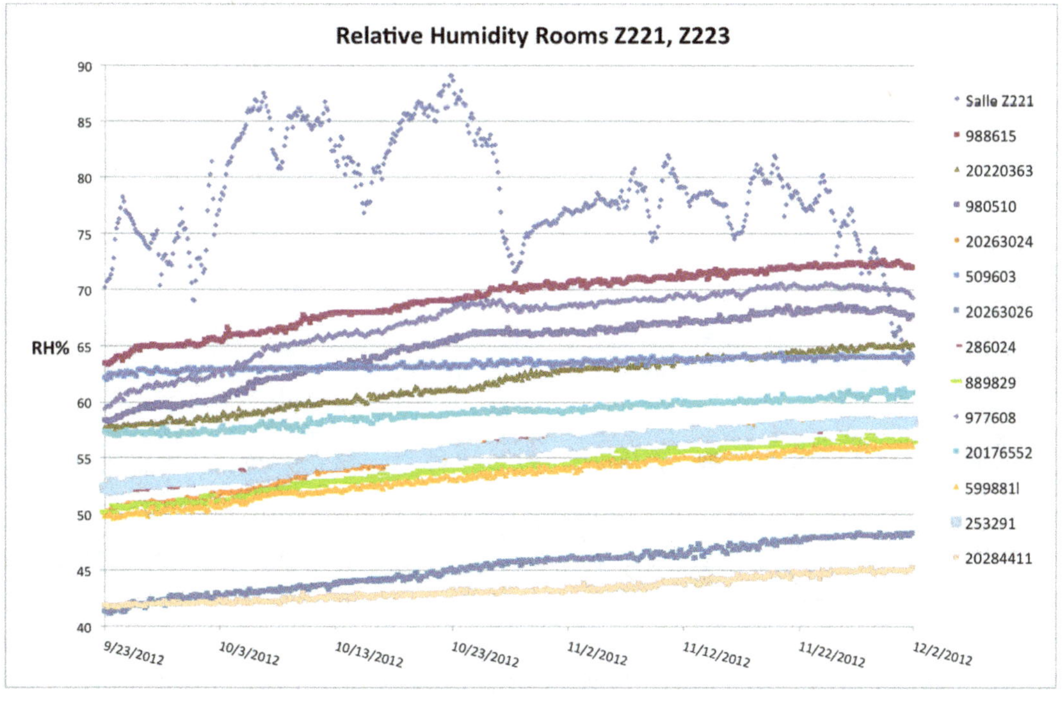


**Figure 2.** Humidity readings inside films cans located in different rooms. The very irregular curves show the RH in the rooms while the almost straight curves represent the RH within films cans.

## Moisture Content of the Films

The ability to release water is related to the moisture content. Using a moisture analyser (Sartorius MA 150), we measured the water content of CTA-based, colour and black-and-white films pre-conditioned at 26°C, 35% RH. For new films, we got 2.1% moisture ±0.2%. For old films in good condition, the water content ranges from 2.3% to 2.61%. For a film affected by vinegar syndrome,

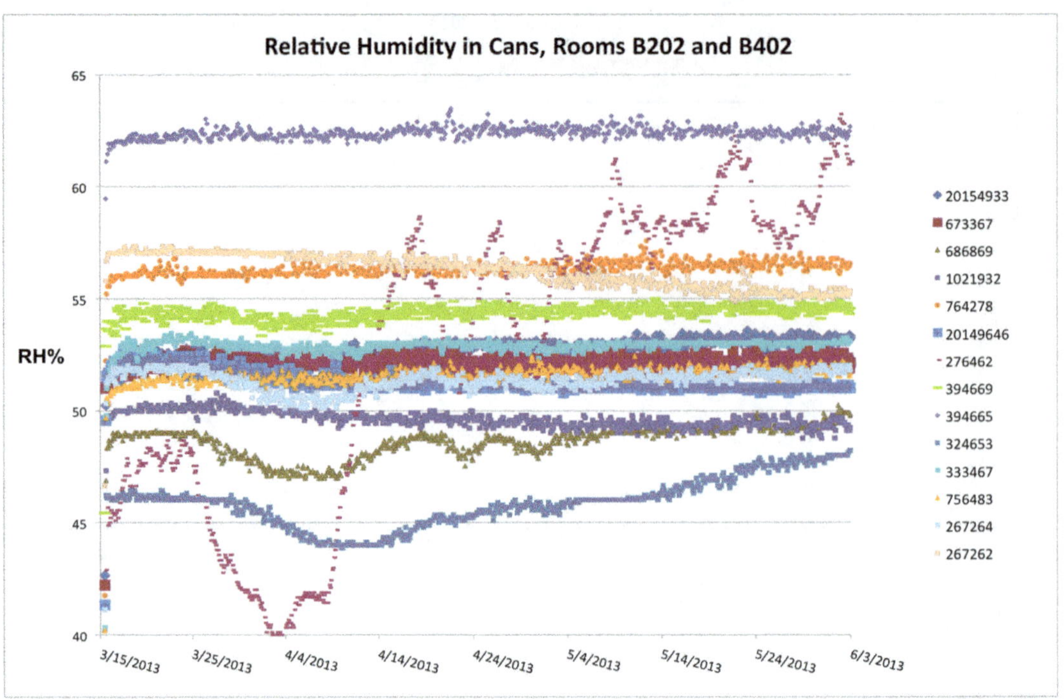


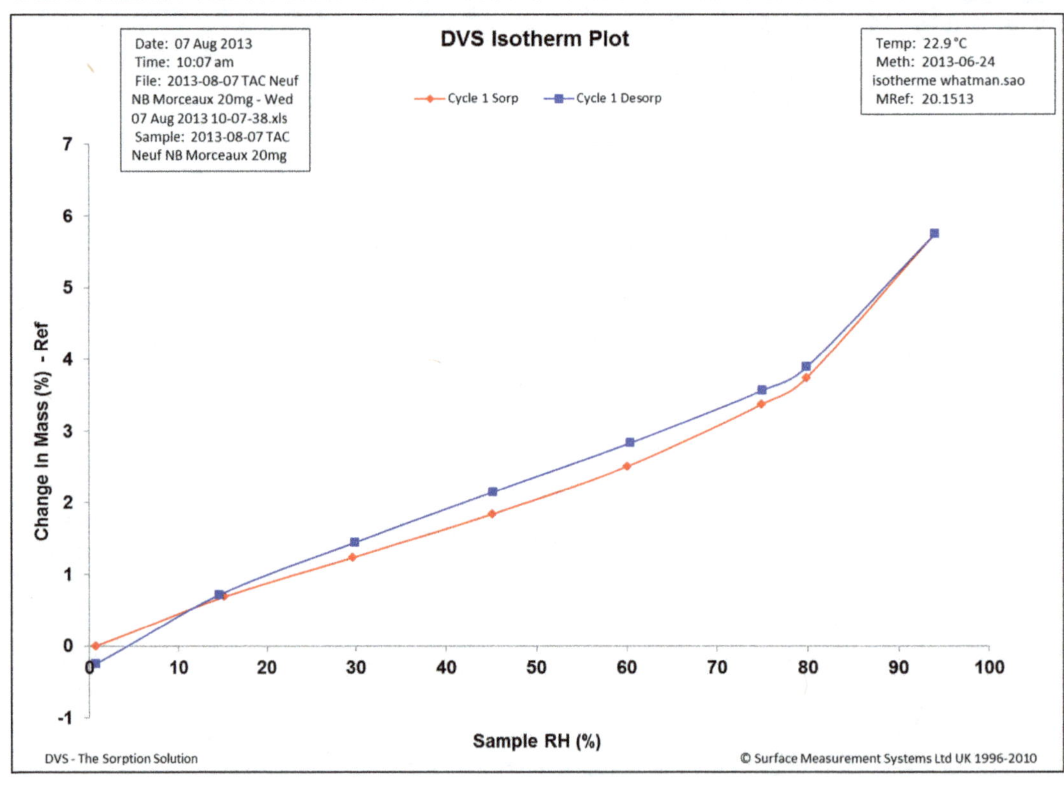


**Figure 3.** A recent film's moisture adsorption isotherm (CTA base).

a higher content of up to 4.55% was observed. To understand this difference, we plotted these films' moisture sorption isotherms using DVS (dynamic vapor sorption). The isotherms differ significantly for new films, old films, and films affected by vinegar syndrome. A new film can contain up to approximately 6% of its mass in water (fig. 3). This capacity increases with old films (fig. 4), and hysteresis is also more significant. Film affected by vinegar syndrome presents particular behaviour (fig. 5). When the humidity increases from 0% to 100%, it absorbs the moisture in a fairly similar manner to a film in good condition, and its mass increases by about 6%. On the other hand, during the reverse operation, when the humidity decreases from 100% to 0%,

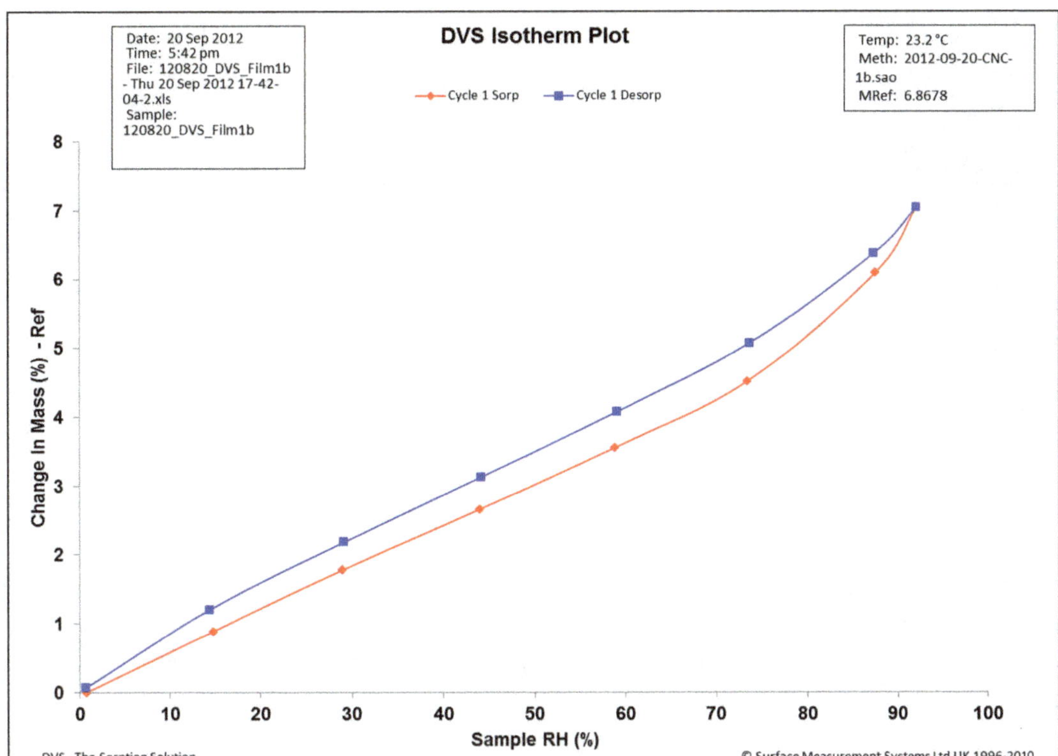


**Figure 4.** An old film's moisture adsorption isotherm (CTA base).

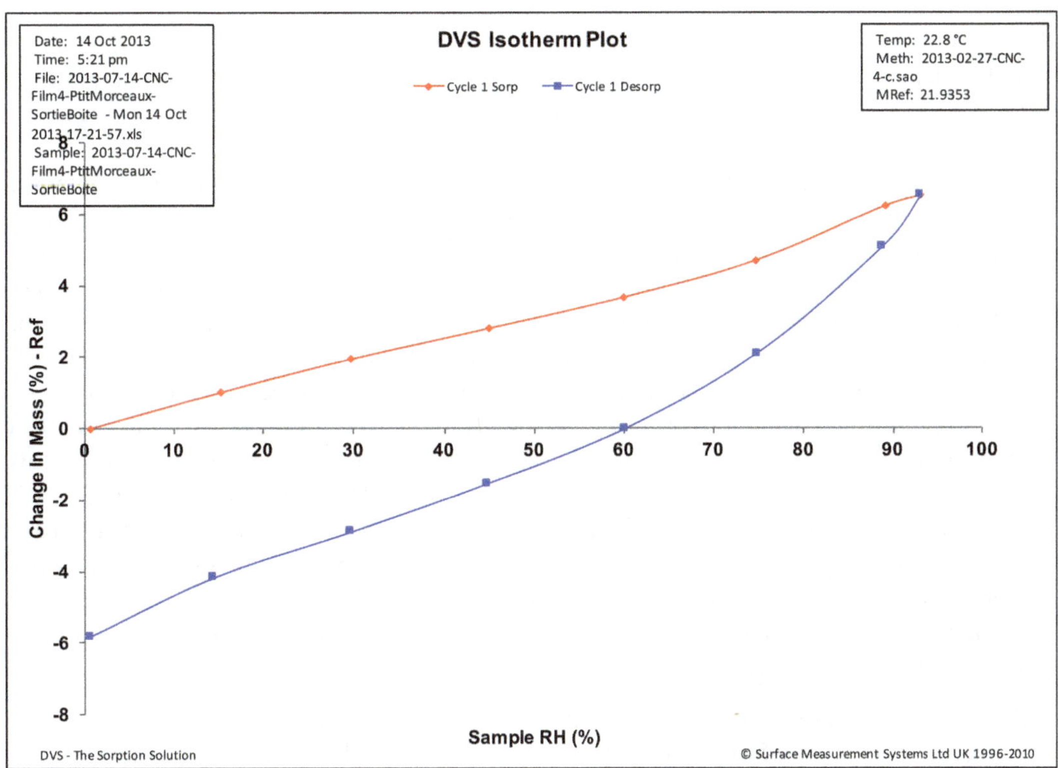


**Figure 5.** The moisture adsorption isotherm of a film (CTA base) with vinegar syndrome.

there is a loss of 12%, well above the 6% humidity that the film appeared to have absorbed. This phenomenon can be explained by the loss of volatiles such as acetic acid or plasticizers that are released with the moisture when the film is dried out. Actually, when we renew this experiment on the same sample of film, (fig. 6), the isotherms then have conventional profiles, but the ability to adsorb moisture has doubled: at 100% RH, the mass of the film increases by 12%. It seems

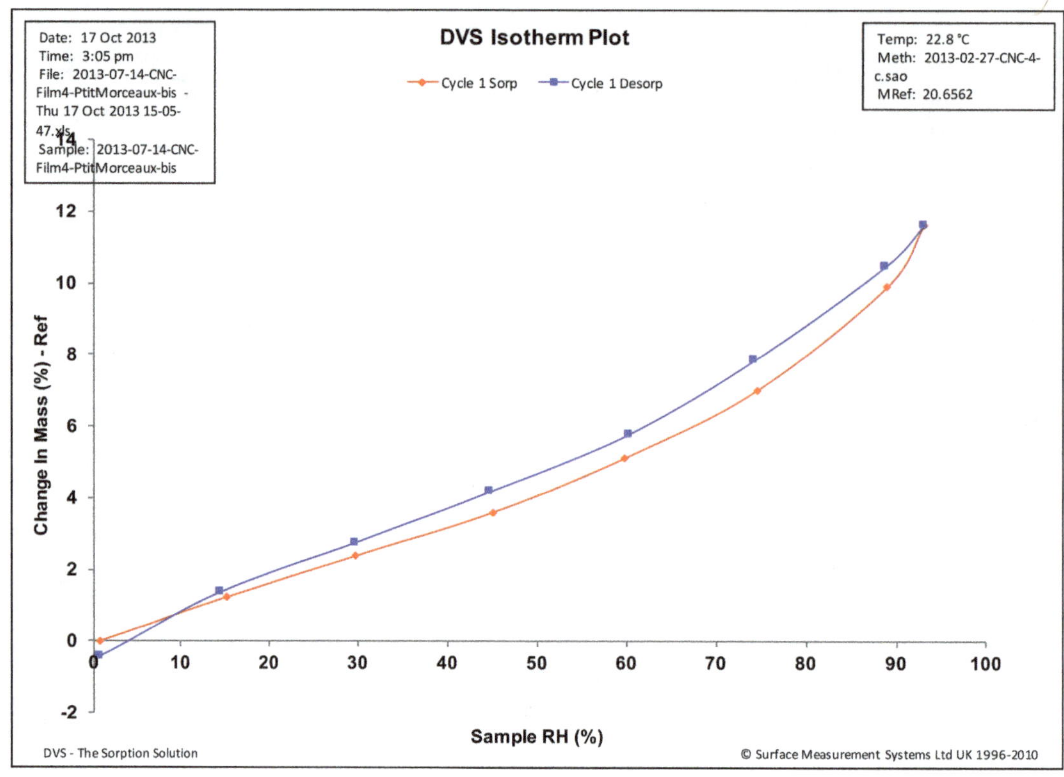


**Figure 6.** The moisture adsorption isotherm of a film (CTA base) with vinegar syndrome, second run.

that sites thus vacated by the release of volatiles will eventually accommodate water vapour. That would explain why deteriorated films can hold more moisture than films in good condition.

## Conclusion

This study was carried out at the CNC film archives to better understand the origin of biological growth in some films cans. There is no relationship between ambient mycelium flora and those analysed inside the film cans with mould growth. It, therefore, seems that this contamination happens prior to the film being placed in the archives. Several cleaning products have been tested—some were rejected, but none at this stage could be recommended. Climate monitoring shows that some storage areas have significant humidity fluctuations during the year with excessive humidity for long periods. In contrast, the humidity within the cans remains relatively stable—it is governed by the buffering effect of the film. However, depending on the moisture content of the film, there are significant differences from one can to another: while relative humidity in some cans stays within a safe range, in others RH can rise over 70%, which will promote the germination of spores. When the film ages, its ability to absorb moisture increases and films with vinegar syndrome have a greater ability to adsorb moisture and create a humid microenvironment in a can. It seems advisable that the can's size fits the reel's size to avoid empty space that promotes internal RH fluctuation and to store films having a low moisture content to avoid high RH within the can.

Bertrand Lavédrine received a doctoral degree from the Faculty of Humanities, University of Panthéon-Sorbonne, with a thesis in art and archeology, and a master degree in organic chemistry. He is Professor at the National Museum of Natural History and head of the Centre de Recherche sur la Conservation in Paris, which is staffed with fifty scientists (http://crc.mnhn.fr/). He has authored papers and books on the preservation and the technical history of photographs and the Autochrome process. He coordinated the POPART European funded research project (for the preservation of plastic objects in museum collections). He teaches at the Sorbonne University and at the National Institute for Cultural Heritage (INP) and is involved in some international initiatives funded by the Mellon and/or the Getty foundations, such as the Middle East Photograph Preservation Initiative, the Hermitage initiative, and the ICCROM training programs (COLLASIA or SOIMA).

Marie Dubail, Chantal Garnier, Martine Gillet, and Malalanirina S. Rakotonirainy are affiliated with Centre de recherche sur la conservation, Ministère de la Culture et de la Communication, Muséum National d'Histoire Naturelle. Daniel Borenstein, Benoit Furdygiel, Geneviève Langlois, and Thi-Phuong Nguyen are affiliated with Centre national du cinéma et de l'image animée, Direction du patrimoine cinématographique.

## Acknowledgments

This research was made possible thanks to the support of the Centre national du cinéma et de l'image animée, film heritage department. We thank all the staff at the film archives for their hospitality and assistance.

## Notes

1. The tests were performed on test strips on a polyester base: Eastman fine grain duplicating panchromatic negative film 2234 (B&W negative), Kodak B&W print film 2302 (B&W positive), Kodak fine grain duplicating positive film 2366 (brown B&W), Kodak vision colour intermediate film 2242 (colour negative); and on a cellulose triacetate base: Eastman fine grain duplicating panchromatic negative film 5234 (B&W negative), Kodak fine grain duplicating positive film 5366 (brown B&W), Kodak vision colour intermediate film 5242 (colour negative).
2. https://www.imagepermanenceinstitute.org/environmental/pem2-datalogger.
3. https://www.eclimatenotebook.com/.
4. http://www.proges.com/plug-and-track/enregistreurs-de-temperature/hygro-bouton-enregistreur-de-temperature-et-d-humidite.html.

## References

Bigourdan, J. L., Adelstein, P. Z., and Reilly, J. M. (1997, April 21–25) Moisture and Temperature Equilibration: Behavior and Practical Significance in Photographic Film Preservation. *La Conservation: Une Science en Evolution, Bilans et Perspectives,* Actes des Troisièmes Journées Internationales d'Etudes de l'ARSAG. Paris, (Paris: Association pour la recherche scientifique sur les arts graphiques, 1997) pp. 154–164.

ISO 18916 (2007). Imaging materials—Processed imaging materials—Photographic activity test for enclosure materials. *ISO.*

Rakotonirainy, M. S., Vilmont, L-B., and Lavédrine, B. (2016). A Methodology for Detecting the Level of Fungal Contamination in the French Film Archives Vaults. *Journal of Cultural Heritage.* Retrieved from http://dx.doi.org/10.1016/j.culher.2015.12.007

Reboux, G., Bellanger, A. P., Roussel, S., Grenouiller, F., Sornin, S., Piarroux, S., Dalphin, R., and Millon L. (2009, December 19). Indoor mold concentration in Eastern France. *Indoor Air*, pp. 446–453.

# Index

# Co-ordinating Council of Audiovisual Archives Associations: Organizations

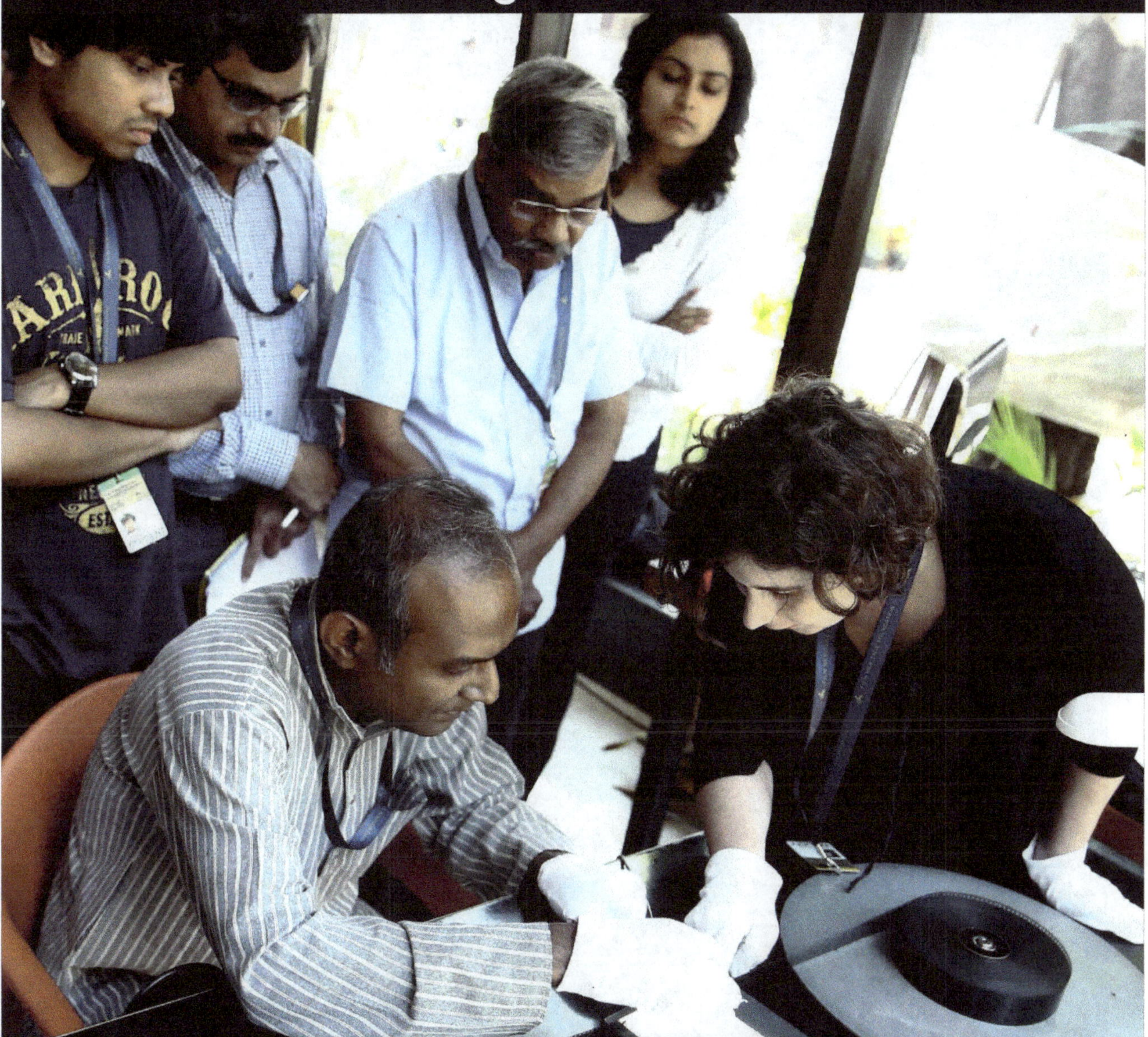

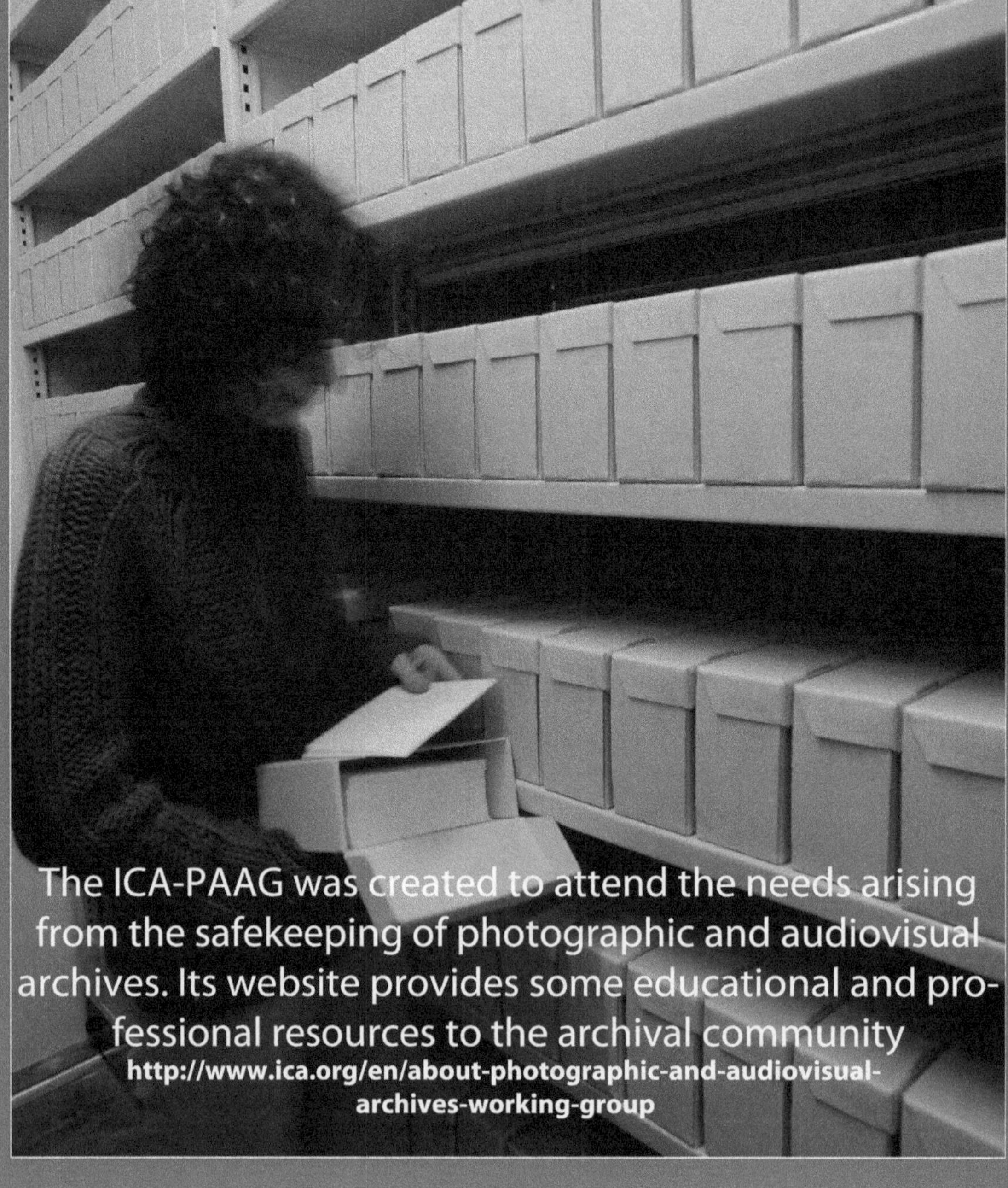

The ICA-PAAG was created to attend the needs arising from the safekeeping of photographic and audiovisual archives. Its website provides some educational and professional resources to the archival community
http://www.ica.org/en/about-photographic-and-audiovisual-archives-working-group

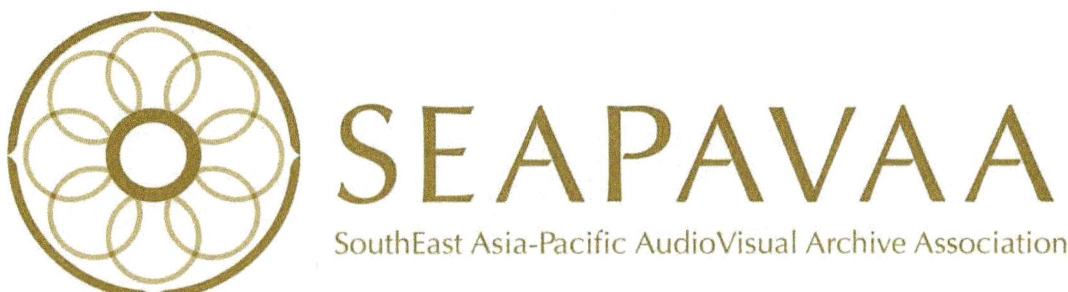


SEAPAVAA is an association of organizations and individuals involved the development of audiovisual archiving in Southeast Asia and the Pacific as to preserve and provide access to the region's rich audiovisual heritage.

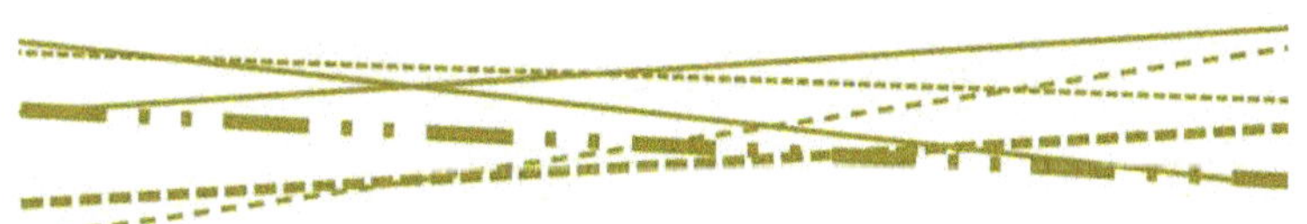

SEAPAVAA Administrative Coordinator
203-R1 Alchemy, 2/F FBR Arcade Bldg
317 Katipunan Ave, Brgy. Loyola Heights
Quezon City 1108, Philippines

Email: seapavaasecretariat@gmail.com

www.seapavaa.net

www.ingramcontent.com/pod-product-compliance
Lightning Source LLC
LaVergne TN
LVHW082004060826
844660LV00031B/1272
* 9 7 8 0 2 5 3 0 2 7 0 2 3 *